Values, Nature, and Culture in the American Corporation

Values, Nature, and Culture in the American Corporation

❏❏❏

WILLIAM C. FREDERICK

New York   Oxford
OXFORD UNIVERSITY PRESS
1995

Oxford University Press

Oxford   New York
Athens   Auckland   Bangok   Bombay
Calcutta   Cape Town   Dar es Salaam   Delhi
Florence   Hong Kong   Instanbul   Karachi
Kuala Lumpur   Madras   Madrid   Melbourne
Mexico City   Nairobi   Paris   Singapore
Taipei   Tokyo   Toronto

and associated companies in
Berlin   Ibadan

Published by Oxford University Press, Inc.,
198 Madison Avenue, New York, New York 10016

Oxford is a registered trademark of Oxford University Press

Library of Congress Cataloging-in-Publication data
Frederick, William Crittenden, 1925-
   Values, nature, and culture in the American corporation / William C. Frederick.
      p. cm.—(Ruffin series in business ethics)
      Includes bibliographical references and index.
      ISBN 0-19-509411-5.—ISBN 0-19-509674-6 (pbk.)
      1. Corporate culture—United States.   2. Business ethics—United States.
3. Social responsibility of business—United States
I. Title. II. Series.
HD58.7.F735 1995   94-38396
302.3′5—dc20

9   8   7   6   5   4   3   2   1

Printed in the United States of America
on acid-free paper

THIS BOOK IS DEDICATED TO

WALTER C. WAGNER

TEACHER, MENTOR, COLLEAGUE, FRIEND

Foreword

The landscape of business and business theory is populated by change. Analyses of global competition, restructuring, total quality management, and other issues are full of advice for how businesses should understand themselves and what lies ahead. Bill Frederick has a very simple answer to these theorists and executives. Business is about values, and understanding values is the most critical task for business thinkers and for business doers.

Bill Frederick has written an important book that will repay many times over the managers and scholars who study it. The executives who take up his challenge will be able to situate themselves and their businesses in the broader social and historical milieu and they will gain a deeper appreciation of the normative power of values that will go far beyond the usual facile statement of corporate values. The management theorists who read this book will begin to see how a whole stream of research on business ethics can be more readily understood as standing at the center of business theory rather than at the margin. The business ethicists who read this book will find a rather brilliant analysis of what they have been doing for the last few decades, and they will find a clarion call to return to the likes of John Dewey and other pragmatists, rather than their cherished philosophical figures.

I believe that this book will substantially alter the conversation that has come to be called business ethics. It represents the wisdom of one of the leading figures in the modern study of the role of business in society. It sweeps across the entire landscape yet it also speaks to executives. It is a rare and wonderful book, one that is a privilege to put in the Ruffin Series.

The purpose of the Ruffin Series in Business Ethics is to publish the best thinking about the role of ethics in business. In a world which there are daily reports of questionable business practices, from financial scandals to environmental disasters, we need to step back from the fray and understand the large issues of how business and ethics are and ought to be connected. The books in this series are aimed at three audiences: management scholars, ethicists, and business executives. There is a growing consensus among these groups that business and ethics must be integrated as a vital part of the teaching and practice of management.

Bill Frederick has given us a method to achieve this integration. He gives us a way to study and pay attention to the natural and social sciences, together with the humanities, to craft a narrative that will allow us to think and live more experimentally, to create the kinds of societies, communities, selves, and relationships that we need for our future.

R. Edward Freeman

Preface

What lies behind and ultimately causes business decisions to be made is the subject of this book. It does not search for the motives of business practitioners as much as it seeks the more fundamental sources that give rise to workplace motives, attitudes, beliefs, and behavior. A deeper layer of business consciousness is brought to light, one that harbors the fundaments of business commitment, business ideology, and business philosophy. The substance of that deep-lying stratum—its active content that comes to the surface of everyday business life—is values.

All people in business—whether highly ranked executives or employees, competitors or suppliers, investors or speculators, customers or salespeople, accountants or marketers—"have" values. Those values constantly come into play as decisions are made, policies are formulated, new markets are entered, weaker firms decline and die, and new products pour out of factories, laboratories, and software design centers. Much is now known about such values, thanks to a widening stream of research undertaken by social scientists and management scientists in the past several decades.

This book draws heavily on that body of research knowledge, but it then takes a step farther out into a realm of explanation not often explored by social scientists or by those scholars who study and teach about business practice. To understand the fundamental forces that undergird modern business, one needs to supplement what social science and management science have revealed by drawing on the natural sciences. The various branches of biological science, especially ecology, genetics, and evolutionary theory, provide stunning insights whose significance cannot be denied or disregarded. So too do some of the physical sciences, including thermodynamics, cosmology, biochemistry, and related disciplines, contain knowledge of central relevance for understanding value phenomena. Relatively newer behavioral sciences, such as ethology and moral development theory, which draw directly and indirectly on natural phenomena, enrich explanations of business behavior and business values. That these regions of science have been largely ignored by business scholars is as well known as it is regrettable. Regrettable for the simple reason that the natural sciences may well contain the several keys that will unlock presently unopened doors leading inward to the core of business decision making. Such, at any rate, is the premise and hope of this book's discussion.

Readers and reviewers should understand that two labels are not apt for describing the naturalistic themes set forth here. One is "natural law"; the other is "sociobiology." There is no intention to invoke laws or principles that are so embedded in the nature of things, so permanent a feature of the universe, or of such overarching superiority that we humans are rendered helpless and supine, unable to act without the inexorable guidance of such laws and principles. The natural law tradition of Western philosophy contains traces of such beliefs, and additionally opposes natural law to positive human-made law, as if the latter could be changed while the former was firmly set on an unswerving course by forces larger and more powerful than human will. Such a notion is explicitly rejected in the present account of business values, which favors a view that gives human actors a positive and affirmative role in determining life outcomes.

Another inappropriate label, which has become an epithet for some critics, is "sociobiology," a term coined and popularized by biologist Edward O. Wilson several years ago. Although the present book is heavily and appreciatively indebted to some of Wilson's later insights about ecological diversity, it does not claim that biological explanations can account for all human behavior or all business behavior. Of course, Wilson did not make that claim either, but some of his harshest critics have misled others to believe so. Because sociobiology thereby acquired a bad odor for seeming to imply that an unyielding natural force removed or greatly imperiled an active human will, all subsequent attempts to draw on the natural sciences for behavioral explanations have been suspect. Readers of this book will not find an unyielding deterministic stance of the kind typically attributed to sociobiological theories of human behavior.

The book's argument begins by noting the remarkable tensions that have long persisted between business and society. It proposes to explain such tensions by showing how business operations encompass two core value clusters, one that drives the firm in economically productive directions and another that imposes a hierarchy of rank order and coercive power on that productive economizing process. Lying outside the precincts of the business firm is yet another core value cluster that is derived from ecological networks and integrated ecosystems. The dynamic interactions of these three value clusters—two inside the firm and one outside—generate the bulk of the tensions and conflicts between business and society. Also found within each business firm are personal, individually "owned" values capable both of mediating some value contradictions and of exacerbating others. Intertwined with all of these value clusters is yet another that acts upon both business and society—a technological value process having a genetic origin and finding sociocultural expression. Describing these matters comprises the core of the book's theory of business values.

The last three chapters offer an alternative approach to business ethics issues. Business ethics, considered as an academic discipline, is one of the premier growth industries of the latter decades of the twentieth century. Although it owes its origin to a continuing round of ethical transgressions by business, it owes its intellectual strength and vigor to academic philosophers who have trained their analytic insights on the kinds of ethical dilemmas that have appeared frequently in recent years. Business ethics philosophers, to an equal or even greater extent than social scientists and management scientists, have ignored or rejected naturalistic explanations of workplace ethical problems. Additionally, their conventional focus on abstract concepts, rules, and principles, rather than on empirically observable behavior, separates them in important ways from others with equal interest in business ethics. These two disciplinary tendencies needlessly deflect and blunt their otherwise indispensable inquiries.

To encourage a more united search for the roots of business's normative behavior, the last four chapters offer a synthesis of the best that can be drawn from four branches of academic science: natural, social, management, and philosophic. Some who are familiar with the history of science will readily recognize the irony of considering philosophy as a separate body of inquiry when once it was itself intertwined inseparably with all of the sciences. Irony aside, we may be witnessing a coming era in which the queen of the sciences will once again reign supreme within all scientific realms. That is the guiding spirit of the New Normative Synthesis and the Culture of Ethics discussed in the last two chapters.

Unlike most discussions of business ethics, this book is neither antibusiness nor probusiness. This does not mean that it straddles or avoids difficult issues. It grants business an indispensable function in society while identifying fundamental features of business that produce antisocial effects. Its arm's-length perspective is intended to shed light on socioeconomic problems emerging from business operations but also to provide ways to recognize and alleviate some of the resultant tensions. Its lessons, if taken seriously by business professionals, would bring fundamental and needed changes to the practice of business.

The book's primary focus is upon business, mainly corporate business in the United States in the last half of the twentieth century. Although aspects of the theory may imply a potentially wider application—for example, to the role that values play in other kinds of institutions or to businesses that operate in other nations—the intention has been to limit the analysis to contemporary business firms in the United States.

Pittsburgh   W. C. F.
October 1994

Acknowledgments

A book is a way of life. At least, so it seems to me. The experience is one that sweeps up many diverse parts of one's life and then enfolds and blends them with cherished and remembered teachers, friends, colleagues, students, spouse, kinfolks, even casual acquaintances who politely inquire about one's progress, audiences who might have heard pieces of the tale, and the anticipated readers who eventually decide the worthwhileness of the entire enterprise.

The first person who encouraged me to continue with what was then a very shaky beginning was S. Lee Jerrell, then a colleague at the University of Pittsburgh. Others might want to note how critically important it is to have one's tentative thoughts endorsed and given a friendly push forward. Support of a related kind was generously extended by a coterie of philosophers whom I count among my closest professional friends: Manuel Velasquez, Norman Bowie, Thomas Donaldson, Richard DeGeorge, Patricia Werhane, and Edward Freeman. They have done what they could to lead me in the correct pathways of philosophy, although, alas, this book may be convincing testimony to my failure to see as clearly as they might have wished. Any emerging book needs the kinds of correctives generated by critical readers, and I am fortunate and grateful to those who read all or parts of the manuscript and offered suggestions: Nancy Kurland, Diane Swanson, James Weber, Denis Collins, Mildred Myers, Rogene Buchholz, and Mike Wagner. Each brought unique and enormously helpful insights to the task, and I am deeply grateful and equally pleased to acknowledge their help in this public way. Another whose steadfast support for teaching and research in ethics has been greatly valued is Dean H. Jerome Zoffer of the Katz Graduate School of Business at the University of Pittsburgh.

The contributions of one person call for special notice. Mike Wagner, to whom the book is dedicated, was my first economics teacher. From that beginning class, I learned that an economic system does not stand alone in grand isolation from the everyday life of ordinary people but is instead a pulsating human organism thoroughly embedded in societal and cultural life. Over the years, our companionship has yielded many other intellectual dividends for me, including his unique interpretation of the venerable concept of economic scarcity on which this book's theory of business economizing is partially based. Needless to say—though I shall say it anyway—he continues to stand as an extraordinary friend and companion, as full to the brim and running over with an apparently inexhaustible fund of ideas as he is with an enthusiastic and contagious zest for life. As is sometimes said of such an exceptional and wonderful person, they don't make them that way anymore.

Contents

Values, Nature, and Culture in the American Corporation

Prologue

But pardon, gentles all,
The flat unraised spirits that hath dar'd
On this unworthy scaffold to bring forth
So great an object: . . .
O, pardon! since a crooked figure may
Attest in little place a million;
And let us, ciphers to this great accompt,
On your imaginary forces work. . . .
Piece out our imperfections with your thoughts; . . .
For 'tis your thoughts that must . . .
[Turn] th' accomplishment of many years
Into an hour-glass; for the which supply
Admit me Chorus to this history;
Who prologue-like your humble patience pray,
Gently to hear, kindly to judge, our play.

WILLIAM SHAKESPEARE
The Life of King Henry the Fifth[1]

1. Stanley Wells, Gary Taylor, John Jowett, and William Montgomery (eds.), *William Shakespeare: The Complete Works,* Oxford: Clarendon Press, 1986, p. 639, by permission of Oxford University Press.

1

Values in Business

This book argues that business values contain the key to much that is troubling the business world today. Understanding those business values—seeing them for what they are and what they do, where they come from, and how they interact with other competing values—can help business leaders and those who study business behavior in two major ways.

Business practitioners toward the end of the twentieth century confront many daunting problems. Some of the more important issues are lagging productivity, burdensome social and regulatory costs, discontented and disloyal work forces, a rising tide of global competition, geopolitical turmoil, unreliable currency systems, and episodic threats of inflation, recession, and general market instability. A deep knowledge of how values impel business practitioners, their workers, and their firms to do what they do might well help them not only to survive present difficulties but also to ride the powerful social and technological currents transforming the world's business systems. It may just be that the values within (as well as those outside) the organization are as important to successful management as a skilled command of financial resources, marketing techniques, accounting controls, and the rapidly advancing computerization of business operations. This is not to say—and this book does not argue in the manner of corporate culture enthusiasts—that there can be "business as usual" if only business managers search for and discover the value roots of their own firms. The task and the challenge are considerably more formidable than some of these simple but salable formulas suggest.

Beyond the potential for managerial gain is the prospect of understanding why business as an institution, and business professionals as a group—in spite of the central, indispensable economic function they carry out—are so thoroughly suspect in the public eye. During much of the twentieth century, business and society have existed in a state of tension and conflict. From a societal point of view, business is frequently believed to have exercised its power and influence to the detriment of particular groups and of society at large. Those in business have just as frequently complained about what they perceive to be unreasonable societal constraints on business operations in the form of burdensome governmental regulations, added costs, and unwarranted intrusions into private decision making. The principal arenas of conflict have been the size and scope of business operations, the size of and rationale for business profits, the extent of government involvement in business decisions, the way business has marketed its products to the consuming public, contentious workplace relations between labor and management, and business operations that impinge on the economic, social, and environmental interests of citizens and communities whose livelihoods are linked to the modern corporation.

The public debate shadowing these tensions has typically found business to be on the defensive. Business motives are often, perhaps usually, suspect. Public confidence in business leadership, as registered in public opinion polls, has remained quite low. A citizenry whose material comfort may well depend upon successful business operations nevertheless doubts the wisdom or sufficiency of profit as an organizational goal and a measure of performance. Many have questioned the probity and ethical sincerity of those who direct business affairs. Narrow-mindedness, a zealous regard for quantity and a somewhat casual attitude toward quality, a pronounced social myopia, and a fixation on today's rather than tomorrow's problems are accusations freely made against business managers and their professional colleagues within the corporation.

These negative, even derisive, traits imputed to business denizens have created a somewhat peculiar business consciousness or mindset. Believing that their work is essential to society's survival and flourishing, and characteristically dedicated to doing the best they can, business functionaries may well ponder why they so frequently are held up to public scorn and condemnation. Such harsh judgments are especially painful to bear when delivered with such gusto by individuals and groups who are themselves not in business and who often know little or nothing about what business operations entail. Little wonder that the venerable question "But have you ever met a payroll?" has been such a comforting retort to fling at the legions of business critics.

Equally baffled have been those very critics who profess not to understand why business managers persist in "putting profits before people." Disbelief and incredulousness about business obtuseness and an apparent absence of simple humane caring have caused many an opponent of some corporate policy to generate a potent mixture of rage and puzzlement. Absent some new perspective, the chances that this all too typical antibusiness attitude will ever be erased from the public mind are no greater than the likelihood that business professionals will be able to comprehend just why their well-intentioned activities are pilloried with such enthusiasm.

One way to lift this veil of mutual ill will, ignorance, and misapprehension—and to create a managerial approach that is equal to the global challenges now facing business—is to take a fresh look at the interface that links business and society together and simultaneously drives a wedge between them. Theories of business and society that attempt to explain some of the conflictive puzzles and to find a way around them first began to appear in the United States during the last half of the twentieth century. Produced for the most part by management scholars lodged in business schools, these theories have become indispensable sources of knowledge about business's relations with surrounding sociopolitical forces in society. For some corporations, they have enabled the building of effective sociopolitical management systems, though many others in the business community have expressed skepticism.[1]

For all of their practical usefulness and scholarly wisdom, these business and society theories, even when considered collectively, fall short of a fully satisfying explanation of why business and society should so persistently seem to be at odds. The root causes of these tensions have yet to be explored in detail. Clarifying the conflict-generating forces will itself not lead to a cessation of hostilities, but by giving all parties a better understanding of the nature of the struggle, a new theory may reveal what is needed to lessen tensions and to find managerial systems that are apt for dealing with complex business problems. Until that task is accomplished, the conflicts will remain as a prominent feature of business operations, and the critics and defenders of business will continue to hurl rhetorical (and perhaps even some nonrhetorical) brickbats at one another.

A THEORY OF BUSINESS VALUES: AN OVERVIEW

The uses of values to understand business and business behavior are rare. Some of this reluctance and hesitation is no doubt caused by a feeling that values are a private and highly personal part of one's very being, not often

1. The most representative of these theories are found in Richard Eells, *The Meaning of Modern Business*, New York: Columbia University Press, 1960; Neil W. Chamberlain, *The Limits of Corporate Responsibility*, New York: Basic Books, 1973; Robert W. Ackerman, *The Social Challenge to Business*, Cambridge, MA: Harvard University Press, 1975; Lee E. Preston and James E. Post, *Private Management and Public Policy*, Englewood Cliffs, NJ: Prentice-Hall, 1975; and Robert H. Miles, *Managing the Corporate Social Environment*, Englewood Cliffs, NJ: Prentice-Hall, 1987. Somewhat more critical assessments of business and society relations have been made—still from within an establishment perspective—by John Kenneth Galbraith, Robert Heilbroner, Ralph Nader and his associates, and various organizations with specific social-interest agendas. Radical left critiques have occasionally stung business consciousness without exerting any appreciable effect on business practice or policy.

enough on public display—and properly so, it is believed—to reveal much about their impact on our behavior. This view receives powerful yet subtle support from a time in Western intellectual history when values are thought—again, properly so—to be embedded deeply within a society's mores and folkways, thereby mirroring the impressively diverse societal values one finds throughout the globe. Thus, to the highly subjective, personal notion of values is added the belief that values are capable of expressing mainly a human diversity that is relative to social time and space. Values, in other words, are acclaimed as a relative property of individual personality and societal conventions. To try to make sense of business operations from such an elusive, remote, and transitory base has seemed a poor prospect indeed. Philosophic, scientific, and religious traditions likewise have turned systematic value inquiry aside by suggesting that the oldest wisdom is the best wisdom, that personal, subjective, relativist values exist in a realm divorced from the factual domain of the scientist, and that whatever values we harbor derive from supernatural sources not accessible through normal human investigation.

These complexities associated with understanding values are not to be taken lightly. Each viewpoint offers, though in varying measure, a perspective worth serious consideration by anyone who wishes to grasp the role of values in human life generally. The same can be said of any effort to clarify the many value issues found in the operation of modern business enterprise. Where appropriate, the following account of business values draws upon what has been discovered about values by others, and it confronts some of the difficult issues that have tended to turn scholars and practitioners away from this value-oriented way of understanding the business institution.

This book develops a theory of business values that explains much of the tension and conflict between business and society. It also provides guidelines for knowing what might be involved in achieving a more economically effective, humanely caring, and ecologically sensitive business organization. The values that are described are derived from the experiences and experienced perceptions of people who work in business, and who live in human social communities, and whose lives are one manifestation of natural and cultural evolution. Not confined to theoretical abstractions, the theory is empirically grounded in what is now known about the behavior of business professionals and the organizational contexts in which they make decisions.

In spirit and intention, the theory is post-Darwinian and post-Einsteinian, meaning that it builds on these landmark orientations and incorporates an outlook congenial to modern scientific inquiry as it is understood toward the close of the twentieth century. It differs from predecessor theories by including a realm of explanation taken from the physical and biological sciences. Additionally, it makes extensive use of burgeoning discoveries in genetic science, ecological science, and biological evolution that have piled up an ever-mounting body of fascinating knowledge about human origins, human development, and environmental potentials and constraints. As will become evident, it is heavily indebted to many scholars who have labored fruitfully to explain just why business and society coexist as they do, sometimes peacefully but often belligerently.

Because the theory draws extensively on several of the natural sciences, as well as some behavioral sciences not normally featured in discussions of human values, some (but certainly not all) readers will encounter concepts and terminology that may seem out of place. That will be especially true in the book's earlier chapters, including portions of this one. In spite of the undoubted strangeness of some of the language and the resulting perspectives that emerge, the risks and discomforts may prove worth bearing if they produce new insights into the workings of the business mind and the normative puzzles that so often dog the footsteps of business practitioners. That is the intention of this new theoretical course that is charted through relatively uncharted intellectual and philosophical terrain.

The theory's central argument is that the source of business and society tension is an incompatibility between three kinds of values: "economizing" values, "power-aggrandizing" values, and "ecologizing" values. The mechanisms through which the tension is expressed consist of three different and opposed value clusters, which are called "Value Cluster I," "Value Cluster II," and "Value Cluster III."

Value Cluster I sustains economizing, which is an essential societal process. All of the values in this cluster support activities that cause individuals and groups to act prudently and efficiently in using resources, thus economizing, husbanding, and processing those resources required for survival and material flourishing. Chapter 2 describes and analyzes these economizing values, which constitute the core values of business.

Value Cluster II sustains the aggrandizement of power, which is a common phenomenon within human organizations. The values in this cluster work toward the acquisition, accumulation, and retention of coercive power by and for those who hold commanding positions within organizations. The several uses of power, for instrumental as well as domineering purposes, are explored in Chapter 3.

Value Cluster III sustains ecologizing, which is a component and an outcome of natural evolution as well as a learned survival trait of human communities. Ecological relationships interweave the life activities of groups in ways conducive to the perpetuation of an entire community, including the flora, fauna, and physical features that comprise the group's ecosystem. While differing from economizing in some very important respects, ecologizing processes exhibit somewhat similar, parallel, and positive evolutionary outcomes. These are analyzed in some detail in Chapter 6.

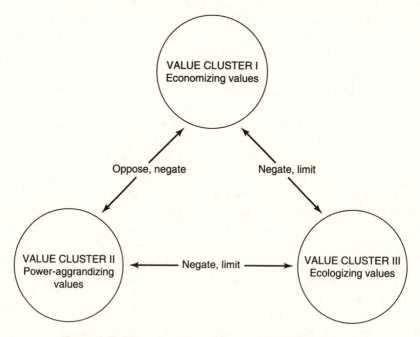

Figure 1–1. Value clusters and the tensions between them

The tensions between these three value clusters are of three basic types, as diagrammed in Figure 1–1. The brief summaries to follow are intended to give an introductory flavor of the kinds of conflicts that typically arise as actions based on each value cluster encounter contrary tendencies and impulses flowing from the other value clusters. Much more is said about each cluster's impact in subsequent chapters.

Economizing/Power-Aggrandizing Tensions

The tensions between economizing values and those that augment the coercive power of organizations and their managers are reasonably familiar to those who follow business affairs on a regular basis. A hostile corporate takeover illustrates these tensions. If such an incursion is undertaken for the sole purpose of expanding the power and influence of the corporate raiders who lack a rational basis for claiming economizing gains, then power-aggrandizing values will have clearly triumphed over economizing values. The result is a loss of economic efficiency and effectiveness for both the acquired and the acquiring firm. On the other hand, economizing-minded raiders, believing that a corporation's resources are being squandered by an entrenched management group more interested in retaining its privileges and power than in using the company's resources efficiently, may promote economizing values and, for the moment at least, relegate power aggrandizement to a lesser status (usually only until they themselves secure the seats of power). Nevertheless, a window of economizing opportunity and enhanced productivity may be opened for a while. There may be occasions when power-aggrandizing activities produce quasi-economizing results, although typically such benefits accrue mainly to the takeover leaders and their confederates. In corporate takeovers, a general economizing outcome is usually claimed by the raiders, whether supported by the facts or not. In the nature of the case, there is a strong tendency for power seeking to overwhelm economizing, a matter discussed later.[2]

The inner precincts of the corporation itself are frequent witness to struggles that pit power-aggrandizing values against economizing values. These struggles may occur as frequently on the shop floor and in middle-management ranks as in top-level executive suites. On these occasions, opposed interests engage in internecine strife that undermines the central economizing mission of the business firm while conveying a sense of magnified glory and esteem to those who seek and wield power for these purposes. Labor–management contests for control of personnel policy, especially when taking the form of strikes or lockouts, provide a well-known illustration, as do the less-publicized but familiar "en suite" turf battles among management rivals for control of company policy. More subtly, the very arrangement of power relations within both business and society—one that allocates overweening influence to business owners and managers—permits those in favored positions to diminish the economic standing and economizing opportunities open to specific ethnic groups, gender classifications, or even whole communities.

Whether occurring inside the company, between companies, or between companies and their various external constituencies, these power contests always tend not only to erode the firm's economizing base, diverting it from the economic mission that justifies its societal existence, but also to weaken and damage the life-support activities of many corporate stakeholders. Neither business nor society gains much, if anything, of positive value from these warlike struggles.

Economizing/Ecologizing Tensions

Environmental crises and near-crises dramatically illustrate the tensions that have arisen between the values of economizing and those of ecologizing. We

2. For skeptical views of corporate mergers, see Dennis Mueller, "Mergers and Market Share," *Review of Economics and Statistics*, 1985, pp. 259–267; David J. Ravenscraft and F. M. Scherer, "Mergers, Selloffs, and Economic Efficiency," Washington, DC: Brookings Institution, 1987; and Richard Roll, "The Hubris Hypothesis of Corporate Takeovers," *Journal of Business*, 1986, vol. 59, no. 2, pt. 1, pp 197–216.

know now with increasing confidence that the economizing values and activities of some individuals, groups, and organizations can negate or diminish the ecologizing values and efforts of other groups and communities. When this happens, the life chances of some communities (human, animal, and floral) are reduced or eliminated, to the survival benefit of the economizing unit(s).

Current examples abound. That part of acid rain that results from the burning of fossil fuels is a clear threat to forest, lake, and stream ecosystems, even though it stems from deliberate economizing activities of power companies and other users of these fuels. On a global scale, the by-products—waste gases, atmospheric heat, and suspended particles—from burning fossil fuels contribute to an entrapment of global heat energy that otherwise would be dissipated. This global warming trend, if verified and extended far into the future, carries the prospect of ecological disruption in the form of climatic shifts, desertification, melting of the earth's ice caps, and rising ocean levels, with an attendant widespread and possibly disastrous rupture of ecological systems in many locations. A third example is found in the rapid utilization of the earth's tropical rain forests and the land they occupy, stimulated by the economizing needs of farmers, miners, land developers, and others. Extended far enough, the destruction of these forests has the potential to change the world's climates in remarkable and probably catastrophic ways. Long-established ecological networks that sustain the life of many plant, animal, and human communities would be at risk.

Conversely, where ecologizing values predominate over opposed economizing ones, the effectiveness and efficiency with which given economizing units operate may be negated, diminished, or made subordinate to the broader ecological functions and needs of a community. The resultant tensions mirror the opposed interests and directions in which economizing values and ecologizing values impel their respective advocates. When the major makers of chlorofluorocarbons agreed to manufacturing and usage restrictions, thereby reducing the threat to the globe's protective layer of ozone, ecologizing needs and values clearly won out over economizing values, at least in principle. Similar costly economizing restrictions have been adopted, albeit sometimes more reluctantly, by auto makers, chemical companies, oil and gas producers, computer chip manufacturers, and industrial and service concerns of all kinds—all in the name of ecological values. These usages have generated potent and strident public policy struggles as economizing and ecologizing values have clashed.

Power-Aggrandizing/Ecologizing Tensions

Power aggrandizement by individuals, firms, and industries can be as threatening to ecosystems as a runaway economizing process. If, for example, a company—a coal mining firm, a housing developer, or an agricorporation—pursues a single-minded strategy of rapid expansion in order to dominate an industrial or market sector or to enhance the prestige and power of its leading executives, then significant environmental damage often occurs. Carelessly contained mine wastes seep into streams and lakes, where they devastate aquatic life or threaten drinking water supplies. Houses and shopping centers located on floodplains or low-lying wetlands may be engulfed by natural forces even as the structures' presence threatens or decimates the living ecosystems they have displaced. Overtilled, overgrazed, overfertilized farmland soils can literally blow away or drain ecologically damaging chemicals into waterways.

Power-aggrandizing values and activities usually negate or limit ecologizing values and opportunities. Thus, the life chances of some communities (human, animal, and floral) are placed at risk by the power-augmenting values and operations of others. The benefits experienced by those exercising power in these ways are, in cosmic and human time frames, fleeting and ephemeral, though momentarily compelling, attractive, and often addictive. The tensions are a function of the obsessive quest for power by some and the subsequently diminished life opportunities felt by the collective membership of a community. A managerial attitude that favors ever more business expansion—often falsely cloaked as economic growth—captures the flavor of this kind of value tension. Bigness of enterprise sought for its own sake, and for the power and prestige it conveys to its managers, produces the same result. If these power-inspired approaches dominate the managerial mind, ecologizing values usually suffer.

Rarely, if ever, are these tensions reciprocal. That is, at this point in world affairs, one only infrequently observes specific instances in which ecological balances are allowed to triumph over power-aggrandizing drives. The reasons are related to the strategic control over economic resources enjoyed by corporations and their confederated governments, plus the diversity of power-related motives and interests that have accumulated in those institutions over time. A desire to dominate or "control" nature, as well as other human beings, has tended to stall or frustrate countervailing ecological tendencies.

Viewed in historical and cultural perspective, the tenacious quality of these business-and-society tensions and the conflicts they induce is truly remarkable. An explanation is wanted and needed about the forces responsible for such enduring and steadfast continuity through time and cultural space. What can be said in a preliminary way is that all three types of values—economizing, power-aggrandizing, and ecologizing—draw from both natural and sociocultural sources that display great persistence. Each value cluster owes something to the evolutionary and genetic processes that have shaped human, animal, and floral development. As such, each of the three clusters expresses an evolutionary outcome that is radically distinct from that of the other two. It will be argued that the tensions and conflicts generated between and among the three value clusters appear to be evolutionarily inevitable. This is tantamount to saying that the values by which humans gain a living, allocate and wield power, and establish communal relations with each other are anchored partially in nature and partially in sociocultural processes.

This view is not equivalent to a simplistic Social Darwinian concept of evolutionary process whereby only those features survive that prove to be the "fittest." Natural selection does indeed produce such outcomes, but that is not the entire story. Morphological and behavioral variation and diversity of flora and fauna appear also as a function of genetic mutations, environmental changes, and—additionally, in the case of humans—cultural interventions. The evolutionary process that extrudes values is not predetermined or teleological, nor is it destined to produce a human ideal or satisfactory outcome. In fact, contrary to the rigidities of Social Darwinian thought, evolutionary process—whether driven by biology or culture, or by some mixture of the two—is remarkably open, variable, and highly probabilistic. For that reason, values extruded by it tend to reflect these same diverse characteristics.[3]

For humans, each type of value-generating process is also a learned human phenomenon transmitted from one generation to the next by sociocultural means. Nature and Nurture exert interwoven effects, leaving their imprint on human values in uncertain but varying proportions. To trace these effects, thus revealing the source of conflict between business and society, and to probe what might be done to deflect or mitigate the negative consequences of these disturbances, is the task ahead.

THE MEANING OF VALUE

As noted at the outset, using values to explain business behavior is relatively rare, and the history of these attempts in the United States is a brief one, traceable not much further back than the 1920s. The pioneers for the most part have been social scientists, some but not all of them affiliated with business schools. A largely unspoken premise has been that the values held by these business leaders—owner-entrepreneurs, top-level corporate managers, financiers, and industrialists—shape the motives, policies, and actions of their firms. Value knowledge of this kind has been presumed to be useful in

3. For a discussion, see Konrad Z. Lorenz, *The Foundations of Ethology* (English translation by Konrad Z. Lorenz and Robert Warren Kickert), New York and Vienna: Springer-Verlag, 1981, pp. 22–33ff. Lorenz has remarked in another place that "Life itself is a steady state of enormous general improbability." See his *Evolution and Modification of Behavior*, Chicago and London: University of Chicago Press, 1965, p. 32.

several ways: to the manager for self-knowledge that might improve decisions made; to a board of directors for selecting top-level leaders; to business scholars for enriching their theories of business operations; and, though probably unintended by the researchers, to critical observers of the business scene whose antibusiness views would then be lent whatever legitimacy social scientific perspectives might provide.[4]

As these scholars set about their studies of business values, they were able to draw on an emerging body of research methods developed largely by psychologists and social psychologists. Additionally, they made use of the intuitive insights, hunches, and logical arguments of other social scientists, historians, and philosophers who, for a much longer period of time, had been exploring the realm of human values and trying to systematize that knowledge so that it could lead to a better understanding of human affairs generally. Thanks to these earlier efforts, it became possible for the latecomers to build on what had been learned about values in the past.

"Value" is a term that has been given many different meanings, some personal, others institutional, some deeply philosophical, many of them conveying an intensely ideological flavor. In one form or another, values have been the subject of deliberation among scholarly people, including artists, poets, and dramatists, for many centuries, just as they have occupied the thoughts and guided the actions of ordinary people as they have gone about the everyday business of living. Values in a sense are a common coinage of humanity, pondered by the serious, elaborated by the studious, but known to everyone. All of this is to say that there is little about values that is remote or mysterious, beyond the mysteries imputed to them.

The positivist tradition in Western thought, reinforced powerfully in this instance by culturally embedded individualist conceptions, has held values to be closely and privately held emotional convictions that are publicly inaccessible. This view, based upon a concept of science that separates "facts" from "values," has perpetuated the belief that values, if not mysterious, are at least difficult to locate in any objective way. Hence, the scientific study of values

---

4. One clear genealogical line of research on values begins with E. Spranger, *Types of Men*, New York: Stechert-Hafner, 1928; continued with Gordon Allport, P. E. Vernon, and G. Lindzey, *A Study of Values*, Boston: Houghton Mifflin, 1960; was extended by William D. Guth and Renato Tagiuri, "Personal Values and Corporate Strategy," *Harvard Business Review*, September-October 1965, pp. 123–132; led to extensive research by George England, beginning with "Personal Value Systems of American Managers," *Academy of Management Journal*, March 1967, pp. 53–68; and continued in the work of such scholars as Barry Z. Posner and Warren Schmidt, "Values and the American Manager: An Update," *California Management Review*, Spring 1984, pp. 202–216, and James Weber, "Managerial Value Orientations: A Typology and Assessment," *International Journal of Value Based Management*, vol. 3, no. 2, 1990, pp. 37–54. A complete family tree of related research would display many other branches too numerous to list here. However, additional sources are cited in Chapter 5.

has lagged attempts to understand other aspects of human behavior that fall into the positivist's "factual" domain. In other words, *what* people do may be discerned scientifically, or even in some cases *why* they may do it, but not *whether* their actions are proper or improper. This positivist view has lain heavily on the corpus of Western economic theory which continues to divine an unbreachable boundary between the description of economic behavior (the "factual") and the prescriptions of economic policy (the "normative").

Given these cultural preconceptions and the array of diverse value outlooks that exist, it will be helpful to be specific about what the term "value" is intended to mean in the present theory of business values. "Value" here is given a fourfold meaning. When business values are described and their functions revealed, they will take these four forms. The two major types of business values mentioned earlier—economizing values and power-aggrandizing values—can be classified as having these four characteristics. The same can be said for ecologizing values, which lie outside the realm of business but interact with business values.

In one sense, "value" is a **belief**. As social psychologist Milton Rokeach says, "A *value* is an enduring belief that a specific mode of conduct or end-state of existence is personally or socially preferable to an opposite or converse mode of conduct or end-state of existence. A *value system* is an enduring organization of beliefs concerning preferable modes of conduct or end-states of existence along a continuum of relative importance."[5] Beliefs of this sort display cognitive, affective, and behavioral dimensions, thus giving insight into the knowing, emotive, and acting-out features of individual persons. Value defined in this way serves well the purposes of psychological theory and psychological analysis by conceptualizing values from the viewpoint of an individual who is looking outward to others in society. Beliefs form an important part of one's personality, and they can help locate and orient one person with respect to others in society. *So, a theory of business values based on this psychological conception of value would be (partially) a theory of the characteristic beliefs held by people in business.* For example, it is commonly believed by most of those in business that economizing is a proper business goal and that expanding the power and scope of a firm is to be expected under normal circumstances. Such beliefs are in a sense the psychological glue that binds a firm's many participants together in a common effort.

5. Milton Rokeach, *The Nature of Human Values*, New York: Free Press, 1973, p. 5. Anthropologist Clyde Kluckhohn's earlier conceptual formulations of value and value processes influenced the thinking of many subsequent social scientists, including Rokeach and Robin Williams, cited here. See Clyde Kluckhohn, "Values and Value Orientations in the Theory of Action," in Talcott Parsons and E. A. Shils (eds.), *Toward a General Theory of Action*, Cambridge, MA: Harvard University Press, 1951.

In another sense, "value" expresses a **relationship** that a person or group has to others or to the environment. Institutional economist Clarence Ayres has said: "'Value' is of course a relational word like 'truth' and 'cause,' to which, indeed, it is closely related. All these words refer to the interconnectedness of things in the universe and to the continuity of human experience which is itself a part of the universe. We speak of causality when we are thinking of the unity of the universe; we speak of truth when we are thinking of the coincident unity of our discourse; and we speak of value when we are thinking of the likewise coincident unity and continuity of our own life process."[6] In other words, values link people to one another by creating and encouraging commonly shared relationships and experiences. Value as relationship thus takes on a social or sociological meaning, as contrasted with the psychological definition of value as personal belief. *So, a theory of business values based on this sociological way of defining value would be (partially) a theory of the characteristic relations and linkages between people in business.* Any business firm consists largely of people working more or less together to achieve the goals declared by those who direct the enterprise. Organizational hierarchy is the typical form employed, although other forms also exist. A strong belief persists that these arrangements are proper, indeed requisite, to getting the economizing job done. Likewise, power aggrandizement rests on this particular business value in ways described later on.

In yet another sense, "value" refers to **judgment**, including the process that is involved in making judgments and the **standards** and **criteria** brought to bear in this judgmental process. This meaning of value is derived from the philosopher John Dewey, who emphasized the importance of the process by which means are appraised, that is, judged, as better or worse for attaining the ends sought. Dewey preferred the term "valuation" or "evaluation" to "value" to emphasize the processual nature of appraisal. Matching means to ends calls for careful judgments, clear criteria, and some way to know whether one is using appropriate means. Since goals, once attained, then become the means to yet other ends, all parts of the process take on a valuational or normative character. This means–ends process is a characteristic human way of solving problems or at least confronting them. Judgments informed by experience, intellect, and the moving frontier of scientific knowledge comprise the values that support this problem-solving process. Dewey's view of valuational phenomena as a judgmental process tied to experiential criteria is supported by sociologist Robin Williams, who maintains that the

---

6. Clarence E. Ayres, "The Value Economy," in Ray Lepley (ed.), *Value: A Cooperative Inquiry*, New York: Columbia University Press, 1949, p. 43.

"core phenomenon [of values] is the presence of *criteria or standards of prefer-ence.* . . ."[7]

So, a theory of business values using this means–ends concept of value would be (partially) a theory of the characteristic judgments made by people in business and the methods, processes, and standards by which those judgments are formed as problems are confronted. Both economizing values and power-aggrandizing values are af-fected by and take much of their everyday meaning from the instrumentalist, utilitarian judgments typical of business thinking. This is not to say that Dewey's conception of instrumental valuation processes has been perfectly mirrored in the utilitarian practices of business, for Dewey had something much broader and more profound in mind, a matter to be touched upon in a later chapter. As an illustrative example, though, there can be little doubt that instrumentalist criteria of success and failure, the utilitarian standards by which firms are judged, and the means–ends processes on which they rise and fall, are a central value component of all business enterprise.

These three meanings of "value," each derived from the scholarly litera-ture, are employed in the theory of business values developed here. One meaning—value as belief—is psychological or personal; another—value as re-lationship—is sociological or organizational; and still another—value as judg-mental standard—is philosophical or logical in construct. As Robin Williams says, "In the enormously complex universe of value phenomena, values are si-multaneously components of psychological processes, of social interaction, and of cultural patterning and storage."[8] Each meaning has a place in ex-plaining the role of values in the business system.

Underlying these concepts is a fourth layer of value significance that re-flects the **experiential nature** of values. Values are derived from human expe-riences that directly and importantly affect our lives. Values emerge from these life-affecting processes. Williams' insights are again useful:

There would seem to be no doubt that the value space of human life necessarily becomes filled with standards relating to all the significant types of objects of ex-

---

7. The Williams quotation is from his "Change and Stability in Values and Value Systems: A Soci-ological Perspective," in Milton Rokeach, *Understanding Human Values: Individual and Societal,* New York: Free Press, 1979, pp. 15–46. John Dewey summarized his ideas about value and valua-tion in John Dewey, "Theory of Valuation," *International Encyclopedia of Unified Science,* vol. II, no. 4, Chicago: University of Chicago Press, 1939. This projected encyclopedia was never published in its entirety; Dewey's contribution was published separately as a monograph. (Another well-known contribution, also published separately, is Thomas S. Kuhn's *The Structure of Scientific Revo-lutions.*) A comprehensive summary of some of the core ideas of Dewey and other American pragmatists is found in Sandra B. Rosenthal, *Speculative Pragmatism,* Amherst: University of Massa-chusetts Press, 1986, and her "Foundations, Rationality, and Intellectual Responsibility: A Prag-matic Perspective," *Reason Papers* 16, Fall 1991, pp. 73–74.

8. Williams, op. cit., p. 17.

perience. Values, accordingly, are always mapped on to the physical world, the human organism, other organisms, the biopsychic personality, social actors and relationships, cultural items, and cosmic or transcendental realms. . . . We know that values are learned. This means that they are developed through some kind of experience. . . . In the long run, values are responsive to changes in social experience; change in values can result from changes in information about oneself and one's social environment.[9]

For these experience-linked reasons, values do not stand apart from us—or we from them. We *experience* values, and they are integral to our existence. They help us to interpret and assign meaning to life's important experiences. "People are not detached or indifferent to the world; they do not stop with a sheerly factual view of their experience. Explicitly or implicitly, they are continually regarding things as good or bad, pleasant or unpleasant, beautiful or ugly, appropriate or inappropriate, true or false, virtues or vices."[10] There is always a connection—sometimes direct, at other times indirect and attenuated—between a life-affecting process and any value. This life-affecting process extrudes or forms values, which both reflect our experience and subsequently take symbolic and conceptual shape in our mind.

In an evolutionary sense, the most basic life-affecting experience is adaptation and survival. Biologists have hypothesized that values, along with the capacity to evaluate, must have been an evolutionary extension of, or supplement to, earlier natural selection pressures that "evaluated" and "selected" survival traits and behaviors in a nondeliberative, unconscious way. Richard Michod, for example, says that, "The adaptive significance of values at least originally, was that they produced fitness enhancing behavior in variable (novel?) environments. . . . [T]he original value must have been inclusive fitness."[11] The inclusive fitness of human extended family groups reflects, quite obviously, the most basic kind of human life-affecting experience possible. It is in this sense that values in the present account are said to be an outgrowth of experience and a first stage of development that eventually leads to their conscious consceptualization as beliefs, relationships, and evaluative criteria.

These extrusions of experience assume the diverse conceptual forms noted above because diverse conceptualizers have experienced these

9. Ibid., pp. 22, 35. This experience-bounded character of values is reported also by anthropologists Florence Kluckhohn and Frederick L. Strodtbeck, *Variations in Value Orientations*, Evanston, IL: Row, Peterson, 1961.

10. Ibid., p. 16.

11. Richard E. Michod, "Biology and the Origin of Values," in Michael Hechter, Lynn Nadel, and Richard E. Michod (eds.), *The Origin of Values*, New York: Aldine de Gruyter, 1993, pp. 265, 266. Michod and other contributors to this volume recognize that biological explanations of value phenomena are only a part of the story.

processes in diverse ways and organize value phenomena in a manner that is congenial to their work. Hence, we have the psychologist's focus on the beliefs held by individual persons; the sociologist's meaning of value that emphasizes interpersonal linkages; and the philosopher's logical construction of value phenomena. These varying conceptual forms are but abstractions of an underlying experiential process that gives meaning to all value forms. For example, business people experience—that is, operationally carry out—economizing functions. They are organized to do so within a familiar, long-experienced, power-aggrandizing system of powerful bosses and the more complaisant bossed. The beliefs, relationships, methods, and standards they rely upon in the workplace—in other words, their job-related values—are directly derived from the way they experience work within a business system.

The general sequence by which values assume symbolic shape is one that begins with an experience relevant to human life, which is then identified and assigned significance, and finally emerges as a conceptual abstraction that describes the experienced phenomenon as a "value." The tripartite sequence of value formation, then, is: first the life-affecting experience, then the assigned normative meaning, and then the conceptual abstraction or value label.

The values that suffuse the business system and that give business its unique function in society may therefore be understood as beliefs, as social relationships, as judgmental processes and criteria, and as manifestations of experience gained as problems are confronted. The specific forms taken by these values, and the way they exert their respective influence on business operations, are explored next.

THE VALUE SET OF BUSINESS

A distinctive set of values is typically found in business organizations. The value set includes the eight types of values shown in Figure 1–2. Three of these distinctive business values serve the firm's economizing function. Four others support power aggrandizement. One type—called "X-factor values"— is a kind of "wild card" or "joker" that can contribute to both economizing and power aggrandizing, or to only one of them, or to neither. X-factor values are described briefly in the following section and more fully in Chapter 5.

The eight types of values shown in Figure 1–2 provide the motivational power of the business firm. They also define its primary goals and determine the methods to be used. They condition and channel the behavior of all who work there. They provide the structure of core business beliefs, the judgmental methods employed, and the standards by which business behavior is assessed. In sum, they comprise the value matrix that causes business to be what

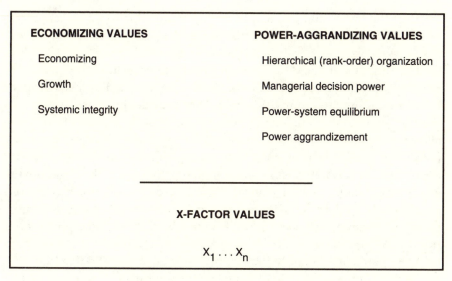

Figure 1–2. The value set of business

it is and to do what it does. Collectively, they present a picture of business values that is far more comprehensive than the one-dimensional notion of maximizing values embodied in much standard economic theory or the equally shallow idea that business values comprise little more than narrowly focused greed and grubby materialism.

It will be useful analytically to distinguish between "found values" and "original values" in business. This distinction identifies those values that are inherently and necessarily—as opposed to typically or characteristically—associated with business operations.

Found Values

The idea of "found values" can be summed up in a question: When one walks into a business firm, what values—that is, what beliefs, interconnecting relationships, and judgmental processes—can be found to be operating there? With keen enough insight and sufficient time, an observer could perhaps make an inventory of all the values at work in that firm. Those values that are "found" are simply the beliefs, relationships, and judgmental methods that prevail within the boundaries of the enterprise. It is the most comprehensive value set that can be described for any given business organization. It includes all of the value types listed in Figure 1–2. Although not found just in business, they will be characteristic of most businesses. As a practical matter, not all found values in a company are necessarily "found," that is, discovered, observed, or known. It may not be important to know or inventory all of them, or the cost of doing so may be unduly burdensome. Quite likely, some values will be hidden from view, although their effects might be felt or seen in behavioral form.

The entire set of found values drives the organization in identifiable channels and toward specific destinations. The operational significance of found values cannot be overestimated because they provide much, if not most, of the concerted motivational power and dynamism of the business firm. They allow it to founder or induce its success. The enterprise will strive to accomplish what it believes in, what it is organized to do, what in its judgment will accomplish its mission, and by those methods thought to be appropriate, which is only another way of saying that it will be driven to its work as a result of its prevailing values. All of these operational values are here called "found" values. Collectively, they sketch in the value character or value profile of a firm.

The operational, found values of one business firm will differ from the found values of another. The differences will appear in a number of ways. Growth in one company may be a stronger belief and practice than it is in another company, or growth in various measures (e.g., market share, return on investment, or gross sales) may be differentially emphasized from firm to firm. Team loyalty and workplace cooperation may dominate the thinking of one firm's employees, while in another this kind of value may be subordinated to the various demands of hierarchical precedence and status labeling. These differences reflect contrasting priority orderings of values within companies.

Besides such differing value priorities among firms, other factors can distinguish the value profile of one company from another's. Competitive market pressures may thrust a firm in the direction of one belief rather than another, as when a company that may prefer to operate in a freely competitive market seeks government protection from foreign competitors who enjoy state subsidies. So too may the specific life history of an enterprise exhibit the imprint of particular values, as frequently happens in entrepreneurial businesses founded by a person or group strongly committed to a particular way of doing business. Wal-Mart's founder, Sam Walton, was well known for a devotion to customer service, low-cost pricing, and a no-frills, no-nonsense "value for money" operation. These practical, experience-based principles became the values on which he built an enterprise of surpassing commercial success.

The element most responsible for variations among the found values in business firms is what is called "X-factor values." X-factor may be pictured as an empty box capable of being filled with a large assortment of beliefs, interpersonal and intraorganizational relationships, and judgments experienced by a company's many employees, regardless of the source from which these values may have stemmed. X-factor values are not simply the "personal," privately held values of those who participate in business life, although these are one important component of this value category. Such personal values are swept up, expressed within, and modified by the many interpersonal linkages that occur during the daily round of business operations. Values that may seem to be quite personal and individually unique tend to acquire a social dimension that deepens, expands, and sometimes inhibits the private meaning they have for any individual carrier. Managers were revealed by one famous study to be personally committed to compassion, tolerance, equality, dignity, honor, and religion but did not believe that these values were often brought into play as they made business decisions. Yet, other research suggests that personal value commitments can indeed influence business outcomes.[12]

For any given business firm, the X-factor box will contain a collection of such values that may or may not be the same as the collection in the X-factor box of another firm. The demographic diversity of a company's work force, and the complex matrix of life histories spawned by those culturally diverse features, combine to produce a vast range of value experiences that are brought into the firm on a daily basis. Since these values are at work in the minds and actions of the company's managers and employees, they exert an influence on what happens there. It is to such an X-factor value box that one must ascribe perhaps the greatest variation in found values from one firm to another, because the possible range of values held by the sum total of all persons at work in an organization is almost infinitely large.

The boundaries and substantive content of any given X-factor box would normally be set by the dominant value system of the firm's host society, but such boundaries can be breached by intruders from other societies or by members of culturally submerged outgroups who carry somewhat different values. Other value dissonances and variations in any given X-factor box can arise from individuals' intellectual explorations, philosophical speculations, psychological-emotional impulses, and the effects produced by broad social changes. So the bounded nature of X-factor boxes is by no means absolute. The potential problems thus posed for the business firm seeking stability and discipline within its work force loom large indeed. These problems are discussed more fully in Chapters 3 and 5.

Original Values

"Original values" in business are the defining beliefs, relationships, and judgmental processes that make business what it is as a human institution. These are the values that are necessary for carrying out the business functions; in that sense, they are the essential or core or first-order values. These beliefs lie

---

12. For the former, see England, *op. cit.* For the latter, see Barbara Ley Toffler, *Tough Choices: Managers Talk Ethics*, New York: John Wiley, 1986.

at the root or foundation of business as a socially approved activity. Of the eight values in the business value set (see Figure 1-2), three are original values. At their most fundamental, archetypal level, they can be identified as **economizing, growth,** and **systemic integrity**. Functionally interdependent, they cluster together to produce an economizing outcome for the business firm. Each is described further in the following chapter.

The associated notion of "origin" as a chronological beginning is less important in defining original values than the related idea of a primary form or type of value—an archetype—from which varieties are subsequently derived. Original values in business, as will be illustrated, do indeed constitute a primary, first-order form of belief-relationship-judgmental process that serves as a model or ideal form from which copies may be derived. Whether, and if so under what kinds of circumstances and with what early effects, these original values appeared together at the now very remote dawning of society's business activities is a tantalizing matter for speculation, but a definitive answer is not essential for grasping the intended meaning of original values. The original values of business necessarily appeared early, paralleling and sustaining certain vital functions that in time were recognized and labeled as "business" activities. But original values are more appropriately understood for their essential, indispensable function in defining what is meant by "business" than for the particular moment in human affairs when they could be said to have appeared. Even though the definition of original values does not rest on chronological precedence, it will become evident that these basic values appeared quite early in human history, but they attained their standing as original values by virtue of their functions and not simply by the fact of their early entry into human affairs.[13]

Original business values are necessarily "found values" because they are essential to the operation of any business firm. For that reason, they will always be present, that is, found to be actively expressed. Other found values, as

13. A large menu of cultural origin theories is available from which almost boundless speculation may be launched about the beginnings of many human practices. While sometimes interesting and relatively harmless, their at times impressive logic in making their respective cases is justifiably classified as speculative and creative. In this sense, they differ from theories of biological evolution, which rest on a more secure, empirically derived base of information. Three representative origin theories are found, respectively, in Leslie White, *The Science of Culture: A Study of Man and Civilization*, New York: Grove Press, 1949; Lewis Mumford, *The Myth of the Machine: Technics and Human Development*, New York: Harcourt, Brace & World, 1966; and Susanne Langer, *Philosophy in a New Key: A Study in the Symbolism of Reason, Rite, and Art*, Cambridge, MA: Harvard University Press, 1942. For White, human origins are rooted in the capacity to form symbols that aided adaptation; Mumford rejects an instrumentalist origin and favors a process that first tamed inner confusions, fears, and emotions arising from dreams; Langer embraces the emergence of symbolic ritual as the hallmark of early humanity. Some of their insights are revisited in later chapters of this book.

will be explained, though present and active, are not central to the business function and hence are not original.

As subsequent discussion reveals, other and more familiar descriptors for the three original values can clarify the intended meanings. The accepted measure of **economizing** success or failure is monetary profit and loss. Although faulty, imprecise, and unreliable, this measure is intended to convey the idea that a firm has (if profitable) or has not (if unprofitable) acted prudently and efficiently in using resources in ways that sustain (or do not sustain) its existence. Nearly all business firms of whatever size or complexity manifest rudimentary economizing—that is, make short-term profits—while only some manage to sustain steady-state economizing over extended periods of time. **Growth** is an outcome of enhanced productivity, which is a sign of ever more successful economizing by the firm. **Systemic integrity** implies organizational bonding of members to the firm and their cooperative interactions to promote the firm's economizing goals. These original values tend to predominate as a business firm operates. Indeed, they must, for they cause a business to be a business. To the extent that these basic beliefs, relationships, and judgmental criteria are present and effective, they define what is meant by the term "business."

The three original values of business *in combination* produce a unique type of function and phenomenon in society. We call that function "business." While other kinds of organizations with other societal functions—for example, a hospital, a charitable foundation, a military brigade—may display some of these same values, such as systemic integrity or economizing, their existence and societal justification rest on other bases, and most likely they draw on other values that distinguish them from the business institution. Values researcher Milton Rokeach has proposed that institutions such as business specialize in "the transmission of certain subsets of values from generation to generation, and as engaging in various activities designed to implement these values."[14] From this perspective, the business institution specializes in and transmits the values of economizing, growth, and systemic integrity. This economizing value cluster is its defining feature, and one mode of approaching and organizing those values involves the use and magnification of coercive power as an aspect of the power-aggrandizing value cluster. The original values that cohere to define the business function may be found also within other nonbusiness institutions. But while other organizations may display economizing features, their *raison d'être* arises from other sources and other

14. Rokeach, op. cit., 1979, p. 260. See also pp. 51–53. Nevertheless, as a theory of the historical origin and emergence of institutions, Rokeach's view partakes a bit too much of a teleologically instrumental, even rational, process of social change for one to be entirely comfortable with its implied preconceptions. But the notion that interrelated values cohere around various important human and social functions is useful and valid.

functions, such as health care, providing for the needy, or military security. Business's *raison d'être* is economizing. Its core values support that function. Business as a cultural function and activity depends on the combined interaction of the three original business values—economizing, growth, and systemic integrity—for its definition and societal justification. They make business what it is by being combined and expressed in the minds and operations of a firm's owners, managers, employees, and associated constituencies.

Four values in the basic value set of business are not original. They are **hierarchical (rank-order) organization, managerial decision power, power-system equilibrium,** and **power aggrandizement**. These four values are typically found in business but are neither the distinctive property of business firms nor determinative of business's unique function in society. Many other kinds of bureaucratic organizations share these values with business, although contemporary corporate business organization is characteristically imbued with them. Their functions and effects are discussed in a subsequent chapter, following a more thorough presentation of the meaning and significance of business's original values in the next chapter.

Before turning to that task, the formidable complexity of the value landscape both within and surrounding business deserves brief attention. It is best described as a constantly shifting melange of original (economizing) values, shaped and constrained and channeled by power-aggrandizing value impulses, penetrated and sometimes destabilized by swirling, never predictable currents of X-factor values, and—as will be seen further along—subject to ecological processes that criss-cross, sometimes supporting and sometimes contravening, the goals and values of business. In this view, business emerges as an institutional-organizational focus of values, a vortex around which diverse values circulate. Some of these values drive business toward economizing, others impel it toward power augmentation, and still others (X-factor) inject occasional diversity and variety into business operations.

Yet the value landscape offers an even more complex and tangled picture. The value set that is *within* business intersects yet another value set whose larger significance is centered in broadly defined communal ecosystems that extend well beyond business's organizational boundaries. The ecologizing values spawned out of these communal ecosystem networks provide yet another means, beyond economizing, for supporting life. Partially attuned to economizing while partially at odds with it, ecologizing undergirds the social value systems seen so frequently to be at odds with business values and purposes. Their fuller meaning is therefore a critical part of the story to be told if the tensions between business and society are to be understood. Immediately ahead, though, is a fuller account of those original business values that cause business to be what it is and to do what it does.

2

The Original Values of Business

The original values of business arise as manifestations of natural evolutionary processes. The forms they take reflect the operation of basic physical processes of the universe. This evolutionary embeddedness gives them their distinctive function in organized life and causes them to be an essential component in sustaining life itself. Although, as will be told subsequently, these values have an acquired cultural meaning, they are rooted firmly in biophysical and biochemical processes that gave them their first significance. As values, they are emergent from, or extrusions of, these natural processes, only subsequently being assigned a conceptual and culturally symbolic significance.

As noted in the preceding chapter, the original values of business are the most fundamental, most archetypal, most basic values present in the business system. Their central position in the business value matrix is testimony to, and largely explained by, their emergence from a natural evolutionary process of the most comprehensive, all-encompassing character. Indeed, the range of phenomena encompassed within that process extends from the microscopic dimensions of molecular genetics to the large-scale phenomena of cosmic evolution. Across that entire spectrum, one finds what appear to be physical constants at work that give momentum and force to evolutionary tendencies. It is those physical constants that have spawned, and continue to justify, the original values of business. Just how that naturalistic process has produced such a result is worth careful attention.

The three original values in the basic business value set—economizing, growth, and systemic integrity—are so interwoven in their meanings and functions that it is desirable, even essential, to define and discuss them together. They are, in fact, an interrelated *cluster* of values and are collectively labeled "Value Cluster I." Together, they sustain economizing. These three values are present in all business organizations, creating a set of motives, defining lines of expected and socially necessary behavior, and setting priorities for the achievement of business goals. They lie at the deepest layers of business consciousness and represent the most fundamental components of business culture. They are rarely if ever questioned. Their existence and continued presence are assumed to define the core purpose—the *raison d'être*—of the business institution. It is through the operationalization of these values that a business firm adapts to its environment and lives to see another accounting quarter. Economizing, when well directed, produces profits; growth manifests enhanced productivity; and systemic integrity achieves the requisite amount of internal organizational integration to make it all possible. Of the three values, economizing is of paramount importance.

FIRST ORIGINAL VALUE: ECONOMIZING

For human beings, "economizing" means the prudent, careful, sometimes deliberately calculated, rational-where-possible actions of individuals, groups, and organizations that are intended to produce net outputs or benefits from a given amount of resource inputs. An "economical" action is one in which this net output has been produced. An "economical" person is one who acts with this intention and result in any given situation calling for this kind of behavior. An economizing objective involves choice among options and a need to judge a range of possible outcomes of these choices. One knows that economizing has occurred when it is possible to observe, estimate, calculate, measure, and verify the output result. A benefit–cost calculus is typically applied as a way of knowing whether or to what extent economizing has occurred.

An illustrative example is Tenneco, a company that had suffered declining earnings and was facing a 1991 loss of $732 million. A newly appointed CEO and chairman took decisive action, according to news reports. He "sought out inefficiencies, such as the 179-mile routes that some parts used to travel *inside* factories. Quality teams . . . re-engineered some manufacturing processes to improve productivity and profit margins. . . . [W]elds on certain car parts [were] shortened, scrap metal previously tossed out [was] recycled, and machines that stamped circular designs from square sheets of aluminum—creating large amounts of waste—[were] redesigned."[1] This search for efficiency, the unrelenting effort to weed out ineffective practices, and the attempt to make better use of materials, machines, and workers' time—all of these are the mark of economizing.

In normal business affairs, a benefit–cost approach is a well-known and widely accepted means of recording the economizing success or failure of

1. "New Blood: Tenneco Hired a CEO from Outside, and He Is Refocusing the Firm," *The Wall Street Journal,* March 29, 1993, pp. A1, A14.

business firms. The net output occurs as "profit" and, according to accounting convention, is recorded on the "bottom line" of the profit-and-loss report. A firm that has failed the economizing test records a "loss," meaning that its actions diminished, rather than multiplied, the potential output from a given amount of input resources initially at its command.

"Profit" and the "bottom line" are ideal abstractions subject to qualification. A firm's profit may be calculated in several different ways, thanks to the never-ending ingenuity of accountants and to the equally never-ending changes made in tax laws and interpretive rules. Hence, what appears as a profit by using one measure may well turn out to be either higher or lower or even a loss if yet another measuring device is used. IBM's accountants, for example, found several ways to record anticipated revenues well before they were to be received, thus presenting a public picture of profits that was said to be more positive than the firm's underlying economic prospects justified. These imaginative accounting initiatives occurred during a period when company losses were mounting—with nearly $5 billion lost in 1992—and stock values had declined sharply. Tenneco proved equally adept, though its accounting maneuvers deliberately *revealed* losses that had previously been recorded as profits. Financial bystanders cheered these accounting miracles.[2] As far as the bottom line goes, the summed columns of a financial report can now be qualified by so many subsequent footnotes concerning various contingent conditions that the "bottom line," meaning the last line of the report, is often found several pages away from the figure that records the firm's profit or loss.

Economizing in the following discussion is not limited to human beings and their organizations. As will be explained, plants, non-human animals, and all other life forms are capable of economizing actions. They take in "resources" and produce a net output of energy, which may be used for survival, growth, and work. These organic economizing activities, which are nonteleological and nonpurposive in any conscious sense, are for the most part an outcome of genetically encoded processes, although human domestication of both plants and animals, and more recently genetic engineering, obviously exert an effect on the amount and direction of this broader kind of economizing activity. The fact that animals, plants, bacteria, and so on do not "know" that they are economizing does not change the economical result of their genetically encoded or domestically induced intake and output activities. This point is made clearer during the subsequent discussion of entropy.

Economizing in this sense can be understood as a value in terms of the fourfold meaning presented in the previous chapter. Business people accept

2. The IBM episode was reported in "Softer Numbers: As IBM's Woes Grew, Its Accounting Tactics Got Less Conservative," *The Wall Street Journal,* April 7, 1993, pp. A1, A6. For Tenneco, see "New Blood," op. cit., p. A14.

economizing as a central **belief**. Economizing also involves and requires that a certain set of **systemic relationships** obtain between employees in a firm and between the firm and its environmental surroundings (these are explained later on). And economizing is attained only after a person or group has made **judgments about the suitability of various means and methods** for achieving economical ends. Moreover, all human (and business) economizing takes place within an **experiential realm** where problems are confronted and solutions sought. Economizing in all four of these senses is a core value of business, indispensable to the firm and to human society generally. Neither firm nor society could long exist without business economizing.

Economizing as an Energy Transformation Process

Economizing occurs as a process of energy transformation. This process is fundamental to life. Each living thing—each life unit—whether a human being, a plant, an animal, or an interrelated group of any of these, must find ways to absorb energy from its environment and convert that energy into forms suitable for its existential needs. Absent this basic, fundamental activity, no life unit can long endure. Those life entities that prove to be adept at this energy absorption-and-conversion process survive. Others less adept do not.

The term "life unit" is used here and throughout the discussion to refer to any entity capable of sustained life, including all biotic forms. A plant, a bacterium, an animal, a human being, all other types of organisms, and interrelated and interdependent groups of each of these that are able to sustain an independent life more than momentarily are considered to be life units. This usage is adopted partially as a more economical way to refer to various types of biota, as well as to acknowledge a large measure of phenomenological uniformity of processes found among wide-ranging life forms. It is also intended to emphasize the adaptive, survival-oriented linkages among members of a given species that sustain life, not just for individual members of these groups but for all members of such communities. Hence, a band, flock, or herd of animals, or a community of plants where some shelter with others—or symbiotic groupings of plants and animals—are life units. So too are human families, organizations, communities, and other forms of human association that sustain life through economizing. Included among these human associations are business firms to the extent that they manifest the original (economizing) values of Value Cluster I. An ability to economize, and to do so on a sustained basis, is normally the minimal distinguishing mark of any life unit. The term thus embraces both biological and cultural meanings.[3]

---

3. Biologists identify five major classifications (called "Kingdoms") of life forms. For a description, see Lynn Margulis and Karlene V. Schwartz, *Five Kingdoms: An Illustrated Guide to the Phyla of Life on Earth*, San Francisco: W. H. Freeman, 1982.

If general life processes among plants, animals, bacteria, and other forms of life are examined in their evolutionary contexts, it becomes apparent that species as well as individual units (i.e., a single plant, animal, or bacterium) are naturally occurring and evolving vessels or devices that are continually engaged in absorbing and converting energy into various forms that run toward a variety of results. In this evolutionary process, it is the flow of energy into and out of life entities that is constantly present, whereas individual units and even entire species ebb and flow, sometimes failing the ultimate test of energy-conversion efficiency and thus dying out. "Nature" seems to be "indifferent" concerning whether any given individual life unit survives or not, the entire matter turning on a unit's ability to assimilate and convert energy into a form useful for its continuation. Energy flow sustains but transcends individual lives.

"Economizing" is the descriptor for this process, whether carried out by a plant, animal, human being, or groups of these. That is, when an individual life entity takes in energy from its environment and converts it into useful work (i.e., generates what are called "outputs"), we say that an economizing process has occurred. It has been economical because net work outputs are produced from resource inputs. In order for this result to occur, the animal, plant, person, or group must have been prudent, frugal, and sparing—that is, economical—in the treatment of energy inputs.

The anthropomorphic language forms used here produce an unfortunate effect. Neither plants nor animals are capable of prudence, frugality, or sparing behavior in any conscious or deliberative sense. In the same way, when economizing is defined as the care and skill with which energy inputs are treated by a life unit, it could be said that neither plants nor animals exercise "care," nor do plants have "skills." What has been called "caringness" and "skills" by human beings is genetically encoded in plants and animals. Hence, the latter two exhibit a process of energy absorption and conversion that runs toward the same ends as the consciously executed and directed care and skills of economizing human beings. In both cases, the economizing result is the same, namely, an economical use of energy inputs that produces a net margin or gain of work outputs sufficient to sustain the life unit.

One can speak validly of energy "inputs" and "outputs" and the creation of an energy "margin" only in reference to and from the perspective of an individual life unit; even then, a misrepresentation of the economizing process can occur. The law of the conservation of energy (discussed in the following section) requires energy inputs and outputs to be balanced, hence ruling out a "margin" or "net excess." A life unit's "margin" of energy is thus illusory because the energy thus acquired and directed toward work in support of that life unit is balanced by an equivalent amount of energy diverted from other life entities or converted into a waste stream of inaccessible energy. Nevertheless, the work inputs that are created from the energy that flows through any

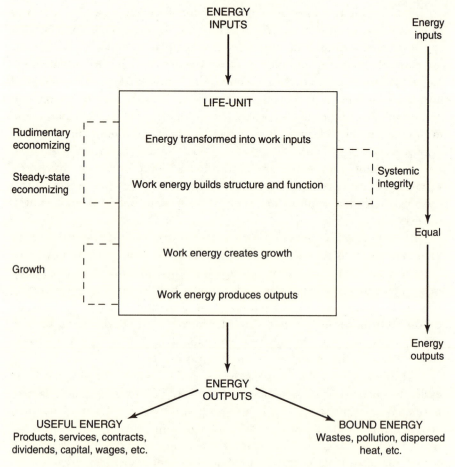

Figure 2–1. Energy transformation within a life unit

given life unit sustain its existence. In this sense, "work" takes on a much broader meaning than usual. It refers to the ordering of processes within the life unit and the movement of energy both *internally*, so as to support the life unit's various functions and operations, and *externally* to mediate its relations with the environment. In drawing energy from the environment, a life unit converts some of that energy into useful (work) inputs that sustain its life, build the unit's morphological structure, and contribute to its various functional processes. Other work inputs create outputs (e.g., goods and services in the case of business firms) that are sent out beyond the life unit's boundaries into the surrounding environment. These relationships are depicted in Figure 2–1. Hence, while life units seemingly disperse "outputs" that exceed their "inputs," thus appearing to have created a "margin" that sustains and amplifies their lives, they do so only by appropriating energy from others and by transforming the overall fund of environmental energy from useful forms to waste forms. The natural forces that produce this peculiar, even puzzling, outcome are discussed next.

Entropy and Thermodynamic Laws

The British author C. P. Snow, in a widely read commentary on the relations between the humanities and science, once declared that most students of the humane studies were quite unaware of the laws of thermodynamics, just as most scientists were probably unversed in Shakespeare's sonnets.[4] Snow's observation, applied to those who study human values, no doubt remains valid some three decades later. Snow's underlying concern was that much of the scientific knowledge that was then revolutionizing human affairs was inaccessible to those in the nonscientific community whose leadership positions gave them great sway over world affairs. Students of the humanities today—through their novels, essays, philosophic studies, commentaries, paintings, plays, films, poetry, music, sculpture, and dance forms—continue to exert significant influence on culture and public life. Hence, any intellectual chasm that separates those who pursue the humane studies from scientists may continue to hobble the efforts of both groups in working to understand the value realm of human behavior.

This problem may be particularly acute among those who ponder the role of values and ethics in business. A deeply rooted antibusiness bias animates much humanistic commentary provided by philosophers of business ethics, who frequently lack scientific training. Nor can scientists, whose discoveries and methods exert such far-reaching influence on business affairs, claim any special, well-developed insight into the moral implications of their scientific work. Few observers of the business scene would want to make the case that business people themselves have any noteworthy insight into the morality of their actions or that they are steeped in scientific know-how. Snow's two-culture gap may appear as a three-culture gap in the world of business values—with humanist philosophers, science workers, and business functionaries mutually alienated by their respective ignorance of each other's sphere of knowledge and expertise. Snow's general perspective and sense of concern are endorsed here in the analysis of values within the business system. Not only the students of business values but especially those persons who occupy leadership positions within business institutions can gain new insights into the values that drive business decisions and policies by drawing on multidisciplinary knowledge from the sciences and from humanistic philosophy. Nor is

---

4. C. P. Snow, *The Two Cultures and the Scientific Revolution: The Rede Lecture, 1959*, New York: Cambridge University Press, 1961, p. 16.

it beyond belief that a reciprocal benefit will accrue to humanist scholars and scientists in the form of their greater understanding of business operations.

Of all the several scientific and philosophic perspectives that have been generated, none equals the significance of the laws of thermodynamics in clarifying business values, especially and fundamentally the economizing values of Value Cluster I. In what follows, two contrasting, and in some ways contradictory, accounts are given concerning the significance of thermodynamic laws. These differing perspectives reflect a deep-seated controversy that rages among cosmologists about the origin and evolution of the universe.

One view, the first to be set forth here, is relentlessly austere. It argues that thermodynamic processes are driving the expanding universe—which is said to have begun with an instantaneous Big Bang—toward a "heat death" characterized by random dispersal and cooling of all matter and energy until none can any longer support life. This view also posits the possibility of an eventual collapse back onto itself of the randomly dispersed matter and energy, which may then begin the process all over again. Obviously, human prospects are not seen to be very rosy in this scenario, although the time scale is so vast that this cosmological Armageddon is not, so to speak, just around the corner.

Others doubt the pessimism implied by the Big Bang theory. In fact, some cosmologists even argue that the Big Bang never happened.[5] This group includes those who believe that the classical, broadly accepted scientific explanations of the universe's origin lack verification and that accumulating evidence is inconsistent with a Big Bang beginning. Rather than a universe that is running down, even as it expands toward random nothingness, some theorists discern self-organizing processes that, taken together, offset any tendency for order and life to be snuffed out on the Final Day at the End of Time.

Paradoxically, both views may be true, and a fair amount of what follows in this book is intended to show how that may be so, at least as far as the controversy bears on an understanding of business values. The key to unlocking this value puzzle is found in the varying scales on which natural processes operate, some of those scales being focused and time-specific, others applying broadly to vastly longer time spans and larger-scale phenomena. As in most attempts to build understandings from an evolving base of scientific knowledge, this one assumes the risks that new scientific discoveries will invalidate the preliminary and provisional conclusions reached here.

---

5. Eric J. Lerner, *The Big Bang Never Happened*, New York: Vintage Books, 1992. Lerner's account is used here to trace some aspects of the controversy. Quite aside from disagreements among scientists, theologians of many different persuasions reject any and all scientific efforts to fathom the origin of the universe, proffering and preferring supernatural explanations.

Entropy I: The Austere View. Economizing takes its meaning from entropy. "Entropy" is a state or condition that is described by the first and second laws of thermodynamics. As first formulated during the nineteenth century, these two linked physical laws were intended to describe the movement or transformation of energy in the form of heat; hence, they became known as the laws of "thermo" (i.e., heat) "dynamics" (i.e., movement, flow, or transformation). Subsequently, these relationships were found to be statable in terms of both information theory and statistical probability theory or statistical mechanics. But the original term "thermodynamics" has remained the standard way of referring to these phenomena. All three ways of stating the laws are recognized and accepted today by science scholars.[6]

The first law of thermodynamics says that the energy in any closed or isolated system may be changed from one form of energy to another but none can be created or destroyed. After any flow, exchange, or transformation of the energy within any such system, the total amount of energy remains the same as it was before these energy movements occurred. Sometimes this law is called the "law of the conservation of energy," because energy is conserved, that is, it remains the same in total amount although it may change in form or type or quality.

While the overall quantity of energy remains the same, its quality may change dramatically. The usual example given is a lump of coal that, unburned, contains energy potentially available to perform work. When burned, it releases that energy in the form of heat, which may then be directed to the water in a boiler that generates heated steam vapor that can be used to turn a wheel or drive a piston. Not all of the coal's energy is converted into heat and put to work; some of the heat energy escapes into the surrounding air, and some is transformed into unusable ash and waste gases. But once the burning process is complete, the total amount of energy remains the same: some of it is transformed into heat energy that is used for work, some heat energy escapes into the air and is not used directly for work (although in cold weather it may be used to warm an enclosure, in which case it constitutes a form of work), and some of the coal's energy is converted into waste gases and some into ash. If all of these energy components were combined, they would equal the amount of energy found in the lump before it was burned, but clearly, the diverse forms of energy released in the burning are of different quality.

This first law of thermodynamics has been generalized and is thought to

6. For a discussion, see Daniel R. Brooks and E. O. Wiley, *Evolution as Entropy: Toward a Unified Theory of Biology*, Chicago: University of Chicago Press, 1986. This is not to say that all now accept the earlier interpretations of thermodynamic processes; for example, see Lerner, op. cit., pp. 117–121.

be a valid explanation of the flow and transformation of energy throughout the universe. This means that energy in the universe is believed to be constant, neither increasing nor decreasing in total amount. But the universe's matter and energy are in a more or less constant state of transformation from one form or manifestation to another: solid fuels are burned, giving up their energy, as in the lump of coal; heated bodies cool, giving up their energy to the surrounding environment; the earth's star, the sun, burns at a ferocious rate, giving up its energy in the form of radiation products, heat, and light; living creatures and plants take in energy from their surroundings and transform that energy into sinew and structure; and the universe has expanded (and apparently continues to expand) at an almost inconceivable speed, spawning galaxies, star systems, and all manner of matter and energy in wondrous diversity and complexity.

Thus is set perhaps the basic condition on which all matter and life turn. We live in, and the physical universe exists in, a condition or sea of energy. The source of most of the energy that presently sustains matter and life on earth is our sun, a star of immensely greater mass than our planet. No creature, whether plant, animal, or human, can exist without drawing on and utilizing this solar energy source.[7] A combination of genetic propensities, biological evolution, and (in the case of humans) cultural innovations has made possible the multiform ways of using energy for survival, growth, and efflorescence. Of energy, there is plenty. It neither decreases nor increases in overall amount. It is neither created nor destroyed, being merely transformed from one state to another. In a way, this is a comforting finding, assuming that adequate and reliable means of energy conversion and transformation can be found and sustained.

Or so it seems. It is not until one ponders the second law of thermodynamics that a somewhat different and unsettling, even ominous, perspective enters into one's consciousness. For the second law of thermodynamics holds that energy and matter move toward a condition of maximum disintegration, disorder, and degradation. This means that energy quality changes significantly. Useful energy (i.e., that which can perform work) is transformed into unavailable energy (i.e., wastes). All energy "runs downhill" into a sink of unusable waste matter. Waste in the form of unusable energy and matter accumulates faster than the products made possible by work energy, which means that pollution outstrips gains in material production. Energy costs outrun energy benefits.

---

7. Other forms of energy reach the earth, such as light and radiation of various forms from other star systems within our own galaxy, and light and energy originating outside our galaxy. Cosmic rays arising from remote energy sources are believed to have the ability to initiate genetic mutations. Heat energy is also present within the earth's molten core and makes its presence known through volcanic action and ocean-floor spreading. Some scientists now speculate that primitive bacteria-like life forms live within and draw energy from compounds associated with magma flowing from crevices created by ocean-floor spreading.

This process of energy degradation is called "entropy." According to the second law of thermodynamics, entropy constantly increases throughout the universe and in any closed or isolated system. Entropy is inexorable and unavoidable. It appears to offer no escape. It is nature's vise. It condemns all matter and energy to the same fate, which is ultimate disintegration and disorder: living things die; metals rust and crumble; stars burn, collapse inward, and sputter out. Worse, these entropic effects are irreversible. A lump of coal, once burned, cannot be reconstituted; entropy has changed it to heat, gas, and ash. Humpty Dumpty cannot be put together again. Living things, once dead, cannot be "raised" or "reincarnated," although their matter and energy are in a sense "recycled." Moreover, time goes in only one direction; "time machines" that permit travel backward (at any pace) and forward (at a pace faster than entropy dictates) occur only in science fiction.

As a foremost physicist once said:

> So the following proposition is true: in any process that is irreversible, the entropy of the whole world is increased. Only in reversible processes does the entropy remain constant. Since no process is absolutely reversible, there is always at least a small gain in entropy; a reversible process is *an idealization* in which we have made the gain of entropy minimal.[8]

Put together, the first and second laws of thermodynamics give this picture: While energy is constant throughout the universe and in any closed or isolated system, being neither created nor destroyed (the first law), energy is constantly transformed from useful to less useful forms, from free energy to bound energy, until it reaches an ultimate destination (a maximum probability) of random disorder and disintegration (the second law). "Time's Arrow," as this process is sometimes poetically called to denote the unidirectional movement of time, points toward this inexorable and irreversible end state.

Economizing and entropy thus stand as polar opposites in nature's evolving theater, posing opposite tendencies in human affairs. Economizing is a process of energy transformation, fundamental to life, permitting life units to assimilate environmental energy. By contrast, entropy degrades all energy, posing the ultimate challenge to all life units. An economizing person or plant or animal thrives only by drawing in and efficiently using energy that by its very use is thereby changed into qualitative forms less accessible for further use (bear in mind the lump of coal). This economizing process is the only way to survive, grow, develop, and flourish. But if entropic processes are at work (and they always are), even the most efficient economizer can hope only to stave off, but not to escape, an ultimate state of disorder and chaos.

---

8. Richard P. Feynman, "[Lecture 44] The Laws of Thermodynamics," *The Feynman Lectures on Physics: Commemorative Issue,* Reading, MA: Addison-Wesley, 1963, 1989, p. 44:12.

The only "outs" allowed by this austere view of the second law are temporary slowdowns in entropy increases. These are temporary fluctuations in the disintegrative process and are situation-bounded. Even though a single creature may find ways to absorb energy, survive, grow, and develop over a long span of time, it cannot do so infinitely and is successful only by increasing entropy at some other point within its total environmental system, for example, by eating plants and/or animals and converting their energy into its own while obviously bringing their victims' existence to an end by appropriating their acquired energy for its own needs. At that moment in time, the creature has "defeated" entropy, but it will prove to be a fleeting victory, perhaps repeated again and again only to eventuate in its own decline and demise.

Genetic traits and processes may play a crucial role in bringing about the finiteness of life for plants, animals, and humans. One leading genetic theoretician has suggested that the fatal infirmities of old age may possibly be a function of "bad" genes being "turned on" by processes not yet recognized or understood. This down side of genetic functioning is thought to be partially offset by the generational transmission of genes from one person (or plant or animal) to another, thus preserving and perpetuating a given gene line indefinitely. But even as the gene line itself is sustained, quite obviously the individual carriers of this gene line successively die off, as they individually succumb to some combination of genetic malfunction, natural selection processes, accidents, and entropic trends.[9]

Different portions of the universe and different processes that govern them experience entropy at diverse rates. Time's Arrow is not uniform at all points in the universe. It may therefore appear that some natural processes (e.g., biological evolution) or some of nature's living things—by sustaining life over very long time periods—have an ability to contradict the second law and its entropic tendencies. But this notion is an illusion that fails to consider the larger disorder (i.e., the entropy) in the overall system that is necessary to sustain a temporary slowdown in the rate of entropy increase at any one point in that system. The higher and more complex forms of life, by utilizing greater amounts of energy, place a higher entropic burden on the ecosystem environment than those life forms that are simpler and less advanced. Their survival is purchased by imposing entropy on others.

The reasons are to be found in the operation of the second law of thermodynamics. That law assures us that for every economizing gain, there is a correlative degradation that diminishes the fund of energy available to support life. In other words, economizing, while life-supporting at its point of occurrence, always increases entropy at some other point within the total environmental system. For example, an electric power plant may generate usable energy for its customers, who thereby slow entropy's effects on themselves,

9. See Richard Dawkins, *The Selfish Gene*, New York: Oxford University Press, 1976.

but the waste products puffed out of the plant's stacks may create acid rain that destroys forests and aquatic life and may produce harmful "greenhouse" effects by warming the earth's atmosphere. The temporary (economizing) respite gained by some is more than offset by the environment's (entropic) degradation. The costs of holding open the entropic vise are therefore large, and the benefits, though welcome at the time, are in a sense illusory, for they can never be as large as the ultimate costs. Energy runs downhill, never up-hill. The process is irreversible. Time's Arrow moves on, varying its rate but not its destination.[10]

Entropy II: Order from Disorder. There is another view of thermodynamic effects. It argues that thermodynamic process provides way stations—life oases—on the road to what otherwise may seem to be ultimate doom. Organization and order emerge in an evolving universe, appearing even to be inherent features of Time's Arrow itself. While an entropic outcome (i.e., maximum disorder) is an inescapable fate of each living form, a countertendency embodying order, organization, pattern, and regularity stands opposed to entropic trends. In the human arena, invention, creativity, self-awareness, social awareness, intellectual exploration, symbolic forms, and technological complexity appear. Out of this organizing regularity, a sustained existence becomes possible.

A short excursion into recently developed cosmological and biological theory indicates, as one source says, "how order can emerge from disorder in terms of a new scientific paradigm [called] 'self organisation.' This argues, contrary to received wisdom, that the Second Law is *not* synonymous with an inexorable collapse into disorder. While this might be the final state of matter and points towards a corrupted and decayed universe at the end of time, the Second Law most certainly does not claim that this trend occurs uniformly throughout space and time."[11] The reason is related to a distinction made by theorists between thermodynamic *equilibrium* (where entropy has

10. Stanley W. Angrist and Loren G. Hepler, *Order and Chaos: Laws of Energy and Entropy*, New York: Basic Books, 1974; and Brooks and Wiley, op. cit. A user-friendly albeit somewhat alarmist account of entropy, its impact on economic problems, and the implications for economic policy is Jeremy Rifkin's *Entropy: A New World View*, New York: Viking, 1980, especially Part Two, The Entropy Law. An Afterword by Nicholas Georgescu-Roegen, a pioneer in bringing entropy into the body of economic theory, contains a summary comment about entropy's broader ramifications for public economic policies. For a critical account of how thermodynamics has influenced the formation of neoclassical economic theory, see Philip Mirowski, *More Heat Than Light: Economics as Social Physics, Physics as Nature's Economy*, New York: Cambridge University Press, 1990.

11. Peter Coveney and Roger Highfield, *The Arrow of Time*, London: W. H. Allen, 1990, pp. 35, 36. Two additional sources are M. Mitchell Waldrop, *Complexity: The Emerging Science at the Edge of Order and Chaos*, New York: Simon & Schuster, 1992; and Roger Lewin, *Complexity: Life at the Edge of Chaos*, New York: Macmillan, 1992. It is, of course, another human conceit to believe that the human species would be around to observe these Armageddon-like conclusions whether they are ushered in cataclysmically or more like a whimper.

been maximized and total disintegration and dispersal of energy and matter have occurred) and *nonequilibrium* states that may be far from an entropic finality.

> The remarkable fact is that while far from equilibrium the global entropy production increases at a furious rate, consistent with the Second Law, we can nevertheless observe exquisitely ordered behaviour. . . . True, at the "end" of time, when no further change can occur, randomness may win. But over shorter timescales we can see the emergence of evanescent structures which survive for as long as the flow of matter and energy continues. Indeed, it is important to appreciate that a system can only be held away from equilibrium if it is open to its environment: this enables the entropy produced by the system to be exported to the surroundings, *thereby permitting the maintenance of organisation* [emphasis added] while allowing an overall increase in the entropy of the system *and* the environment. . . . In such a universe, irreversible non-equilibrium thermodynamics allows for the possibility of spontaneous self-organisation leading to structures ranging from planets and galaxies to cells and organisms.[12]

Both genetic and cultural functions that slow entropy's relentless erosion of life prospects—in other words, those features that, occurring far from thermodynamic equilibrium, keep entropy at bay—are clearly observable. Some have argued that the earth itself has become increasingly hospitable to life by capturing energy flows and converting them into a self-replicating life process.[13] Genetic mutations, the emergence of species, and morphological and functional adaptations that exhibit a similar kind of survival value are widespread among both plants and animals. These counterentropic processes seem to occur in all living entities. In some species, they are genetically encoded. In others, including humans, they are an admixture of genetics and of consciously learned and invented behavioral disciplines. In all cases, they are markers of what cosmologists have called self-organization ten-

---

12. Ibid., pp. 164, 168. These authors provide a quite readable summary of the remarkable, even revolutionary, theoretical and empirical work that accounts for the simultaneous existence of entropy and these counteracting, life-sustaining processes; see especially Chapters 5, 6, and 7. Another account is found in Ronald F. Fox, *Energy and the Evolution of Life*, New York: W. H. Freeman, 1988, which describes the theory of self-assembly of rudimentary life forms, another manifestation of this counterentropic phenomenon. This kind of patterning and organizing regularity is not limited to life forms, for various chemical compounds appear to be organized and in some cases are thereby rendered stable by the same self-organizing processes, which is yet another indication that thermodynamic laws operate across the full spectrum of biotic and nonbiotic phenomena.

13. James E. Lovelock, *Gaia*, New York: Oxford University Press, 1979; and Lerner, op. cit., pp. 306–318. For a skeptical view of the Gaia concept, see Paul Ehrlich, "Coevolution and Its Applicability to the Gaia Hypothesis," in Stephen H. Schneider and Penelope J. Boston (eds.), *Scientists on Gaia*, Cambridge, MA: MIT Press, 1991, pp. 19–22.

dencies that, albeit temporarily and provisionally, keep life forms away from thermodynamic equilibrium.

As noted earlier, these two cosmological viewpoints frame a controversy that conditions the theory of business values developed in this book. It is quite possible that each perspective, though opposed to the other, is meaningful in forming a picture of the values that are central to the business function as we know it. That will be a working hypothesis in the pages ahead.

Economizing as Process and Value

Most, and certainly the most fundamental, processes that allow economizing to proceed in humans are genetically encoded, taking the form of "involuntary" processes that operate according to DNA instructions. These include the digestive system (literally an input–output process), the heart-lung-circulatory system (also input–output), the immune system (which defends the integrity of the whole), the neural system (which detects, comprehends, coordinates, and defends), ovarian function (egg production, fertilization, gestation, birth, lactation, menstruation, menopause), sexual stimulus–response and function (arousal, receptivity, erection, insemination), the muscular and skeletal structures, the diurnal-nocturnal pattern of waking and sleeping, and other such functional processes and features. Each of these can be affected positively or negatively by an overlay of sociocultural instructions and supplements. These cultural processes condition, but do not substitute for or eliminate, the gene-based instructions embedded in a person's DNA.

Beyond (but also linked to) this genetic base, humans display a capacity for symbol creation and symbol manipulation—to which the label "culture" has been attached—that outruns related processes found in other species. By combining its own highly generalized biological and physiological features with a neural-based sociocultural symbol system, the genus *Homo*, particularly *Homo sapiens*, has proved to be a remarkably adept economizer. Now numbering nearly 6 billion, earth's human population continues an expansive growth that is only a few million years in process and that promises to spawn even greater numbers. In sheer survival capability and fecundity, discounting an unevenness by geographic region (revealed by famine, massive floods, volcanic eruptions, epidemic diseases, warfare, and various other natural and sociocultural events), human economizing has indeed demonstrated overwhelming success.

Noting human population growth as an index of gross adaptive success need not mean, nor does it here, that sheer numbers are a measure of human adaptive needs. Current and projected population pressures on human ecosystems, when linked with culturally driven processes that produce acid rain, atmospheric warming, rain forest clearing, and depletion of stratospheric ozone, sketch potential problems of terrifying proportions. For all of its adaptive support, human culture vies with more ancient, highly successful genetic processes. Hence, cockroaches have been around at least 340 million years longer than humans, and their numbers unquestionably are greater than ours, so a case might be made for a gene-based adaptive ability that may well outrun culture-based adaptation. Survivability of either individuals or entire species rests to a large extent on the competitive traits and/or skills they manifest in an evolutionary process of natural selection. Both cockroaches and humans seem to be reasonably successful in finding survival niches within their respective (and regretably overlapping) ecosystems.

In its earliest and simplest phases, economizing is rudimentary and survival-oriented. Each life unit functions in ways that permit it to assimilate energy in sufficient amounts to begin life-supporting activities, however precarious and fleeting that life may initially be. In most life forms, genetics plays a key role, often the only role, in instituting rudimentary economizing, being responsible for the DNA-embedded information bits that specify diverse routes for energy absorption and assimilation.

Rudimentary economizing among humans, though impelled forcefully by similar genetic-encoding processes, is supplemented by culture and powerfully extended through the traits of conscious awareness, foresight, a high degree of intelligence, and supportive familial bonds. Thus, long before there was anything remotely resembling what we now call "business," rudimentary economizing was an extruded human value, manifesting and reflecting the natural evolutionary process that spawned it. Only much later was it to be conceptualized as such a value, then rationalized as a sought value to be placed within an organizational, institutional frame, and eventually evolved as a focused functional institution described as "economic" or labeled "business."[14] Economizing thus passed from its initial, rudimentary, unstable phase into a more permanent, sustained economizing process, deliberately sought and cultivated by its human sponsors. Today, economizing among humans is clearly a blend of genetic process and sociocultural symboling, the latter much elaborated beyond a genetic level but still resting on and continuous with that underlying genetic process and capability.[15]

Sustained, steady-state economizing—whether achieved by a single life unit or by a group, a species, or a business firm—carves out of an entropic

14. See Milton Rokeach, *The Nature of Human Values*, New York: Free Press, 1973, pp. 24–25, 327, and Milton Rokeach, *Understanding Human Values: Individual and Institutional*, New York: Free Press, 1979, pp. 51–53, for a discussion of this specialized functional concept of institutions.

15. For a discussion, see Michael Conrad, *Adaptability: The Significance of Variability from Molecule to Ecosystem*, New York: Plenum Press, 1983, pp. 356, 366–370; and Niles Eldredge and Marjorie Grene, *Interactions: The Biological Context of Social Systems*, New York: Columbia University Press, 1982, pp. 182, 186–187, 198–201.

universe an island of order and life. Entropy is thus temporarily outwitted, life is balanced against disorder, and life units create a platform that makes possible the further realization of genetic potentials and, additionally for humans, sociocultural opportunities.

Where these life units are business firms, one finds economizing values present in all meanings of the term. Few beliefs are more firmly and deeply embedded in the modern business firm than the commitment to economizing. All is grist for the company's economizing mill—capital, labor (known in management argot as "human resources"), land (now "environment"), management process, aesthetics, taste, time. Once within the firm's orbit, all components become subject to the economizing process, each is fitted into the whole in ways that (at least, ideally) promote economizing, and all are measured by a benefit–cost calculus, their acceptance or rejection turning upon an ability to contribute to the firm's economizing goals. Thus, as belief, as method, as organizing principle, and as judgmental outcome, economizing assumes its rightful place as the foundation value of the business order.

SECOND ORIGINAL VALUE: GROWTH

A belief in growth dominates the business mind. The mark of a successful business firm is said to be its ability to expand operations. The firm that cannot do so is threatened with extinction or, at best, stagnation and slow decline. This modern business belief is an adumbration of the ancient process of life struggling against entropy. It is in fact a replication of that vital activity, so far as any given business firm is ideally concerned.

Growth takes any given life unit a step beyond mere survival. Rudimentary economizing is but a platform from which growth, expansion, and development can potentially occur. Steady-state economizing is a condition of homeostasis, in which the life unit simply maintains itself, staving off entropic tendencies. Growth and development require a margin of energy that can take a life unit beyond mere maintenance of its immediate form and functions. Homeostasis permits the performance of work that sustains life, but a net margin of energy greater than mere sustenance creates conditions for growth, development, and expansion. The existence of this life margin is at once an indication that economizing is proceeding effectively and that a (temporary, provisional) balance of economizing and entropy has been attained by the life unit. In many organisms, this net margin permits an unfolding of genetic potentialities embedded within the organism's DNA, transforming its size, form, functions, organic traits, and behavior. This kind of growth—the realization of genetic potentials—can occur only if economizing by the life unit produces a margin sufficient to sustain the organism over an extended period of time. If full development is to occur, somehow the margin must multiply the organism's life-sustaining power beyond mere survival, must enhance and expand its ability to economize in an enduring fashion, so that entropy can be overcome on an extended, sustained, and expanded basis.

Some life units—families, clans, villages, tribes, and many contemporary forms of human association—are not entirely dependent upon genetic encoding for the direction and quality of their growth. Human inventiveness resting on creative intelligence supplements and greatly extends, almost in the manner of what might be called a cultural mutation, the growth potentialities of many human groups. Economizing and growth in these cases are more a matter of deliberate calculation and the result of intelligent, goal-directed behavior. When growth of either kind occurs, it means that the life unit has an ability to add to its immediate stockpile of needed energy and that it can continue to do so beyond the point of mere survival for the moment.

So it is with the modern business firm. In an ideal sense, from which there are now many exceptions, a business firm is considered to be successful because, through its own economizing activities, it has attained a margin of work-energy outputs from its resource inputs. This margin permits the firm to grow, with this kind of growth taking several well-known forms: enhanced productivity rates, increased production, greater sales volume, larger market share, penetration of new markets, new-product developments, technological innovations, an expanded work force (whether human or technological), more capital assets, greater usage of transportation and communication networks, and all other such augmentations of productive and distributive functions that result from and contribute to the firm's economizing processes. Where this kind of growth has occurred, the firm is said by conventional economic lore to be "rewarded" with profits for its ability to be economical, prudent, and frugal in managing the resources under its supervision. Much praise is then heaped on the heads of those who manage firms that gain this kind of growth margin in their operations.

In business—by contrast with the unfolding of genetic potentials seen in organisms—growth arises from culture-based learning and inventive processes. When there is present a belief in the desirability of growth, when a rational calculation of appropriate methods for growth is made, and when there exists an organizational system appropriate for these purposes, the conditions for growth are laid down. In other words, when growth is accepted as a value—when it is believed in, when the necessary methods and means are created, when components of the firm are organized for that purpose—the firm embarks on a growth path.

Whether business firms are unwaveringly devoted to growth as a value may well be doubted by some who have read of or have lived through the retrenchments, massive layoffs, and "downsizing" efforts of well-known American corporations during the 1980s and 1990s. However, close examination of this phenomenon by careful researchers reveals little or no contradiction or inconsistency with the permanence of growth tendencies found in business. In a study of the automotive industry, researchers concluded that downsizing strategies were adopted as a way to restore the firms' growth potentials. They reported that "Downsizing was interpreted in some firms as an admission of failure or weakness. More commonly it was considered a temporary, protective mechanism that would help the firm weather the storm *until a normal growth orientation could be resumed.*"[16] Further evidence that corporate retrenchments are undertaken to restore economizing vigor and subsequent growth potentials is offered in another study, which provides these two revealing definitions: "Strategic turnaround: Efforts of a financially troubled firm to pursue *a return-to-growth strategy*" and "Turnaround response: Once-successful firms . . . overcome their troubles and return *to match or exceed* their most prosperous periods of predownturn performance."[17] The available evidence and insights from experienced research scholars seem only to verify, rather than to question, the dominance of growth as a core, much-desired business value.

Intersecting and Conflicting Growth Paths

Important qualifications attach to growth as a business value. Growth in nature is not unbounded, nor does it occur without imposing burdens on oth-

16. Kim S. Cameron, Sarah J. Freeman, and Aneil K. Mishra, "Best Practices in White-Collar Downsizing: Managing Contradictions," *Academy of Management Executive*, vol. 5, no. 3, 1991, p. 68, emphasis added. In what is apparently an inexhaustible (but generally unrecognized) business talent for inventing soothing euphemisms to describe unpleasantries, the authors go on to say, "For example, a number of substitutes for the term downsizing were used in these firms to avoid negative connotations: resizing, right-sizing, rationalizing, rebuilding, rebalancing, reassigning, reorganizing, reallocating, redeploying, streamlining, slimming, slivering, functionalizing, demassing, downshifting [as in a truck?], consolidating, contracting, compressing, ratcheting-down [my favorite], and even leaning-up [a close second]."

17. D. Keith Robbins and John A. Pearce, "Turnaround: Retrenchment and Recovery," *Strategic Management Journal*, vol. 13, May 1992, pp. 287–309, emphasis added. This much reported but not yet very thoroughly researched phenomenon deserves more scholarly attention, as noted by Cameron et al., op. cit., p. 58, who say that "Despite its pervasiveness, downsizing has rarely been investigated . . . [and] [f]ew systematic studies have been published." Any standard strategic management textbook reflects the canon that retrenchment's goal is the resumption of growth, as the following typical passage reveals: "[T]he corporation is likely to emerge from this strategic retrenchment period a much stronger and better organized company. It has improved its business strength/competitive position and is able once again to expand the business." J. David Hunger and Thomas L. Wheelen, *Strategic Management*, 4th edition, Reading, MA: Addison-Wesley, 1993, pp. 185–186.

ers. The limits to growth, and therefore to reliance on this business value, devolve from thermodynamic forces.

Growth encounters thermodynamic limits on two different levels of existence. The growth path of one species may spell doom and dissolution for the efforts of others to live and grow, as when a young robin snaps up a worm, or when animals grazing in a field crop vegetation so close to the turf as to kill it, or when a human group pursues food animals with such vigor that the supply is exhausted or eliminated entirely. When conflicting growth paths intersect in this way, the more effective economizer survives, unless economizing is pursued so vigorously that it decimates all food targets. For example, farmers may overtill, overfertilize, and overgraze land until yields drop drastically. But there is a far more important growth constraint. In their efforts to grow, all species—the totality of life units of all kinds—confront the unyielding limits of entropy. All growth is purchased at the price of environmental degradation, as energy is inexorably converted into less accessible and qualitatively less desirable forms. This condition affects all economizing life units, whether they prove to be successful competitors or not. In fact, successful economizing itself, while sustaining life, also renders it more precarious for all.

In modern business, with its characteristic competitive struggles, the emphasis is normally placed on the former limit to the firm's growth. That is, one company's growth (Robin Redbreast Corporation) may be another's competitive demise (Lowly Worm, Inc.). The other kind of limit—the one dictated by the long-term consequences of entropy—is typically pushed into the background of day-to-day business thinking, if in fact it is a conscious thought at all. The value of and belief in growth tend to be held so strongly in some business enterprises that its entropic limits are not grasped, even though these are the most important factors limiting business growth.

An island of order, growth, and prosperity may indeed be created by successful business units, but to do so the firm must directly destroy or diminish the fortunes of others, as well as place an increasing burden on the surrounding environment. The potential economizing efficiencies of business competition are often purchased at a price that lessens the economizing possibilities of others. An example comes from Europe, where small food shops are reported as being pressed to the brink of extinction by much larger "superstores" offering more diverse and lower-priced products. "Downtown and corner stores are threatened with extinction, as suburban superstores selling 'everything under one roof,' from food and cosmetics to clothing and electronics, become more popular."[18]

---

18. "Europe's Smaller Food Shops Face Finis," *The Wall Street Journal,* May 12, 1993, p. B1. A similar story is told in "Barnes & Noble's Boss Has Big Growth Plans That Booksellers Fear," *The Wall Street Journal,* September 11, 1992, pp. A1, A4.

In addition to less efficient competitors, others who may feel the bite of an effective economizing firm are consumers whose incomes are constrained by low-cost wage policies, workers whose jobs are exported to low-wage Third World regions, and a citizenry that suffers negative health impacts when industrial pollution costs are not internalized and thus not constrained by a company. The second law of thermodynamics tells us that growth is sustained only by extracting entropy's price, which takes these and other forms of greater environmental disorder and dissolution.

Carl Madden's relatively early account of this process, drawing on the work of Nicolas Georgescu-Roegen, who developed the link between economic theory and entropy, was remarkable for its perceptive insight into the entropy-bounded limitations of economic growth.[19] Madden's basic message to business was a simple but powerful one: economic growth is limited by entropic forces that cannot be ignored. Traditional business values that favor unbounded growth clash with the forces of both nature and culture. That his well-intentioned warning to the business community was all but ignored by business practitioners and management scholars alike is even more remarkable. Madden himself was an unlikely source for these advanced ideas, having served earlier as a business school dean, as economist for a Federal Reserve Bank, and as chief economist for the U.S. Chamber of Commerce, none of these being founts of revolutionary thinking. Members of the National Planning Association's Business Advisory Council on National Priorities, which sponsored publication of Madden's book, were careful to distance themselves from some of Madden's most revolutionary perspectives, and one council member felt compelled to record his view that "thermodynamic law . . . clearly has no meaning in social/economic relationships."

In spite of the destructive and disruptive consequences of some economic growth, it remains true that protective, nourishing, mutually supportive relations often exist between different organisms, species, and human groups, as each strives in its own ways to economize, thereby offsetting entropy. This phenomenon has been extensively observed in the plant and animal worlds and is discussed in considerable detail in Chapter 6. A similar relationship is frequently seen in any industrial or commercial cluster of business units, where some smaller firms tend to be satellites of or parasites on larger host firms. These communities of life units may thus coexist as oases of economizing order and growth, where intersecting growth paths reinforce one another rather than running toward the annihilation of one group by another. An example comes from UCLA's Lewis Center for Regional Policy Studies:[20]

19. See Carl H. Madden, *Clash of Culture: Management in an Age of Changing Values*, Washington, DC: National Planning Association, 1972, especially Chapters IV. and V. The passage quoted at the end of this paragraph is on p. viii.

20. Gary Stix and Paul Wallich, "The Analytical Economist: Is Bigger Still Better?" *Scientific American*, March 1994, p. 109.

[R]esearchers are studying the means by which industrial districts such as Silicon Valley, the southern California aerospace industry or the agglomeration of textile firms near Florence . . . achieve "external" economies of scale. Once a regional industry has begun to grow, it attracts a skilled labor force and a supporting infrastructure of city streets, expressways and airports. Small specialty firms then may coexist with giant production houses. The scale factors can involve hundreds of thousands of workers spread over a few square miles rather than single plants or pipelines.

Nevertheless, these symbiotic communities too are subject to the overriding force of thermodynamic laws because their successful and integrated efforts to grow merely push the entropic consequences of growth into other regions and later time periods. As in all similar cases, their victory over entropy is fleeting.

Growth, therefore, while moving all life units well beyond steady-state economizing in ways thought to be desirable at the moment, is by no means an unmixed blessing. As a process, growth is essential for releasing both genetic and cultural potentialities for all life units. On the other hand, the very process of growth for some denies both growth and life to others. As a business value, growth is firmly implanted within business consciousness, guiding the firm toward goals that both serve and diminish life for the firm and for others within its orbit.

THIRD ORIGINAL VALUE: SYSTEMIC INTEGRITY

Many business firms go to considerable lengths to identify, to label, and thus to distinguish their activities from those of other enterprises. Slogans, mottos, logos, and brands are meant to signal that one company stands for something unique among its competitors. This labeling activity reflects and symbolizes a third original value of business which is called "systemic integrity."

Systemic integrity in a generic sense refers to the essential organizational integrity and identity of any given life unit. Among plant and animal species, entity integrity and identification are genetically determined, as forms and functions evolve according to the genetic messages contained in the organism's DNA. Hence, the organism assumes its characteristic shape and size, and its internal life-supporting processes are organized and integrated into a whole capable of functioning within the genetically encoded potentialities and limitations. The resultant organizational integrity allows economizing to occur and, if that economizing is done well and long enough, allows growth to occur as well. In this sense, organizational integrity—or what might also be called "unit wholeness"—has obvious adaptive value.

Beyond this kind of integrity of single life units that is a function of genetic potentials, one finds functionally similar effects in groups of animals.

Collective and functionally cooperative behavior among members of a species has been frequently observed by ethologists and is believed to have adaptive survival value for the species. Konrad Lorenz has identified three such distinct patterns of social interaction among animals: the flock or herd of animals, where pairing and attachments among individuals are random; social organizations, where interactions and some pairing are built around the common enterprises of nesting and reproducing offspring but where few or no lasting attachments among individuals are evident; and bonding that brings pairs of individuals into enduring relationships with each other.[21] These forms of social organization contribute to the solidity, stability, and integrity of such groups and thereby to the economizing activities essential to the survival of their individual members as well as the entire group. This kind of unit wholeness, as applied to a group of individuals, therefore works toward the same general economizing result as do genetic potentials in the lives of individual organisms. The collaborative, cooperative behavior often seen among social animals is largely, but not entirely, attributable to phylogenetically imprinted genetic messages.[22]

Unit wholeness assumes a similar importance as a business value. In order for a business organization to be efficient in economizing, its employees, in combination with whatever technology is used, must form a coherent whole in which interrelated working parts and functions mesh together. Here, one sees the importance of work discipline, specialization of tasks (division of labor), organizational bonding, and all forms of integration that promote an exchange of information, free flow of work processes, and an interchange of workers and functions among needed economizing tasks.[23] This need for organizational integration and coherence is a major reason why "team play," "team loyalty," and "team spirit" are thought to be so important by managers. Teamwork obviously contributes to coherence and thence to a company's economizing efforts. For this reason, there will be a desire and tendency to preserve that integrated wholeness as a means of continuing the company's economizing ways. Top-level corporate managers have frequently declared that the worst thing that can happen to a company is to have an employee, or perhaps more than one, who does not "fit" and who does not work in tandem with others.

---

21. Konrad Lorenz, *On Aggression* (English translation), New York: Bantam Books, 1967, Chapters 8, 9, 10, and 11 (the original German-language version was published in 1963 in Vienna).

22. See Konrad Z. Lorenz, *The Foundations of Ethology* (translated by Konrad Z. Lorenz and Robert Warren Kickert), New York and Vienna: Springer-Verlag, 1978, 1981.

23. For a discussion, see Rodolfo Alvarez and Leah Robin, "Organizational Structure," in Edgar F. Borgatta and Marie L. Borgatta (eds.), *Encyclopedia of Sociology*, vol. 3, New York: Macmillan, 1992, pp. 1399–1401. The authors draw on Talcott Parsons, *Structure and Process in Modern Society*, New York: Free Press, 1960.

Organizational science has devoted much time and no small amount of imaginative thought to helping companies achieve a satisfactory degree of internal organizational coherence. A leading authority on such matters notes with apparent approval that companies typically "attempt to screen out those whose personal styles and values do not make a 'fit' with the organization's culture." Called "deselection," this step is followed by others: one is "a carefully orchestrated series of different [humility-inducing] experiences" whose purpose is to help new entrants "to decide whether or not they can accept the organization's norms and values" and "to make newly hired personnel vulnerable and to cause them to move closer emotionally to their colleagues, thus intensifying group cohesiveness." (The similarity of these corporate practices to collegiate fraternity hazing and military boot camp routines is striking.) Training in a work discipline then follows; rewards and controls are applied to channel an employee's work toward economizing goals; personal value dissonances are overcome "by connecting the sacrifices to higher human values such as serving society with better products and/or services"; company "folklore"—tales of organizational success and failure—circulates to reinforce dominant organizational values; and, the final step on the ladder of organizational coherence, promoting as "role models" only those who display the desired degree of company loyalty by serving the firm's economizing goals.[24]

When a company therefore attempts to instill loyalty and corporate pride in its employees, it is replicating a form of behavior that is more easily and naturally displayed in those animal species whose identity and functioning are genetically established. Organizational discipline is particularly difficult to achieve where human culture opens up so vast an arena of behavioral and attitudinal possibilities among those who go to work in business firms. The X-factor value alone (noted in Chapter 1 and discussed in greater detail in Chapter 5) can inject a frightening, even nightmarish range of potential attitudes and behaviors for an organization's managers to confront in their efforts to induce sufficient uniformity for economizing to occur. But without such unity, economizing and all that flows from it—growth, efflorescence, and continued life—are neither attainable nor sustainable.

---

24. Fred Luthans, *Organizational Behavior*, 6th edition, New York: McGraw-Hill, 1992, pp. 570–573. Luthans relies partly on Richard Pascale, "The Paradox of Corporate Culture: Reconciling Ourselves to Socialization," *California Management Review*, vol. 27, no. 2, Winter 1985, pp. 26–41. The literature of organizational socialization, though voluminous, tends to be focused on promoting the original business value of systemic integrity, with scant attention given to broader behavioral and normative issues that are raised by strict adherence to this value. Two classic exceptions are William H. Whyte, Jr., *The Organization Man*, New York: Simon & Schuster, 1956; and William G. Scott and David K. Hart, *Organizational America*, Boston: Houghton Mifflin, 1979. Neither of these works is mentioned or referenced by Luthans, whose long-lived textbook may plausibly be considered to be widely representative of received wisdom concerning organizational matters.

Any efforts, therefore, directed toward encouraging those associated with the firm to see it as "their" company, to believe that one's working associates are part of one distinctive corporate "family," and that one's loyalty is to this particular "team" in its competitive struggles with others are moves well taken by any business enterprise intent on economizing. All such efforts conduce toward the firm's organizational integrity—its unit wholeness—and this condition is a prerequisite for economizing. To the extent that a firm's managers and employees believe in their company's economizing mission, organize themselves and their work to promote that mission, and make correct appraisals of the means for carrying out that mission, a company has embraced one of the original values of business. As will be subsequently noted and discussed, this devotion to systemic integrity can be dangerously excessive if organizational learning and creativity are suppressed or if the price of internal coherence is environmental inflexibility.

IS PROFIT AN ORIGINAL BUSINESS VALUE?

Some, probably most, students of business will want to believe that profit is an original value of business. What, after all, is more closely associated with the business institution, and what seems more genuinely to be its hallmark, than profit? Whether praised as a central motivator or flung contemptuously as the ultimate epithet, surely, it will be argued, profit deserves a place among business's original values. That is not the position taken here.

Profit is a purely derivative concept, not an original process from which business values were extruded in the course of natural and cultural evolution. It is a consequence—an outcome—of economizing. In primitive and early stages of economizing among simple life forms, profit in the sense of an energy margin need not exist at all. Long stretches of time may ensue as life units achieve rudimentary economizing that permits life to become established; and even longer periods of time may be spent in a state of homeostasis or steady-state economizing where no margin of energy beyond that necessary to stabilize and sustain the life unit is present. Only when these two phases of economizing have been secured will a net energy margin be available for growth and development. Even then, one must be careful not to impute more to "profit"—this energy margin—than it functionally deserves. For growth among human life units occurs as a function of three components, not just one. These are an available margin of energy not devoted directly to either rudimentary or steady-state economizing, a life unit's systemic integrity, and the availability and skillful use of appropriate technology.

Business firms may sustain themselves over quite long periods of time without showing a profit from their economizing efforts. External supplements—such as borrowed funds, money from new stock issues, deferred payments to creditors, government-guaranteed loans, cross-subsidies of one business unit by another, even extended bankruptcy proceedings—can allow a company to operate indefinitely without profit. Though desired, profits appear not to be essential to any particular firm, although some minimum (varying) number of companies need to be profitable if their host economy is to grow. Profits emerge from, and are dependent on, successful economizing that goes beyond mere homeostasis; hence, profits for individual businesses are never a certainty.

In fact, neoclassical economic theory holds that profits are zero in perfectly competitive markets, a condition which that same theory sacralizes. Profits may arise from monopoly, from innovations, from entrepreneurial efforts, from market imperfections such as barriers to entry into a market, or from information asymmetries—but all of these are considered to be either undesirable or temporary. Thus, profits at best are elusive and constantly imperiled by competitive pressures. To counteract this tendency of profits to approach zero, a cottage industry of "strategic management" techniques has evolved to help corporations seize as many (temporary) profits as possible by escaping the clutches of competitive markets.[25]

In the business lexicon, profit takes its meaning largely from ideology, not from evolutionary process. In this sense, profit is seen as a reward for services rendered, as noted by an authoritative source: "[Profit is a] payment or commitment to a person (entrepreneur) undertaking the hazards of enterprise; remuneration or reward for uncertainty-bearing."[26] Additionally and most importantly, in economic lore and business legend, profit looms as a larger-than-life component that drives economic progress. When accumulated in sufficient amounts—and invested as "capital"—it is said to be "the goose that lays the golden eggs." As such, profit is seen as the wellspring of economic productivity and material progress. Those responsible for bringing forth this economic fecundity acquire a hallowed and much respected standing, and they are thought to deserve whatever rewards they might appropriate from the hoard of golden eggs. Just as surely, these profit-based prizes are typically condemned as being unfairly large when compared with the shares of others more remote from the firm's economizing center. For example, periodic uproars are heard protesting executive salaries, bonuses, retirement payments, and privileged perquisites and deploring the gap between executive pay and that received by lower-ranked personnel. Capitalist ideology enshrines these

25. For a summary of these ideas, see Robert Jacobson, "The 'Austrian' School of Strategy," *Academy of Management Review*, vol. 17, no. 4, 1992, pp. 782–807.

26. W. W. Cooper and Yuji Ijiri (eds.), *Kohler's Dictionary for Accountants*, 6th edition, Englewood Cliffs, NJ: Prentice-Hall, 1983, p. 400.

twin myths of profit-as-creator and profit-as-just-reward, although neither myth finds a counterpart in the economizing-growth processes of natural evolution. Economizing, if carried beyond its rudimentary and steady-state phases, produces profit, which is then potentially capable of enhancing the productivity and growth of life units, including individual business firms as well as entire economies. In all cases, profit rests on a base of economizing.

In neither sense of profit—as net energy margin available for growth or as reward for economic progress—is profit an original value of business. Though sought as a desirable business goal, it can exist only when economizing—an original value—makes it possible. It *arises from* economizing and is thus entirely derivative. As an imposed ideological income share and an imputed agent of productivity, profit enjoys a long, contentious history, though not so long and not so functionally integral as to qualify it as an original value of business.[27]

In a curious, paradoxical way, both the detractors and supporters of business share a vested interest in the belief that profits are an inherent, original business value. Detractors, questioning the fairness of profit as an income share, are guaranteed a perpetual case against this detested feature of capitalist business. Supporters, putting their faith in the imputed fecundity of profit, can celebrate an economic order inherently capable of outstripping others in economic achievement. Neither of these ideological forays hits the mark. Both commit the same kind of error. Each, in its own way and for its own purposes, reads into an institutional feature or trait a function whose source lies elsewhere. Profit, far from being the productive, creative core of business, is a sometime consequence of a productive process identified here as economizing. Profit, when calculated in a reasonably honest way, is a mere sign that economizing has occurred. The fecundity it signals has its source in economizing, not in profit seeking or profit making. Economizing owes its existence to material and technological processes that undergird all kinds of sociocultural economic systems, some of which generate profits more successfully and consistently than others. Looking for economic creativity by tracking profits is a misguided search, impelled by an ideological fervor that diverts one's gaze from fecundity's source.

So, too, with those who rail against the evils of profit taking. Were profits not to be made—which is another way of knowing that productive economizing is *not* well and securely underway—a given business firm would indeed

27. Among the many accounts that have been critical of the conventional version of economic progress is Clarence E. Ayres, *The Theory of Economic Progress*, Chapel Hill: University of North Carolina Press, 1944; 2nd edition, New York: Schocken Books, 1962. Ayres built upon and extended the earlier critiques of Thorstein Veblen, who traced economic progress to technology-based productivity rather than to the institutional trappings of capitalism, such as private property, profits, and so on. A later chapter considers these possibilities in some detail.

have reason to worry about its longer-term future. The venerable debate over the relative desirability of "true" profit, "competitive" profit, "monopoly" profit, "administered" profit, "maximum"-"optimum"-"satisficing" profit, and so on, should not be allowed to cloak the functional need for an economizing process that, when effective, spawns profit. An antipathy for business that is rooted in a disdain for or a rejection of profit misses the mark and is closely equivalent to a rejection of the nature-based economizing process that sustains all life. One critical account of life within the business corporation has declared that "corporations remain *shackled* to the task of achieving profitable growth," as if this practice is not only undesirable but a burdensome constraint best dispensed with altogether. The authors prefer a corporation whose main business is the "emancipation" of those who dwell and work there, without explaining how emancipated lives are to be sustained absent economizing growth.[28]

Profit is not the essence of business, though it is one of its expected and socially desirable traits. The ideological furor over the size, type, source, and use of business profit, while understandable, nevertheless tends to mislead by implying that profit should be tied to and defined by a society's income-share system (one that favors the propertied groups and their allies) rather than its economizing system. That might well bring economizing into the service of an institutional order that elevates status-income shares above a society's own collective economic and material welfare. If such a development were to be consolidated, business's ideological detractors would have achieved the same ends sought by its ideological boosters—namely, to denigrate economizing by claiming too much for profit. Thus, for all of these several ideological reasons, profit is claimed, both by its advocates and its detractors, to be more central to economizing and growth than it deserves.

Some may protest that business profits are frequently the result of activities that appear to have little or no redeeming economic or social value, thus reflecting something less than productive, life-supportive economizing purposes. Two responses to this objection may be noted. The first is to acknowledge the wide variety of profit-making initiatives that are condemned by the varying laws and social mores of societies around the globe, such as slavery, prostitution, criminal enterprises of great variety, fraudulent sales, commerce in child labor, manufacturing and selling defective or ineffective products, and exploiting the marketing weaknesses and vulnerabilities of others. Every society must grapple with what it considers to be productively acceptable and thus to bring its own meaning to nature's economizing processes. The nor-

---

28. Mats Alvesson and Hugh Willmott, "On the Idea of Emancipation in Management and Organization Studies," *Academy of Management Review*, vol. 17, no. 3, 1992, pp. 432–464. The quotation, with emphasis added, is from page 459.

mative choices and issues involved in assigning sociocultural significance to economizing practices are thoroughly discussed in the last three chapters of this book. For the moment, it may suffice to note the tendency of societies everywhere to place limits on a life unit's self-seeking, economizing behavior, including a wide range of profitable business practices.

The second response to the notion of nonproductive, profit-seeking economizing is less appealing but no less consistent with thermodynamic laws and the functions of economizing as an entropy offset. Even the most dubious forms of economizing that yield profits represent a productive function for the life unit that initiates and carries the activity forward. Energy is taken from the environment, processed, and converted to forms that support that particular life entity. Economizing is typically focused within an individual life form and is carried out in ways that serve the economizer's need to offset entropic pressures. The stark, even brutal, reality of a naked economizing process, unclothed by protective sociocultural garments, is shocking and frightening. This possibility lends particular urgency to the need for socially regulative constraints on economizing's potential excesses. Some of these regulatory controls are found within the business order itself—the market process is an example—while others are expressed through various sociocultural institutions. All of these social buffers receive much attention in subsequent chapters of this book.

The present discussion should lend additional force to the idea that profits and profit-making attempts are not properly considered to be original business values. Profits can indeed arise from questionable activities that outwardly may bear a resemblance to productive economizing but that may represent little more than shifting (by market theft, deception, or fraud) existing income or wealth from one person or group to another. While profits can indeed signal the presence of productive economizing, they need not. Economizing, not profit, is the bedrock business value.

ORIGINAL BUSINESS VALUES—A SUMMATION

The distinctive value set of business is centered on the three original values of **economizing, growth,** and **systemic integrity.** These three natural processes, when recognized and conceptualized as values—that is, as beliefs, relationships, and methods of appraisal and judgment reflecting human experience—identify business as a unique and analytically separable activity in human affairs. Although business is not the only institution in which these values may be observed, no other human arrangement combines them so consistently and so enduringly or pursues them so assiduously as does business.

The presence of these values is one reason why business firms are so determinedly resistant to external forces that are perceived (rightly or wrongly) to be antieconomizing or noneconomizing in their effects. Also explained by the presence of these values is the strong pragmatic orientation of business managers who, if well trained, consider everything as grist for the firm's economizing mill. Few truths are more lasting in the business world than the notion that economizing and its associated values should be observed and preserved at all costs.

The kind of economizing behavior induced by Value Cluster I is imperative for all life units, including business firms. These three original values—economizing, growth, systemic integrity—are rooted in the nature of the physical world and in the operation of the first and second laws of thermodynamics. Their role is vital and indispensable if life is to continue. They make possible an essential phase in the evolution of all life units.

In one sense, the undesirable and disagreeable aspects of business behavior—the dissonant societal, environmental, and personal chords—tend to emerge from other-than-original business values. This is not to say that competitive economizing itself is free of societal dissonances, which may arise for example when socially disruptive unemployment accompanies a plant-closing decision made for economizing reasons. Nevertheless, a major part of the negative social impact of business operations stems from the power-aggrandizing values that comprise Value Cluster II—**hierarchical (rank-order) organization, managerial decision power, power-system equilibrium,** and **power aggrandizement**. These values deserve the close study they are given in the following chapter.

3

The Power-Aggrandizing Values of Business

The central idea of this chapter is that business operations, based originally on economizing values that promote productive outcomes, are typically hampered by a competing set of values focused on coercive power, its acquisition and augmentation. Power-focused values, while usually found in most business firms, are not inherently necessary for business's economizing mission to be carried out successfully. Giving allegiance to such values almost invariably diverts a company from making effective use of resources.

The presence of these values also creates and multiplies an aura of invidious personal and social discrimination within the business organization, such as that between the managers and the managed, the leaders and the followers, the managers and the workers, the (conventionally male) dominants and the subservient male and female subordinates, the (typically white) commander-generals and all other ethnic-minority corporate soldiers. In all of these distinctions, one side is found to possess dominant workplace power over the other side. In spite of these power differentials, a surprising consensus tends to sustain the prevailing distribution of power, even though subdued grumbling continues to be heard from those who wield little power.

This entire structure of power-related values—that is, the beliefs, relationships, and experience-based judgmental criteria—conditions life and work within the business firm. These values are one of the principal features of corporate and business culture. Their prevalence also poses a question of central importance: whether power might be, or ever is, used instrumentally to promote a company's economizing goals, in spite of a tendency among power wielders to take purely self-interested actions to preserve their power and privileges. That question is taken up at a later point in this chapter and receives even greater attention in a later chapter.

This chapter also draws an important distinction between business growth and business expansion. Growth, being one of the original values of business, is a manifestation of successful economizing by a business firm. Growth occurs when steady-state economizing produces a margin of energy that can be fed back into the firm's already successful economizing activities, thereby multiplying and enhancing the company's productivity, its productive output, and its chances for even greater economic success in the future. Expansion, on the other hand, is merely an increase in the size or scope of operations, normally without an attendant improvement in economizing activities. This kind of expansion, it is argued here, is typically inspired by a desire to increase the power accruing to those in charge of the company. By aggrandizing their personal organizational power, along with the power of the firm, they are able to influence a larger circle of events both within and outside their company. Some will wonder if economizing growth and power-inspired expansion must always be distinct and separate. Might they not be achieved simultaneously? That question is best addressed within the context of the power-aggrandizing value cluster itself, to which we now turn.

As noted in the preceding chapter, the original values of business, while defining the core meaning and economizing mission of business, do not tell the entire story of values to be found within the business institution. Sharing value space within the business firm is another cluster of interrelated and intertwined values that, while characteristic, are not the exclusive possession of business. Four values comprise this cluster: **hierarchical (rank-order) organization; managerial decision power; power-system equilibrium;** and **power aggrandizement**. Each will be described in detail. These found values are widely shared with other institutions. Standing by themselves, they are no more characteristic of business than of many other types of human institutions and organizations. However, contemporary business—particularly the large-scale corporate enterprise—has become identified with these four found values to a very great extent, and justifiably so. When they are linked with the three original (economizing) values of business, the entire value set reveals the typical value profile of modern business enterprise. To review the value set, see Figure 1–2 in Chapter 1.

The effect of this value cluster is to sustain a process of power aggrandizement expressed from deep within the firm's culture, directed both inward to augment the power of those who direct and manage the firm and outward to expand the range, scope, and influence of the firm within its environment.

As with original business values, these power-aggrandizing values reinforce one another, being a functional cluster of accepted beliefs, interlocked social relations, and judgmental methods and standards reflecting the existential experience of those who inhabit business firms. Each of the four values therefore helps to define the others, so intermingled are their effects and functions. Their prominence and omnipresence deserve careful consideration if one is to understand the various ways by which values influence business affairs.

FIRST VALUE: HIERARCHICAL (RANK-ORDER) ORGANIZATION

In every business organization, there is a discernible pattern of authority and a related distribution of power. Authority is the warrant for holding and wielding power within the firm; it is the justification that permits some rather than others to be powerful. In Western capitalist economies, private ownership has been the ultimate authority upon which the legitimacy of business decisions and policies has rested. The private owner has been understood to stand at the center of the enterprise, directing its fortunes in ways thought to be desirable and profitable for the owner. The English philosopher John Locke provided all the justification needed by capitalist merchants and landlords for using their property to enrich themselves and to accumulate those riches for further investment. The authority that permitted them to occupy powerful positions and thus to be able to instruct others to follow their wishes was their ownership of shops, factories, ships, farms, and all the accompanying paraphernalia of economic production and distribution. Absent a socially acceptable theory of ownership, their acts and decisions might have been seen simply as the brute exercise of power, to be challenged at will by those who might have believed themselves to be even more powerful and deserving, though propertyless. An attack upon private property threatens the very basis of authority on which business power is held and exercised, and so must be guarded against at all costs if the business institution as we know it is to be upheld.

The appearance of the professional manager of large-scale corporate enterprise, who holds operational power by virtue of organizational position and managerial skills rather than by ownership, has seemed to pose a challenge to the traditional authority derived from business ownership. This controversy, which has alarmed many who speak both for and against the business establishment, continues to manifest itself in fascinating ways even today. The position accepted here is that a sufficient community of interest—in pre-

serving the functional features and privileges of a private property–based social order—prevails between owners and managers as to render the controversy less central and vital than is often claimed.[1]

The configuration or pattern of managerial power within business organizations is hierarchical, appearing as a rank ordering of persons and roles.
This rank-order arrangement permits some to be dominant over others regarding all significant matters facing the firm, including decisions about the
specific goals to be sought, the work to be performed, the way work is to be
organized, and related operations. In fact, dominance over others is an archetypal trait of business organization. Commenting on this facet of organizational life, one notable social scientist who has studied many corporations at
close range observed that "The process of stratification in human systems is
typically not as blatant as the dominance-establishing rituals of animal societies, but it is functionally equivalent in that it concerns the evolution of
workable rules for managing aggression and mastery needs."[2]

The resultant status hierarchy that emerges provides the organizational
spine around which the affairs of the firm are arranged and mediated. "Hierarchy," as used here, should not be confused with "specialization of function." Some organization theorists tend to use these two concepts inter-
changeably. The root meaning of "hierarch," traced etymologically from
Middle Latin through Greek, is one who is the steward of sacred rites or a
chief priest who rules or has authority in sacred things. This ancestral meaning, though losing some but perhaps not all of its explicit sacral character,

1. The classic sources are Adolf A. Berle, Jr., and Gardiner C. Means, *The Modern Corporation and
Private Property*, New York: Macmillan, 1932; and James Burnham, *The Managerial Revolution: What
Is Happening in the World*, New York: John Day, 1941. Berle extended his ideas in *Power Without
Property: A New Development in American Political Economy*, New York: Harcourt, Brace, 1959, Chapters I, II, and III; and *The American Economic Republic*, New York: Harcourt, Brace & World, 1963,
Part One. Both confirming and disconfirming studies of the Berle and Means thesis of ownership and control have appeared, the most notable being Robert J. Larner, *Management Control
and the Large Corporation*, New York: Dunellen, 1970; and Philip H. Burch, *The Managerial Revolution Reassessed*, Lexington, MA: Lexington Books, 1972. A rather impassioned, not to say hysteri-
cal, reaction to the Berle and Means thesis is found in Robert Hessen, *In Defense of the Corporation*,
Stanford, CA: Stanford University Press, 1979. A worthwhile insight into the share ownership
stake of corporate directors and managers, and the subsequent community of interest that prevails between managers and owners, is found in Harold Demsetz, "The Structure of Ownership
and the Theory of the Firm," *The Journal of Law and Economics*, June 1983, especially pp. 387–390.
The entire June 1983 issue of the latter journal is devoted to a discussion of the Berle and Means
thesis. John Kenneth Galbraith has offered two amendments to the structure of power proposed
by Berle and Means; these are found in *The New Industrial State*, Boston: Houghton Mifflin, 1967;
and *The Anatomy of Power*, Boston: Houghton Mifflin, 1983.

2. Edgar H. Schein, *Organizational Culture and Leadership*, San Francisco: Jossey-Bass, 1985, 1988,
p. 72.

now refers to a system of persons or things existing in a graded (rank) order.[3] Specialization of function, while distinguishing the activities of one person from those of others, need not be based on a graded rank order of invidious distinction. In most business organizations, both rank-order hierarchy and specialization of function are present as organizational components and hence tend to be commingled (and generally confused by organization theorists). A later chapter that discusses technology as a value component takes up this matter again, emphasizing the close association of functional specialization, that is, division of labor, and technology. The present emphasis of this chapter is on the invidious status-rank distinctions spelled out in the business hierarchy.

In corporate organizations, the chief manager, or at times a small group of managers who share chieftainlike power, occupies the pinnacle of the status hierarchy. From that point down, power lessens level by level throughout the organization, matching a decline in the status ranking of those on successively lower levels whose organizational roles are classified as being relatively inferior to those in the upper reaches of the pyramid. The classical model of this type of hierarchy is military organization, with its highly formalized and ritualized rank orders. In such stratified systems, a rich display of symbols distinguishes one status level or rank from others. Clothing, manner of address, precedence in speaking during meetings, seating order, location and size of office, quality of office furnishings, pay and diverse perquisites, and other such features of the workplace acquire great symbolic meaning as tokens of status rank, whether one looks at business firms, hospitals, universities, labor unions, or other hierarchy-based organizations. An early lesson urged on organizational newcomers is to absorb the meaning of these symbols and the rank-order reality they represent.

An example comes from the testimony of a professional manager who was describing the culture of the company where he had worked:[4]

> [It was] a bureaucratic "caste system." There were multiple layers of management and many outward symbols of the authority and relative importance of each of the levels of management. The Director, for example, had a large office, his own reception area and conference room, which were encased in lead walls to ensure his privacy. Other managers' offices were scaled in size based on their relative posi-

---

3. C. L. Barnhart (ed.), *The American College Dictionary*, New York: Random House, 1960, p. 570. In some scientific fields, "hierarchy" refers to levels or degrees of complexity without invidious comparison of better or worse, higher or lower.

4. This passage is from a description of his company's culture by a business manager. Though anonymously presented here, the account is of an actual corporation, given in a personal communication to the author.

tion in the structure, but all tended to be lavish in decor, and were furnished with pictures and plants. Professional and clerical areas, on the other hand, were designed to be functional and resembled "bull pens."

Each manager had his own individual parking spot, while parking for the rest of the employees was on a "first come, first serve" basis. Managers were frequently addressed as "Mr." or "Mrs.," while the professionals and employees were addressed by their first names.

Decision making was discouraged at the non-management levels. Employees were expected to take their problems and questions to their managers, and lower level managers in turn were expected to consult with higher level management before making more than routine operating decisions.

This hierarchical trait of business organization comprises one of the central values of contemporary business. It is a **belief** widely shared in business, in the sense that most will declare that there is no realistic alternative to hierarchy in organizing business affairs. This view remains remarkably stable, although fashions and fads touting various "horizontal" schemes—matrix, networks, participatory systems, empowerment methods—come and go, waxing and waning as their advocates are able to play upon the frustrations and powerlessness felt by those caught up in stable, long-lasting rank-order systems. Commenting on the hold that this belief has on the managerial mind, organization theorist Edgar Schein refers to "one major, deeply embedded cultural assumption [of managers] so taken for granted that it is difficult even to articulate. This is the assumption that all organizations are fundamentally *hierarchical* in nature, and that the management process is fundamentally hierarchical. We need new models [of organization], but we may have difficulty inventing them because of the automatic tendency to think hierarchically."[5]

The acceptance of hierarchy as a central business value goes beyond simple belief, which is only one of the meanings of value. The status hierarchy, with all of its deferential and ceremonial display of rank, is also the way in which people in business are **related to one another** for the purpose of getting the firm's work accomplished. The hierarchy itself is valued for bringing a certain kind of order and certitude into human relationships in the workplace, providing a means of sorting out, separating, and relating workers— who display highly diverse backgrounds and interests—to one another and to the prime source of organizational authority. It is probable that a kind of psychological comfort and reassurance is experienced by many employees, who thereby "know their place" within the larger system of authority and power that typifies corporate enterprise.

5. Edgar H. Schein, "Reassessing the 'Divine Rights' of Managers," *Sloan Management Review*, Winter 1989, p. 63.

"Knowing one's place" tends to be a constant source of interest, concern, and perhaps even anxiety for many who labor in the corporate vineyards. Over a period of years while consulting for a large company, my primary contact would always begin our sessions by telling me of changes in organizational position that had occurred among the upper-echelon managers to whom he reported. A large organizational chart, with pictures of those at the summit, was on the wall of his office, and he would tell me in some detail how and, according to company scuttlebutt, why these shifts had occurred. They never appeared to have any relation to the work I was being paid to do, but they were often uppermost in my contact's mind. Robert Jackall, author of *Moral Mazes*, who had extensive interviews with many corporate executives, has reported a similar anxiety among those he studied. Their need to prove themselves to their organizational superiors, to their peers, and to themselves, according to Jackall, "produces a profound anxiety in managers, *perhaps the key experience of managerial work*."[6]

Rank-order superiority and deference likewise constitute the **standards** by which **judgments**—two other meanings of value—tend to be made within the enterprise. Appraisals of what is appropriate to get the job done are always filtered through those favored managerial members of the organizational hierarchy whose fortunes and rank are most directly and importantly involved and who have the organizational ability to veto or modify any such appraisals. Career outcomes thus turn on one's success in being judged to have performed in ways consistent with the needs of the enterprise, as defined by those in authority.[7]

SECOND VALUE: MANAGERIAL DECISION POWER

Few doubt that the central authority figures in the modern corporation are managers who dominate the organizational hierarchy, occupy its prime positions, and wield what power those positions permit. Managerial power, as developed here, is akin to what John Kenneth Galbraith has labeled "conditioned power," which arises from the largely unconscious acceptance by members of an organization of the power differentials that are part of the organization's structure.[8]

As noted earlier, the professional manager was brought to this exalted status as the business unit grew in size, complexity, and command of resources.

6. Robert Jackall, *Moral Mazes: The World of Corporate Managers*, New York: Oxford University Press, 1988, p. 40, emphasis added.

7. Ibid., Chapters 3 and 4.

8. See Galbraith, *The Anatomy of Power*, op. cit., Chapter III.

Within a capitalist order, various motives asserted themselves in support of this trend toward professional managerialism. On a micro level, the desire of investor-owners for multiplied gain while sheltering from the risk of total loss made the limited-liability feature of corporate stock ownership attractive. On a macro level, the need of capitalist enterprise for ever-larger sums of capital that could be concentrated in one place and subjected to a disciplined routine of investment for gain all but required an organizational device such as the corporation. When, in the course of time and judicial wisdom, the corporation was declared to be an artificial legal person, capable of entering into contracts and seeming to enjoy a prolonged life, the future was made even more secure for this way of organizing business activities that had lain relatively fallow for several centuries.

Of all those who have questioned the propriety and justification of the professional manager's power and prominence, none seems to doubt the fact of power that is centered in the executive suite and delegated from there in measured amounts downward through the descending levels of the hierarchy. The point is confirmed, or at least reinforced, even in the bland, oblique language of what might fairly be called establishment economics:

> Strategic position is the crucial underpinning of management control of the large corporation. It rests on daily and direct management command over personnel and resources, knowledge, the importance of managerial and organizational skills, and the structural and social relationships that develop on the basis of proximate command.

> The power lacunae left by the diffusion of ownership is [sic] gradually occupied by those who exercise power on a daily basis and who are thereby well positioned to consolidate it more firmly over time.[9]

Whether the exercise of that power is final or qualified, and who does and who should do the qualifying, have occupied the attention of many alert intellects, and the issue is worth clarifying for purposes of this present account of business values. Those said to be potentially capable of checking or even withdrawing the power of top-level corporate managers include the board of directors, large-bloc minority shareholders, majority shareholders, creditors in bankruptcy proceedings, and, in rare instances limited to specific business functions, governmental (i.e., executive, regulatory, and judicial) agents. Large-scale institutional shareholders, given much prominence in recent decades as a new type of corporate owner, may play a key role in corporate power struggles, but they typically do so as minority shareholders, sometimes allying themselves with other minority shareholders to build collective power

---

9. Edward S. Herman, *Corporate Control, Corporate Power*, Cambridge: Cambridge University Press, 1981, p. 52. For "strategic position," read hierarchical rank; for "direct management command," read managerial power; for "structural and social relationships," read rank-order system.

and influence. The legal character of all these power players is noteworthy, suggesting a widespread, socially approved acceptance of an orderly system for the modification of managerial power, if indeed it is to be modified at all.

The stories are too well known to be retold here of the overweening advantages accruing to entrenched management in its struggles to retain control over corporate affairs. Unorganized shareholders owning a majority of a company's stock have little prospect of eroding executive power. Even when well organized, their sometime appearance during annual shareholders' meetings is acknowledged to be a farce or, at best, a public relations event intended to create propagandistic media messages.[10] Without question, large-bloc minority shareholders, particularly the managers of pension funds and mutual funds, can make their influence felt on corporate matters affecting the pecuniary value of their stock holdings.[11] So too can beleaguered creditors, acting singly or together as a pack or gang during bankruptcy proceedings, at least block or partially checkmate managerial cunning intended to escape the worst consequences of unwise financial decisions of the past. Recent history has even recorded a few instances of managerial reversals suffered at the hands of an activist, not to say impudent, board of directors who, uncharacteristically, may seize the initiative from a company's chief managers.[12] An even more notable and imaginative way of rearranging and consolidating prevailing managerial power is through the leveraged buyout; one version allows an entrenched executive group to seize the very source and authority of managerial power itself by becoming owners of that which they previously managed only by proxy. In effect, they replace themselves as managers with themselves as manager-owners, perhaps sloughing off less favored former colleagues in the process of drawing power into a tighter circle of trusted fellows.

A number of other parties and diverse methods are available for counteracting the power of corporate managers, including aroused stakeholder groups, trade unions, host governments of multinational corporations, and others. These rarely are able seriously to diminish centralized managerial power, nor do they enjoy the advantage of legal standing as owners, owner-agents, or creditors that would make their counterclaims more appealing to judicial minds who settle such quarrels. A more serious contender for countervailing the power of an *existing* corporate management is the aggressive investor, often ungenerously labeled a "corporate raider" by some, who, advised by investment banking houses and cheered on by watching financial

10. David Vogel's *Lobbying the Corporation: Citizen Challenges to Business Authority,* New York: Basic Books, 1978, provides the best view of the possibilities and limitations of shareholder activism.

11. For a skeptical view of shareholder power, see "Shareholder Activism, Despite Hoopla, Leaves Most CEOs Unscathed," *The Wall Street Journal,* May 24, 1993, pp. A1, A5.

12. "Eminence Grise: Behind Revolt at GM, Lawyer Ira Millstein Helped Call the Shots," *The Wall Street Journal,* April 13, 1992, pp. A1, A6.

interests with a stake in the outcome, bids for sufficient stock to oust the ruling management clique. In these cases, though, one finds that the replacements quickly adopt similar methods of managerial control, deriving their power and authority from the same ownership principles that sustained the claims and booty of their predecessors.

One interesting contest between top-level management and technical personnel for control of corporate policy and directions occurred at Autodesk, Inc., a U.S. computer software firm. A "cabal of programmers" long associated with the company were reported to be all-powerful, drawing on their accumulated and acknowledged expertise to exert overweening influence on corporate affairs. Top officers were forced out and others had their executive powers clipped by this "theocracy of hackers." This revisionist plot is spoiled somewhat by the fact that the firm's founder, who was once the CEO and had remained the principal majority shareholder, was a prime support and even the leader of some of the cabal's rebellions, thus suggesting that ownership retained its privileges and powers even in this high-technology company.[13]

The overall effect of all these incursions into managerial power tends to be marginal, though sometimes spectacular in outward appearance. Such contests demonstrate that the power of specific managers at specific points of time and under specific circumstances is not unassailable. *However, in all cases, managerial power is replaced by managerial power.* Only the faces change. For example, an aroused board appoints a new chief executive officer thought to be more malleably inclined to the board's wishes. In Autodesk's case, a new CEO believed to be able to overcome infighting and divided responsibility between technical factions was selected. Or creditors acting through a bankruptcy court force a reorganization that brings in yet another top executive to breathe new life into a moribund corporation. In some cases, a disgruntled large-bloc minority shareholder, having successfully breached the walls of corporate power through a takeover, hires its own champion, usually a manager with experience in such matters. The dance of managerial power and dominance continues, in the main without a break in the music. Also prevailing is the general warrant of managerial authority—private ownership—inasmuch as all those who would control corporate affairs turn in the end to the legally sanctioned ownership principle to justify and defend their grip on power.

All of this testifies to managerial decision power as a central business value. As a belief, it is widely prevalent within business, although held with varying degrees of enthusiasm and fealty. Managerial decision power also becomes a focus of organizational relationships, as all look to the managerial cadre for work directives. Among managers' duties is the establishment of

---

13. "'Theocracy of Hackers' Rules Autodesk, Inc., A Strangely Run Firm," *The Wall Street Journal,* May 28, 1992, pp. A1, A14.

standards of performance and making judgments about success or failure in adhering to those standards. This tripartite template that defines the meaning of value fits like a glove around the hand of managerial decision power. The uses of this power are several. Some involve the promotion of organizational purposes, such as market dominance. Other uses are more personal, such as securing the privileges and perquisites that accrue to those of higher rank. Additionally, at some point in business life, the power exercised by managers enters the plane of economizing, upon which the organization's continued existence depends. Just how power conditions economizing is discussed further along in this chapter and again in Chapter 5 where managerial work is considered.

THIRD VALUE: POWER-SYSTEM EQUILIBRIUM

The primary referent of organizational (rank-order) hierarchy and its associated managerial decision power is dominance over others. This trait poses a special problem of the greatest significance for business firms. The logic of managerial dominance can be sustained only as long as the hierarchical structure of power is preserved. Raw, brute power is less readily accepted than the same power enfolded within a socially approved framework. But the very pursuit and exercise of managerial decision power by individual managers has the potential to rupture the graded ranks that comprise the hierarchy. Were that to occur, the manager's warrant of authority to dominate others, which is granted by the organization, would be undermined. The dilemma is simple but profound: power on which the system rests must somehow be contained so that the power network itself is safeguarded against dissolution without suppressing the power-seeking motives that activate the system and draw adherents to it.

The dilemma arises largely from the dynamics of business operations. A business life is an active life; transactions occur constantly. Many of these transactions are required by the very nature of the firm's economic mission, as a variety of resources flow into and out of the organization. Labor market exchanges occur; resource inputs from suppliers are converted into outputs; manufactured products and services enter the marketplace in search of a compensatory return; and financial and technical information flows from point to point within the firm and to and from its many external stakeholders, including government, the media, local communities, and others.

The fate of managerial and professional careers turns on the outcome of these many transactions within and outside the firm. Indeed, one's position within the company's rank-order system determines the kind and amount of transactions permitted to any given status-role occupant, and one is judged by how successfully these transactional responsibilities are discharged. A correct amount of diligence skillfully applied qualifies one for advancement to higher status levels within the company. This organizationally sanctioned quest for enhanced status and power becomes one of the prime motives acting on those in business. The rewards are considerable for those who persevere: higher pay, a more spacious office, more support services, and all of the little subtle behavioral deferences granted to a "fast tracker." In addition, there is normally much jockeying for power among those who chafe under the sometimes slow pace of transaction-based advancements. Still others watch enviously as their rivals move up faster than seems justified or because they take advantage of interpersonal relationships having little to do with the firm's workaday transactions. Envy, tension, stress, hostility, trap setting, and a host of even less admirable emotional displays and maneuvers are spawned, seething just beneath the formally placid surface of organizational life.

If not contained, these two kinds of power enhancement—one an organizationally approved way of advancing oneself, the other a kind of individualized brute rivalry—threaten to collide with the enduring nature of the organization's status-power hierarchy. In most companies, status power acquires a meaning *sui generis;* it becomes an end in itself. The preservation of the existing power arrangements of the organizational hierarchy, not just the safeguarding of any given *individual's* power, becomes centrally important. Though often rivals with one another, managers see their collective warrant of authority as bound up in the hierarchy itself. A threat to the hierarchy is a threat to their power *and* their authority. Nothing must be allowed to challenge the basic structure of prevailing rank-order arrangements, neither disobedience, disloyalty, lack of enthusiasm, nor lack of conformity to organizational norms. When the day's work ends in a business firm, it is expected that nothing will have been permitted to breach the rank-order system with which the dawn was greeted.

One business executive confirmed, in a private communication to the author, the prevalence of this value in his own company: "The organization focused on maintaining the status quo. Change could involve risk, and risk could mean problems and mistakes which could upset the organization balance. The staffing reflected this organizational value. All managers had long tenure, and were employees who had come up through the ranks and were recognized experts in their area of accounting or systems."

Many proverbs and aphorisms capture the essence of the several ways by which corporations keep their minions "in their places." These include "playing by the rules," "obeying orders," "being a team player," "being a regular guy," "someone I can count on," "knowing how it's done around here," "not overstepping one's authority," "not going over the boss's head," and "staying within channels." These tags, when attached to one's colleagues and subordinates, label them as trustworthy guardians of the power pyramid.

Ideally then, and from a managerial point of view, organizational power would be maintained as an equilibrium. Power would not pass to unauthorized persons in unauthorized amounts. Service to the firm's goals would be rewarded by movement through the hierarchy's stable levels. Power struggles occurring as an adjunct to these transaction-based awards, though frequent, would not be permitted to rupture the power structure itself.

Status-power equilibria of the kind described here are not limited to the internal transactional dynamics of any given business firm. Anthropologists have long studied social reciprocity as a mechanism or process that permits exchanges of power among different levels of a society's class system without endangering the structure itself. Since business power is so frequently the centerpiece of a society's social class order, the power exchanges that occur inside corporations have ramifications far beyond the firm. Individuals who qualify for top corporate rank quite often thus find themselves tacitly nominated and eventually tapped for positions of similar influence in other spheres of life, ranging from university trustee to cabinet posts in government to public-service commissions to board member of churches or private foundations and even occasionally to such clearly superior positions as top commissioners of professional sports leagues. One result is the cultivation of outlooks and world views generally supportive of the maintenance of power relations throughout a society's leading institutions. Thus, an equilibrium within the corporation is echoed outside the corporation, and vice versa.[14]

The desirability of having and maintaining a stable system of managerial power is deeply embedded in business consciousness. All who work in business come to accept this idealized power equilibrium as a cardinal belief in the ways things should be done. Though some chafe under its strictures, most agree to abide by the behavioral implications of the existing distribution of power, not wishing to be accused of breaching company rules regarding advancement, fearing for their own chances. In doing so, they exhibit the kinds and qualities of judgment and demonstrate that they adhere to the standards thought to be appropriate for the firm. The idea of an organizational power equilibrium thus takes its place as a found value in business.

---

14. For a classic anthropological study of social reciprocity, see Bronislaw Malinowski, *Argonauts of the Western Pacific*, New York: E. P. Dutton, 1922. The importance of reciprocity as a redistributive mechanism was recognized by Karl Polanyi in *The Great Transformation*, Boston: Beacon Press, 1944, especially pp. 269–273. C. Wright Mills, *The Power Elite*, London: Oxford University Press, 1956, is another classic that describes the interlocking character of social and corporate elites. An economist with insight into the relationship of business power and social power is Neil W. Chamberlain, *The Place of Business in America's Future: A Study in Social Values*, New York: Basic Books, 1973; *The Limits of Corporate Responsibility*, New York: Basic Books, 1973; *Remaking American Values: Challenge to a Business Society*, New York: Basic Books, 1977; and *Social Strategy and Corporate Structure*, New York: Macmillan, 1982.

FOURTH VALUE: POWER AGGRANDIZEMENT

A central goal and preferred tendency of business firms is expansion, whether of sales; assets; factories; retail outlets; number, location, and proportional share of markets; diversity of products and services; number of employees; capital invested; revenues accrued; and/or profits secured. Many business corporations expand to great size, commanding a large and diverse array of resources. Not infrequently, such aggrandizement seems to become the main purpose and goal of those who direct the enterprise.

As such expansion occurs, the power of the firm and its managers is augmented in a linear fashion. More employees require the issuance of more managerial directives and a related expansion in the ranks of subordinate supervisors who carry out those directives. Larger sales bring enhanced revenues and associated financial wealth that can be turned to the firm's advantage in various ways. Expanding operations into new markets establishes a new sphere of economic and geographic influence for the company. Greater accumulations of capital give access to advanced technology, thereby opening up greater market opportunities, producing even more geographical expansion, leading to increased sales, the accumulation of yet more capital, and so on through a continuing cycle of corporate activity that swells the size and extends the orbit of the firm.

Managers who direct, or are thought to be responsible for, this kind of expansion are typically rewarded with higher salaries, special bonuses, and other executive perquisites. Not infrequently, a measure of organizational genius and business acumen is attributed to them, swelling the general esteem with which they are viewed and doubtless bringing magnified psychological and emotional satisfaction. Honor, prestige, and larger portions of social influence within their own circles accrue. Prominent political and social roles, with whatever influence they imply, may be offered to those corporate executives whose firms have markedly amplified their command of the financial and commercial worlds. These rewards are powerful stimulants to executive action. They can and probably often do cause corporate managers to accept this kind of power aggrandizement as the main purpose and goal—the sustaining rationale—of the enterprise. Expansion of size per se becomes "the name of the game." Merger and acquisition may appear to be more attractive, far easier, and a more certain way of reaching this expansionist goal than improving the company's actual productive abilities. The occasional spectacular collapse of one of these bloated corporate empires reveals the extent to which its managers are often driven to expand their own power by augmenting their company's size. Two examples told in the business press are instructive, as well as colorful.

Circle K's attempt to expand into a convenience store giant big enough to compete with rival 7-Eleven eventually pushed the firm into bankruptcy. *The Wall Street Journal* reported that "some directors came to believe that [the CEO] had concentrated so much on expansion—adding roughly 500 new stores a year—that he didn't have an adequate knowledge of what was being sold in his 4,700 stores. . . . What he has striven for are power and recognition."[15]

Another corporate managerial cadre whose "lust for growth at all costs" drove their firm into bankruptcy and ruin worked at Laventhol & Horwath, the nation's seventh largest accounting firm before its fall. According to *Business Week*, it experienced "dizzying growth," beginning in the mid-1980s, by engaging in a "merger binge" that scooped up many smaller accounting practices and resulted in a doubling of revenues by 1990. Never able to integrate these diverse, widespread operations, top management created a work climate that the head of one office said "brought out the worst in people: fiefdomism, lack of cooperation, and avarice on the part of some." These aggressions, released by the expansionist frenzy, blended with other values to generate over 100 malpractice lawsuits against L&H, defaults on bank loans, and "a client roster that often looked like a rogues' gallery." A new CEO brought in to rescue the company in its final days was "overwhelmed by business pressures beyond his control," according to *Business Week*. The expansionist push that began in 1985 thus ended in ignominy in 1990 as the overstuffed empire collapsed under its own weight.[16]

Aggrandizement and growth—the latter identified earlier as an original value of business—are sometimes confused. "Growth," which is a consequence of effective economizing, refers to the multiplication of a firm's productive potential so that its life may be extended into the future through repeated economizing acts. Growth is thus antientropic. "Aggrandizement' is an enlargement of the firm's size, usually motivated by the potential dilation of personal and organizational power accruing to its chief operators. Aggrandizement is proentropic, diverting vital energy inputs from economizing to power seeking. A company may become larger through internal expansion or by merger or acquisition without experiencing an increase in productive output or profits; and a company may grow in productive output and productivity without expanding. Power aggrandizement may come closer to explaining the motive for many corporate mergers than does growth. Recent history records many instances of mergers thought to have been founded on economizing gains that turned out to be economizing disasters. The certain outcome of corporate aggrandizement is an amplification of the power centered

---

15. *The Wall Street Journal*, March 28, 1990, pp. A1, A14.

16. "Behind the Fall of Laventhol," *Business Week*, December 24, 1990, pp. 54–55.

in the firm and wielded by its chief managers. Only rarely, perhaps never, does this ballooning of power signal the kind of economizing that can lead to productive growth.[17]

It is difficult to find a more fervently held business belief (i.e., value) than this commitment to aggressive expansion. It can produce in its devotees a frenzied, frenetic mien. Its attainment approaches the zenith of business accomplishment. A company's rank in the *Fortune Directory*, and those of its competitors, are eagerly scanned and held up to scorn or praise as the case may be.[18] "Expand or die" in the corporate world is the proverbial equivalent of "sink or swim." As a business value, it haunts the dreams (and nightmares) of many executives, inspiring in them deeds of valor in the competitive fields of business endeavor. Their judgments and all of their organizational skills are bent to the pursuit of ever greater power and influence for themselves and their company. This addictive hedonism of power is the defining trait of corporate managerial culture and personality.[19]

As one views the prevalence of aggrandizement yearnings within the business system, and particularly the self-reinforcing character of the entire clus-

17. For a discussion of the internal executive psychodynamics that drive some merger decisions, see Diane L. Swanson, "Dysfunctional Conglomerates: An Explanation Provided by Linking Ontological Individualism to Social Relations within an Open Systems Context," *Behavioral Science*, vol. 37, 1992, 139–150; and Richard Roll, "The Hubris Hypothesis of Corporate Takeovers," *Journal of Business*, vol. 59, no. 2, pt. 1, 1986, pp. 197–216.

18. A diverting variant of this type of invidious display occurs when university business schools are ranked by summing the opinions of alumni, business representatives, faculty, students, and others with presumed knowledge of the respective schools' educational excellence. Unlike businesses, though, rarely if ever are these schools praised for their size or growth rate, although the size and splendor of a school's sponsored-research budget may figure in its ranking. However, a presumption of those devoted to this game is that the achievement of high rank can produce a larger flow of high-quality student applicants, a greater likelihood of attracting desirable faculty members, more companies to interview and offer jobs to the school's graduates, and perhaps a measure of favorable publicity that is believed to carry weight as learned groups (usually drawn from the leading business schools themselves) deploy grant funds of government agencies and private foundations. To the extent that business school ranking attracts the attention of faculty members and students, it becomes part of the mental and attitudinal conditioning that contributes to the inculcation and generalized attractiveness of expansion-oriented values. In this way, students are, perhaps inadvertently, prepared for the rigors of the competitive expansionist struggles that lie ahead.

19. The point is made and illustrated by Jackall, op. cit.; Howard Schwartz, *Narcissistic Process and Corporate Decay: The Theory of the Organizational Ideal*, New York: New York University Press, 1990; Charles M. Kelly, *The Destructive Achiever: Power and Ethics in the American Corporation*, Reading, MA: Addison-Wesley, 1988; and Manfred F. R. de Vries and Danny Miller, *Unstable at the Top: Inside the Troubled Organization*, New York: New American Library, 1987, 1988, especially Chapter 6, The Compulsive Organization. Speaking after losing a merger contest to a rival, one executive said, "They pulled out every stop. After a while, you had to realize he was going to do anything to win." The winner of this mega-merger battle exulted, "We're going to build a global super powerhouse." Paul Farhi, "Viacom Beats QVC in Paramount Deal," *Washington Post* (reprinted in *Pittsburgh Post-Gazette*, February 16, 1994, pp. A1, A5).

ter of values that comprise Value Cluster II—rank-order hierarchy, managerial decision power, power-system equilibrium, and aggrandizement itself—an explanation is wanted. Why, it might be asked, is this value cluster rooted so deeply within the business psyche? To what area of human experience is it related that can explain its persistence and the fervent loyalty it commands from so many?

The evidence is compelling, if not entirely conclusive, that power-seeking and its magnification reflect a genetically embedded process operating within the confines of cultural elaboration. Ethologists who study animal behavior have reached no definitive or general conclusions on the debt that aggressive power owes to nature. They do report widespread instances of phylogenetically based aggression and dominance, as well as rank orders that occur widely among many different animal species. In those cases, rank order rests primarily on phylogenetic processes encoded in DNA, although learning by the young also occurs.

Ethologists also stress that conceptual learning in the human species creates the possibility that the preference for rank order and power seeking goes beyond phylogenetic origins, expressing an *acquired* yearning for power over others. Where that is found, as one ethologist has said, "[Human] striving for power is particularly problematical since it is not turned off by biological control mechanisms as are, for example, hunger and thirst when the organism is satiated. . . . [By contrast with animals] our striving for power is insatiable." Yet opinion is divided; another leading ethologist maintains that "the lust for power, the striving for status [are] irresistible tendencies of phylogenetically programmed behavior."[20]

These perspectives are echoed by a leading organization theorist:

> The core issue of power distribution derives from the underlying biological nature of the human organism. Culture eventually covers over with a veneer of "civilization" the underlying biological roots of human behavior. But we cannot ignore the fact that all human beings have to learn to deal with their biologically based aggressive feelings, their needs to dominate, control, and master others and the environment. Only when we recognize that cultural norms regarding the handling of aggression help us deal with feelings that might run out of control, endangering us and others, can we understand why those norms are not easily changed.[21]

A postulate offered here is that the power-aggrandizement feature of corporate life is a blend of nature and culture. There is little reason to believe

---

20. The first quotation is from Irenaus Eibl-Eibesfeldt, *Human Ethology*, New York: Aldine de Gruyter, 1989, p. 719. The second is from Konrad Lorenz, *The Waning of Humaneness*, Boston: Little, Brown, 1983, 1987, p. 141.

21. Schein, *Organizational Culture and Leadership*, op. cit., p. 73.

that gene-based selective processes that made power seeking and aggression so much a part of the life of animals and of our prehuman ancestors—and that operated over millions and millions of years—were simply displaced when conceptual thought and culture arrived on the scene. Nature offers few instances of such breaks in selectively advantageous evolutionary processes. The argument over these matters continues, some maintaining that culture has crowded out or overridden genetic propensities, others favoring the view that power seeking and aggression continue to reflect both phylogenetic encoding and cultural patterning.

The view here is that the power-aggrandizing value cluster we see at work in the modern corporation is an overlay of patriarchal culture imposed on a base of phylogenetically encoded instructions. The extent to which patriarchy owes a debt to genetically encoded male aggression and assertiveness is an open, intriguing question. Successive waves of cultural evolution over many millennia appear to have added a multitude of power permutations to the simple melding of rudimentary patriarchy with gene-based, aggressive power impulses. Untangling and identifying the separate biological and sociocultural strands that make up the present picture may be less important than being aware that both elements continue to play compelling roles.

The role of female hierarchies has been studied, but insufficiently so, to ascertain how and to what extent matriarchal rank ordering might have contributed to the emergence and consolidation of institutionalized aggression and power aggrandizement. One group of research scholars reached no definitive conclusion about whether females characteristically form hierarchies (from either biological or sociocultural impulses) or whether extant female hierarchies are based on biological or sociocultural factors or some combination of the two.[22]

What can be said with some confidence is that the process and the values of power aggrandizement have penetrated deeply into business consciousness and business practice. The quest for power and its augmentation are ever present, guiding decisions, shaping policies, setting priorities, and conditioning the firm's economizing operations.

ON THE INSTRUMENTAL USES
OF COERCIVE POWER

It would be difficult to argue that coercive power of the kind found in business organizations is never turned to economizing purposes. The reason is simple: all business economizing takes place within an institutional context of

---

22. Lionel Tiger and Heather T. Fowler (eds.), *Female Hierarchies*, Chicago: Beresford Book Service, 1978. For an account of patriarchy's appearance and spread, see Gerda Lerner, *The Creation of Patriarchy*, New York: Oxford University Press, 1986.

power relations. No firm can be found where coercive power is absent. As business is presently organized, if economizing is to occur at all, it must go forward in the presence of power. When, for example, a company must pare down its work force in order to enhance its productivity, or when another firm introduces technologically superior machines or methods, a directive must be issued. Such an order normally comes from "the top" and is interpreted as a fiat to be obeyed. The hierarchy is speaking with the clear voice of an organizational authority backed by law, custom, and accepted practice. Those who disobey or who deplore the "human costs" of layoffs or who resist the new technology may soon find out what the term "coercive power" can mean: a discharge slip, a demotion, a side-tracking job change, a subtle labeling as uncooperative.

So, in one sense, coercive power is used instrumentally to achieve an economizing outcome *simply because that is the way business is organized.* In this sense, all business economizing is conditioned by the presence of a coercive power system. Managerial power, the motivations it activates, the compelling addictions it cultivates in those who wield it, the impressive amounts of organizational time and energy given to its pursuit and consolidation—all of these traits greatly qualify and constrain any economizing gains that might be achieved through the instrumental use of coercive power by managers. One might well wonder how much greater the economizing gain might have been had those status and power-seeking diversions of organizational energy not driven the decision. The dubious economizing outcomes of many power-driven corporate mega-mergers suggest that the purported gain for the merged companies ranges from modest to nonexistent, not to mention the negative economic results sometimes experienced by other groups (e.g., laid-off workers, creditors, and stockholders).

It is not at all clear that business economizing *must* be so organized and directed. The establishment of power may not need to be a prelude to organizational economizing, nor in fact *is it* actually a functional requirement at any given moment in the life of most business firms. An organizational consensus leading toward economizing might well emerge from methods and procedures that do not rely on the use of coercion. A fascination with power—probably induced by genetic and cultural conditioning—cloaks and hides from view the underlying reality of cooperative, technologically induced consensual behavior required for effective economizing. If economizing has an organizational imperative, it lies here with technology rather than with power. Managerial directives need not be fiats coercively enforced. They can be, and frequently are, an expression of technological intelligence accepted as a tested judgment that has been made by those who know what they are talking about. A later chapter explores in some detail the linkages between business economizing and technological intelligence that may provide an alternative to the power-constricted economizing that tends to prevail in modern business.

The yearning expressed here, and by many others through the years, for an alternative to power-based organization may well be frustrated by the simple facts of biological function and ingrained cultural habit. Rank-order hierarchy may *in fact* be impervious to reform. What that would mean, for the value profile of business, is that economizing values would always operate through a screen of power values. The presence of this power filter is what has caused organization theorists to conclude, with some justification, that managers striving for economizing's rewards must use the power they have in these instrumental ways.[23] What may be missing from this formulation is that the energy costs of sustaining such an organizational hierarchy would subtract from economizing gains that otherwise might be realized as productivity and growth. Whether that cost is imposed by nature or culture is a question worth pondering by those who seek alternative ways to organize business.

VALUE CLUSTERS I AND II—A SUMMATION

The four values in Value Cluster II function together in interwoven fashion in much the same way as do the three original (economizing) values of business. Only the ultimate effect is different. Here, all is power—its definition, justification, allocation, maintenance, and expansion. There, in Value Cluster I, the focus is on economizing as an offset to entropic trends. Here, organizational dynamics bind employees together with sinews of power and of deference to superior authority. There, a firm's identity and organizational integrity serve, not power and deference but the survival needs of the company as a type of life unit. Here, one pursues the magnification of personal and organizational power. There, one seeks a growth path that might sustain the firm's economizing processes indefinitely.

Taken together, these two subsets of business values—Value Cluster I and Value Cluster II—comprise a behavioral, attitudinal, ideological, judgmental, and methodological structure that explains much about the operations, decisions, and policies of the standard business firm. These two value sets are driven so deeply into business consciousness that they are all but invisible to their carriers, who adhere to them with a conviction not unlike that of a young child who sees its parents as an extension of its own self. When one steps into the precincts of a business firm, these values are put on as one dons a uniform to perform specified tasks; they, so to speak, "go with the job." They shape the mentality one brings to business chores and functions. They create attitudes that ease the actions and, at times, salve the conscience of business functionaries who make hard decisions. They sketch the broad out-

23. Jeffrey Pfeffer, *Power in Organizations*, Marshfield, MA: Pitman, 1981.

lines of business policies and purposes, its strategies and tactics, its goals and means, its methods and standards, its measure of success or failure. The pursuit of economizing values and the expression of power-aggrandizing values are part and parcel of business life, the be-all and end-all, the supreme goal and central purpose, the core meaning that business has acquired as one manifestation of evolutionary process operating in both nature and culture.

The view that the defining values of business are limited to these two clusters might understandably draw objections. Some would want to insist that the typical business firm manifests a far larger range of indispensable and characteristic values. Others who define values with somewhat different conceptual categories than those used here would be likely to discover a different range of values.[24] It remains true, though, that a close examination of such other values usually reveals them to be either X-factor values (defined provisionally in Chapter 1 and discussed further in Chapter 5) or subsidiary values that derive their significance from their relationship to economizing and/or power aggrandizement.

Few of these other values are found to be essential to the normal operations of most business firms, although they may contribute importantly to the *operational style* that is characteristic of particular companies. An example is seen in Hewlett-Packard's reputation for treating its employees with respect and dignity, encouraging open communication among all ranks, and its focus on honesty and integrity in dealing with external stakeholders.[25] Such values might well make life in that firm less stressful, more pleasant, and open to greater creativity than one finds in other companies. It might even be argued that the style itself, by deemphasizing rank-order distinctions, contributes to the company's productivity (i.e., its economizing). But in any event, style does not displace or substitute for the need to economize, nor does it entirely remove the shadow of power aggrandizement that is cast broadly upon all business firms. In general, any such subsidiary values, whether held as purely

24. For examples, see Elizabeth C. Ravlin and Bruce M. Meglino, "Issues in Work Values Measurement," in William C. Frederick and Lee E. Preston (eds.), *Research in Corporate Social Performance and Policy*, vol. 9, Greenwich, CT: JAI Press, 1987, p. 162 (thirteen values are listed); Bruce M. Meglino, Elizabeth C. Ravlin, and Cheryl L. Adkins, "A Work Values Approach to Corporate Culture," *Journal of Applied Psychology*, vol. 74, no. 3, 1989, p. 426 (four values are listed); Jeanne Liedtka, "Organizational Value Contention and Managerial Mindsets," *Journal of Business Ethics*, vol. 10, 1991, p. 549 (fifteen values are listed); Cathy Enz, "The Role of Value Congruity in Intra-organizational Power," *Administrative Science Quarterly*, vol. 33, 1988, p. 292 (nine values are listed); and Barry Z. Posner and Warren H. Schmidt, "Values and the American Manager: An Update," *California Management Review*, vol. XXVI, no. 3, Spring 1984, p. 208 ("more than 225 different values, traits, and characteristics were identified [and reduced to] 15 categories"). These various lists exhibit some overlap and duplication but are quite diverse overall.

25. Kirk O. Hanson and Manuel Velasquez, "Hewlett-Packard Company: Managing Ethics and Values," in *Corporate Ethics: A Prime Business Asset*, New York: The Business Roundtable, February 1988, pp. 65–76.

personal commitments or appearing as matters of organizational style, achieve their importance in the business arena by the extent to which they either reinforce or compete with the core values that comprise Value Clusters I and II.

Business values from either cluster do not appear willy-nilly within their host firms. They are regularized and patterned in distinctive ways, exhibiting a structure of beliefs, relationships, applied methods, and criteria of performance. Understanding that patterned structure of values, which directs business behavior into characteristic channels, is the task immediately ahead.

4

The Structure
of Corporate Values

The journey through evolutionary time from the rudimentary economizing activities of early life forms to present-day business values has been an extremely long one. The full story is untraceable, concealed by and within evolutionary complexities of great magnitude and ancient lineage. The one constant that has prevailed through all of the evolutionary permutations that have accompanied life on earth—and that links those earliest struggles to gain and maintain life with contemporary business activities—is economizing. All successful life forms have reached out into the environment for vital energy, have directed that energy toward the building of their own internal systems, and have then developed their biological and/or cultural potentials. This indispensable economizing constant, when taking a form shaped by cultural evolution, lies at the root of the modern business institution. Economizing not only sustains the societal legitimacy of the business function but does so as a culturally modulated expression of some of the most basic laws of nature. Time's Arrow has pointed in this direction, driving this particular human enterprise to assume the shape and perform the functions we recognize today as business.

Within that broad evolutionary spectrum and over the course of many centuries, business practice has taken many diverse forms. The preeminent form today, at least in the industrialized centers of Euro-American culture, is corporate enterprise. There is no intention here to suggest that the corporate form is a foreordained outcome of evolutionary process or that its appearance and prominence at this point in time represent a superiority over alternative ways of organizing business operations. Numerically, other business forms—individual proprietorships and partnerships—are predominant. Historically, the corporate form is relatively recent. Long before the corporation, there was bartering of several varieties; simple trading; face-to-face exchanges; family-, tribal-, clan- and village-based trading practices; and a great diversity of other economizing ways recorded by anthropologists and economic historians. These have served their respective societies well, often supporting complex and farflung trading practices and exchange systems.[1]

It is in the modern corporation that one can expect to find business values at their fullest and most characteristic expression. To the extent that the corporate system, taken as a whole, is able to spread its influence beyond the cultural centers that spawned its original development, then to that extent will the values embedded in corporations hold sway over other business forms, as well as many other types of human endeavor found in diverse societies around the world. That means that the modern corporation has become the primary home—the ever-active fount—of both economizing and power aggrandizement. Its culture, because it harbors these two master value sets, is the key to understanding the way values influence business behavior and decisions.

THE CONCEPT OF CULTURE AND ITS MISUSE

The notion of "corporate culture"—the idea that a corporation could have a "culture," much as societies have been said by anthropologists to possess distinctive cultures—began to take shape in the popular mind around 1980. The idea had been lurking in the deeper intellectual recesses of a few scholars and management consultants during the 1970s and was given its first popular expression in a landmark article in the business press entitled "Corporate Culture: The Hard-to-Change Values that Spell Success or Failure."[2] This account tended to equate culture and values and seemed to suggest that corporations differed from one another in the kinds of values they promote to their employees, customers, competitors, and the attentive public. The article's subtitle also hinted, rather darkly, that these values might well lead a

---

1. Claude Mosse, *The Ancient World at Work*, New York: W. W.Norton, 1969; Karl Polanyi, Conrad M. Arensberg, and Harry W. Pearson, *Trade and Market in the Early Empires*, Glencoe, Ill.: Free Press, 1957; George Dalton (ed.), *Tribal and Peasant Economies*, New York: Natural History Press, 1967; Melville J. Herskovits, *Economic Anthropology: A Study in Comparative Economics*, New York: Alfred A. Knopf, 1952; and Fernand Braudel, *The Wheels of Commerce: Civilization and Capitalism 15th–18th Century*, vol. 2, New York: Harper & Row, 1979, 1982.

2. *Business Week*, October 27, 1980, pp. 148–151 ff.

corporation to ruin, although a brighter side implied that, with proper guidance, companies with dissonant values might reform their ways and thus thrive after all. Anthropologists everywhere snapped to attention, some pleased that their theoretical contributions might now find this new practical outlet, while others pondered how they might be directly helpful to corporate clients eager to secure the right values that could promote corporate interests and purposes.

It was not long before a horde of management consultants, most of them without anthropological credentials, came forward to fill this vacuum. Speaking now the somewhat exotic but appealing language of anthropology—"tribes," "clans," "rituals," "shamans," "myths," "legends," "value orientations," and other intriguing terms—this new breed of management consultant brought a hopeful message to corporate enterprise. It was that the corporation could be studied just as one observes a primitive tribal society. The corporation's culture could thus be revealed as a network of "rites and rituals," in the somewhat redundant phrase of one leading source. The company's core values, being exposed through anthropological analysis, could then be seen as either supportive or inhibitive of the firm's basic goals; and a program of "managing culture" might then be recommended to set the company on a firmer path toward "success" and away from "failure."

Since, for the most part, this new consultancy enterprise was not undertaken by anthropologists, the idea of "culture" suffered considerably from the exigencies one encounters in corporate consultancy practice. Consultants are hired to promote corporate interests, whatever they may be at the moment. Many of these interests require direct, practical, and reasonably short-term actions. The anthropologist's painstakingly planned and executed field work, often carried out over a period of years and that involves living closely with the group being studied, is not a model readily welcomed by corporate clients. The immediate pressures may be too compelling, and the thought of an outsider taking up residence in the corporate precincts invokes uncertainty in the executive mind. For a corporation's managers seeking consultancy help, failure may be just around the corner; the next quarter's success may need to be recorded within a few short weeks. A consultant under these circumstances will need to come up with a picture of a corporation's culture that falls far short of the detailed and often subtle understanding that is available to the field anthropologist. The unfortunate and disappointing result was predictable: the concept of corporate culture was to become a simplified and far from complete version of what anthropologists had spent their entire professional careers trying to understand, and the idea was to be turned into a serviceable instrument to promote the self-interested purposes of consultants and their corporate clients.[3]

Clearly, there is a quantum difference between the anthropologist's idea of "culture" and what is popularly called "corporate culture." In spite of this lapse, an understanding of business culture need not rest on a superficial misuse of this powerful concept.[4] Culture can indeed clarify the practices and policies of modern corporations, as well as the sometimes bizarre and distressing behavior of those who work in corporations. It can do so because culture constitutes the bedrock of humanness, being responsible for all of the nongenetically programmed phenomena believed to be uniquely "human." Therefore, capturing culture's meaning may unlock many doors within the corporate citadel.

Three perspectives on culture will be helpful to this present effort to understand business values.

First, culture is conceived as consciously transmitted, cumulative, symbolic learning, which enjoys an established continuity with precultural, naturalistic processes and forces.[5] Symbolic learning of this type is made possible

3. Some rather remarkable claims can be found in the resultant literature on corporate culture. One instrument, consisting of a brief questionnaire plus accompanying explanations, offers organizations the prospect of having their employees identify the central components of their company's culture, the inconsistencies that are present in it, the degree of change needed to overcome these gaps, and (with the help of the consultant) ways of changing the culture that create a more effective organization. If one thinks of such anthropological stalwarts as Bronislaw Malinowski, Franz Boas, Margaret Mead, Ruth Benedict, Alfred Kroeber, and others of their stature—all of whom spent several years in arduous field work—it seems a pity that they did not have the wits to develop such a simple, straightforward device. It would have enabled them to avoid such field research risks as exposure to rare tropical diseases and icy Arctic winters, finding themselves the targets of curare-tipped arrows, winding up in the cooking pot of cannibals, or having their shrunken heads impaled at the entrance of a chieftain's house, not to mention escaping the tedium of observing, recording, transcribing, analyzing, and reporting the many complexities of the economic, religious, political, kinship, and language systems that comprise the cultures of most societies. *Sic transit gloria* classical anthropology.

4. A refreshing, if somewhat turgidly presented, review of the possibilities is found in Mary Jo Hatch, "The Dynamics of Organizational Culture," *Academy of Management Review*, vol. 18, no. 4, 1993, pp. 657–693. Hatch explicitly notes (p. 660) that she "follow[s] the lead of eminent cultural anthropologists such as Redfield, Kroeber, Malinowski, and Herskovits." A somewhat similar point of view is found in J. R. McLeod and J. A. Wilson, "Corporate Culture Studies and Anthropology: An Uneasy Synthesis?" in Tomoko Hamada and Willis E. Sibley (eds.), *Anthropological Perspectives on Organizational Culture*, Lanham, MD: University Press of America, 1994, pp. 279–291.

5. Leslie A. White, *The Science of Culture: A Study of Man and Civilization*, New York: Grove Press, 1949, was an early advocate of the symbolic basis of culture. His Chapters II, III, IV, and VII present a particularly useful account of this view. The current tendency of some organization theorists to define culture as "shared values" falls seriously short of capturing important components of culture. Culture, when seen as symbolic learning, embraces both tangible aspects (technology and other physical artifacts) and intangible aspects (mental symbols of all kinds) involved in human life. This matter is discussed further in Chapter 7, The Values Within Technology.

by the specialized human neural system, especially the impressively complex brain, which supports the coevolution of physical tools and a wide variety of other human symbols. This evolution has been shaped by genetic, chemical, and physical processes similar to those responsible for all of our other structural and functional features. This is not to deny a possible reciprocal relationship between the evolution of the human brain and the symbolic uses to which it has been put by its human carriers. Tool use and mental development more than likely coevolved, each reinforcing the other. The human use of symbols emerged as part of an evolutionary process rooted firmly in nature.

The presumed Great Divide between humans and prehumans has not been found by paleontologists, physical anthropologists, ethologists, or biologists. Their discoveries reveal more continuities and parallels than discontinuities and differences, more degrees of distinction than absolute opposites, more subtle similarities than remarkable oppositions. Establishing the time, place, and manner of the first appearance of culture, once thought to be the marker of the Great Divide, has proven to be an increasingly elusive matter. These gropings into the past may well be telling yet another story of even greater significance, namely, that the Great Divide cannot be found because it does not exist. Is it not possible that culture emerged as a continuous, though probabilistic, process of natural evolution, *sans* marker, eventually thrusting its human carriers forward equipped with an adaptive feature different in degree and potentially more effective in the struggle of life impulses against entropic forces? This query, too, though intriguing, finds no definitive answer but is explored again in Chapter 7.

Human culture is a partial expression of those natural forces that have been associated with the evolution of all biotic and nonbiotic components of earth's ecosystem. This evolutionary embeddedness of culture has played a central role in bringing forward the core value components of business, for culture is only another manifestation of the regularity and patterning that accompany the operation of thermodynamic laws. As such, culture makes possible a great diversity of economizing modes, as noted further on in this account.

A second perspective developed here is that culture is, among other things, an amalgam of experience-based efforts to solve perceived problems as its human carriers adapt to their environment. It is through cultural lenses that we perceive problems and attempt to grapple with them. Tools are a major component of human culture for a very good reason—they are indispensable in solving problems. Culture also is a repository—a vast memory storage bank—of previous efforts to cope with the environment. This instrumental, adaptive function of culture is typically clouded by misperceptions about the nature of some problems and is cluttered with many false starts, maladaptive processes, blind alleys, and a gloss of misguided and futile means for coping with environmental forces. The operational dimension of culture, flawed though it is by maladaptive factors, underscores the experiential dimension that is a defining trait of all human values, including business values.

A third perspective adopted here is that culture gives form and meaning to human values. Because culture is a phase in natural evolution and because culture has adaptive functions, it extrudes values that reflect human experience in coping with an environment that either sustains or diminishes life. These extrusions of human experience, which we call "values," provide meaning, significance, order, priorities, and guidance for human actions taken in a world of impressions, stimuli, and forces that otherwise would be seen as entirely and overwhelmingly confusing, hostile, complex, and overpowering.[6] Value structures order perceptions of one's environment. Those patterned perceptions become the experiential basis for understanding environmental forces. There is no guarantee that this perceptual screen of values—the beliefs, relationships, standards, and judgments that prevail among individuals and groups—will filter environmental information accurately, and the history of human culture records many episodes where perceived experience has misled and misdirected human problem-solving efforts. Indeed, these misperceptions and misinterpretations of environmental information lie at the root of many of the difficulties posed by the full operation of business values, as will be told subsequently.

This broader view of human culture provides the platform from which one might grasp the significance of those patterns that bear the "corporate culture" label.

CORPORATE CULTURE

The account of what has been called "organizational culture" most nearly consistent with the anthropological meaning of culture—and therefore the one most useful for clarifying business values—is found in Edgar Schein's *Organizational Culture and Leadership*. Not surprisingly, Schein draws on the work of anthropologists Florence Kluckhohn, Frederick Strodtbeck, and Edward T. Hall, and he specifically observes that the concept of organizational culture is distinct from the more comprehensive construct of culture. Others

6. For a related discussion, see Lewis Mumford, *The Myth of the Machine: Technics and Human Development*, New York: Harcourt, Brace & World, 1966, 1967, Chapters 2 and 3.

also have recognized the distinction between "local organizational cultures" and "the depth and richness of socially shared understanding characteristic of the paradigmatic cultures studied by anthropologists."[7]

According to Schein, an organization's culture expresses the same kinds of experienced-based instrumental functions as culture generally. His words are worth recalling: "What [organizational] culture does is to solve the group's basic problems of (1) survival in and adaptation to the external environment and (2) integration of its internal processes to ensure the capacity to continue to survive and adapt."[8] These two operational outcomes of organizational culture—external environmental adaptation and internal integration—are the functional equivalents of the core economizing values that comprise Value Cluster I. By reaching out into the environment for the requisite energy resources, an organization acts to counter entropic forces in an adaptive, *economizing* way. Its success in doing so will depend largely on the degree of *systemic integrity* it is able to sustain. Productive *growth* may then follow. An organization's culture therefore enfolds the three value orientations that are most important for its continued life. Schein once again, on the leading role played by the environment:

> Although these [external and internal] issues are highly interdependent in practice, for purposes of analysis, it is important to note that they reflect very different sets of functional imperatives. The external issues are concerned with survival in what must be assumed to be a *real* environment that is, in part, beyond the control of group members. *These external realities define the basic mission, primary task, or core functions of the group.* The group must then figure out how to accomplish the core mission [**Author's note: The core mission of business is economizing**], how to measure its accomplishment [**by using economizing criteria**], and how to maintain its success in the face of a changing environment [**through constant appraisal of means and ends**]. But survival over any length of time requires internal integra-

7. Edgar H. Schein, *Organizational Culture and Leadership*, San Francisco: Jossey-Bass, 1985, 1988. The quotation is from Alan L. Wilkins and William G. Ouchi, "Efficient Cultures: Exploring the Relationship between Culture and Organizational Performance," *Administrative Science Quarterly*, vol. 28, 1983, pp. 468–481. Another, somewhat less successful effort to array comparative concepts of culture developed by anthropologists and organization theorists is found in Linda Smircich, "Concepts of Culture and Organizational Analysis," *Administrative Science Quarterly*, vol. 28, 1983, pp. 339–358. Hatch, op. cit., pp. 657–658, lists much of the work on culture done by organization theorists in recent years, as do Harrison M. Trice and Janice M. Beyer in *The Cultures of Work Organizations*, Englewood Cliffs, NJ: Prentice-Hall, 1993. For a flavor of the differing meanings of culture that emerge from the work of anthropologists and organization theorists, see James R. McLeod, "Ritual in Corporate Culture Studies: An Anthropological Approach," *Journal of Ritual Studies*, vol. 4, Winter 1990, pp. 85–97.

8. Schein, op. cit., p. 50.

tion [i.e., **systemic integrity**], and such integration is, of course, aided by external success. . . .

However, one must never forget that the environment initially determines the possibilities, options, and constraints for a group, and thus forces the group to specify its primary task or function if it is to survive at all. The environment thus initially influences the formation of the culture, but once culture is present in the sense of shared assumptions, those assumptions, in turn, influence what will be perceived and defined as the environment.[9]

For the business corporation, the entropic environment sets the basic conditions that define the firm's functions and purposes. Unless armed with values that allow it to draw energy from this environment, it will languish and eventually perish, thus reaching a lifeless thermodynamic equilibrium. While Schein's culture concept is applicable to many diverse types of organizations, it is particularly apt for characterizing the value set found in business firms. Value Cluster I, which includes economizing, growth, and systemic integrity, is found at the core of corporate culture. Interpolating Schein's phrase, these survival values exist as a result of "a *real* [i.e., an entropic] environment that is, in part, beyond the control of group members. These external realities [i.e., **the need to find energy**] define the basic mission, primary task, or core functions of the group."

Value Cluster II, which includes the values of power aggrandizement, also is operative in corporate culture. They too are linked to environmental adaptation and internal integration but in far different ways and with remarkably different effects. That story should be preceded, though, by a brief encounter with an even more fundamental aspect of organizational culture noted by Schein.

For him, culture can be conceptually parsed into three analytic levels.[10] "Artifacts and Creations" are the most visible and tangible components of an organization's culture; they are the technology, art, and "visible and audible behavior patterns" that are present and in use. These artifacts are what one sees and hears on entering an organization's precincts.

"Values"—"the sense of what 'ought' to be"—are less visible but detectable; some are made explicit through the statements and actions of the organization's leaders; also, values "will predict much of the behavior that can be observed at the artifactual level," although one must be careful to dis-

9. Schein, op. cit., p. 51. Emphasis added, except for the word "real."

10. Schein, op. cit., pp. 13–21. The several quotations that follow are taken from these pages. Figure 1 on p. 14 of his book is particularly helpful.

tinguish espoused values from actual operational values. A corporate chieftain who advocates "cooperative team play" as a company value but who then acts autocratically and arbitrarily sends, at best, mixed signals about the company's true values. The same can be said of managers who tolerate or actively encourage unethical behavior that benefits their company (e.g., price-fixing or bid-rigging schemes) while promulgating a written code of ethics that warns against such practices.

The deepest level of culture Schein calls the organization's "Basic Assumptions." Largely invisible and "preconscious" (in the sense of explicitly felt awareness of their presence), these are the foundational preconceptions that underlie the organization's basic purpose and functioning. If one of these basic assumptions "is strongly held in a group, members would find behavior based on any other premise inconceivable." These assumptions are driven so deeply into the consciousness of organizational members that they "are, by definition, not confrontable or debatable." For example, making a profit would be accepted by most business people as this type of Basic Assumption. Another, in Western capitalist business systems, is private ownership of property. The desirability of free market exchange is yet another. Most observers of American business would agree that none of these assumptions is normally "confrontable or debatable."

It is in this latter sense—the presence of a deeply embedded and largely unquestioned set of preconceptions of organizational purpose—that business values have been defined in the preceding three chapters of this book. What Schein calls "Basic Assumptions" are here called, in the case of business firms, "business values." By "value," Schein means a provisional proposition or assertion that is fully shared or accepted as valid by others only when it has met the test of aiding problem resolution. Hence, values have instrumental effects, a trait that is consistent with the view of values expressed in earlier chapters of this book. For Schein, only when values have achieved a level of social consensus and acceptability based on their instrumental validation can they be transformed into the fundamental beliefs that may eventually become Basic Assumptions. For example, a chief executive officer might proclaim as a value that "This company ought to plan its future strategically and deliberately rather than being simply market-driven." If enough others in the company agree with the CEO and act to promote this proclaimed (provisional) value, then it may eventually be so well accepted by everyone in the company that it becomes an unquestioned Basic Assumption. The terminological differences between Schein's and this book's way of describing values should not obscure the more important agreement that organizational cultures rest on a bedrock of submerged preconceptions—whether called "Basic Assumptions" or "values" matters little—that have the effect of orienting the organization to its environment and to ways of dealing with it.[11]

These core assumptions and values tend to be interlocked to form "cultural paradigms" that differ from one company to another.[12] Such patterns create, for their organizational members, ways to "perceive, think about, and judge situations and relationships." Consistency among a firm's basic assumptions and values is said at times to produce a strong culture, which has been claimed by some to be a symbol of organizational health. The successful building of consistent cultural paradigms, where values mesh with one another in internally supportive ways, does indeed play a key role in helping business organizations to achieve their purposes. However, as will be made obvious in later chapters, cultural paradigms spawned within corporations may and frequently do work at cross purposes with competing value paradigms of the larger society. For the moment, though, it is sufficient to be aware that a corporate culture is, as Schein notes, an integrated pattern of basic assumptions, values, and artifacts that sets the stage for action, belief, and policy.

Another intriguing, if partial and perhaps even unintended, conceptual characterization of corporate culture has been advocated by the philosopher Peter French.[13] The main burden of his account is the argument that corporations should be considered to be moral agents in their own right, capable of taking on moral responsibilities for their actions, much as individual persons are thought to be moral agents responsible to others for a range of decisions and activities having moral import. That argument, which rages with considerable passion among philosophers, may be set aside for the present, and attention focused instead on an interesting and insightful concept introduced by French that has implications for understanding the normative aspects of corporate culture.

11. The "archetypes" described by Ian Mitroff, in his brilliant exposition, *Stakeholders of the Organizational Mind*, San Francisco: Jossey-Bass, 1983, are quite closely related to both Schein's notion of basic assumptions and this book's concept of original values. Mitroff's extension and application of Jungian concepts is more psychologically focused and it explores more fully the organizational and societal implications of archetypes than Schein's or this book's approach. More than one passage in Mitroff's account could stand virtually without significant modification in its meaning by substituting the term "value" (in the sense used here) for his use of "archetype." See the second full paragraph on page 163 of Mitroff's book for an example.

12. Schein, op. cit., pp. 109–111.

13. Peter A. French, *Collective and Corporate Responsibility*, New York: Columbia University Press, 1984, especially pp. 41–43, where the following quotations may be found. The argument for corporate moral agency has been extended in Peter A. French, Jeffrey Nesteruk, and David T. Risser, with John M. Abbarno, *Corporations in the Moral Community*, New York: Holt, Rinehart & Winston, 1992.

French believes that, in his words:

> Every corporation has an internal decision structure. CID [Corporate Internal Decision] Structures have two elements of interest to us here: (1) an organizational or responsibility flowchart that delineates stations and levels within the corporate power structure and (2) corporate-decision recognition rule(s) (usually embedded in something called corporation policy). The CID Structure is the personnel organization for the exercise of the corporation's power with respect to its ventures, and as such its primary function is to draw experience from various levels of the corporation in a decision-making and ratification process.

"Recognition rules," which are of two kinds, simply recognize that workplace decisions are ostensibly made for and on behalf of the corporation. One such set, called "procedural rules," specifies that those decisions are to be reached by well-understood corporate routines and according to approved ways. "Policy rules" generally lay down general guidelines and rationales that define the directions and goals to be sought by corporate managers as they go about their daily work. These two types of rules provide the logic of corporate decision making. They stand apart from the actual persons who work within this structure (this being the main point of French's argument that corporations deserve standing as moral agents because the organization's rules motivate managers and employees to act). Their combined effect is to direct the actions of corporate functionaries in ways thought to be congenial to the corporation's goals and purposes.

Thus, without directly engaging in an analysis of corporate culture, French has in fact captured some of its meaning through his notion of a CID Structure. One component of the structure—the organizational flowchart—invokes the rank-order hierarchy that is so typical of corporate bureaucracies. The recognition rules, which specify approved corporate procedures and identify goals and policies, embody the bulk of the values to be found in Value Clusters I (economizing) and II (power aggrandizement). This CID Structure functions to "exercise . . . the corporation's power" and to express "a decision-making and ratification process" for the pursuit of corporate purposes. These functions are among the normal operational expressions of corporate culture, as discussed by Schein, and of business values, as set forth here.[14]

---

14. French should not to be faulted for not carrying the tale of corporate culture further, although his argument for corporate moral personhood would have been considerably strengthened had he done so. As Edgar Schein's concept of organizational culture makes plain, a corporate culture encompasses much more than an organizational system and the rules to guide its operations. A company's culture also exerts a massive influence on the values and behavior of those who live within its presence daily. If one is to assign moral responsibility for the actions of corporations, this behavioral and moral influence of culture cannot be ignored or omitted.

THE VALUES OF CORPORATE CULTURE

There have been surprisingly few systematic, comprehensive attempts to describe the main values and basic assumptions that undergird business policy and practice in the modern corporation. Accounts of business values are not lacking, although they tend not to be focused on the integrated *system* of values that is found within corporate culture. Some of these studies have been mainly interested in the interplay between business values and competing social values. Other scholars have sought to reveal key values in the workplace without placing them explicitly within the context of corporate culture.[15]

For present purposes, the insights of James O'Toole are most fruitful. Drawing on his consultancy experience in advising corporations, O'Toole has identified a "dominant managerial culture that most American corporate executives share to at least some degree. . . . [This] culture is characterized by a congeries of mutually supporting and complementary values." They include, in O'Toole's words, economic efficiency, growth, short-term profitability, loyalty to the system, managerial authority, camaraderie, security, power, and stability. These values are said to suffuse corporate cultures everywhere.[16]

O'Toole's corporate culture value list overlaps to a very large extent the seven values found in Value Clusters I (economizing) and II (power aggrandizement):

- O'Toole's **economic efficiency** is equivalent to **economizing**.
- **Camaraderie** in O'Toole's account can be seen as a partial expression of **systemic integrity**.
- **Loyalty to the system** invokes both **systemic integrity** and **organizational (rank-order) hierarchy**.

15. Examples of the first group include Gerald F. Cavanagh, *American Business Values*, 2nd edition, Englewood Cliffs, NJ: Prentice-Hall, 1984; William G. Scott and David K. Hart, *Organizational America*, Boston: Houghton Mifflin, 1979; and Neil W. Chamberlain's books cited earlier. Charles S. McCoy's *Management of Values: The Ethical Difference in Corporate Policy and Performance*, Boston: Pitman, 1985, is a thoughtful but diffuse discussion of diverse normative components found in corporations; it gives only the most elusive insights into the actual values at work there. Various noncontextual studies of "work values" and managers' personal values are part of the story to be told in the following chapter of this book.

16. James O'Toole, *Making America Work: Productivity and Responsibility*, New York: Continuum, 1981, pp. 119–126. O'Toole recognizes other cultural and organizational features that distinguish corporations from one another: internal stratification, roles, associations and networks, systems of sanctions, career paths, and structural integration. Each of these cultural components finds a counterpart somewhere among the values of Value Clusters I and II, although not all of these relationships are explored here. See James O'Toole, *Vanguard Management: Redesigning the Corporate Future*, New York: Berkley Books, 1987, where the emphasis is on identifying values and goals that he believes corporations should cultivate, rather than those they should avoid. By identifying the reciprocals of these preferred "vanguard" values, a reader can develop a list that roughly parallels O'Toole's earlier version of questionable values. Interestingly, O'Toole has an anthropological background, which goes far to explain and validate his grasp of corporate culture's value system.

- His **managerial authority** and **power** match **managerial decision power**.
- The **power-system equilibrium** discussed here rests on what O'Toole refers to as **managerial authority, loyalty to the system,** and **camaraderie**.
- O'Toole's **power** component is roughly equivalent to **power aggrandizement**.
- **Growth** for O'Toole appears to include both **economizing growth** and **power-augmenting expansion**.

Altogether, it is not a perfect match, but the parallels are intriguing and highly suggestive. O'Toole's anthropological insights appear to be fully consistent with what one might expect to find within the culture of most large-scale business firms. The prime focus of that culture is on economizing, efficiency, growth, productivity, expansion of operations, the magnification of power, and stability of operations—all directed by managers who wield decision power within a relatively stable status hierarchy that grants them the various rewards that accompany aggrandizement of the firm. We turn now to the patterns formed by these characteristic value components within corporate culture.

Economizing Values in Corporate Culture

The economizing core of the modern business corporation's culture relies on personnel who assume a pragmatic posture toward problem solving, exhibit a practical turn of mind, take a logical-rational analytic approach, and measure results by a utilitarian cost–benefit calculus. When applied with vigor and determination, these core elements lead to growth and greater productivity. The economizing activities and outcomes are more likely to be achieved when the values of systemic integrity are given full sway. That means a focus on cooperation, teamwork, free information flows, open decision making, and other similarly functional means of binding workers together into a common economizing effort. Like all life units, business firms need to display large measures of systemic integrity if they are to draw energy from the environment and focus it effectively to promote their economizing purposes and goals.

In these fundamental ways, the values of the firm's economizing core— Value Cluster I—shape, regularize, and focus the activities of those who live within the confines of corporate culture. Corporate actions are structured actions, occurring according to whatever logic and pattern that may be embedded in a company's culture. Whether by means of Schein's cultural paradigm, French's corporate internal decision structure, or O'Toole's common managerial culture, one finds corporate actors answering to cultural cues. The cues signal the presence of a regularized pattern of expectations that, for most. becomes an imperative call to duty whose strength is too great to be forsworn.

Power-Aggrandizing Values in Corporate Culture

The patterned values that comprise the core of corporate culture are not limited to economizing values. Sharing the value space of the business firm are power-aggrandizing values. Augmenting and preserving the power of individual managers, as well as that of the entire enterprise, become central goals. Expansion that magnifies managerial and corporate power may, and frequently does, replace economizing growth as an organizational goal. When that happens, the economizing function and its values are placed at the service of the power-aggrandizing function and its values. The expansionist misadventures of the Circle K convenience store chain and the accounting firm of Laventhol & Horwath, told in Chapter 3, are worth recalling as cautionary tales; each company suffered economic ruin after unleashing expansionist urges.

A similar threat may endanger another of the economizing values. The systemic organizational integrity that is essential to sustained economizing may be contaminated and weakened by the necessity of preserving managerial and corporate power by resort to rank-order privilege and coercive commands. It is not unusual for a company's executives to fall prey to the allures of power aggrandizement, thereby smothering potential innovations and economizing initiatives under a blanket of rank-order protocol or abusive power.

Most corporate managers face an organizational dilemma rarely emphasized in training manuals, workshops, MBA programs, or other management preparation exercises. Daily, they must trade off economic efficiency for rank-order status claims. Typically, these claims arise from above as top-level managers demand organizational fealty to high-level commands, whether economically sensible or not. In one instance, perhaps an extreme one, a group of corporate executives revolted after allegedly suffering "frequent harangues and erratic, autocratic behavior" by the chief executive officer of their company. Claiming that they "were pitted against one another, publicly hazed, humiliated, and even physically intimidated," the officers appealed to the firm's board of directors, who then fired the CEO, who denied the charges. Knowing the risks to themselves of such "disloyalty," the executive rebels "pledged themselves to a 'blood pact' . . . and agreed that 'if one of us gets shot, we all get shot."[17]

---

17. "Fired Sunbeam Chief Harangued and Hazed Employees, They Say," *The Wall Street Journal,* January 14, 1993, pp. A1, A8. A similar story was reported from another leading corporation, whose CEO's style of management was so abrasive that he was known to insiders as the "Wrecking Ball." Several high-level executives were alleged to have left the company after being publicly humiliated and hazed by the CEO, who denied their allegations. See "At Procter & Gamble, Brands Face Pressure and So Do Executives," *The Wall Street Journal,* May 10, 1993, pp. A1, A8.

At other times, and increasingly so, a diverse lot of stakeholders, some inside and others outside the company's precincts, demand attention, special treatment, and status entitlements based upon race, gender, religion, national origin, and so on. That these latter groups occupy low levels of the status pyramid does not lessen the status-based authority that they assert for themselves. The effect of these incursions can, and frequently does, lower the company's economizing potential, although others maintain that a diverse corporate citizenry can boost a firm's overall productivity.[18] The contradictions and inconsistencies that prevail between these two master value sets—economizing and power aggrandizement—thus create much of the internal drama of corporate and managerial life and set the stage for many of the economic, social, and ethical dilemmas that occur there. These dilemmas receive much attention in later chapters of this book.

For the moment, it will be instructive to examine the various ways by which power-aggrandizing values make their presence felt in the daily work life of the corporate citizenry. Two views are particularly useful. One is given by Robert Jackall, a sociologist and anthropologist, who by means of multiple interviews and participant observation made an in-depth study of 143 executives in three corporations from 1980 to 1985. The other tale is told by Howard Schwartz, who has drawn on psychoanalytic concepts to analyze executive behavior at General Motors Corporation and at the federal government's National Aeronautics and Space Administration. Their research is helpful in comprehending how the structure of corporate culture, especially the power-aggrandizing value cluster, shapes business behaviors and outlooks.[19]

Jackall found that power seeking and power keeping dominate the lives of corporate managers, often (perhaps even typically) overriding the firm's economizing needs, as well as teaching managers and their corporate colleagues a moral code that subordinates all to the ingrained system of power aggrandizement.[20] He explains it this way:

> The hierarchical authority structure that is the linchpin of bureaucracy dominates the way managers think about their world and about themselves. . . . [It] creates

18. Taylor H. Cox and Stacy Blake, "Managing Cultural Diversity: Implications for Organizational Competitiveness," *Academy of Management Executive*, vol. 5, no. 3, 1991, pp. 45–56. In spite of the widely popular claim that diversity enhances the economic prospects of corporations, the authors state that "we are aware of no article that reviews actual data supporting the linkage of managing diversity and organizational competitiveness" (p. 45).

19. Robert Jackall, *Moral Mazes: The World of Corporate Managers*, New York: Oxford University Press, 1988; and Howard S. Schwartz, *Narcissistic Process and Corporate Decay: The Theory of the Organization Ideal*, New York: New York University Press, 1990. An earlier, condensed version of Jackall's study appeared as "Moral Mazes: Bureaucracy and Managerial Work," *Harvard Business Review*, September-October 1983, pp. 118–130.

20. The following passages are quoted from Jackall's book, op. cit., pp. 17, 19, 21, and 23.

a chain of commitments from the CEO down to the lowliest product manager or account executive. . . . In this world, a subordinate owes fealty principally to his immediate boss. . . . The shrewd subordinate learns to efface himself, so that his boss's face might shine more clearly. . . . In short, the subordinate must symbolically reinforce at every turn his own subordination and his willing acceptance of the obligations of fealty.

Sitting atop this bureaucratic status structure is the chief manager, who, in Jackall's words,

carries enormous influence in his corporation. If, for a moment, one thinks of the presidents of operating companies or divisions as barons, then the CEO of the corporation is the king. His word is law; even the CEO's wishes and whims are taken as commands by close subordinates on the corporate staff, who turn them into policies and directives. . . . The CEO becomes the actual and the symbolic keystone of the hierarchy that constitutes the defining point of the managerial experience. Moreover, the CEO and his trusted associates determine the fate of whole business areas of a corporation.

All corporate employees are caught up within the toils of this rank-order system. It has particular meaning for managers, especially those who covet favorable positions within the hierarchy. Their work life becomes one long round of securing the good thoughts and support of their superiors, colleagues, and subordinates, so that they may be known as loyal team players, ready to offer fealty to the boss and to receive it from lower ranks. Only in that way may one advance upward to whatever glories and power that high corporate position offers. One top-level executive was credited with saying, "I'd cut off my right arm for my leader" and "I have only two words for [my CEO]: 'Yes, sir.'"[21] Overstepping—breaching the established system of power and privilege—carries severe penalties, including personal ignominy and banishment from upper-level ranks, which is tantamount to career-ending professional failure.

The quest for power and, once gained, its preservation can and frequently do prevail over the corporation's economizing needs, as noted by Jackall:

Surely, one might argue, there must be more to success in the corporation than appearances, personality, team play, style, chameleonic adaptability, and fortunate connections. What about the bottom line—profits, performance? After all, whole forests have been demolished to print the endless number of tracts designed to ensure and extol "results-oriented management."

21. "The Grand Pilferer?" *Business Week*, June 7, 1993, p. 39.

Unquestionably, "hitting your numbers"—that is, meeting the profit commitments already discussed—or achieving expected levels of performance in other areas is important, but only within the social context I have described. . . . More generally, there are several rules that apply here. First, no one in a line position—that is, with responsibility for profit and loss—who regularly "misses his numbers" will survive, let alone rise. Second, a person who always hits his numbers but who lacks some or all of the required social skills [in negotiating his way through the rank-order system] will not rise. Third, a person who sometimes misses his numbers but who has all the desirable social traits will rise.[22]

Thus does the system of power aggrandizement, in which all managers are encapsulated, enfold and shape the firm's economizing functions.

A similar outcome has been reported by Howard Schwartz but with even more severe consequences that can threaten not only economizing efficiency and adaptability but a company's very existence. Drawing upon published reports and the shared knowledge of insiders, he attributes the organizational and competitive decay of General Motors Corporation to what he calls "totalitarian management" run amok. Schwartz's explanation for the obsessive character of General Motors' culture, as well as that of NASA, runs along psychoanalytic lines, as follows. Corporate managers identify their narcissistic selves with their company's goals and organizational needs; they then become addicted (literally) to serving those organizational ideals, regardless of the directions in which that pursuit carries them and their company. In the process, they lose sight of all other considerations and are unable to serve other purposes.

Schwartz asks: "How is it possible . . . that work organizations ceased valuing work? Indeed, it appears that there is something about the culture of the work organizations . . . that seems to impede the work process."

That "something," it becomes obvious, is the rank-order feature of the organization's culture:

. . . individuals become obsessed with organizational rank. They become compelled to beat down anyone whom they see as threatening or competing with them in their pursuit of higher rank or threatening the rank they have already acquired. Thus, ironically, behind the display of the organization ideal, of everyone working together to realize shared values, the real motivational process becomes a Hobbesian battle of one narcissism project against another narcissism project. . . .

When work, the productive process, becomes display, its meaning becomes lost. Its performance as part of the organizational drama becomes the only meaning it

22. Jackall, op. cit., p. 62.

has. Accordingly, the parts it plays in the organization's transactions with the world become irrelevant. When this happens, work loses its adaptive function and becomes mere ritual.[23]

Were it not for the presence of the rank-order "totalitarian management" system within corporate culture, managerial energy and skill would appear to be potentially able to carry a company toward the higher summits of economizing, increased productivity, and enhanced profits. Rather, as in the case of this well-known corporation, an obsessive managerial quest for power can carry the firm ingloriously downward toward competitive weakness and industrial decline. Schwartz also concludes that the National Aeronautics and Space Administration revealed similar value priorities that seriously damaged its reputation when NASA's top-level managers sought to preserve the space agency's image, authority, and political influence by overriding its own engineers' safety recommendations, thus leading to the *Challenger* space shuttle's explosion and loss of life.

These scholarly studies are constantly affirmed in the popular business press, as any regular reader of *The Wall Street Journal, Fortune, Forbes,* and *Business Week* can testify. *Business Week* has spoken of "CEO disease" that is epidemic in corporate suites, infecting its carriers with bloated egos, a can-do-no-wrong attitude, a dependence on supportive sycophants, an addiction to status symbols and privileges, and a reluctance to consider (and sometimes a deliberate campaign to frustrate) the selection of a successor. A case in point is the earlier than expected resignation of the vice chairman of Chrysler Corporation, who had been a leading contender to succeed Chairman Lee Iacocca until "he sent a memo to board members that criticized Mr. Iacocca." The aspiring vice chairman clearly had not learned to accept what Robert Jackall calls the "obligations of fealty," which include absolute loyalty to one's boss.[24]

---

23. The preceding quotes are, respectively, from Schwartz, op. cit., pp. 129, 58, and 61. Others have made studies of the power complex that seems to grip the managerial mind: Anne Wilson Schaef and Diane Fassel, *The Addictive Organization,* San Francisco: Harper & Row, 1988, especially Section III; Charles M. Kelly, *The Destructive Achiever: Power and Ethics in the American Corporation,* Reading, MA: Addison-Wesley, 1988; and Diane L. Swanson, "Dysfunctional Conglomerates: An Explanation Provided by Linking Ontological Individualism to Social Relations within an Open Systems Context," *Behavioral Science,* vol. 37, 1992, pp. 139–150, the last being a theoretical account of the role played by managerial power and grandiosity in conceiving and implementing corporate merger policies.

24. See "CEO Disease," *Business Week,* April 1, 1991, pp. 52–59. Two related stories are "Trying Harder to Find a No. 2 Executive," *The Wall Street Journal,* June 19, 1989, p. B1; and "Predecessor's Presence Clouds Power Transfer," *The Wall Street Journal,* March 17, 1992, p. B1. The Iacocca incident is reported in "Some Holders in Chrysler Back Lutz for Chief," *The Wall Street Journal,* March 6, 1992, p. A4.

Another instructive morality tale comes from General Electric Corporation's CEO, John Welch. When he declared (rather imperiously) in his company's 1992 annual report that autocratic management styles would no longer be tolerated within GE, *The Wall Street Journal* considered it remarkable enough to give the announcement prominent coverage.[25] Welch, who spoke in a voice that few in GE's managerial cadre would have misunderstood, told of a promising future ("onward and upward" were his words) for the manager who "delivers on commitments—financial or otherwise—*and shares the values of our company.*" But "the autocrat, the big shot, the tyrant" who "suppresses and intimidates" would no longer be tolerated. The autocratic delivery of this seemingly antiautocratic message makes one wonder just how large a dint will have been put in the authoritarian rank-order system of GE's culture, particularly since CEOs are said to be role models for their underlings. The unintentional inconsistency projected by Welch's decree reminds one of the U.S. Army officer during the Vietnam War who claimed that his troops had had to destroy a village in order to save it.

The pragmatic authoritarianism that suffuses corporate culture typically turns the company's power brokers toward expansionist goals. Expansion can bring tangible rewards of greater influence, larger domains of authority, pecuniary prizes, symbolic glory, and magnified psychological satisfactions to those who direct and can claim credit for leading their companies toward expanded fields of business endeavor.[26] Just as often, though, one reads of the ruination of careers and entire companies whose executives reached too far, driven as they were by power-aggrandizement urges. Among the many examples, in addition to the demise of Circle K and Laventhol & Horwath mentioned in Chapter 3, the case of Days Inn reveals some of the perils of unbridled expansion.

Following a leveraged buyout of the motel chain in 1984, which saddled the company with $700 million of debt financed largely with high-interest junk bonds and eventually led to a bankruptcy filing, the new owners agreed on what business school scholars like to call a "strategic decision." They switched from being the owner of at least half of their motels to being an exclusive franchiser of the Days Inn name; by 1992 the parent company did not own a single motel. Relying for revenue on royalties from franchisees, the company embarked on an expansion binge that, according to *The Wall Street Journal,* franchised the Days Inn banner to many motels whose standards of cleanliness, guest security, and maintenance of facilities were near the indus-

25. "GE Is No Place for Autocrats, Welch Decrees," *The Wall Street Journal,* March 6, 1992, p. B1. Emphasis is added in the following quotation.

26. Aspects of this story are told in Ralph Nader and William Taylor, *The Big Boys: Power and Position in American Business,* New York: Pantheon Books, 1986.

try's lowest. With the expansion fueled by handsome commissions paid to company personnel for signing up new franchisees, the total numbers of motels in the chain increased fourfold in less than eight years, most of the additions being older motels that purchased the Days Inn name. In the expansion's early years, some 600 of these motels joined the chain. As the expansion continued, performance standards seemed to decline, as acknowledged by present and former company officials. From a national chain known for its high-quality operation and its careful choice of franchisees, Days Inn's "strategic decision" to seek the glories to be found in expansionism brought the firm to the brink of financial ruin and badly tarnished its image in the minds of many travelers.[27]

That corporate culture need not always lead companies to these misfortunes is made obvious by the example of Eaton Corporation, a producer of diverse industrial equipment. Utilizing a gain-sharing compensation system for its employees, who also are given cost and production data not often released by a company's inner financial circles, Eaton boasted an enviable productivity record, increased earnings, and enhanced stock value during a recessionary period marked by sharper foreign competition. Here is a company whose growth-oriented economizing values appear to be nearer the center of its corporate culture than the crippling expansionist values of power seeking found in many firms.[28]

The contrast is instructive for understanding the relationship between corporate culture and business values. The specific culture found in any given company may vary greatly from that of another firm. Companies display contrasting styles of management and give over varying proportions of corporate life to productive economizing and to expansionist power seeking. Such differences may arise from a lingering value tradition originally imposed on the firm by its founders, or from accepted practices and competitive conditions typical of the firm's industry compared with another, or from the technological matrix employed, or from the demographic and ethnic mixture of the company's personnel, or, as noted in the book's opening chapter, from the prevalence of diverse X-factor values. Though the proportions may vary,

---

27. "How a Motel Chain Lost Its Moorings After 1980s Buy-Out," *The Wall Street Journal,* May 26, 1992, pp. A1, A10. Such stories are routinely reported by this newspaper; see also "Playtex Goes Through 4 Buy-Outs Since 1985, Enriching Top Officer," December 17, 1991, pp. A1, A5; "A Shadow of Itself, Drexel Comes Back From Bankruptcy," April 30, 1992, pp. C1, C13; "Barnes & Noble's Boss Has Big Growth Plans That Booksellers Fear," September 11, 1992, pp. A1, A4; "A Defective Strategy of Heated Acquisitions Spoils Borden's Name," January 18, 1994, pp. A1, A4; and "Its Acquisition Binge Has Loaded Banc One with Maze of Branches," April 11, 1994, pp. A1, A6.

28. "A Manufacturer Grows Efficient by Soliciting Ideas from Employees," *The Wall Street Journal,* June 5, 1992, pp. A1, A5.

some blend of economizing values and power-aggrandizing values is present in the culture of the typical business firm.

The Value Core of Corporate Culture

Edgar Schein's tripartite classification of organizational culture is useful for understanding both the differences and the similarities in the value profiles of business organizations. As noted earlier, Schein says that Artifacts and Creations are the most visible aspects of culture, Values are provisional beliefs tested and validated through experience, and Basic Assumptions are the fundamental preconceptions that give meaning to an organization's existence.

The theory of business values being presented here contends that as one moves from the most visible level of Artifacts and Creations to the more deeply embedded Basic Assumptions, the cultural differences among firms lessen. This occurs because the need to economize is the *most basic* Basic Assumption shared by *all* businesses, regardless of differences in other features of their cultures. Technology, management style, group interactions, the many provisional personal values and beliefs held by managers and employees—all of these offer opportunities for immense distinctions among companies. Even though companies also approach their environments with diverse Basic Assumptions about the nature of reality, human nature, and human relationships generally—a point made by Edgar Schein—*each one eventually has to come to grips with the problem of entropy*. The chances for cultural variation thus become smaller as one approaches the most fundamental defining components of a company's culture. It is true that many diverse pathways lead different business firms toward economizing outcomes, and these will distinguish one from another. But whatever differences their separate cultures may display, Time's Arrow points them all toward their most basic need and function—to acquire environmental energy sufficient to fend off entropic trends.

Important as their cultural differences may prove to be in the life (and survival chances) of business firms, it remains true that all such firms, of whatever specific cultural makeup, manifest the operation of both economizing and power aggrandizing at their vital center. Driven deeply into the organizational structure by the forces of both nature and culture, economizing values and power-aggrandizing values reign as the supreme arbiters of business decisions, policies, and practices. The resultant workplace climate, whatever the relative balance achieved between these two master value sets, enables managers and other employees to know what is expected of them as they perform their assigned tasks.

The key figures in this corporate drama, as noted previously, are managers and top-level executives. The specific values they hold and project onto their work and into the consciousness of their peers and subordinates are worthy of special attention. For the most part, their *managerial* values are drawn from and help to express the particular character of their companies' cultures. Some of their value commitments, however, also are strongly shaped by their own individual life histories and so bring us into the realm of X-factor values mentioned but not fully explained in the earlier chapters of this book. What is known about the general matrix of corporate values when blended with managers' personal values, along with the effects they produce in the business firm, receive careful attention in the following chapter.

5

The Values of Managers

The prominence given to managers' values is explained by the manager's commanding position and decisional dominance within the corporation. Saying so is not meant to justify, defend, or otherwise rationalize this state of affairs but only to acknowledge one of the brute facts of business life. Hence, if one wants to understand the value system of the modern corporation, one turns attention to the kinds of values carried in the psyche and projected onto the corporate scene by the firm's chief managers.

The term "manager" is used here and throughout the book in a generic sense to denote one who holds a formal organizational position with managerial duties and responsibilities attached to it. "Managerial" means having the power and ability to direct or persuade others to undertake some work-related activity. In recent years, it has become fashionable to distinguish invidiously between "executives" (or sometimes "leaders") and "managers," with the idea of describing their work activities as involving distinct functions and operations, and with the further notion that the former are somehow more advanced and generally more important to the firm than the latter. These invidious distinctions reflect rank-order status gradations to a greater degree than actual operational differences in getting the firm's work done. More is said about these matters, particularly concerning the nature of managerial work, further along in this chapter.

One needs to distinguish carefully between what are frequently called the **personal values** of managers and the structure of **organizational values** comprising a large portion (but by no means all) of corporate culture. As told in the preceding chapter, the organizational value structure is patterned in ways that serve both the **original (economizing) values** of business and the **power-aggrandizing values**. All managers, in the course of their daily work routines, render tribute to these two corporate value systems. Lying outside this structured system of corporate values is a quite complex and varied group of values called **X-factor values**, so designated because their precise nature and number cannot be known a priori. Managers and all other employees bring these "personal" values into the workplace, where they exert varying effects on what happens there, and so they must be understood if one is to grasp the totality of value influences within the firm. An additional component of corporate life that deserves attention is the prevailing **ethical climate** of any given firm—those intuitions and feelings regarding normative expectations that pervade any particular workplace. These climates of opinion-attitude-expectation frequently give tangible form to embedded organizational value systems, disciplining managerial and employee approaches to problems and decisions.

Within this cocoon of interwoven value elements, the manager works. Figure 5–1 graphically displays the major valuational components of the business workplace and reveals the somewhat porous walls of the firm as it interacts with external social, natural, and personal forces. Just what managerial work is and how it is affected by the firm's values-in-place tells much of the story of modern business life. The managerial decisions that are forthcoming from the corporation's decision centers shape the lives and fortunes of many people both inside and outside the firm's precincts. To clarify the links between managers' decisions, their work, and their values is the task now at hand.

MANAGERS' VALUES: THE RESEARCH PICTURE

What is empirically known about managers' values and the role they play in business life presents a less precise picture than one might wish. The research findings, considered as a whole, are diffuse, clouded, uncertain, and sometimes contradictory. The reasons are varied: different motives have activated researchers' interests in knowing more about values and communicating that knowledge to interested audiences; values have been variously defined; diverse methods have been employed; and many researchers have been hampered by a widely shared belief that values are inherently difficult to study, thus rendering both researcher and audience skeptical and tentative about the interpretations of what is revealed through systematic research. Probably as important as any of these factors, the findings themselves may deliver unwelcome normative messages about the nature and impact of business operations, lessons that constitute what Robert Jackall has called, in a related context, "invitations to jeopardy," thus causing scholars with varying allegiances to the corporate system to render diverse interpretations of their research results.[1]

---

1. Jackall's phrase appears as the title of Chapter 19 of his *Moral Mazes: The World of Corporate Managers*, New York: Oxford University Press, 1988.

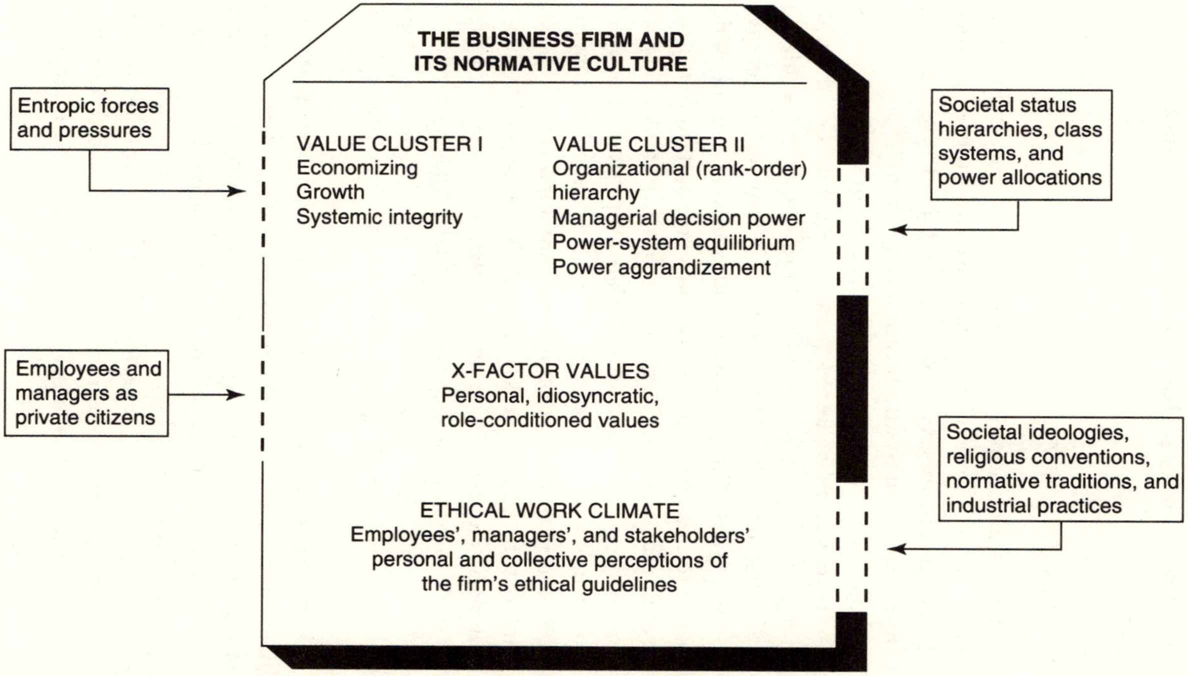
THE BUSINESS FIRM AND
ITS NORMATIVE CULTURE
Entropic forces and pressures
VALUE CLUSTER I
Economizing
Growth
Systemic integrity
VALUE CLUSTER II
Organizational (rank-order) hierarchy
Managerial decision power
Power-system equilibrium
Power aggrandizement
Societal status hierarchies, class systems, and power allocations
Employees and managers as private citizens
X-FACTOR VALUES
Personal, idiosyncratic, role-conditioned values
Societal ideologies, religious conventions, normative traditions, and industrial practices
ETHICAL WORK CLIMATE
Employees', managers', and stakeholders' personal and collective perceptions of the firm's ethical guidelines

Figure 5–1. The value arena of managerial work

Value knowledge therefore comes in several different forms and makes possible a wide array of interpretations about its overall normative significance within the business realm. It may be helpful preliminarily to chart a path through this knowledge base to reveal the distinctive themes that emerge from it.

Empirical Values Research

Four reasonably distinct empirical approaches are discernible, although no attempt is made here to provide an exhaustive inventory of all such studies. The greater part of this research has been conducted by scholars working in and/or in close collaboration with business corporations.

The **first** approach, both chronologically and in continuing popular acceptance, posits **managers' values as personal attributes or traits** that shape character and personality. Early research here was aimed at identifying the character traits that are reflected in managers' expressed preferences for different personality types. These might include personalities focused primarily on *theoretical* interests (such as discovery and systemization of truth), *economic* interests (useful, practical knowledge and action), *aesthetic* values (form and harmony), *social* orientation (altruistic, philanthropic love of people), *political* interests (power motives), and *religious* interests (mystical orientation to life), or some combination of these ideal types. From a manager's choices among these personality types, researchers constructed a value profile showing a preferred orientation. The resultant value profiles were presumed to give clues to the kinds of decisions, policies, and goals that managers would be likely to choose for their firms. The Allport-Vernon-Lindzey value scale, which posits the six character types, was the prime research instrument employed to elicit respondents' preferences.[2]

From this base, research on managers' values became an attempt to find those individually unique personal values that are hypothesized to have an influence on a manager's approach to corporate strategy, the formulation of company policy, and the kinds of managerial decisions likely to be made. Being congenial to the general purposes and goals of corporations, this way of understanding managers' values found its way into mainstream management theory. Having originated, or at least having found fertile ground early on, among scholars at the Harvard Business School and then continuing to

---

2. W. Gordon Allport, Philip E. Vernon, and Gardner Lindzey, *Test Booklet: Study of Values*, 3rd edition, New York: Houghton Mifflin, 1960. The six personality types were derived from Eduard Spranger's *Types of Men*, 5th edition (translation by Paul J. W. Pigors), Halle: Max Niemeyer Verlag. For a summary, see Allport, Vernon, and Lindzey, *Study of Values Manual*, Boston: Houghton Mifflin, 1960, pp. 3–5.

enjoy further receptivity there, the personal-values approach might justifiably be labeled the "Harvard values approach."[3]

Sharing an affinity with the Harvard Business School's focus on personal values but arising from different intellectual sources is values research grounded in the discipline of social psychology. Here, too, the quest is to understand the value commitments and preferences of individual persons. A similar assumption is made that these personal values influence both the perceptions and behavior of managers, thus having an impact on corporate affairs. This approach, which spawned newer and more sophisticated methodological instruments, has proved to be quite popular among research scholars and can be rightly said to have produced a majority of the extant empirical knowledge base about managers' values.[4]

Some of the most important research arising from the personal-values approach has focused on large populations of managers in an effort to identify characteristic value patterns or value profiles of managers in general. These might be called macro-population studies, to distinguish them from organization-specific, *in situ* research where the population is specifically associated with a given company or department or division of a company. Hence, a general managerial typology of characteristic values is one product of macro-population research. Where managers' values are investigated *in situ*, they may be expected to reflect the particular influences rooted in a given company's culture; therefore, the managers' value profile in those cases is likely to vary somewhat from the general values typology revealed in macro-population studies.

George England's widely respected and replicated research on managers' values set the pattern for macro-population studies. In view of its early and continuing importance, it is odd indeed that he does not offer a substantive

3. For examples, see William D. Guth and Renato Tagiuri, "Personal Values and Corporate Strategy," *Harvard Business Review*, September-October 1965, pp. 123–132; and Renato Tagiuri, "Value Orientations and the Relationship of Managers and Scientists," *Administrative Science Quarterly*, vol. 10, 1965, pp. 39–51. Both of these studies used the Allport-Vernon-Lindzey instrument. The work of Kenneth Andrews, Raymond Bauer, Robert Ackerman, Robert Miles, and Kenneth Goodpaster—all at one time or another faculty members of the Harvard Business School—has been influenced by this personal-values approach.

4. Representative works are George W. England, "Personal Value Systems of American Managers," *Academy of Management Journal*, March 1967, pp. 53–68; Barry Z. Posner and Warren H. Schmidt, "Values and the American Manager: An Update," *California Management Review*, Spring 1984, pp. 202–216; and Posner and Schmidt, "Values and the American Manager: An Update Updated," *California Management Review*, vol. 34, no. 3, Spring 1992, pp. 80–94. The research methods developed by Milton Rokeach, though not originally designed to elicit managers' values, have been used by several researchers for that purpose; see Milton Rokeach, *The Nature of Human Values*, New York: Free Press, 1973. A review article that, along with other aspects of this field's literature, traces the origins of the Rokeach approach is Ralph H. Kilmann, "Toward a Unique/Useful Concept of Values for Interpersonal Behavior: A Critical Review of the Literature on Values," *Psychological Reports*, vol. 48, 1981, pp. 939–959.

definition of values. His research instrument attempts to "get at a manager's values through the use of a carefully specified *set of concepts.*" Since he does not study values directly, England and those who use this method can only *infer* values from the choices that respondents make in considering the set of concepts. The way respondent managers arrange and rank the concepts comes to "represent" managers' values.[5]

The **second** most prominent stream of empirical research focuses on the **values found in corporate culture**. As noted in the preceding chapter, this novel concept took the scholarly world of management studies by storm during the 1980s. Thrust forward mainly by management consultants, it stressed the importance of identifying a firm's key values, which were to be found within the minds and actions of top-level managers, as well as in the conventions and traditions making up the history of the company. Finding ways to identify and promulgate these values with clarity could lead to what was called a "strong" organizational culture that was more apt than others to cause its host firm to be an effective, even "excellent," market performer. As this line of research was pushed forward, the notion of "shared values"—subsequently to be labeled "value congruence"—was said to be a further key to getting all employees of a company to work for the firm's goals, and several studies seemed to demonstrate the general validity of such thinking.[6]

The corporate culture/shared values approach was a departure from seeking values solely within the managerial psyche. It signaled a sociological-anthropological way of conceiving values, which carried value analysis beyond the individual's personal commitments and into the realm of organizational values. This broadened approach was clearly a gain that promised a richer and deeper picture of the values that influence managerial actions.[7]

A **third** line of empirical research, appearing in the 1970s, seems to bear little direct relation to those already mentioned and in fact is rather broader in its search for value meaning in the workplace. **Work values** are said to be those values that suffuse the internal job environment of the firm, although

5. England, op. cit., p. 55.

6. For two examples, see Cathy A. Enz, "The Role of Value Congruity in Intraorganizational Power," *Administrative Science Quarterly*, vol. 33, 1988, pp. 284–304; and Charles A. O'Reilly III, Jennifer Chatman, and David F. Caldwell, "People and Organizational Culture: A Profile Comparison Approach to Assessing Person–Organization Fit," *Academy of Management Journal*, vol. 34, no. 3, September 1991, pp. 487–516.

7. Edgar H. Schein, *Organizational Culture and Leadership*, San Francisco: Jossey-Bass, 1985, 1988, is the primary scholarly source. Popular and widely read sources include Thomas J. Peters and Robert H. Waterman, *In Search of Excellence: Lessons from America's Best-Run Companies*, New York: Harper & Row, 1982; and Terrence E. Deal and Allan A. Kennedy, *Corporate Cultures: The Rites and Rituals of Corporate Life*, Reading, MA: Addison-Wesley, 1982. See also John P. Kotter and James L. Heskett, *Corporate Culture and Performance*, New York: Free Press, 1992; and Cathy A. Enz, *Power and Shared Values in the Corporate Culture*, Ann Arbor, MI: UMI Research Press, 1986.

they may owe their origin and derivation to broad ideological orientations prevalent in the company's host society. For example, public and business concern about a reputed decline in the (Protestant) work ethic initially stimulated some of this research, although later studies show an affinity with both the Harvard values/social psychology approach and the organizational culture approach. In any event, the focus has not been on managers per se but on the broad range of employees (though also including managers) whose work is thought to be affected by their attachment to various value orientations.[8]

Standing somewhat apart from these three research streams is the empirical work of Geert Hofstede, who has identified "four value dimensions" present in the workplace: Power Distance (acceptance of power differentials), Uncertainty Avoidance (discomfort with ambiguity and a preference for institutional conformity), Individualism-Collectivism (orientation toward loosely knit or tightly knit social systems), and Masculinity-Femininity (achievement, assertiveness, material success versus caring relationships and quality of life). These are said to be present in all societies in varying degrees. They influence the way work is organized and carried out within any given business firm. This **fourth** kind of empirical research—like that on work values—emphasizes **the link between organizational value components and the broader national value systems of the host society.** Hofstede also maintains that the early history of a firm, along with the dominant values of the founding group, have much to do with the values that become characteristically associated with any given company. His approach is clearly compatible with an anthropological tradition that finds values, both personal and organizational, to be rooted within cultural systems. In this sense, it parallels the approach and tenor of Robert Jackall's landmark study, *Moral Mazes*, referred to in the preceding chapter.[9]

An oddity—some would call it an artifact—of the empirical research tradition on values, including research on managers' values, is its tendency to define values in positive, affirmative terms. This tradition can be traced at least back to Clyde Kluckhohn's renowned definition of value as a "concept of the desirable." It is echoed in Milton Rokeach's notion that a value is a "preferable" be-

8. An early example is Stephen Wollack, James G. Goodale, and Jan P. Wijting, "Development of the Survey of Work Values," *Journal of Applied Psychology*, vol. 55, no. 4, 1971, pp. 331–338. Later representative research includes Bruce M. Meglino, Elizabeth C. Ravlin, and Cheryl L. Adkins, "A Work Values Approach to Corporate Culture: A Field Test of the Value Congruence Process and Its Relationship to Individual Outcomes," *Journal of Applied Psychology*, vol. 74, no. 3, 1989, pp. 424–432.

9. See Geert Hofstede, *Culture's Consequences: International Differences in Work-Related Values*, Beverly Hills, CA: Sage, 1980; and Hofstede, "The Interaction between National and Organizational Value Systems," *Journal of Management Studies*, July 1985, pp. 347–357.

lief about means and ends, and by those who urge corporations to develop and communicate clear pictures of the positive, forward-looking values they espouse so as to enhance overall company performance. Allport, Vernon, and Lindzey also cautioned users of their method that their six ideal personality types were based on Spranger's "somewhat flattering view of human nature."

The result of this methodological artifact is seemingly to rule out all notions of value that carry a negative connotation. Hence, managers or other employees may display avariciousness and a preference for self-centered power-seeking, power-possession, and power-wielding behavior. They may seek profits for themselves or their firm, even though acquired in doubtful or even criminal ways, or they may promote their company's interests (whether economizing or power-aggrandizing) in the face of clear-cut negative social impacts. Employees may sabotage company operations for personal gain or out of private pique. Many similar questionable goals, motives, and negative values tend not to be registered in the notebooks and data banks of empirical researchers because the research tradition in which they work has caused their methodological tools, designed as they are, almost automatically to treat such values as more or less "out of bounds."

For example, a research project in which I was involved a few years ago once approached a group of activists who were protesting the plant-closing policies of western Pennsylvania steel companies during the mid-1980s, asking them to cooperate by responding to the Rokeach Value Survey (RVS). After mulling it over for a day or so, the group's leadership refused to let their members participate in the research, saying that the RVS failed to specify some of the core values that this group of dissidents believed to be at the heart of the steel companies' policies and actions, including "greed," "profits before people," "power," and "union-busting tactics." Because they did not fill out the RVS forms, the values they had identified informally were not included in the formal data analysis. One unfortunate and highly misleading consequence of such research procedures, which are quite commonly used, is that personally and/or socially undesirable or nonpreferred values are made to appear nonexistent in the workplace. Thus, they drop from the researcher's sight, falling into some statistical and methodological never-never land, sometimes to be revealed during face-to-face interviews (and then only cautiously) when the respondent has been assured of complete confidentiality regarding ethically sensitive topics. Even then, some researchers appear reluctant to bring these values forward as equal in significance to socially approved values.[10]

A complete mapping of a corporation's value space requires that *all* val-

---

10. An exception is James A. Waters, "Catch 20.5: Corporate Morality as an Organizational Phenomenon," *Organizational Dynamics*, Spring 1978, pp. 3–19.

ues present in the workplace—in earlier chapters these were called "found values"—be represented, including those that are antibusiness, antiorganizational, and antisocial. Many of these will be X-factor values brought to the job by employees. Others will be part of the embedded organizational value system and the corporate culture. Since these fugitive negative values are presumably present though not often verified empirically, their influence can be attested only by attribution, by inference, and through interpretive studies such as those by Gerald Cavanagh, Barbara Toffler, James O'Toole, Howard Schwartz, and others whose methods, while not rigorously empirical, have been models of professional clarity and common sense.

Nonempirical Critical Commentary

Tangential to these four empirical approaches to understanding managers' values, one finds a set of **nonempirical critiques of business values** that, on the whole, verge on being ideological commentaries about the function of business values within society. They too have been produced largely by business school faculty members. Useful for their historical and social insights, these works shed little direct light on the way in which values affect the day-to-day or even year-to-year operations of business managers. Rather, their function is to call attention to the ideological currents and conventions that surround the firm and its managers, adding a fair amount of speculation about the future fate of those companies that fail to heed social changes and shifts of public opinion.[11]

Standing almost alone as an early exemplar of a nonempirical social science–based discussion of business values is *The Value Issue of Business* by Alvar O. Elbing and Carol J. Elbing. Remarkably insightful, this commentary argued that business values are given their meaning by society rather than by or through the market, as classical and neoclassical economics had posited, and that values suffuse all realms of business operations.

> All business acts, being human acts, are social responses, having social implications and social consequences. Economic activity is inescapably social activity. Economic events are social events, and business history is social history. Business produces not only economic consequences—goods, services, profit, and wealth—but a great variety of other social consequences. The firm as a social system acting

11. See Francis X. Sutton et al., *The American Business Creed*, Cambridge, MA: Harvard University Press, 1956; George Cabot Lodge, *The New American Ideology*, New York: Knopf, 1976; Lodge, *The American Disease*, New York: Knopf, 1984; Gerald F. Cavanagh, *American Business Values*, 2nd edition, Englewood Cliffs, NJ: Prentice-Hall, 1984; Neil W. Chamberlain, *The Place of Business in America's Future: A Study in Social Values*, New York: Basic Books, 1973; and Neil W. Chamberlain, *Remaking American Values: Challenge to a Business Society*, New York: Basic Books, 1977.

upon a larger social system is a vast producer of social relationships and molder of social values. Today's continuous technological revolution *is* social revolution in which value issues *inhere.*[12]

Not only was the Elbings' discussion of value methodology far advanced for its time, but a retrospective reading discloses that they anticipated all of the major theoretical trends that were to become the principal body of theory comprising the business and society field.[13]

This brief survey of research approaches suggests that the picture of managerial value phenomena that has emerged is a created one, shaped importantly by the general approach and the specific methods employed by researchers. Their own normative orientations toward business and business managers may well have influenced the investigators' preferred approach and adopted methods. Where the normative stakes are large, as they are in any study of a society's dominant institutional order, research clarity is often difficult to achieve, and one must be alert to both the institutional constraints and the subsequent intellectual limitations possibly manifested in research reports and conclusions drawn. All who study business values and comment upon their significance (including the author of this book) are influenced in these ways by their institutional and societal affiliations and allegiances.[14] Given the normatively bounded nature of research knowledge, the following account of managers' values is sketched with full awareness of its tentative, partial, and idiosyncratic character. Others with different normative commitments undoubtedly would be likely to render a different interpretation of the overall significance and impact of managers' values than the one given here.

MANAGERS' EMBODIED VALUES

Managers' values are embodied in their perceptions, attitudes, and behavior. These perceptual, attitudinal, and behavioral components, in turn, are an ex-

12. Alvar O. Elbing and Carol J. Elbing, *The Value Issue of Business*, New York: McGraw-Hill, 1967, p. 77.

13. Two other early contributions to value analysis in the business realm are C. West Churchman, *Prediction and Optimal Decision: Philosophical Issues of a Science of Values*, Englewood Cliffs, NJ: Prentice-Hall, 1961; and Wayne A. R. Leys, *Ethics for Policy Decisions: The Art of Asking Deliberative Questions*, Englewood Cliffs, NJ: Prentice-Hall, 1952. Both books foreshadowed the later entrance into the business ethics field of large numbers of applied ethics philosophers.

14. See William C. Frederick, "The Empirical Quest for Normative Meaning: Introduction and Overview," pp. 91–98, and "Epilogue: Whither Method?", pp. 245–246, in *Business Ethics Quarterly*, vol. 2, no. 2, April 1992. All of the articles in this special issue discuss various empirical methods used in research on business values and ethics.

pression of the forces—both natural and cultural—involved in the formation and operationalization of values. Value commitments, value judgments, value standards, value relationships, and valuational experiences are the day-to-day expression of symbolic human meanings that bring order and significance into human transactions. One would therefore expect that managers' values—like the values of all others—would be revealed by observing their expressed perceptions, work attitudes, and on-the-job behavior.

Since business managers work within structured organizations whose major value systems are devoted to both economizing and power aggrandizement, and since those value systems are given their regularity and patterning by corporate culture, the value-conditioned outlook and behavior of managers can be expected to be aligned more or less consistently with the economizing and power-aggrandizing values found within the firm's culture. Extant research on managers' values confirms the general outlines of this expectation, as the following discussion reveals.

Managers' Organizational Commitments and Attitudes

The macro populations of managers studied thus far commonly share a wide range of values, as well as behavioral traits and attitudes closely associated with those values. The value profile that emerges is one of a manager committed to organizational effectiveness, productivity, efficiency, high organizational morale, and concern for organizational reputation. Each of these value orientations either contributes directly to or is an expression of the firm's economizing activities. By contrast, direct concern about the company's value to the community or its service to the public ranks low in a typical hierarchy of managers' organizational goals.

Research shows that these value inclinations tend to be stable over time. Managers' goal-value commitments did not change appreciably over a ten-year period during the 1980s, which was characterized by many shifts in the general economic environment and greater competitive pressures. The more intense competitive environment apparently brought about a greater focus on quality of product, customer service, and organizational stability, and these economizing features became more prominent in the general value profile revealed in one large-scale study of 1,000 American managers.[15] In an earlier study, these researchers spoke of "the remarkable similarity in the val-

15. Posner and Schmidt, "Values and the American Manager: An Update," op. cit., pp. 203–205; and Posner and Schmidt, "Values and the American Manager: An Update Updated," op. cit. The quotations in the following paragraph are from Schmidt and Posner, *Managerial Values in Perspective*, New York: American Management Associations, 1983, p. 45; and from the second paper listed above, p. 84.

ues held by managers, regardless of age, organizational level, gender, or nationality." This comment was virtually identical to their finding in a later study, where they refer to "the striking similarity in the relative ranking of organizational goals across the decade [of the 1980s]." Goals, of course, are not the same as values, but it is reasonable to assume that the goal rankings of managers represent, in some general approximation, their beliefs (i.e., values) about what is important within the workplace while they are acting out their roles as corporate functionaries. Other researchers have reported similar value congruence within the managerial class: "Overall, the data suggest that all managers, regardless of level or organization, share common values."[16]

Managers' value preferences also are revealed in the attitudes they adopt toward their colleagues within the company and toward others both inside and outside the company. These stakeholder rankings generally reveal a manager who takes seriously those who are most important and critical to getting the job done, including customers, "myself" (which ranks high at all times), subordinates, bosses, coworkers, and others who populate the company's ranks and role structure. Those with more tenuous links to the manager's workaday activities—the general public, owners, stockholders, even elected public officials and government bureaucrats—are considered to be less important and less worthy of managerial attention than one's colleagues who are directly instrumental to the daily round of work.[17] Whether this inward-looking attitude is wise or not is considered in a later chapter of this book.

Again, these ingrained managerial attitudes are testimony to the sway of organizational economizing within the managed business firm. There is a sense in which one would not wish it to be otherwise, given the critical and indispensable function that economizing performs for the firm and for society generally. One would want to object if economizing managers were competitively diverted from their central (economizing) function, blocked by countervailing power games, narrowly channeled toward a firm's exclusive glorification, directed in ecologically destructive ways, or otherwise motivated to diminish other vital human values. Generally speaking, the manager's positive acceptance of organizational goals is a clear index of an enduring commitment to the economizing principle whose value roots reach deeply into both natural and cultural soil.

16. Donald A. Clare and Donald G. Sanford, "Mapping Personal Value Space: A Study of Managers in Four Organizations," *Human Relations*, vol. 32, no. 8, 1979, p. 662.

17. See Posner and Schmidt, "An Update Updated," op. cit., Table 3, p. 85. The mean scores of the five less highly regarded groups increased from 1981 to 1991, but as a group their relative rankings remained lower than other more directly involved groups.

This managerial economizing value trait was affirmed by George England's research. He demonstrated that managers' "operative values"—those that "should influence the behavior of managers more than [any other component] in the Value Profile"—were headed by organizational efficiency, high productivity, profit maximization, organizational growth, industrial leadership, and organizational stability. Each of these goal-values promotes the firm's drive toward an economizing outcome.

England also empirically established that managers' primary decision-making approach is pragmatic, focused on whether any given decision is likely to accomplish a practical purpose for the manager and the organization. A majority of his respondents revealed their devotion to an active pragmatism by giving high ranking to ability, ambition, and skill, and favoring achievement, success, and creativity as personal goals. The impact on the achievement of organizational goals is obvious: "Pragmatists have an economic and organizational competence orientation . . . , will be more responsive to the economic aspects of behavior and decisions . . . , [and] are more apt to be influenced more by training, persuasion and leadership approaches which focus on the notion of whether or not a particular act or decision will work or is likely to be successful."[18] Clare and Sanford, using a truncated version of the Rokeach Value Survey, reported an identical result: "The [value] profile which emerges . . . is one of a managerial value pattern dominated . . . by personal, achievement-oriented goals . . . and . . . by competence and individualistic means." Moreover, three-quarters of over 400 managers studied by James Weber registered a strong preference for what Milton Rokeach has called "competence values"—meaning those that promote a feeling of adequacy through behavior that is logical, intelligent, or imaginative.[19]

Although wearing, often proudly, the indelible mental tatoo of organizational pragmatism, the manager who survives the rigors of corporate life need not, and typically does not, dedicate this talent solely to organizational economizing purposes and needs. As many observers have pointed out, managers struggle for their own professional survival, as it were, in a corporate setting not unlike a jungle populated by hostile creatures and displaying tangled webs of political intrigue and self-seeking combat where a critical mis-

18. England, "Managers and Their Value Systems: A Five-Country Comparative Study," *Columbia Journal of World Business*, Summer 1978, p. 41. For the pragmatic traits, see England, "Personal Value Systems of American Managers," op. cit., pp. 58–65.

19. The Clare and Sanford quotation is from Clare and Sanford, op. cit., p. 662. The Weber data are in James Weber, "Managerial Value Orientations: A Typology and Assessment," *International Journal of Value Based Management*, vol. 3, no. 2, 1990, pp. 37–54. Weber's paper also identifies other research that yields similar results.

step or miscalculation can easily threaten one's career and organizational standing. Pragmatism, wielded as a personal weapon, therefore has uses that go well beyond the firm's official need to economize. It can be and frequently is brought to bear in the continuing round of power struggles and conflicts whose source is the firm's power-laden organizational (rank-order) hierarchy. Weber's study recorded managers' strong orientation to personally pragmatic instrumental values: when asked to rate the importance of predominantly *personal* values and predominantly *social* values, 72 percent of the management respondents registered a preference for personal, ego-centered values.[20] Thus, the pragmatic inclination to produce workable economizing outcomes for the firm competes with a pragmatic desire to protect one's organizational turf, power, and privileges. In either case, the manager's behavior tends to mirror the two value systems—economizing and power aggrandizement—that dominate the workplace.

A similar devotion to these two master value clusters was observed in the qualities that managers seek in their workplace colleagues. Posner and Schmidt asked their respondents, "What values (personal traits and characteristics) do you look for and admire in your superiors [and in your colleagues and subordinates]?" From a final list of fifteen categories, they found that "integrity (truthful, trustworthy, has character, has convictions)" was the most often chosen response, with "competence (capable, productive, efficient, thorough)" ranked third by all managers. Relative rank within the hierarchy moderated the respondents' second choices along expected lines: in one's subordinates, managers preferred "determination (industrious, hardworking, motivated)"; from superiors they wanted "leadership (inspiring, decisive, provides direction)"; and they looked for "cooperativeness (friendly, team player, available, responsive)" in their peers. As the authors emphasize, "The two qualities cited most often in all three categories—integrity and competence—are perhaps *the qualities most basic to doing a good job.*"[21] In other words, managers at all levels and ranks want to work with others whose personal and professional traits can promote commonly shared organizational

20. Weber, op. cit., p. 49.

21. Posner and Schmidt, "Values and the Manager: An Update," op. cit., pp. 208–210, emphasis added. The entire list is worth consulting. The traits of "fairness," "maturity," "straightforwardness," and "sensitivity" were chosen least often. In their 1991 follow-up study, "Values and the Manager: An Update Updated," op. cit., the authors provided fewer details of these characteristics than in the 1981 report, and there were subtle changes of wording and phrasing of some questions that reflected their greater interest in the concept of leadership ("honest" replaces "integrity" and "leader" replaces "superior"). Nevertheless, they point out (p. 86) that "These findings are remarkable for their consistency over time, across organizational levels and demographic characteristics. The problems may change, the context may become more complicated, and the situation may be increasing [sic] tempestuous, but the guiding forces required in people we would be willing to follow remains constant."

goals and purposes. Quite obviously, some of the most highly favored traits contribute directly to the firm's *economizing* goals.

A similar orientation toward acceptance of managerial power and authority was revealed by this research. Within managerial ranks, according to the researchers, "[a leader] has *referent and expert power*. These kinds of power influence people's attitudes as well as their behaviors."[22] The fealty (or in the language of management theory, the "loyalty") accorded by managers to their organizational superiors does indeed, as noted in earlier chapters, influence on-the-job behavior. That deference to authority simply means that economizing is pursued within a domain of managerial power.

Just how firmly these values and attitudinal traits are rooted within what might be called the generic managerial mind, thus appearing in some form wherever any managerial work is performed in any society or culture, is not entirely clear. The theory of business values offered in this book would posit such genericism among management values. The extant comparative research on managers' values in different societies is suggestive, though not conclusive, that this hypothesized picture is at least in the right direction. Geert Hofstede's previously mentioned study of national work-related value systems among respondents in over fifty countries permitted him to identify four value dimensions "that together explain about 50 percent of the differences among work-related value patterns." Organizational value systems mirror, to varying degrees, the relative emphasis placed by a host society on Power Distance, Uncertainty Avoidance, Individualism-Collectivism, and Masculinity-Femininity. At least two of these value orientations—Power Distance and Masculinity-Femininity—contain or express power relations commonly found in the corporate workplace. Hofstede additionally believes that the nationality of an organization's "founder and dominant elite" will have much to do with the values to be given warrant within any given organization's culture. Founders and dominant elites occupy the most favored ranks within a company hierarchy and express managerial decision power. Hence, Hofstede and other researchers seem to have observed key elements of the power-aggrandizement value cluster in a variety of social and cultural settings.[23]

England's comparative research in five different nations also established a link, though a varying one, between societal cultures and the respective value profiles of the managers studied. For example, managers in the United States, Japan, and Korea demonstrated large measures of pragmatism, while Australian and Indian managers registered a moralistic value orientation. The attention given to employees varied from a high-priority value among United States managers to a low-priority value among Korean and Indian

22. Posner and Schmidt, "Values and the American Manager: An Update," op. cit., p. 210.

23. Hofstede, "The Interaction," op. cit., pp. 347–351.

managers. Managers' devotion to competence, organizational growth, competition, and achievement also was quite diverse from nation to nation. Nevertheless, England concluded:

> Despite the value differences among managers in the five countries and the value diversity within each country, there is a common pattern of translation of values into behavior across the countries. . . . The important generalization that emerges is that values get translated from states of intention into behavior outcomes in a similar way across countries. Our results argue strongly for the possibility of generalization across countries. . . .[24]

England's cautious claim suggests—but does not establish—that managers everywhere approach their workplace tasks with a broadly similar orientation. But quite clearly, a society's deeply embedded value systems tend to channel and constrain managerial behavior, so that it conforms in broad terms to socially approved norms.

Research on values therefore seems to confirm that managers assume a pragmatic posture toward their workplace tasks, pursue goals congenial to their company's mission, choose character and behavioral traits in their fellow workers that will promote their own and their company's goals, are ever alert to safeguard their personal interests and status within the rank-order hierarchy, and appear to share these orientations to varying degrees with managerial counterparts in other nations, cultures, and societies. The cumulative consequence of these channeled behaviors is to move the business firm toward achievement of its (at times contradictory) economizing and power-aggrandizing purposes.

Ethical Climates and Organizational Values

As noted at the outset of this book, values display contrasting levels of abstraction. They may appear as beliefs of individual persons; as social links that relate people to one another; as measures or standards of worth; and as judgments about the desirability of an object, event, or process. Values may assume or may be given these conceptual forms, depending on the use to which any given observer plans to put them. Also, as the preceding chapter made clear, business values are structured into systems or paradigms that make up the patterned regularities of corporate culture.

Yet another way of conceiving values is through the perceptions of those who have a need to identify and understand the force of values in their own lives, both personal and professional. It is in this perceptual sense that the

---

24. England, "Managers and Their Value Systems," op. cit., p. 41.

concept of **ethical work climates** can be useful. These climates are not like corporate culture, whose reified components run the gamut of group belief systems, accepted behaviors, conventions, traditions, legends, stories, and technology and other physical appurtenances of production. An ethical work climate exists solely in the minds of those who perceive it to be what they believe it is. "The prevailing *perceptions* of typical organizational practices and procedures that have ethical content constitute the ethical work climate." These collective perceptions are "*only a segment* of . . . organizational culture"—the part that is *perceived* to outline "the ethical dimensions of organizational culture."[25]

In their landmark study, Bart Victor and John Cullen uncovered five different types of ethical work climates residing within the perceptions of managerial and nonmanagerial personnel employed by the four companies they studied. These climates varied from those in which ethical norms were seen as promoting a caring climate to others emphasizing laws and codes, organizational rules, individualistic instrumentalism, and self-defined moral independence. Companies could be distinguished from one another by these five types of climate. Caring climates and instrumental climates appeared most uniformly among the four firms studied. An instrumental climate is one, not only where "people protect their own interests above all else" and "people are mostly out for themselves" but also where "People are expected to do anything to further the company's interests, regardless of the consequences." This "general sanctioning of instrumental norms" in these companies was offset somewhat by the simultaneous presence of caring climates which, the authors somewhat optimistically opined, "implies that societal norms require organizations to develop at least a minimal caring [work] environment."[26]

Because they are products of employees' perceptions, ethical work climates pervade business organizations and exert effects on workplace behavior. They provide critically important clues to expected and approved behavior. The climate is a personal as well as a collective interpretation of a company's culture, a translation into operational terms of the behavioral implications embedded in that culture's values. The perceptual distinctions that comprise ethical workplace climates are necessarily affected by the moral habits of thought and the moral sensitivities of employees. As with personal values, these personal moral orientations owe much to previously experienced religious conventions, social ideologies, normative traditions, and perhaps an awareness of ethical attitudes thought to be typical for any particular industry.

25. Bart Victor and John B. Cullen, "The Organizational Bases of Ethical Work Climates," *Administrative Science Quarterly*, vol. 33, 1988, pp. 101, 103, emphasis added.

26. Ibid., p. 119.

Managers are as subject to the effects of ethical work climates as all other employees. As holders of privileged power positions within the firm's organizational (rank-order) hierarchy, they have much to do with creating the climate itself because they are constantly perceived by their subordinates as authoritative sources of the company's goals and ethical attitudes. Indeed, in the purview of management consultants, managers are said to be primarily responsible for detecting, predicting, articulating, expressing, and—through their own actions and words—embodying the company's ethical climate. Looking downward from the pyramidal organization's top layers, the manager properly sees himself or herself as the author of ethical climates. Looking upward through the layered ranks from any lower point in the pyramid, employees, including managers of varying status rank, seek ethical guidance by searching for the climate's major dimensions, as defined by higher-ranking organizational superiors. Since the manager serves this dual function of author and subject, creator and responder, the manager's own perceptions constitute a feedback process that continually renews and extends the meaning of ethical climates in the workplace.

These climates make their presence felt in tangible ways, often posing a dilemma for managers who find their personal values at odds with the ethical and performance expectations of their companies. When asked during the early 1980s whether "they felt that they sometimes have to compromise their personal principles to conform to their organization's expectations," managers responded according to their rank-order level. The lower their rank, the greater was the pressure they felt. Ten years later, the pressure had increased for mid-level and upper-level managers. "Pressure to conform to organizational standards" was thought to be strong and relatively constant by three-fourths of managers studied. The researchers concluded that "the vast majority of managers believe that unethical behavior is largely dependent on the organizational climate—especially the actions of one's immediate boss and peers."[27]

Ethical workplace climates, as perceptual reflections of embedded cultural values, register in yet another form the manager's orientation to the dual disciplines of economizing and power aggrandizement. That these two goals must be pursued within the strictures of a defined ethical climate may add a touch of moral elegance to a sometime grubby professional career, although the climate's presence is not expected to divert such managerial goal seeking from the main targets embodied in Value Cluster I and Value Cluster II.

27. Posner and Schmidt, "Values and the American Manager," op. cit., 1984, pp. 210–211, 215; and Posner and Schmidt, "Values and the American Manager: An Update," op. cit., 1991, pp. 12–13 and Table 6.

Value Uniformity and Variety: X-Factor Values

Managers project their values onto the corporate landscape through several perceptual and behavioral screens. These filters include the norms and values of the larger societal culture, the generic business values of economizing and power aggrandizement, the distinctive shape given to these values by corporate culture, the particular ethical climate that prevails in a manager's company, and the personality structure of the individual manager. The general effect of this filtering process is to let through only those values, whether negative or positive in their impact, that seem to serve or can be made to rationalize societal, organizational, and institutional purposes. Exceptions, however, can and do occur. A further result is an observable uniformity of values expressed and acted out by managers within the confines of the business corporation.

Value Uniformity. Although managers as a group—in terms of their value preferences—can be distinguished from other inhabitants of the workplace, as well as from external stakeholders, the value differences are not great.

In his well-known research, Milton Rokeach has distinguished two basic kinds of values: "terminal values" are end-states preferable to others, and "instrumental values" are preferred means and methods for achieving desired end-states.[28] Adopting this distinction, James Weber and I compared the value profiles of managers, union members, and community activists. To our surprise, union members and managers were found to share four of five top-rated terminal values (self-respect, family security, freedom, and happiness) and the same ratio of high-ranked instrumental values (honest, responsible, capable, and independent). The same general picture emerged when the value preferences of community activists who had been critical of business performance were compared with managers' values; these two groups expressed the same strong preference for three of the five top-rated terminal values (family security, self-respect, and freedom) and three of the highest-ranked instrumental values (honest, responsible, and capable).

Value differences among these three groups did exist, running along expected stereotypical lines. Executives sought an exciting life, self-respect, and a sense of accomplishment. Unionists preferred pleasure, a world of beauty,

---

28. Rokeach acknowledges that the relationship of terminal values and instrumental values is more complex than implied here. The link is not necessarily a direct, straightforward, one-to-one association between all terminal values and all instrumental values because each respective value group is further subdivided into personal and social values and into moral and competence values. For a discussion of these complexities, see James Weber, "Exploring the Relationship Between Personal Values and Moral Reasoning," *Human Relations*, vol. 46, no. 4, 1993, pp. 437–440. Nevertheless, for purposes of identifying a uniformity of major types of managerial values, Rokeach's basic distinction is useful.

and inner harmony. Community activists emphasized equality, true friendship, and a world at peace. Nevertheless, Weber and I were unable to conclude that the value preferences registered by these three groups were sufficiently different to explain their obvious policy differences concerning plant closings, unemployment issues, and related matters. We concluded that the three groups' sharp policy conflicts perhaps were driven, not by *personal* value preferences but by a corporate (i.e., an *organizational*) value system that pitted managers against the institutionalized value systems of unions and community activists.[29] Such a corporate value system is one of the large filters mentioned above, which has the effect of channeling managers' perceptions and actions more or less uniformly toward promotion of their organizations' purposes and goals, with less concern for other groups or the general public.

Yet another indication that managers display a uniformity of value-driven behavior is the pattern of moral reasoning they bring to bear in the workplace. Here, too, one sees few significant differences in the general level of sophistication of moral logic employed by managers when they are compared with the general adult population.

Lawrence Kohlberg's concepts of moral development and moral reasoning, based on earlier research by Jean Piaget, have been applied to various populations of managers. Kohlberg posited six levels of moral development through which individuals move as they mature cognitively and socially. The progression is generally from an ego-centered moral reasoning to one that is group-centered, then society-centered, and finally humanity-embracing. One also moves from specific rule-governed moral reasoning toward a broad, more abstract and universalized, principled moral logic.[30]

Research by Kohlberg and others seems to show that socialization processes widely at work throughout the larger society tend to bring most people, including managers, to a uniform level of moral calculus. The authoritative sources of moral guidance at this general level are *organizational rules and norms* and *society's laws and generally accepted behavioral rules*. In other words, managers (and most adults), when faced with a moral quandary such as deciding whether to pad an expense report or whether to hire a relative as

29. William C. Frederick and James Weber, "The Values of Corporate Managers and Their Critics: An Empirical Description and Normative Implications," in William C. Frederick and Lee E. Preston (eds.), *Research in Corporate Social Performance and Policy*, vol. 9, Greenwich, CT: JAI Press, 1987, pp. 131–152. The Rokeach value definitions are described in Milton Rokeach, *The Nature of Human Values*, New York: Free Press, 1973, Chapters 1 and 2.

30. For a full description of these stages, see Lawrence Kohlberg, "Stages of Moral Development as a Basis for Moral Education," in C. M. Beck, B. S. Crittenden, and E. V. Sullivan (eds.), *Moral Education: Interdisciplinary Approaches*, New York: Newman Press, 1971, pp. 86–88. The bulk of Kohlberg's work is found in Lawrence Kohlberg, *Essays in Moral Development: The Philosophy of Moral Development*, vol. 1, New York: Harper & Row, 1981, and *Essays in Moral Development: The Psychology of Moral Development*, vol. 2, New York: Harper & Row, 1984.

an outside contractor, would look to company rules and policies for moral guidance, and would also want to be assured that their actions and decisions were legal.

Managers, though tending to gravitate toward this conventional level of moral reasoning, do not always attain it. For example, one study revealed that managers in large and medium-sized enterprises displayed a stunted, truncated moral reasoning ability—lower than the social average—when they were asked to consider a series of simulated ethical dilemmas. They also tended to reason at a simpler and lower level of morality when facing an ethical problem in the workplace than when considering a moral choice not related to their work.[31] These findings seem to reinforce the idea that managers, though similar to others in general moral logic, become distinctive, and perhaps less admirable, moral reasoners when doing their jobs as managers.

The general impression emerging from research on managers' values, ethical attitudes, and moral reasoning is that members of this important business group share common views of right and wrong, seek and encourage similar responses from their professional colleagues, and apply an on-the-job moral logic near, or in some situations lower than, the social mean.

Value Diversity. In spite of a sameness imposed on the managerial scene by personal, organizational, and societal value filters, variety exists. This value variety has several sources, some of a personal nature and others stemming from diverse contextual features. These value distinctions are what an earlier chapter called "X-factor values." (See Figure 1–2 in Chapter 1.)[32]

The personal, individualistic, uniquely configured, and idiosyncratically weighted values of those who work in corporations exert an indeterminate, variable influence on events in any given firm. An inventory of all the personal value commitments and preferences of all managers and employees in any sizable business firm would reveal an astonishing array and range of ethical and moral viewpoints. Moreover, another firm's inventory would be likely to display a different personal value profile because its personnel would have been recruited from other sources with varying demographic traits (ethnic identity, gender, age, national and regional habitat, professional-technical qualifications, educational level, work experience, political affiliation, etc.).

---

31. James Weber, "Managers' Moral Reasoning: Assessing Their Responses to Three Moral Dilemmas," *Human Relations*, vol. 43, no. 7, 1990, pp. 687–702. The most detailed examination of how managers' personal values interact with and influence their moral reasoning is found in Weber, "Exploring the Relationship Between Personal Values and Moral Reasoning," op. cit.

32. X-factor values, which occupy a central role in theories of business ethics, also receive further attention in Chapter 8, where those ethics theories are discussed.

Such demographic variety makes it virtually impossible to know or to predict with any certainty the precise mixture of personal values that may be brought into the workplace of any given firm; hence, their influence on corporate events is elusive and difficult to trace.

Contextual features also determine the amount and kind of decisional and policy influence exerted by personal values. Firm size, competitive industrial patterns, conventions within given industries, a firm's technological profile, its market structures, geographic locales, linkages with other firms (such as joint ventures), life cycle status (whether early or late, growing or declining), and the shape and nature of the organization's role structure—all of these and other situational traits may create opportunities for, or close the door on, the active expression of personal values on the job. But in which precise direction and with what particular force these values may work their influence are matters to be determined rather than granted by assumption.

For all of these reasons, the X-factor value box of one firm may contain quite a different sorting of values than that of another company. The socialization challenge that this kind of value diversity presents is formidable if the firm is to pursue its goals successfully. The varying value content of the X-factor box may also contribute to the presence of what might be called underground or latent value systems that operate for many corporate inhabitants just under the surface of their publicly displayed organizational masks or personae.

The most likely pathways through which X-factor values might find operational outlet in the business firm—and therefore may be thrust into the policy and decision realms—are probably located within and shaped by the architectural design of the company's role structure. For example, a company may divide its work force along divisional lines; by geographic areas; by functional specialties such as marketing, finance, or personnel; and so on. In each case, various roles or functional responsibilities will need to be specified and individuals chosen to fill those roles. Any given role is an idealized bundle of expected behaviors and attitudes. It is "occupied" by an actual person, who then is expected by others to perform according to the role's idealized pattern of duties, obligations, and responsibilities. In doing so, this particular person brings personal values to the role, along with an expected commitment to promote the firm's goals and to show allegiance to its embedded value systems.

It is at the point of acquiring and discharging role responsibilities that an individual's personal values are modified and reshaped by organizational demands. Such values begin to lose their distinctive, unique, "personal" character, gradually shading into a form compatible with the duties of one's organizational role. The process is so subtle that many, even those who might have imagined their own values to be at odds with business's materialistic values, may come eventually to see no difference at all between the two. For others, the journey may be longer, even painful. Some, of course, never attain this organizational nirvana.

Role configurations vary considerably from company to company; some define role obligations severely, while others permit much latitude to the role occupant. In the latter case, the value space of any particular role could conceivably be occupied by the dominant value obligations that stem from economizing and power aggrandizement, as well as by the personal value commitments brought to the role from outside the firm. A close reading of Barbara Toffler's interviews with thirty-three corporate managers reveals varying amounts of role and task latitude permitted to role occupants in confronting workplace ethical issues. In fact, many but not all of their "tough choices" stemmed largely from conflicts they felt between their personal values and what they sensed was expected of them in their organizational roles.[33]

George England's research also revealed the presence of personal values that might or might not be activated by a manager carrying out organizational duties. "Intended values" are those "considered highly important by the manager throughout most of his life [but] do not fit his organizational experience" and therefore do not find ready outlet on the job. On the other hand, "adopted values," though "less a part of the personality structure of the individual . . . affect behavior largely because of situational [i.e., workplace] factors." "Nonrelevant or weak values" that are not strongly held or do not fit the pragmatic orientation of managers have little prospect of being activated by role occupants. "Operative values" are those most likely to "influence the behavior of the managers more than any other [values]"; they are the more or less official values attached to the manager's formal role.

England emphasized the differences to be found among individual managers:

> Some managers have a very small set of operative values while others have a large set and seem to be influenced by many strongly held values. The operative values of some managers include concepts which are almost solely related to organizational life while other managers include a wide range of personal and philosophical concepts among their operative values. Some managers have what might be termed individualistic values as opposed to group-oriented values. Some managers appear to be highly achievement-oriented as compared with others who seem to value status and position more highly. . . .[34]

33. Barbara Ley Toffler, *Tough Choices: Managers Talk Ethics*, New York: Wiley, 1986. For Toffler's views on the influence of role structure and personal demographics, see pp. 28–44.

34. England, "Personal Value Systems of American Managers," p. 67.

John Kotter's research on general managers led him to the same general conclusion about the unique personal dimensions of "effective executive behavior":

A large number of motivational, temperamental, interpersonal, and other personal characteristics are important; experiences, literally starting from birth, are important; some degree of specialization, commitment, and fit with the local environment is important; complex, subtle, and informal behavior are important. All of this is so because of the very nature of executive jobs today.[35]

Hence, within the established patterns of value-driven behavior that are typical of corporate life, one finds a fair amount of variation and a range of choice and personal preference. These wrinkles on the face of the embedded corporate value system are manifestations of X-factor values at work in the managerial mindset.

The workplace presence of these different types of values makes plain the potential, whether realized or not, for individualistic emphasis on one value type rather than another. Within the general confines of expected role behavior, one manager might easily, and perhaps subtly, shift the proportional balance among operative, intended, and adopted values. Role structures are not simply iron cages that imprison their occupants and fetter their choices. Given the variations found within the cultures of different companies and given the personal value diversity England discovered in the managers he studied, decision latitude and idiosyncratic choices are possible and are to be expected. Some of these choices are deliberately undertaken to move the firm toward its goals; others may be simply style variations introduced into the daily round of work by managers who are granted decision-making leeway. Some correlation is to be expected between the expression of these personal role interpretations and the amount of formal power and authority imputed to the respective roles by the organization's conventions, history, and general value system.[36]

A variant of role-linked personal value involvement is the influence almost universally accorded to the personal values and ethical beliefs of corporate chief executive officers. They are said to be the fount of ethical culture

---

35. John Kotter, *The General Managers*, New York: Free Press, 1982, p. 131.

36. The actual carryover of personal values into the workplace may be of lesser magnitude than theoretically possible than or feared by employers. One study has shown that employees' organizational commitments (to do their jobs well and as expected) were not significantly affected by their involvement in and commitment to non-work-related activities such as family obligations, participation in religious and political organizations, spending time on hobbies, and so on. See Donna M. Randall, "Multiple Roles and Organizational Commitment," *Journal of Organizational Behavior*, vol. 9, 1988, pp. 309–317.

within their companies, serving both symbolically and behaviorally to define the outer limits of ethical expectations for all. This trait is named as the most critical component of ethics awareness and training programs that have been described as exemplars among large U.S. corporations.[37] CEOs attain this glorified ethical posture, of course, as a function of the hierarchical ordering of status ranks rather than from any imputed superiority of their ethical insights. Their position atop the corporate pyramid lends special significance to their personal value commitments, and their idiosyncratic views (if any be left after their long trek to the summit) are given special hearing within the corporation's halls.

As prime architects of the firm's ethical climate, which as noted earlier is the perceived reflection of the firm's operative value system, top-level managers are in a unique position vis-à-vis their own role obligations. While unable to disregard the constraints imposed by the firm's history, by its present momentum and inertial direction, or by external environmental forces, the chief managers are granted a degree of freedom and initiative in creating the expectations that others will (and, according to organizational mores, should) have of them that others of lower rank within the role structure do not enjoy. The personal values that they import to their roles will therefore be of particular importance and are likely to carry special weight in the creation and projection of the company's ethical climate. This perceptual interlinking of ethical work climate and top managers' roles reveals once again how the bureaucratic structure of corporate enterprise gives effect to both the personal values carried by managers and the collective organizational values of the company's culture.

Values and Character. The strategic position and potential influence of managers' X-factor values have caused some scholars to emphasize the importance of personal character as a critical moderator of managerial work. The analytic case they make, while standing somewhat outside the realm of empirical research, is nevertheless quite consistent with what other researchers have demonstrated empirically. They stress the obvious links between a manager's personal character, value commitments, and approach to the work at hand. The impact of character on managerial decisions is seen in the way that a manager marshals his or her moral commitments and moral outlooks, as well as the purposes and goals they seek.

Clarence Walton, a seasoned observer of the management scene, puts it this way:

---

37. The Business Roundtable, *Corporate Ethics: A Prime Business Asset*, A Report on Policy and Practice in Company Conduct, New York: The Business Roundtable, February 1988, pp. 4–5.

Character, therefore, is more complex than a character trait. When directed toward developing a constellation of qualities like sensitivity, loyalty, courage, fairness, honesty, and openness, the manager reveals a particular and visible moral identity. Direction, determination, movement—all reflect the operation of a developed character guided by a developed conscience. . . . What we do morally is determined not solely by rules or responses to one particular situation but by what we have become through our past history. . . . Emphasis on character shifts attention from the act performed to the performer of the act, from emphasis on thinking to emphasis on being, from the single act to the series of acts. Character becomes the conduit through which an individual's past and present flow and the future is designed; while shaped by conviction about what is right and wrong, significant and insignificant, tolerable and intolerable, the connection must explode in deeds.[38]

Whether seen through the prism of personal character or as the acting out of personal value commitments, one finds that X-factor values manifesting ethical import may be expressed by role occupants who labor within the confines of corporate cultures. At some indeterminate point, these personal values unavoidably intersect with the dominant values of economizing and power aggrandizement. The outcome, while also indeterminate in any given episode, may lend a degree of variety to the way in which the core values of business are pursued and promoted.

THE VALUE DIMENSION OF MANAGERIAL WORK

The arena in which corporate managers do their day-to-day work is saturated with values and normative components of several kinds, as depicted in Figure 5–1. In spite of this massive normative presence, the value dimension of managerial work has received less attention from management scholars than it deserves if one wishes to have a full picture of the manager's job. To clarify just how values enter into managerial work is the next task.

Although few doubt that the work of managing is important, even critical, to corporate success, there is less agreement on the precise nature of that work. The main argument runs between those who have identified the substantive functions said to be performed by managers and those who emphasize that managerial work is relational in form, whatever the operational functions may be. The former group projects a picture of rational calculation

---

38. Clarence C. Walton, *The Moral Manager*, Cambridge, MA: Ballinger, 1988, p. 177. A similar approach is found in James E. Liebig, *Business Ethics: Profiles in Civic Virtue*, Golden, CO: Fulcrum, 1990, which chronicles the development and expression of personal character in twenty-four top-level business executives. Both Walton and Liebig acknowledge the strong influence of culture in shaping personal character.

and careful deliberation about feasible alternatives prior to (and as a plat-form for) decision making, policy formulation, and strategic implementation of corporate goals. In this work, the manager is said to play a key role as plan-ner, organizer, staffer, motivator, controller, and general director, thereby driving and leading the firm toward rationally conceived goals.[39]

Others dispute the neat picture of rationality and orderly progression im-plied by this conception of managerial work. Their research tells them that managers concern themselves less with the actual substantive operations of their companies and spend most of their "work time" engaged in continuous but fleeting, irregularly paced contacts and relationships with the persons and groups who are positioned to cause the firm's substantive operations to be performed. Decisions and operational commitments are made quickly and, in many cases, almost unobtrusively but in ways well understood by those familiar with the firm, its mission, its key personnel, and its culture.

An advocate of this view put it this way:

> In other words, these effective executives did not approach their jobs by planning, organizing, motivating, and controlling in a very formal sense. Instead, they relied on more continuous, more informal, and more subtle methods to cope with their large and complex job demands. The most important products of their approach were agendas and networks, not formal plans and organizational charts. These agendas were not inconsistent with formal plans, but they were different. Agendas tended to cover a wider time frame than did most formal plans; they tended to be less numerical and more strategic in nature; they usually dealt more with "people" issues; and they were typically somewhat less rigorous, rational, logical, and linear in character.[40]

The task of defining managers' work has been complicated—and the shape of the argument has been affected—by a felt but often unexpressed ideological need to defend against the charge that managers are only the guardians of corporate property, serving as simple hired agents of the own-ers. Whereas in the older annals of economic theory it was possible to ratio-nalize the income shares paid to landowners (rent), laboring people (wages), and capital providers (interest), serious questions were faced when that body

39. A useful summary of this and related views is found in Henry Mintzberg, *The Nature of Man-agerial Work*, Englewood Cliffs, NJ: Prentice-Hall, 1973, Chapter 1. A defense of the functional ap-proach is mounted in Daniel A. Wren, "The Nature of Managerial Work: A Comparison of Real Managers and Traditional Management," *Journal of Managerial Issues*, Spring 1992, pp. 17–30. Henri Fayol, Lionel Urwick, and Luther Gulick are considered the original authors of this func-tional version of managerial work.

40. Kotter, op. cit., p. 127. The other major source is Mintzberg, op. cit. See also Allen I. Kraut, "The Role of the Manager: What's Really Important in Different Management Jobs," *Academy of Management Executive*, vol. III, no. 4, 1989, pp. 286–293.

of theory was called upon to justify payments to managers who own little or no significant proportion of a corporation. "What do managers do?" became a most difficult and ideologically awkward question. If they serve only as caretakers and groomers of capitalist-owners' property, why not have their shares taken from that of the provider and owner of capital? Were this view to prevail, perhaps managers should be lumped together with bookkeepers, file clerks, lawyers, property conveyers, and others who labor to shore up the claims and augment the wealth of property owners, and who at the end of the pay period line up to receive their reward directly from the owner-employer. Their work would thus find its meaning and justification as a service to ownership.

The continuing presence and active expression of ownership rituals—for example, annual meetings of the "owners," "election" of directors, proxy contests for control of shareholders' votes, and dissenting shareholder resolutions offered by disaffected owners—reinforce the belief that managers are little more than employees hired by the owners to promote and preserve ownership interests. Most annual shareholders' meetings invoke the dead language of ownership: individual shareholders speak, sometimes with pride, of the past year's achievements of "our" company; top managers and board members who address the assembled owners refer in deferential tones to "your" company; dissenting shareholders, by buying shares of "their" company, gain entrance and the right to criticize present management; votes are tabulated as if each one sounds the authoritative voice of the "owner."

Beneath this ceremonial mask, one finds the reality of managerial power and control discussed in an earlier chapter. The directors collectively hold the largest number of shareholder votes, having gathered them by proxy. The firm's chief managers, some of whom also serve as directors, have typically chosen the other directors for their posts, thus creating a community of interest that seldom gives rise to contrary or threatening thoughts. Most owners may safely be considered a passive lot, unable, unwilling, or uninterested in serious challenges to entrenched management power. To be sure, large minority-bloc shareholders such as pension funds, or determined corporate raiders, or even an occasional rebellious board may make dents in the power of managers or even displace them, only to appoint yet other executives more amenable to promoting the interests of the disaffected group. Hence, managerial power reasserts itself in circular fashion, suggesting the presence of a residual work function that goes beyond mere guardianship of property.

The pragmatic, goal-focused, organization-centered proclivities of managers—well documented by research—bespeak a unique type and level of necessary skill and talent that contrasts sharply with that of owners and corporate outsiders generally. The company's goals must be charted, operations planned, resources gathered and reallocated to support the firm's economizing mission. Employees need to be persuaded to join the overall effort. The organization's strategy and tactics must be adapted to a shifting environment. Seeing that these and related tasks are performed—finding pragmatic solutions to these organizational needs—is the work of managers. Few owners, even the largest ones, possess these managerial talents or are close enough to the operational scene to promote or directly engage in these economizing activities.

Research as well as casual observation tells us that managerial styles vary greatly from one person to another. Some managers prefer the rationalistic, functional approach described earlier. Others take the relational route, also noted above. The management work of economizing can therefore produce its results in diverse ways. Whether done directly, with rational deliberation and forethought, or with all of the relational skills of expediency and superficiality matters less than that it occurs in some systematic and orderly fashion that produces economizing outcomes. Regardless of the style employed, the primary work of management—organizational economizing—rests securely on the values that comprise Value Cluster I (economizing, growth, and systemic integrity).

Henry Mintzberg, in explaining "why organizations need managers," describes the way in which these economizing values are served by managerial work:[41]

1. The prime purpose of the manager is to ensure that his organization serves its basic purpose—the efficient production of specific goods and services. . . . [Author's note: This is the form taken by business economizing.]

2. The manager must design and maintain the stability of his organization's operations. . . . Essentially, he must ensure that the organization functions as an integrated unit. [Author's note: This activity is equivalent to what in this book is called "systemic integrity" and to Schein's internal integration function of organizational culture, which was discussed in Chapter 4.]

3. The manager must take charge of his organization's strategy-making system, and therein adapt his organization in a controlled way to its changing environment. . . .

5. The manager must serve as the key informational link between his organization and its environment. . . . The two-way flow of information [to and from the environment] is continuous, real-time, and specific in its detail. . . . [Author's note: Items 3 and 5 refer to the necessity of taking energy from the organization's environment and incorporating it into work energy that supports the firm; this is equivalent to Schein's external adaptation function of organizational culture, also discussed in Chapter 4.]

41. Mintzberg, op. cit., pp. 95–96.

At the same time and as might be expected, managers find themselves in the service of other organizational values as well, namely, those associated with power aggrandizement. Again Mintzberg provides a partial clue:

4. The manager must ensure that his organization serves the ends of those persons who control it. The manager must act as the focus for organizational values. Influencers exert pressures on him to have the organization serve their ends. *The manager must interpret the values of each influencer, combine all these to determine the true power system, and then inform his subordinates of this in the form of organizational preferences to guide them in their decision-making.* Should growth or profit or some other value be preeminent, the manager must ensure that these ends are achieved as a result of the decisions taken. . . .

6. As formal authority, the manager is responsible for the operating of his organization's status system. . . .[42]

The added emphasis in this passage is a commentary on the reach of managerial power within the corporation. Anyone who is permitted to interpret others' values, combine them into a single power system, and then issue preferences based on that self-interpreted value-and-power system that "guide" others' decision making does indeed occupy a position of overwhelming organizational influence.

An example of just how important that influence can be in shaping the actions of others and guiding their decisions is revealed in an astounding declaration—astounding for its openness in advocating lying and other forms of dishonesty as an acceptable managerial technique— by Chester I. Barnard, the ultimate management guru. Barnard once told an audience of faculty and students at Princeton University that

the truth could not ordinarily be conveyed by stating it exactly. . . . Not only do words mean different things to different people or under different circumstances; but there is a tendency unintentionally to discount or to read into statements what is not intended. It is consequently necessary to say things in a form which is not correct from the standpoint of the speaker or writer, but which will be interpreted by the listener or reader in a sense which will be true. To do this often becomes a matter of habit. Hence, a speaker must often be dishonest in statement from his own point of view in order to achieve honesty of result, although he ceases to be aware of it. It is a fatal dilemma for many people, who are unable to withstand either the moral or intellectual strain.

. . . Yet, the practice of short-cutting explanations, of using false analogies, of suppressing confusing qualifications, which are practical necessities, tend to destroy sincerity by creating a habit of misstatement from the speaker's point of view. In

---

42. Ibid., emphasis added.

the intellectual difficulty of working in two personalities at once, I think I see the moral deterioration and finally the intellectual collapse of more than a few men.[43]

That Barnard acknowledged the moral perils (to "more than a few men") of blatant lying to achieve management purposes did not deter him from urging this technique on his audience of students, some of whom might plausibly have been expected to assume managerial posts during their professional careers, and of their teachers, some of whom might plausibly have absorbed and passed Barnard's lesson on to future generations of students who also might have been expected to join the ranks of corporate management. In any event, young minds were being conditioned to know and accept the various necessities that accompany the presence and use of managerial power within organizational life.

A pronounced tendency of the literature on managerial work is to sidestep a direct discussion of the role of values. To some extent, this reluctance reflects a sensitivity regarding the presence, the use, and sometimes the abuse of power by managers. Partly, it stems from a defensive posture of not wishing to acknowledge or emphasize that business corporations are organized along status-rank lines and are drawn up into pyramids of hierarchical power. The obverse may exist also: that is, an unquestioning scholarly acceptance of rank-order hierarchies as the only rational way to organize business activities, further commentary or notice not being needed. In other cases, values are thought to be merely subjective, idiosyncratic, and arbitrary preferences that, while present, serve mainly to inject arbitrariness and irrationality into an otherwise orderly economizing process.

The latter view is held by Mintzberg who nevertheless explicitly acknowledges the presence of values in the work of managers. He says: "Chief executives, particularly those in large organizations with fragmented groups of 'influencers,' are able to assume much power over organizational values." It is odd, though, that he sees values entering directly into managers' work only through one of the ten roles that he assigns to them, namely, the Disseminator Role.[44] But surely, as Figurehead, Leader, Liaison, Monitor, Spokesman, Entrepreneur, Disturbance Handler, Resource Allocator, and Negotiator

---

43. Chester I. Barnard, "Mind in Everyday Affairs," A Cyrus Fogg Brackett Lecture before the Engineering Faculty and Students of Princeton University, March 10, 1936, reprinted in Chester I. Barnard, *The Functions of the Executive*, Cambridge, MA: Harvard University Press, 1950 (1938, 1968), p. 319. Barnard's blithe acceptance of lying as a "practical necessity" of business life shocks because it comes from such a highly respected source of management thought, long believed to be the fount of management wisdom. For a comprehensive, arm's-length evaluation of Barnard's contributions to management theory, see William G. Scott, *Chester I. Barnard and the Guardians of the Managerial State*, Lawrence: University Press of Kansas, 1992.

44. Mintzberg, op. cit., pp. 73–74, 97.

(Mintzberg's other managerial roles), the manager's actions and decisions are also largely affected by both personal and organizational values.

Yet another hint of how values and managerial work intersect was given by a study that compared and contrasted managerial success and managerial effectiveness.[45] "Success" was defined as holding high rank in an organization; "effectiveness" meant the "quantity and quality of the performance of a manager's unit and his or her subordinates' satisfaction and commitment." This kind of "success" is equivalent to having acquired upper-level managerial decision power, which is one of the power-aggrandizement values, while "effectiveness" refers to a business unit's economizing performance made possible by internal integration as part of the economizing value cluster. The most "successful" (power-holding) managers in the study spent a significant amount of their work time "networking," which meant "interacting with outsiders" and "socializing/politicking" both inside and outside their company. The "effective" (economizing) managers, by contrast, focused their efforts mainly on (routine) "communication" and on "human resource management," which referred to task-oriented personnel matters. The networking ("successful") manager made few direct contributions to the firm's economizing activities but held high rank and thus significant power. The effective managers produced the work that enabled their company to achieve its economizing mission but engaged in little of the socio-political networking. These correlations and contrasts have been observed by others, including Robert Jackall, whose corporate executives learned to thread their way through their companies' "moral mazes" by being both politically adept and able to "hit their numbers" (i.e., reach their assigned organizational production or financial targets).

The overall picture that seems to emerge from this large body of theory and research is that managerial work goes forward in expected ways to promote the values of economizing and power aggrandizement but does so with all of the variety and style differences that X-factor value orientations might be expected to contribute to the process. With a retrospective sigh, Mintzberg once asked, "Might we not just as well say that people throughout the organization take actions that inform managers who, by making sense of these actions, develop images and visions that inspire people to subsequent efforts?"[46] In its simple elegance, this comment sums up the essence of managerial work, which does indeed help the business firm to achieve its purposes, goals, and values.

---

45. Fred Luthans, "Successful vs. Effective Real Managers," *Academy of Management Executive*, vol. II, no. 2, 1988, pp. 127–132.

46. Mintzberg, "Retrospective Commentary," *Harvard Business Review*, March-April 1990, p. 170.

As noted at the outset of this chapter, those who believe that values comprise a central component of managerial activity have much confirming research to bolster their conviction. These value orientations assume a wondrous diversity of forms and they exert varying influence within the workplace. The interweaving of personal and organizational values is itself a highly complex process that can produce a wide spectrum of decision possibilities. Ethical climates, being the perceptual product of numerous employees, managers, and external stakeholders, enfold the manager within a set of normative expectations whose subtle messages often whisper softly in the managerial ear. As all of these value components come together in the workplace, managers feel, and know they must respond to, the hovering presence and domineering commands of the two master value clusters—economizing and power aggrandizement—they have learned to know best.

It is time now to place these managerial goals and values within a larger context that lends them a significance far more profound than if they are understood only by and for themselves. It should now be apparent that business values are central to human existence, appealing psychologically for the rewards they bestow, and capable of driving behavior in both desirable and questionable directions. The task immediately ahead is to show how business values intersect other natural and sociocultural value systems to produce complex effects both frightening and hopeful for present and future human prospects.

6

Ecologizing Values
and the Business Dilemma

The central proposition of this chapter is that ecological processes provide a large natural and sociocultural framework whose normative significance extends beyond that of both economizing and power aggrandizement. For business, that poses a dilemma of unbelievable complexity and difficulty, for it is equivalent to saying that the core values of business are encompassed within a normative system that threatens to override all that has been central to and characteristic of the business institution and the business function in society. For the global citizenry, arguing that ecology trumps both economy and business power seeking potentially creates a public policy agenda that could easily pit business against society on many fronts. It is easy to believe that the first skirmishes of such a public policy debate began during the last half of the twentieth century, if one bears in mind the widespread public concern about environmental pollution, depletion of the earth's ozone layer, the possibility of global warming, and other ecological crises and trends.

However, the view here is not one of unremitting doom and gloom about the world's environmental prospects or the future of business enterprise. Rather, the major thrust is to grasp the meaning and function of ecological processes, which are seen as a third major evolutionary source of human values. The parallels, as well as the distinctions, found between ecologizing, economizing, and power aggrandizing harbor some of the answers to the puzzles that plague business and society. Resolving these public policy puzzles is more likely to be achieved if policy rests on a reasonably valid understanding of ecological process, for it is from that process that a set of distinctive human values has emerged.

Equally important is the need to know more about the several ways in which the three major value systems interweave with one another, and how those interweavings affect human, and particularly business, affairs. It will be argued that the larger significance of values and value systems is found at the intersections where they meet. Values often converge and combine peacefully, thus providing stable platforms for human affairs. Frequently though, and perhaps even characteristically, these value junctions are the scene of collision and competition between incompatible and contradictory value phenomena. When this happens, strife, stress, and powerful emotional surges can tear at human relationships, often ripping through the tissue of vital social linkages. In the worst cases recorded by historians, organized efforts to eliminate hated values and their human carriers accelerate toward wholesale destruction of one group by another. Short of such bellicose drama, one finds more subtle socialization pressures brought to bear in ways intended to promote one value system or set of values over another differing set. It is the latter kind of value competition that is most often encountered by most people.

Earlier chapters have recounted the collisions sometimes witnessed between economizing values and power-aggrandizing values. In these struggles—both sets of values being energized in varying proportions by the combined forces of nature and culture—value outcomes are never quite certain. Where economizing predominates, life entities achieve temporary respite from entropic trends, thus surviving and becoming integrated living systems capable of growing and realizing their genetic (and additionally in humans, their cultural) potentials. If power aggrandizement wins out, the economizing outcome is less certain than the indisputable consolidation of power residing in the hands of those who advocate and wield society's power instruments.

As important and central as these value clashes are, they do not by themselves tell the whole story of business values and the influence they exert on human affairs. A third major value cluster, comprising **ecologizing values**, intersects the two master value clusters that lie at the heart of business operations. The clashes engendered there dwarf the collisions between economizing and power aggrandizement. These three value systems move as if they were massive tectonic plates grinding against one another to form the drifting normative platforms on which human events are played out. The ethical fault lines thus created generate enormous normative tensions that pose questions of fundamental import for the future of business and society relations.

The task now at hand is to clarify the meaning of ecological processes and systems, followed further along by an attempt to characterize how economy, power, and ecology mingle in both nature and culture. Unavoidably, some of the discussion traverses technical ground that at times may seem to be somewhat remote from the everyday problems typical of the corporate workplace.

The major aim, however, is to elicit overarching *principles of ecological process* that, taken together, begin to define the kinds of value issues that require an increasing amount of attention from those who direct business affairs.

THE NATURE OF ECOLOGIZING VALUES

The first task is to grasp the overwhelmingly profound meaning of an evolutionary process that has extruded ecologizing values. In ecologizing processes, one finds the root value orientations that both create and sustain human collective life. These life-conserving values have emerged from an evolutionary dynamic that expresses in yet another form the second law of thermodynamics, whose entropic force these values momentarily hold in abeyance. Thus, the Arrow of Time is bent and blunted—delayed and deflected, so to speak, though not arrested—in its inexorable flight toward decline and decay.

In what follows, we visit these ecologizing values, probing the interfaces they share with both economizing values and power-aggrandizing values, and seeking explanations for the curious and fascinating links one discovers among these three master value sets that preside over human (and business) affairs. Four values comprise the ecologizing value cluster. It will be helpful to describe each briefly. Collectively, they are referred to as "Value Cluster III" and are listed in Figure 6–1.[1]

First Ecologizing Value: Linkage

A widely accepted definition of ecology is that it consists of the study of life forms, the interactions between and among them, and the totality of their relationships with both their biotic and abiotic (nonliving) environments.[2] When ecologists look at nature they see connections, interrelationships, linkages, an interwoven web of life, networks that relate life forms to each other and to their physical environment. This ecological web that pulsates with life, that arrays nature in wondrously complex patterns, and that brings cohesion and order out of seeming chaos within nature is itself a constantly changing and evolving phenomenon. This fluidity means that evolution is at work as surely within these interwoven webs as it is within the genetic systems of all

---

1. An earlier published account described a slightly different, albeit largely parallel, group of ecologizing values. The present version is more consistent with current ecological theory. Cf. William C. Frederick, "Anchoring Values in Nature: Toward a Theory of Business Values," *Business Ethics Quarterly*, July 1992, pp. 283–303.

2. For an example, see Eric R. Pianka, *Evolutionary Ecology*, 3rd edition, New York: Harper & Row, 1983, p. 3.

```
┌─────────────────────────────────────────────┐
│                                               │
│              VALUE CLUSTER III:               │
│             ECOLOGIZING VALUES                │
│                                               │
│                                               │
│         Linkage                               │
│                                               │
│         Diversity                             │
│                                               │
│         Homeostatic succession                │
│                                               │
│         Community                             │
│                                               │
└─────────────────────────────────────────────┘
```

Figure 6–1. Value Cluster III: Ecologizing values

life units. An evolutionary continuum stretches from genome to phenome, from genotype to phenotype, and from these organismic levels outward to the various associated groupings, populations, and phyla that constitute the forms of evolved life on earth.[3] Natural selection nonconsciously and continuously channels this genetic-phenotypic-organismic change process in ways that permit some to survive, others to perish, all to answer sooner or later to the fateful call of entropy.

But until they hear that summons, ecological linkages give life, provide shelter, create safety nets, extend the realization of genetic potentialities, permit an efflorescence of life forms, succor collectivities of organic beings, and regularize and pattern the interactions that life units have with and within their oftentimes threatening environments. As one school of ecological thought has put it, natural life process may be more accurately characterized

3. For a comprehensive classification of living systems, see James Grier Miller and Jessie L. Miller, "Introduction: The Nature of Living Systems," *Behavioral Science*, vol. 35, no. 3, 1990, pp. 157–163. A "genome" is all of the genes of an organism. It is an organism's hereditary material. A "genotype" is the genetic makeup or constitution of an organism, prescribing such traits as blood type, flower color, petal shape, and sex. A "phenome" is all of the observable traits that are characteristic of a particular type of organism or species. A "phenotype" is the observable traits or characteristics of an organism that are a result of the interaction between genotype and environment. In simple terms, a phenotype is what one sees physically (e.g., a rosebush with red blossoms). A genotype is primarily responsible for producing a particular kind of physical phenotype (e.g, a rosebush instead of a palm tree). Over the long run, a physical phenotype can be affected by the environment (e.g., a rosebush in an area being transformed into a desert climate may evolve new ways of absorbing moisture from the increasingly dry soil). A genotype is enclosed within a phenotype, whose shape and function are largely determined by the genotype. Got it?

as "green in root and flower" than "red in tooth and claw."[4] Life is magnified and augmented as its multitudinous forms are interrelated and interwoven with each other. This life-sustaining trait of ecologizing is, one can note, similar in evolutionary consequence to economizing, which enables a given life entity to draw energy from its environment in entropy-deflecting ways. Further along in the analysis, the intriguing parallels to be seen between economizing and ecologizing are clarified. For now, the emphasis is on the life-augmentation capabilities of ecological networks.

The values—that is, the beliefs, relationships, judgmental-appraisal processes, and the sustaining experiential base—that have emerged from ecological phenomena now occupy an increasingly important place in human awareness and human affairs generally. This is the manner in which all values enter the human realm. They are extruded from natural processes, incorporated into human experience, and eventually conceptualized as values. And so it is with the value of **linkage**. The realization that human beings, far from standing alone and apart from nature, are bound together in and are part of evolving environmental and creaturely webs is a revolutionary idea, only in relatively recent times systematically recorded, debated, and (partially) accepted. Its full significance has yet to be firmly grasped. This is not to discount or to denigrate the anciently held intuitive sense, often felt more keenly in earlier times than now and more often in non-Western and nonindustrial cultures than in ours, of a bond that ties human fate to nature. It is plausible to believe that such mythical, legendary orientations toward nature reflect, though imperfectly and often inaccurately, a primitive acceptance and emergent awareness of the value of linkage. Thus, from multiform human experiences amid nature's cycles a value was extruded. This value was at once a **belief** that nature mattered in human affairs, an awareness of the **close ties** that bind humans and nature together, a **judgment** that nature's forces might be either beneficent or threatening, and an orientation toward nature based on **shared experiences**. The twentieth century's contribution to this emerging value concept—largely through ecological science—would appear to consist of clarifying the kinds of ecological linkages that are found and—of special importance—recognizing those linkages as a type of human value.

The remarkable growth of ecological awareness is roughly measured by today's common usage of the term "ecology," which at mid-twentieth century was an arcane concept known and used mainly by a handful of biologists. Our linkage with the natural environment, with plants and animals, with each

---

4. The phrase and a related discussion are in Douglas H. Boucher, "The Idea of Mutualism, Past and Future," in Douglas H. Boucher (ed.), *The Biology of Mutualism: Ecology and Evolution*, London: Croom Helm, 1985, pp. 23ff.

other in ever-widening circles of humanity throughout the globe, and now beyond earth with the nearby planetary system is common knowledge, no longer questioned or doubted. Linkage as a human value has come of age.

Second Ecologizing Value: Diversity

Life's flight from entropy has made diversity a central feature of nature. Thermodynamic process produces this effect throughout both biotic and abiotic realms. From the beginning of the universe, energy flows have produced an astonishing mosaic of physical elements, chemical interactions, climatological processes, wave phenomena, nested linkages, attractant and repelling forces, energy-to-matter and matter-to-energy transitions, sentient and nonsentient forms, conscious and nonconscious entities, mobile and immobile forms of life, amphibious, airborne, and land-anchored creatures, particles so tiny and elusive that we call them microscopic after the instruments used to sense their presence and so large and remote that we calculate their dimensions and distance from us in light-years and "see" them through a varied set of energy impulses that transit the intervening space.[5]

This kaleidoscope of natural phenomena is an outcome of evolution operating on thermodynamic principles. The tiny part of this vast, still expanding, and presumably still diversifying process that we experience on earth lies at the center of our growing ecological consciousness. Life forms—both present and extinct—are almost incomprehensibly numerous and variegated. Each such form, in one way or another and for varying lengths of time, has managed to extract energy from its surroundings long enough to begin and then to sustain life. The diversity of these life-support systems is as impressive as their numbers, frequently giving rise to the claim that their very complexity must be the work of some superior force far exceeding anything else known or humanly comprehensible.[6]

Throughout life's multiple manifestations, from gene to phyla, diversity reigns. One witnesses a diversity of life forms, of physiological functions, of survival "strategies," of linkages among life entities, of time scales on which different life units exist, of evolutionary potentials and opportunities embed-

5. Any standard textbook in the ecology field gives ample evidence of diversity, for example, Daniel D. Chiras, *Environmental Science: A Framework for Decision Making*, 2nd edition, Menlo Park, CA: Benjamin/Cummings, 1988, especially Part I, Principles of Environmental Science, pp. 1–104. For a more thorough discussion, see Edward O. Wilson, *The Diversity of Life*, London: Allen Pane, the Penguin Press, 1993 (and Cambridge, MA: Harvard University Press, 1992).

6. It was this claim that gave rise to Richard Dawkins's book, *The Blind Watchmaker*, Harlow: Longman, 1986, which argues that it is the very complexity and variety of natural phenomena that support the concept of an evolved life system on earth *sans* guidance.

ded in genotypes and spelled out in gene-driven phenotypes, of interactions and transactions between and among life forms and their environments. Variability and diversity of life phenomena are simply one outcome of thermodynamic energy flows. Within this overarching thermodynamic framework, natural selection's mechanism of evolutionary change contributes to the variegation of life by favoring organisms (and their underlying genomes) whose energy extraction processes excel those of others.

Thus the sources of biodiversity are "genetic variation within species and differences among species," the latter an outcome of natural selection pressures exerted over time on a given population. Going on to describe the resulting efflorescence of life, one biologist puts it this way:

> This principle of evolution stems from the immense variety made possible by rearrangements in the sequence of nucleotide letters of the genetic code. The code contains about a million nucleotide pairs in bacteria and between 1 to 10 billion nucleotide pairs in higher plants and animals. Evolution proceeds mostly by the accidental substitution of one or more of the letters, followed by the winnowing of these mutations and their combinations through natural selection. Because mutations occur at random, and because natural selection is affected by idiosyncratic changes in the environment that differ from one place and time to the next, no two species ever follow exactly the same path for more than a couple of steps. The real world, then, consists of species that differ from one another in infinitely varying directions and distances.[7]

Rather paradoxically, diversity binds life forms together within an ecological context. This feature is what makes **diversity** a value. The links established between life units and their surroundings are founded in and are dependent upon the presence of diverse life forms. The greater the variability, the larger and more expansive are the life potentials and life opportunities to be realized within the whole. This is partly due to elaborately interlinked food chains and varying levels of biomass displayed in most ecosystems, where a multiplicity of life types extends the life chances of the whole. Expressed more bluntly, there is more to eat in a diverse environment, and mutual

---

7. Wilson, op. cit., pp. 88, 156. Wilson goes on to say (pp. 161–162) that "The true, ultimate measure of genetic diversity is nucleotide diversity" which he conservatively estimates to be "a total of 10^{17} (100 quadrillion) nucleotide pairs specifying the full genetic diversity among species. . . . That figure, 10^{17}, is in one sense the entire diversity of life. Yet it still does not take into account the differences among individuals belonging to the same species. When that dimension is added, the potential grows still more. . . . [I]n the whole genetic makeup of the species there would be 10^{18} possible combinations for each species. This immense figure is still an underestimate." In Chapters 5 and 6, Wilson summarizes the various processes that operate within natural selection and genetic variation and that contribute to biodiversity. His account presents complex ecological theory in accessible terms without the shallow generalizations sometimes found in popularized versions.

bonds between various life forms are greater in number and variety. Ecological uniformity and ecological shallowness—a barren seascape or landscape scoured of most of the variety that once might have filled it with teeming life of all kinds—severely reduces the evolutionary potential of an ecosystem. Rachel Carson's careful studies warned of this problem in the awakening days of ecological consciousness.[8]

Life depends upon diversity of life. That is simply the way evolution has occurred, the path taken by thermodynamic process. Evolutionary logic suggests—indeed, seems to establish—that ecological links among diverse life forms have been a necessary part of biotically related thermodynamic transactions. Life-unit economizing that proved successful in staving off entropy has always occurred within a context, a network, a web of surrounding forces and events and other life entities. The more diverse that life web is, the greater are the prospects for life within it. No better illustration exists than a tropical rain forest where literally millions of diverse species interact in a dense network of life forms.

The emerging human awareness of this feature of ecological systems signals that the conceptualization of diversity as a value is well underway. As a naturalistic process, diversity has anciently accompanied the evolution of life forms—and appears not only to have made life possible but to have vastly enriched the makeup and content of life's accumulated manifestations. The same can be said about human experience within a cultural regime: sociocultural forms exhibit manifold variety, in this case demonstrating how widely and how comprehensively it has been possible to arrange human affairs. Taken as a whole, human culture mirrors the same diversity-dependent trait that is seen throughout all natural evolution (as it should since culture is part of that same process).

Awareness of diversity as a value is partially and importantly a function of the scale of cultural experience encountered by an individual or a society. Single cultures, particularly those either isolated from others or capable of mounting strong defenses against incursions from other cultures, may severely limit the experiences of their denizens. Homogeneity, not heterogeneity, may prevail. Ideological systems rooted within cultural traditions frequently discourage explorations and contacts outside the boundaries of a given culture. For these reasons, the view from inside a particular culture may not convey the notion of cultural diversity at all or may view cultural variety as a form of deviation from the True Way, best avoided if obliteration of the of-

8. Rachel Carson, *Silent Spring*, Boston: Houghton Mifflin, 1962. Two earlier books that laid the groundwork for the sense of concern that she expressed in *Silent Spring* were *The Sea Around Us*, New York: Oxford University Press, 1950, 1951, and *The Edge of the Sea*, Boston: Houghton Mifflin, 1955.

fending practice or belief is not possible. Thus, a generalized intercultural blindness may be and frequently is reinforced by a similar intracultural myopia that limits the life chances of unfavored groups within a society who may be encouraged to believe that their station in life is foreordained by larger-than-life supernatural powers.

Diversity as a human value proclaims that differences matter. Variety is more than "the spice of life." It *is* life. Moreover, **diversity** and **linkage** coexist. Each natural process and each value depends on the other, is augmented by the other, multiplies the likelihood that each will prevail in the course of evolutionary change. This functional convergence or reinforcement plays a significant role in the formation of communities, which is given fuller attention further along in this chapter.

Third Ecologizing Value: Homeostatic Succession

Observed over time and in sufficient depth of detail, ecological networks are found to be dynamic. These life webs are active, ever-shifting continuua of diverse components fused together in functional ways. The bonds are pathways along which life impulses continuously and restlessly move, thereby shifting the sometimes delicate and often precarious balance achieved among life forms that seek life-sustaining energy. Here one encounters the underlying dynamic principle of ecological process. Life webs are constantly living, aging, renewing, dying, continuing, evolving, adjusting, adapting, revolving, cycling, pulsating, merging, thriving, speeding up, slowing down, emerging, declining, oscillating, extinguishing, diminishing, augmenting. Overall, there is no balance or equilibrium, no moment when living systems and their inhabitants find surcease from change or the prospect of change. The cycles and regularities that govern ecosystem life and that appear superficially to be stable are themselves irregular in magnitude, timing, and impact. This is true of abiotic elements (geothermal factors, climate, nonterrestrial radiation, planetary revolution, etc.), as well as of the living components subject to population fluctuations, genetic drift, genetic mutations, phenotypic adjustments to natural selection pressures, and so on.

The nature of ecological change is not easily captured in a phrase, but perhaps "homeostatic succession," though an unfamiliar and cumbersome usage, conveys as well as any other what appears to be happening. "Succession" has acquired a special meaning within ecological science, referring generally to the chronological replacement of one biotic community by another, as might occur when desert plants and animals replace temperate-zone flora and fauna as a region slowly becomes drier. As used here, succession refers also to a generalized process of transition within many of the interconnected levels of an ecosystem where these changes transform the life potentialities of the affected life units. Emphasis is on the depth and comprehensiveness of these transitions that occur throughout any given ecosystem. These systemwide movements tend to occur over relatively long time periods, partly because they entail disruptions in well-established survival linkages and partly because many life units exhibit flexibility in their economizing habits and thus have an associated tolerance for shifting environmental conditions. The outward appearance is one of inertia, although change may be deep, fundamental, and far-ranging within the system. For example, as groundwater levels drop in an area undergoing desertification, the soil conditions affecting different plants' moisture-uptake capacities are slowly transformed, thus leading the way to plant succession plus changes in all other related species whose existence depends upon either the invading desert plants or the waning temperate-zone plants.

"Succession" therefore is "homeostatic"—that is, ecological networks attain a regularity, display a pattern, that tends toward stability while moving constantly away from a fixed equilibrium state. There is a sense in which these results are accomplished through what might be called, with some caution, self-correcting interactions. Life units preserve their way of life by resisting rapid or radical change. Their genomes will therefore tend to "correct" or make allowance for environmental changes that threaten established life routines (as in the desertification example above). This inertial impulse gives a superficial impression of a "self-correcting" system. Various pressures—natural selection, genetic, environmental—act to offset radical shifts in the linkages. But a lasting "balance" among these self-correcting forces is elusive, rarely if ever attained, and a function of the magnitude of the change-making forces at work within the web.

Homeostatic succession is a process of change that occurs within continuity. The continuity is the prevailing pattern of interlocked-life-and-abiotic-environment that comprises an ecosystem, such as a coral reef or an open savannah. The rate of change is not uniform within such ecological contexts; some species may be declining, others expanding. Neither does change occur at all points simultaneously inside the web. Nor can ecological change be described as strictly linear; the transitions often follow convoluted pathways, some circular, others cyclical, still others episodic. Hence, the amount, rate, direction, and kind of ecological change perceived at any one moment are very much a function of the position of an observer within the system. Ecological dynamics can therefore be said to be relative—or at least, understanding the process is best attained from what might be called an ecologically relativist perspective.

Homeostatic succession is the least developed and least understood of the values that make up the ecologizing value cluster. The entire human experience has been one of change and of adjusting to ecological changes that are neither continuous, uniform, nor entirely linear. At base, the changes reflect and are a function of the second law of thermodynamics—the flow of energy through living systems (biologists call them dissipative systems) that dissipate energy into an environmental (entropic) sink.[9] Where that flow is captured and diverted into pools of organic substance, life prevails. Entropic process in this way postpones its own logical outcome by making possible the inter-linked life webs that we lately have recognized as ecological in nature. Ecological bonds are thus life-giving and life-sustaining survival systems capable of restraining the rush of energy toward entropic equilibrium. This feature of ecological networks appears to be a manifestation of the self-organizing, order-producing effects of thermodynamic process discussed in Chapter 2.

"Succession within continuity" implies that ecological change is con-strained by existing life-net survival functions. Radical shifts tear at the web and diminish its support function. Massive and usually unpredictable envi-ronmental events—volcanic eruptions, earthquakes, prairie and forest fires, widespread radiation releases, sunspot flares, asteroid impacts—catastrophi-cally disrupt or possibly demolish long-prevailing life linkages. Edward O. Wilson cites five major "extinction spasms," the first beginning some 450 mil-lion years ago, that have decimated living species. He makes an impressive case that another, even vaster extinction of global species has been set in mo-tion by human environmental impacts (pollution, habitat destruction, pesti-cides, herbicides, etc.).[10] More typically, though, ecological networks display remarkable staying power through time. Populations of particular species wax and wane, come and go; predators overkill their prey populations, only to face extinction themselves; genetic drift carries a group to a dominant po-sition within its ecosystem, while genetic mutations may lessen or quicken the prospects of another group; temperature gradients within a stream slowly make life unfeasible for some aquatic life forms, while others find the new cli-mate more supportive. As these changes go forward within an ecosystem—both giving life and taking it away—the system itself resists radical change. This is the nature of homeostatic succession as a change process.

As a value, homeostatic succession seems now to have crept into human consciousness on a new scale. A quickening awareness of the life-supporting features of ecological networks *qua* life webs has spread with remarkable speed into many societies. Global or regional warming, rain forest destruc-tion, ozone depletion, chemical dumping, and accidental radiation releases from nuclear plants are now seen as threats to human, animal, and plant life

9. For a clarifying discussion, see Ronald F. Fox, *Energy and the Evolution of Life*, New York: W. H. Freeman, 1988, pp. 2, 152–155. See also Niles Eldredge and Marjorie Grene, *Interactions: The Bio-logical Context of Social Systems*, New York: Columbia University Press, 1982, p. 165.

10. See Wilson, op. cit., pp. 187–194 and Chapters 11 and 12.

that bring unwelcome and unwanted change. It may be ironic that this new-found orientation to nature has, so to speak, "come in the back door" due largely to the perceived negative impacts that recent cultural practices have engendered within ecosystems. Ancient and simpler societies perhaps sensed long ago that life skeins resist radical transformation, even when such orientations emerged dimly from a mystical, and therefore misconceived and misguided, grasp of nature's forces. Mainly, though, it is only in our time that human cultural artifacts and practices seem capable of initiating ecological change on a scale large enough and far-reaching enough to sound a trumpet of alarm throughout the earth. Certain vital strands of the global web of life are under much stress, imperiling human enterprise on a grand scale.

That warning is the best evidence we have that homeostatic succession has taken its place in the domain of human value concepts. This value acknowledges the life-support features of ecosystem networks, along with the diversity of interlinked life forms that make those networks possible. Change or succession within ecological systems is more or less continuous though slow-moving because life-threatening to some. Within the whole, diversity reigns and life pulsates as thermodynamic energy flows into and out of the entire network. While stable (thus being "homeostatic"), ecosystems evolve (and thus display a "succession" of life forms and life patterns). In these ways, natural process, having made its impact on human experience, provides the base for a conceptual device that is increasingly accepted as a widespread belief, that expresses a relationship of humans to nature, that creates a new standard for appraising and judging ecological and economic issues, and that is anchored securely within a human experiential realm. In all of these respects, homeostatic succession qualifies as a human value.

Fourth Ecologizing Value: Community

Ecological processes and their conceptualized values cluster together, converging toward and culminating in certain evolutionary outcomes. This tendency toward convergence is present also in the other two value clusters discussed in earlier chapters. Economizing, growth, and systemic integrity work together in ways that produce life-sustaining economizing outcomes, just as hierarchical (rank-order) organization, managerial decision power, power-system equilibrium, and power aggrandizement lead to augmentations and uses of power whose evolutionary effects are problematic. The same convergence is seen in the interweaving of linkage, diversity, and homeostatic succession that produces what may be usefully called "community." **Community** is an evolved outcome of the operation of these three ecological processes. It is a homeostatic network of diverse life units with a survival potentiality that turns out to be dependent on the linkages and diversity within the web. As one ecologist stated, "even the simplest communities contain an enormous reservoir of potentialities and an enormous potentiality for new adaptation."[11]

For most species—perhaps all except humans—this survival potentiality of a community is solely a function of the interaction of biotic and abiotic environmental components, as genotypes produce phenotypes through natural selection. The most prominent of these community-creating processes in nonhuman animal populations are four in number: genetically determined species-mating-recognition-systems, which permit members of a single species (lions) to recognize and mate with one another rather than with members of another species (tigers); subsequent mating and sexual reproduction; affiliative bonds among mating pairs and their offspring; and various inborn and learned group defense mechanisms that protect a population from unwanted or life-threatening forces.[12] These are the sinews that bind animal species into recognizably distinctive groups of life units. These and similar natural processes occurring among other organisms appear to be the biological rudiments of community aggregations among most animal life forms.

Communities of plants (and fungi) are a response to somewhat different combinations of natural processes, although similar communal outcomes tend to be produced through gene-driven sexual reproductive systems, species defense mechanisms, and even a "bonding" effect in the sense of individual life units responding more or less uniformly to environmental conditions. Obviously lacking animal consciousness and active-expansive learning capacities, plants and fungi do not "recognize" or "choose" mates nor do they develop deliberate affiliative ties to others of their kind.[13]

Ecological communities that include humans display—in addition to gene-based processes that create distinctive groups and species—symbolico-cultural components as an integral part of the linkages and diversity that comprise the community. These symbol-based cultural systems apparently

11. Michael Conrad, *Adaptability: The Significance of Variability from Molecule to Ecosystem*, New York: Plenum Press, 1983, p. 286.

12. For group defense, see Thomas Caraco and H. Ronald Pulliam, "Sociality and Survivorship in Animals Exposed to Predation," in Peter W. Price, C. N. Slobodchikoff, and William S. Gaud (eds.), *A New Ecology: Novel Approaches to Interactive Systems*, New York: Wiley, 1984, pp. 279–308; and Jeremy J. D. Greenwood, "The Evolutionary Ecology of Predation," in B. Shorrocks (ed.), *Evolutionary Ecology*, Oxford: Blackwell, 1984, pp. 236–240ff, who lists forty sources.

13. An undue focus or emphasis on the differences between "conscious" human awareness and "nonconscious" plants, fungi, bacteria, and other forms of life most probably reflects a kind of anthropocentric thinking that seeks both similarities and distinctions between humans and various other life forms. A close examination of natural processes leads one to doubt the presumed homeocentric significance of these differences and parallels. They are, however, perhaps helpful as a taxonomic tool when used for nonteleological comparative purposes. For a related discussion, see Paul A. Keddy, *Competition*, London: Chapman and Hall, 1989, pp. 160–171.

occur only where humans are present, adding yet another kind of naturally evolved dynamic to the interconnections that make up a community. Culture may either enhance or diminish the life potentialities experienced there; terminal outcomes traceable to culturally inspired motivations and practices (such as warfare, urban violence, and homicide) if not *as* likely to occur as the enrichment of life, are nevertheless present and active. As with nonhuman communities of plants or animals, the extent of survival potentiality within the community network depends on the extent, strength, and magnitude of the three interacting values—linkage, diversity, and homeostatic succession. No particular outcome is foreordained.

Contrary to popular, often uninformed opinion, ecologists and ethologists routinely acknowledge the significance of human culture as a factor in human evolution and human communities, as demonstrated by the following quotations:

> Before the appearance of humans and human societies life developed under the aegis of natural selection. . . . But with the evolution of human beings the possibility of cultural transmission of acquired information became orders of magnitude more significant than at any previous time. Linguistic mechanisms, methods of training, and use of information processing methodologies are some of the tools which make human and social model development and problem-solving increasingly important after this point.[14]

> . . . a language user enters a whole new world, a totality of symbols and therewith symbol-imbued behaviors that, for all our biological kinship, remains unique.[15]

> . . . conceptual thought—with syntactic language accompanying it—constitutes a new kind of life. Except for the one great evolutionary step leading from non-life to life, the coming into existence of conceptual thought certainly creates the most essential distinction known to science.[16]

> Niko Tinbergen [one of the major founders of the field of ethology] . . . wrote for example that "our unique position in the modern world is due to the consequences of our cultural evolution, which . . . has . . . progressively . . . superimposed (itself) on our still ongoing genetic evolution" and that "we transfer . . . , from one generation to the next, not only our genetic heritage but also (our) accumulated non-genetically acquired . . . experience."[17]

14. Conrad, op. cit., p. 369.

15. Eldredge and Grene, op. cit., p. 177. See the entire chapter on Human Sociality.

16. Konrad Lorenz, *The Foundations of Ethology* (English translation by Konrad Z. Lorenz and Robert Warren Kickert), New York and Vienna: Springer-Verlag, 1981, p. 340.

17. Juan E. Delius, "The Nature of Culture," in M. S. Dawkins, T. R. Halliday, and R. Dawkins (eds.), *The Tinbergen Legacy*, London: Chapman & Hall, 1991, p.75.

These several passages are quoted to counteract the view that ethologists and biologically trained ecologists attribute all significant human behavior and attributes to biological factors.

Human community, when achieved through the ecologizing values of linkage, diversity, and homeostatic succession, depends heavily on the basic symbol systems that comprise human culture everywhere: language, tools, and a play-curiosity-experimental capacity that may be expressed either as dramatic myth making or as technical trial-and-error tinkering.[18] From the interplay among these symbolic cultural rudiments, a human group may enhance its survival potentialities by applying its collective foresight, imagination, intelligence, information, and tools to the environmental situation it encounters. In general, evolutionary process embodying linkage, diversity, and homeostatic succession brings human groups to a symbolico-cultural threshold that offers immensely expanded opportunities for forming collective ecological wholes. An extended discussion of this cultural-value threshold and the possibilities it holds for human prospects is found in the following chapter.

Hence, **community** as a conceptualized value arises from—is a product of—the other three ecologizing values of **linkage, diversity,** and **homeostatic succession**. Together, they comprise Value Cluster III. Humans value (i.e., believe in) community life that relates them to each other; they frequently measure and appraise their success (or failure) in achieving the necessary degree of integration and cooperation to make life tolerable; and they root their acceptance of this value solidly in the collective experiences they have had. In all of these senses, community has long been a central human value. We now move closer to seeing it as one more outcome of an evolutionary dynamic that leans against the entropic winds otherwise blowing us and all living forms toward a silent terminus.

ANTHROPOCENTRIC INTERPRETATIONS OF ECOLOGICAL PROCESS

It will be helpful to compare the foregoing view of ecological process with current popularized versions, which frequently or perhaps even typically project a skewed picture that hampers the search for value clarity in business and society. There is no little irony in such a critical review, for it is through the widely circulated notion of an ecologically threatened planet that ecologizing values now enjoy increasingly broad acceptance.

18. For a discussion of the play and curiosity elements in animal and human behavior, see Lorenz, op. cit., pp. 329–335; and Irenaus Eibl-Eibesfeldt, *Human Ethology*, New York: Aldine de Gruyter, 1989, pp. 580–593, 665–702.

One can easily gain the impression from some popular as well as scholarly accounts that humans are set apart from their natural surroundings, viewing nature, so to speak, from the outside and from a superior, deserving, or even exalted position, as if from an evolutionary pinnacle. Several easy if erroneous claims may then follow: Humans are pitted against their environment. Humans "control" the natural environment (e.g., the weather) or "predict" natural events (e.g., earthquakes, cyclones, tornados, floods). Human impacts are said to create environmental "disturbances" or cause environmental stress and degradation. Human actions are claimed to bring a loss of environmental "balance" or to disrupt naturally occurring ecological cycles. An expanding human population, by diminishing an environment's "carrying capacity," is thought to threaten its "sustainability." Humans are said to "intervene" in nature, thereby contravening what an otherwise unfettered "nature" seemingly dictates.

These concerns and alarms stem from an "us against them" mindset, where "us" is humanity and "them" is Nature. Nature tends to be personified, often carrying a feminine label such as Mother Nature or Her Bounty, and some have sought to establish that the entire idea of a hegemony over nature is yet another manifestation of masculine attitudes and behavior gone (typically) berserk. Whether these particular views and grammatical usages are valid is, for the moment, less critical than to see the Humans versus Nature formula for what it is. All too subtly, the notion is insinuated into the dialogue that there is, on the one hand, human purpose and, on the other, natural process—and never the twain shall meet save on the environmental battleground where both sides take their determined stands, one to conquer, the other to resist. Thus, one encounters an anthropomorphic, teleological conception of natural process that views the environment in homeocentric terms and thereby creates a divide between humans and nature, and thus between humanity and an evolved universe. That this outcome should have been deliberately promoted by some ideologues is no surprise, but that it has been partially (though perhaps inadvertently) encouraged by ecological scientists themselves, along with their ecological popularizers, is unfortunate.[19]

As the foregoing discussion of ecological process has attempted to establish, nature knows no "balance." Natural cycles and oscillations, however stable they may seem from one (or any) particular space-time perspective, are not immutably fixed in their swings. "Disturbance" and variation are normal in nature. A fixed "equilibrium" of natural forces is a phantom created by

19. For a revealing discussion of how ecological scientists have often manifested this skewed perspective, even as they have pursued rigorous field studies, see J. S. Kennedy, *The New Anthropomorphism*, Cambridge: Cambridge University Press, 1992. It is dismaying to find frequent, though presumably unintended, teleological phrases and passages used by such leading biologists as Edward O. Wilson in *The Diversity of Life*.

human imagination. To speak of human "intervention" in natural affairs is to posit a grievous misconstruction of the human condition. To "intervene" is to enter nature from the outside; such a view overlooks the embeddedness of humans within nature. Humans *are* nature, in the sense of being one manifestation among many of natural evolution. They and their human culture are as surely an outcome of natural forces as any phenome produced by any genome.

In transactions with their environment, humans quite clearly slice through ecological cycles and regularities that have life-sustaining functions for other life entities, as can happen when a chemical spill kills hundreds of fish in a stream or along a seashore. (Other species, of course, do the same, as when sheep overgraze and therefore kill pasture grasses.) In that sense only, humans "intervene in" and "disrupt" nature, or they upset "equilibria" and create "imbalances." But they do so as full-fledged participants in nature itself, just as viruses invade human tissue, just as tornados and earthquakes wreak havoc in urban centers, just as the wolf slays the lamb.

Environmental "carrying capacity" and the associated idea of "sustainability," as discussed in both popular and scientific literature, often emerge as little more than anthropocentric distortions of the connections between humans and their environment. An ecosystem, such as may be found in a prairie or an isolated mountain valley, may be abundantly rich in complex life forms and thus display an impressive "carrying capacity," and it may sustain that life-preserving trait for long periods. But that the natural forces that brought such ecosystems to such a life-sustaining plateau should be thought to have reserved a special place for its human inhabitants is only a wistful fantasy. Nature evolves complex *systems* of interconnected life entities, and on global and geological scales relatively few of the participating life forms are or have been human. Nature does not exist to "sustain" human existence, nor does it define a human "carrying capacity." Completely aside from the specific culture-bound definition of "carrying capacity" and "sustainability" (cast largely in terms of the envisioned fate of advanced industrial Western societies), neither nature nor the second law of thermodynamics plays favorites among life forms.[20]

What *does* occur is human adaptation within natural environments. This adaptation is a consequence, not a purpose or goal, of evolutionary process. Purpose is a human invention, not a built-in feature of natural evolution. Na-

20. An account of environmental carrying capacity and sustainability that is remarkably free of environmentalist dogma and cant is found in Andrea Baranzini and Gonzague Pillet, "The Physical and Biological Environment—The Socioeconomy of Sustainable Development," in Beat Bürgenmeier (ed.), *Economy, Environment, and Technology: A Socio-Economic Approach*, Armonk, N.Y.: M. E. Sharpe, 1994, pp. 139–162.

ture evolves; humans, from within nature itself, impose meaning on and may impute purpose to nature. Human adaptability to environmental change, like the adaptability of any organism, is enhanced by both a diverse range of human types and a generality of genome in projecting phenome. Human attempts to "control" or "command" nature—as may occur in business economizing and corporate power aggrandizement, *as well as in some well-intended ecologizing initiatives*—frequently, perhaps typically, overlook and may damage vital ecosystem linkages that sustain human life and culturally created human purpose. Examples are the unplanned clearcutting of forests that destroys habitats, construction of mammoth power-generating dams (such as the Aswan High Dam in Egypt) that obliterate riverine ecosystems, and the extensive overuse of chemical fertilizers on farmland that damages soil and pollutes streams. These and other homeocentric attempts to "control" nature are human purpose gone astray from the natural processes in which humans are rooted. The consequence may well be ecological catastrophe on a grand scale, thus defeating the proximate goals putatively driving the human control efforts. Such are the wages of anthropocentric attitudes toward ecological process.

THE INTERFACE OF ECONOMIZING AND ECOLOGIZING

One of the central issues facing both business and society today is how to reconcile economics and the environment, economizing and ecologizing—those two forces of nature, each magnified and extended by human culture, that make our life possible. The relationship between economizing and ecologizing is no simple matter, as a deep knowledge of ecology soon makes very apparent. It is not even clear that the two are distinct and separable processes. But to the extent that they are, the dynamics that occur at their interface pose grave and perhaps intractable problems for the business system and for organized human life everywhere. We now explore this uncertain and sometimes bewildering ground.

Close examination of both ecological theory and field data reveals that economizing and ecologizing are unavoidably linked together as a part of evolutionary process but that they are separable in the respective *scale* of evolutionary effect each displays. This means, first of all, that economizing cannot and does not occur, nor has it ever occurred, absent an ecological context—because that context, even an abiotic one, is the source of economizing energy needed for life. But it also means that while economizing can occur at the tiniest and most rudimentary particle-points and life-levels, ecological life webs (however small or large they may be) exert their influence over a comparatively broader range of life. It would be only suggestive and not quite accurate to say that an ecological system can be thought of in macro terms, while economizing's effects can (but need not) occur at a local and relatively delineated point (e.g., within a single organism that is successful in absorbing the energy it needs for metabolic functions). As two ecological authorities point out, "all but a few specialized cells . . . lead an economic existence, that is, require a source of energy to maintain themselves and perform whatever metabolic functions are peculiar to them. All organisms . . . are economic machines."[21] Hence, economizing does indeed take place within very small organic locales.

Put another way, any economic transaction is inherently ecological—that is, it occurs within a context of biotic and abiotic forces that exert an influence on the outcome—and this has been so since the beginning of life on earth. Some ecologists have argued that a rudimentary ecological process may be discerned even at a prelife molecular level where thermodynamic energy flows organize increasingly complex chemical interactions that may in turn lead toward life.[22] The captured flow of life-sustaining energy that *is* economizing is itself part of the life unit's environmental context (i.e., its ecological setting). In fact, some ecologists say that the very substance of ecological process is little more than a pattern of economic transactions occurring among life units within any ecosystem. Such a view is closely equivalent to saying that economizing and ecologizing are but different sides of a single process. This close blending of ecology and economy is revealed in the following passages:[23]

> . . . large-scale biotic systems arise purely as an effect of the economic activities of organisms. . . .

> Thus a simple consequence of interaction—*economic* interaction involving energy flow—is that complex, coherent biotic systems are formed. . . .

> The notion of energy flow, which is seen to connect variegated elements of any well-analyzed ecosystem in an intricate web, lies at the heart of this concept. It is this very form of interaction that coheres economic biotic systems. . . .

And what is true of ecosystems in general applies equally to human phenomena, as one learns from the perspective of ecological theory: "economic behavior . . . on the whole dominates human existence, as it does that of almost every other organism. . . . Most human interactions—and especially

21. Eldredge and Grene, op. cit., p. 68.
22. See Keddy, op. cit., pp. 24–27.
23. Eldredge and Grene, op. cit., pp. 114–115.

the sorts of interactions that integrate social systems—are economic, or quasi-economic, in nature."[24] But being economic, they also are simultaneously ecological inasmuch as economic transactions occur within ecosystems.

While economizing and ecologizing activities are not identical—because of scale differences in the way each works—the two processes *are* interdependent. They occur simultaneously, with much interactive feedback between the two and between the living biotic components and the abiotic surrounding forces. This somewhat bizarre interface is therefore more complex and more subtle than is sometimes realized. These two vital natural processes along with their extruded value systems, in their very makeup, are at the same time mutually supportive of one another and of life processes *and* capable of exerting contradictory effects on each other and on those who live within their respective orbits. Though having evolved together and in parallel as life-sustenance systems, each has the potential to counteract and cancel out the other's evolutionary effect.

Such odd, unexpected, and somewhat paradoxical outcomes can be better understood if one is aware of the different forms taken by economizing within complex ecological networks. These ecological mosaics reveal certain patterned regularities in the modes by which life units seek and process the energy they need for survival. They tell much about the intersection where economizing and ecologizing touch one another, sometimes with harmonious and life-sustaining results, at other times bringing life forms, including humans, nearer to their ultimate entropic fate.

VARIETIES OF ECOLOGICAL PROCESS

Ecologists' studies have established that the economizing activities comprising ecological webs take various forms. Some economizing is competitive, while cooperative or concerted interactions prevail elsewhere. Sometimes, both occur simultaneously and in overlapping fashion. The goal now is to show how these diverse patterns both sustain and deny life to individual life units within ecological networks while simultaneously preserving the collective whole that is an ecological community.

Nonecologists should be aware that ecological science is young enough still to be in a stage characterized by taxonomical debate and definitional uncertainties not unlike that of other disciplines. Fierce debate and barbed exchanges occasionally surface in the literature as ecologists struggle for theoretical clarity. Some of these unsettled matters edge into this present account

24. Ibid., p. 195.

of the various ways by which life units go about their economizing business, and they will be noted where appropriate.[25]

Competitive Economizing

Ecological science has, according to some of its major proponents, placed competitive striving at the center of its conceptual and theoretical framework. According to these accounts, competition between species is "a potent organizing force in communities."[26] Ecology textbooks give "substantial treatments of competition and predation," an observation verified by one study showing that the attention given to these two topics outweighed discussions of mutualisms by a ratio of 9 to 1.[27] There has been good reason to do so, for reasons related to the quest of organic life for needed energy. That ceaseless search frequently goes on where others are equally bent on the same task and where access to resources is limited either by (abiotic) environmental conditions or by unequal organic facility in doing what is necessary to obtain and absorb those resources. Darwin's emphasis on natural selection as the evolutionary dynamic through which some forms of life adjusted to their environments and survived, while others less adept died out, has lain at the center of ecological thinking about the importance of competition in nature. Genetic theory has done nothing to lessen this bent, for it outlines the process by which some genotypes prove superior to others by transmitting coded instructions to organic phenotypes in a way that contributes to the organism's competitive success.[28]

The case for competition in nature may be even more basic than that which is reinforced by natural selection and genetic information. One ecological theorist posits that a type of competition (for energy resources) may occur among nonliving chemical molecules in some types of rudimentary compounds, largely as a function of the flow of energy through these compounds.

> There are therefore good thermodynamic reasons for expecting competition in nature. They are based on the observation that the accumulation of more-com-

25. For a summary of this conceptual flux, see Peter W. Price, "Alternative Paradigms in Community Ecology" in Price et al., op. cit., pp. 353–379.

26. Ibid., pp. 354ff, who attributes this view to three of the field's leading theorists, namely, Howard Odum, Eric Pianka, and Robert Ricklefs.

27. John Vandermeer, "The Evolution of Mutualism," in Shorrocks, op. cit., p. 221. The results of the textbook study are shown in Keddy, op. cit., pp. 161–162.

28. The process is discussed at length in Richard Dawkins, *The Selfish Gene*, New York: Oxford University Press, 1976, and Dawkins, *The Extended Phenotype: The Gene as the Unit of Selection*, Oxford: W. H. Freeman, 1982.

plex molecules is limited by, among other factors, the pool of resources. The variety of life-forms is staggering, and it is so easy to get caught up on fascinating details of form, function and natural history. However, if the systems were stripped of all detail, they would look very much like the thermodynamic model . . . [of] the behaviour of simple chemical systems.[29]

Competition in the organic realm is, in a sense, a form of economizing, or perhaps more accurately, it is an interactive process *between* organisms that are impelled by genetic coding, learned habit, or enculturated behavior toward economizing outcomes. Where access to needed energy resources is unequal, this kind of economizing supports the life of a single organism or a group of organisms by diminishing the life prospects of one or more other organisms. It is nature's zero-sum game, played in deadly earnest. The members of one species living within reach of a given resource pool compete among themselves for what may be taken from the pool; the "fittest" survive (or survive long enough) to perpetuate their genes, while the less "fit" die or have less favorable chances of extending their genetic structures to future generations. Ecologists describe an almost limitless number of permutations of this kind of competitive economizing within a single species, between different species, and as one species diverges to form two or more distinctive species.[30]

Plants do not compete with one another in quite the same way as do animals. One plant ecologist points out that "the proximity of neighbors" is the crucial element in competitive economizing among plants; where crowding occurs, one plant's roots or leaves may interfere with another plant's need for sunlight or nutrients. In these cases, he has suggested that "interference" might be preferred to "competition" as a descriptor of competitive economizing. Regardless of the label adopted, one observes a negative impact on one organism brought about by another organism's superior access to a resource needed by both.[31]

Predation between species is yet another variety of competitive economizing extensively studied by ecologists. Interestingly enough, these predator–prey relationships in which a representative of one species directly ends the life of a member of another species constitute a large (but not the largest) portion of what goes on in most ecosystems most of the time. The stuff of wildlife films where lions are shown chasing, catching, and devouring zebras; grizzly bears scooping salmon from a river; even carnivorous plants

---

29. Keddy, op. cit., pp. 25–27. Keddy goes on to say, that "Of course, even if this is true, it does not prove that competition is universal."

30. Cf. Wilson, op. cit., Chapters 7 and 9.

31. See Keddy, op. cit., pp. 2–3ff, for further discussion.

capturing and absorbing insects—these and countless other examples bring home the ubiquity of predation in nature. Little wonder that it has been seen as the competitive glue that paradoxically binds ecological communities together. Life taking life is as ubiquitous as it is unavoidable if there is to be life at all. While life-denying *inter*species competition and predation are common in nature, humans appear to be one of the very few organisms—and the only one to do so deliberately and consciously—to systematically practice life-taking *intra*species competition such as warfare, genocide, and ethnic decimation.

For competitive economizing to produce its life-sustaining effects, all four of the basic ecologizing forces must be in place. Life forms must be **linked** together. A **diversity** of biotic and abiotic forces magnifies these competitive strivings. **Homeostatic succession** constantly reshuffles the chances for competitive success and failure. A **community** is structured and knitted together to a very large extent by the competitive pathways established among the members that group together there. Positive evolutionary outcomes for many (but obviously not all) individual organisms, species, and populations are an outgrowth of competitive economizing.

But this entropic offset is not the whole story. Prey plants and animals suffer directly, usually losing their lives entirely. Moreover, competitive economizing for some can be carried too far for the ecosystem's overall stability. An ecologist points out that ecological communities, though continually changing within, must be reasonably stable entities. "But the individual species does not know this. What is optimal from its short-sighted point of view may not be optimal for the community and therefore [for] its own advantage in the long run. This is the conflict between the evolutionary stability of the community and the evolutionary stability of species." The implications for human ecosystems are obvious: If human well-being is to be safeguarded, judgments and decisions that preserve the stability and integrity of human ecosystems are essential. Overzealous competitive economizing by a few individuals or by a large organized group may undermine the ecological foundations for all inhabitants of an ecosystem. From the point of view of their own environmental adjustment and survival, some species do take competitive economizing to this point of diminishing returns as they become "too efficient. The advantages of efficiency wring out unexercised adaptability. . . . At first the community appears more capable of conserving itself because of more effective cycling and because of the quenching of less fit variations among the dominant forms. But in reality it has traded potentiality for efficiency."[32]

---

32. The quotations are from Conrad, op. cit., pp. 283, 342, who provides extended discussion of the adaptability–efficiency trade-off on a global basis on pp. 352ff, applying its lessons to human society.

This trade-off of community adaptability for economic efficiency leads to a decline of collective life chances and fewer prospects for preserving the flexible and diverse linkages that are found in survival communities. So, in spite of economizing's antientropic thrust, it is capable of showing a proentropic facet where it erodes the essential components of ecological life networks. The interface of these two powerful and inherently life-giving natural processes is therefore an uneasy and troubling one.

Human communities around the globe now dimly see how a failure to reconcile economizing efficiency and ecological systems poses hazards of immense significance for life at all levels. The direct rupture of vital life cycles, in the name of economic need and economic growth, can be seen in the clearcutting of forests, industrial pollution that contributes to global warming, consumer and industrial products that thin out the earth's protective ozone layer, environmental dumping of hazardous wastes, and many other such environmental insults. It does indeed appear that human adaptability potentials on a global scale are thereby being lowered by a relentless drive for economizing efficiency that operates on a narrower dimension. This clash of economizing values and ecologizing values becomes hard to ignore when so many life interests are at stake. But given the life-supporting thrust of each value system, the steps toward reconciliation are not easily taken because they are not delineated within either of these two processes.

Mutualistic Economizing

As important as competitive economizing is within ecosystems, another kind of ecologizing process may well be more significant. "Mutualism" has enjoyed a renaissance among ecological scientists, one of whom comments as follows:

> Different kinds of organisms help each other out. This, in brief, is the idea of mutualism, and it is an idea which has been reborn in the last decade. Never entirely absent from ecological thought, it none the less fell out of favour as modern ecology grew, and only since the early 1970s have we begun to find it important again. No one can be sure that its recent renaissance will not in turn fade away, but at least today it is an idea which is steadily gaining ground. Ecologists once again find it interesting.[33]

Strictly speaking, Boucher's definition of mutualisms as "helping" behavior is not accurate since many (and most nonhuman) organisms do not consciously or otherwise attempt to "help" one another. Rather, each organism pursues its own genetic program as shaped by natural selection within a given

---

33. Boucher, op. cit., p. 1.

environment. The *behavioral outcomes* of these forces take on the appearance of "helping" but in fact are only self-driven economizing activities of each separate organism. As another ecologist points out, "Mutualism—just as competition, predation and other isms—is a property of the interaction, not the organism. . . . There is no gene for mutualism. . . . Organisms do not seek (or avoid) mutualisms any more than they seek to avoid competition."[34]

Several research scholars have noted the relative paucity of research on mutualisms as compared with competition and predation. One says, "of the three, mutualism is certainly the most commonly observed in nature. . . . [A] host of . . . spectacular mutualisms are readily observable in every corner of the globe. Yet the less frequently observed predation or the almost never observed competition have received most of the attention."[35] Another claims that "Mutualism . . . has hardly been studied as an organizing influence in natural communities."[36]

Several thoughtful ecologists have speculated about the reasons for this disciplinary bias that favors competitive and predatory activities. Little can be done here with their viewpoints other than to list some of the more prominent and intriguing possibilities. Most agree that general cultural features that idealize and promote competitive striving as an admirable human trait have created a climate of inquiry conducive to exploration of competitive urges and expressions. Grant money has been more frequently available for these purposes than for other routes of ecological inquiry. Darwinian emphasis on natural selection of the "fittest" types produced an intellectual aura or paradigm that has turned investigations in the general direction of a struggle for survival amidst hostile environments. Another has posited a gender bias within the community of predominantly male ecologists that may have drawn greater attention to aggressive actions than to "nurturing-cooperative interactions." Another type of bias—this time a taxonomic one—may have skewed ecological field studies to focus mainly on species that exhibit competition and predation. Once established and underway, such a given direction for approved research topics may then set patterns for younger scholars to follow if they wish to make a reputation for themselves, a phenomenon widely known in other disciplines as well.[37]

This intellectual ferment among ecological scientists is responsible in part for the relatively unsettled state of conceptual agreement on the nature of

34. See D. H. Janzen, "The Natural History of Mutualisms," in Boucher, op. cit., p. 82.

35. Vandermeer, op. cit., p. 221.

36. Price, "Alternative Paradigms in Community Ecology," in Price et al., op. cit., p. 376. See also the earlier reference to Keddy, op. cit., pp. 161ff.

37. For further discussion of these intriguing ideas, see Vandermeer, op. cit., pp. 221ff; and Keddy, op. cit., pp. 160–171. Keddy's analysis is especially fruitful.

mutualism. A growing number of ecologically sensitive members of the general public have long been familiar with the ecological notion of symbiosis, whereby two or more organisms—plants, animals, or some mixture of these—intertwine with each other to their respective benefit. That idea lies at the root of what is now meant by mutualisms in nature. However, the literature of the field reveals varying usages of the term "symbiosis"—some referring only to a close association between life entities, others specifying the need for actual physical contact (as in parasitic mistletoe growing on a tree), and still others wanting to call symbiotic *all* classes of closely associated natural linkages whether reciprocally beneficial or not.[38]

The key element in all symbiotic contacts is a functional association between organisms that contributes to the fitness or adaptability of at least one of the organisms. For example, pollen-gathering bees and the flowering plants whose blossoms they visit are symbiotically linked, each gaining a life-enhancing benefit. "In all mutualism birth rate is enhanced and/or death rate decreased as a result of mutualism, whether it be directly or indirectly."[39] The particular fitness advantage is one that presumably cannot be gained without the symbiotic tie. When the fitness gain is enjoyed on both sides of the equation (as in the bee–flowering plant illustration), it is appropriate to say that a mutualistic linkage exists. In the fine-grained analysis found in ecological theory and empirical studies, a further distinction is made by delineating "commensalisms" whereby one organism benefits but the other is not harmed. Then there are the widely reported "parasitisms" (such as the mistletoe) in which one party benefits at the expense of another.[40]

These kinds of mutualisms are, as noted earlier, extremely widespread in nature, as seen in the following passages:

> Consider—each cell in our body is possibly a symbiotic association of prokaryotes [organisms whose cells are without well-defined nucleii; bacteria are an example]. A large proportion of the world's biota is made up of multicellular organisms—a mutualistic association of unicellular components. We all breathe oxygen that is produced by plants. Studies of mycorrhizae [nitrogen-fixing fungi on plant roots] suggest that plants are joined by extensive mycorrhizal networks. All multicellular

---

38. See, for example, D. H. Lewis, "Symbiosis and Mutualism: Crisp Concepts and Soggy Semantics," in Boucher, op. cit., pp. 36–37ff; Price, op. cit., pp. 376–377; and John F. Addicott, "Mutualistic Interactions in Population and Community Processes," in Price et al., op. cit., pp. 438–439.

39. Carole L. Wolin, "The Population Dynamics of Mutualistic Systems," in Boucher, op. cit., p. 252. See also Kathleen H. Keeler, "Cost:Benefit Models of Mutualism," in Boucher, op. cit., p. 122.

40. One ecologist has said that "parasitism is predation in which the predator eats the prey in units of less than one. Being eaten one small piece at a time and surviving, often well, a host organism is able to support an entire population of another species." Under this arrangement, parasitism could be said to be one-bite-at-a-time predation. See Wilson, op. cit., pp. 176–177.

organisms have endosymbionts in their guts, which may assist with digestion and/or manufacture of vitamins. Many plants require insects for pollination and seed dispersal. Predators kill herbivores which otherwise would eat plants.[41]

Mutualistic symbioses offer striking examples such as these: the fungus and alga that compose a lichen; the ants and ant-acacias, where the trees house and feed the ants which, in turn, protect the trees; and the fig wasps and fig tree, where wasps, which are obligate [necessary] parasites of fig flowers, serve as the tree's sole means of pollination and seed set.[42]

Any average human, for example, is normally host to billions of symbiotic organisms belonging to perhaps a thousand different species.[43]

These examples make plain the economizing nature of all symbiotic mutualisms. Through these life-sustaining linkages, organisms enhance their prospects for gaining energy needed for metabolism and growth. Their fitness potential rises. Their birth rate rises or their death rate declines. They are able to absorb greater amounts of environmental energy than would otherwise be possible if these symbiotic-mutualistic ties did not exist.

However, the *ecological* significance of mutualisms is far greater than the *evolutionary* potential gained by individual pairs of symbiotically linked organisms. *Mutualisms convey a survival potential for all components of an ecosystem that far outruns the strength imparted to individual organisms, important as the latter may be.* Some field research shows that mutualisms possess a multiplicative effect that, in a sense, provides an umbrella of life support throughout an ecosystem. Such is the interconnected nature of life within any given ecosystem that mutual-support processes, which themselves are very widespread, constitute a support system going well beyond the directly involved symbionts. And ecologists have been challenged by one of their members to establish through research that if key mutualists are removed from or introduced into an ecological community, the relative abundance of life within that ecosystem may be radically altered. Another likely finding from research yet to be undertaken on a large scale is that "biomass production [i.e., the total weight of all living

41. Keddy, op. cit., pp. 161–162. Footnotes omitted.

42. Robert Axelrod and William D. Hamilton, "The Evolution of Cooperation," *Science*, vol. 211, 27 March 1981, p. 1391. Footnotes omitted.

43. Delius, op. cit., p. 85. This latter quotation puts a somewhat different cast on what is usually referred to as an "individual" human being. Although only one distinct person may be discernible, that individual human being is quite clearly a collectivity of life forms, all or most of which make life possible for the entity we label "human," and vice versa. Another way of saying the same thing is that each individual human entity *is* an ecological community, exists *within* an ecological community, and has no way of either coming into existence or continuing life absent such ecological ties.

matter] of natural or artificial communities is increased by the addition of mutualisms . . . and decreased by their elimination." It is known already that the diminution of biodiversity based largely on mutualistic ties can decimate life within an ecosystem, such as a tropical rain forest or a tidal estuary.[44]

The human significance of this umbrella-like life-support trait of mutualistic networks is twofold. On the one hand, the survival of humans (as a species) is enhanced where mutualisms prevail widely, as is true for all other species. Of parallel importance for humans is the *quality* of that survival, an issue that thrusts values forward and into the center of judgments about how and for what humanly created purposes that quality of life can be secured.

While mutualistic linkages themselves directly augment life, their presence sustains still other traits of ecological communities that likewise extend life chances for all. This effect can best be seen by visualizing what life would be like without mutualisms, as in the following passage:[45]

> In short, a world without the four common mutualisms would be less species-rich, less ecologically and life-form diverse, richer in extreme specialists and incompetent generalists, and have population patterns based more on monospecific stands (lower within-habitat diversity). Competition would be more intense among the survivors, and the survivors would expend more resources on it than they do now.

Simply and directly put, life in the natural world is more probable, more expansive, more supportive of greater biomass, more efflorescent in general, and channeled along pathways with greater potential for even greater variety of life in the future when characterized by complex and plentiful mutualisms. *There is every reason to believe that when compared with competitive economizing, mutualistic economizing far outstrips the other in antientropic effects.*

This finding carries enormous significance for value inquiry that seeks ways to expand, extend, and enrich human life. It is equivalent to recognizing that concerted, mutually beneficial, reciprocal relationships that saturate the natural world are, in fact, the very sinews that bind a community together into an integrated whole. Since humans are an integral part of the natural world, there is every reason to believe that these same forces are at work in creating and sustaining human communities within their respective ecological settings. Thus is the circle of ecologizing values closed: **linkage** of **diverse life forms** within a process of **homeostatic succession** produces **community**, a mutualistic antientropic network that, while manifesting thermodynamic

---

44. The challenges are presented in Boucher, op. cit., p. 23. The effects of reduced biodiversity among mutualisms are extensively discussed in Wilson, op. cit.

45. Janzen, op. cit., p. 89.

process, also turns that very process toward positive evolutionary consequences.

POWER AGGRANDIZEMENT AND ECOLOGIZING

Another great value intersection where the pathways of evolution encounter and cross one another is found where power confronts ecology. Unlike the intertwining of economy and ecology each of which, though at different levels of magnitude, promotes life prospects, power in nature and culture delimits and sometimes denies life opportunities for those subject to its hegemony. This value interface is therefore fraught with risks and dangers to human enterprise generally—and perhaps uniquely so in the business realm where power and its attractions have assumed such a central role.

If it is true that the world is now passing through a sixth, human-inspired "extinction spasm" that threatens to diminish biodiversity on a massive global scale, it is worth pondering how much of the destructive trend is due to overzealous, suboptimal economizing and how much may be the result of institutional power aggrandizement. Seeking an answer permits one to clarify the ways in which power phenomena intersect ecological process. Additionally, a peculiar and invariably obfuscating association of power aggrandizement and economizing can perhaps be better understood if seen against the screen of ecological phenomena outlined above.

As described in earlier chapters, power aggrandizement appropriates energy and incorporates it within hierarchical status-power systems, preserving the rank-order hierarchy and its extensive symbol system *and* sustaining the life units who command and operate the entire enterprise. This energy-appropriating activity simulates economizing by seeming to support and extend the life prospects of the power wielders, their surrogates, and all associated sycophants. From the outside, it takes on the appearance of any ordinary economizing process. It is best described, though, as quasi-economizing or pseudoeconomizing because its evolutionary outcome is the gathering and hoarding of power and its perquisites rather than the absorption of energy that makes possible and extends life opportunities. The controllers, though enjoying the fruits of the power system's energy-acquiring functions, which in a modern large-scale business corporation may be quite impressive, devote themselves to power acquisition, power retention, and power enlargement to the neglect of economizing per se. Employees' tasks are expected to be carried out in ways that are compatible with the power needs of the system and its controllers. Some economizing *effect* may well be achieved in these ways but typically as a by-product of power seeking, which remains "the name of the game."

This kind of power-conditioned pseudoeconomizing falls short of evolutionary economizing to the extent that it also typically ignores the total (social) costs—standard economists call these "externalities"—that frequently accompany expansionist corporate operations. Various forms of environmental pollution, such as the careless dumping of hazardous wastes, are social costs that might not be "booked" by a firm. Accounting for such costs might well reveal that the pollution-generating operation could not be claimed to be an economizing one, that is, total costs might be found to outrun productive benefits.

Power-inspired quasi-economizing of this kind is rarely if ever dependent on the operation of ecologizing values. Often, these values are defeated or diminished as power wielders lord it over their respective ecosystems. **Diversity** within corporate ranks—whether of personnel, thoughts, opinions, work-relevant ideas, methods, means of measuring organizational success, or modes of communication—may well be seen as anathema to corporate purpose and goals. Diversity, pluralism, and lack of a focused organizational discipline can loom as a decided threat to an established corporate power system. The same rejection of diversity occurs if an ecosystem's diverse natural components stand in the path of a sought-after corporate project, whether a parking lot, a shopping center, a power line, a timber supply, or an increased share of the annual tuna catch. In these and similar cases, ecological diversity stands well below the organization's top priority of expansion and "development," which usually leads to augmentation of the company's power base by shifting part of production costs from the company to the environment.

Linkages, on which natural ecologizing processes rest, are turned within the corporation to the needs of preserving internal power rather than to strengthening symbiotic ties. Employees are linked into the stair steps of the status ladder, each one expected to occupy a proper place and to proceed upward (if possible) by observing the power system's rules of the game for advancement. Externally, ecological linkages are imperiled if they are not consistent with internal corporate purpose, as may be seen when electric power companies and agricorporations combine to "control" or "tame" a river by damming it, thereby destroying or drastically transforming a riverine ecosystem rich in diverse life.

In depressingly similar ways, both **homeostatic succession** and **community** may be freely disregarded in favor of decisions and policies that promote more narrowly focused power goals centered in the corporation. Sponsored corporate change may be rapid and disruptive, and homeostasis of ecological systems disregarded, just as community process and community values may play second fiddle to the major rhythms of corporate expansionist strategy. Communities from Love Canal to Bhopal to Kiev bear witness to such ecological crimes of devastating magnitude.

The best that can be said for the operation and effect of power-aggrandizing values, when they confront ecologizing values, is that the power and privileges of an oligarchic group (along with their supporters) are promoted and protected, hence expanding their delimited life chances. Without question, quasi-economizing gives life to some while diminishing it for others. To that extent, it is evolutionarily supportive of specific life units where brought to bear. But the entropic price paid by all who are not swept up in the circle of power or not suckled on power's tempting teats is indeed a high price. The general magnification of power appears to loom large over all four ecologizing values, perhaps poised to pulverize each one if power's purposes dictate that outcome.

Once again, it is possible to discern differences of scale in the operation of nature's three major value clusters. Ecological process proceeds across wide horizons, taking its meaning and function from an interconnected network that in many respects is truly global in dimension and generating an ecological community of organisms integrated through intricately interwoven natural (and additionally, for humans, sociocultural) processes. Economizing too is global in scope though focused within individual organisms, as well as operating in reproductive groups, genealogical populations, species, and ecosystems of varying size and complexity. Less diffuse than ecologizing and more directly centered on survival, sustenance, and development, economizing's effective scale is less encompassing though still life-supporting.[46]

As widespread through nature as power aggrandizement appears to be, it nevertheless exerts its influence within relatively contained systems, whether being a function of phylogenetic impulses leading to dominance behavior or of socially acquired and psychologically implanted urges to dominate others. To be expressed, power needs actors to wield the hegemonic instruments of control, just as those actors require organizational structures through which their power can be channeled and implemented. The exercise of power is thus delimited to specific locales and must be directed to identifiable purposes. Power is focused, not diffuse; concentrated, not widespread; and

---

46. Eldredge and Grene, op. cit., distinguish between genealogical (reproductive) systems and ecological (economizing) systems, but they go on to argue that the former is dependent upon the latter. For them, economic activity is a "matter–energy transfer process" that occurred first at simple cellular levels and later at an organismic level, which makes their concept consistent with the thermodynamic definition of economizing adopted in the present account. In time, economic activity of this sort then supports increasingly complex manifestations of life (such as genealogical groups), as well as interlinked life forms that are not genealogically related but that depend for their survival upon the mutually supportive ecosystems in which they dwell. The authors maintain that social systems among organisms, including humans, arise when the genealogical (reproductive) system and the economic (ecological) system, separately organized and evolved in parallel, are reunited. For the full story, see op. cit., especially Chapters 3, 5, and 7.

grants its rewards narrowly rather than expansively. In these ways, the power-aggrandizing value cluster appears to operate at a scale of lesser scope and magnitude than either of the other master value clusters. The corporate form is marvelously fit to focus power in specific operational ways. Its rank-order hierarchy ensures deference to managerial authority. Its reward and punishment rules secure broad general compliance from both aspiring and cowed employees. The psychological and financial bonuses accruing to the power holders are sufficient to sustain continuing efforts to preserve the entire structure.

Of the three value clusters, ecologizing is the most comprehensive. Ecological process enfolds economizing, drawing its anti-entropic tendencies into a broader realm of diverse life that displays mutualistic survival consequences. Ecological networks also overarch the institutionalized particle points where power is focused and its magnification is pursued. The value dynamics of both nature and culture reveal that economizing and power aggrandizement can work against or even contradict ecological potentials. These value intersections thus become the forcing bed of issues that pose some of the most fundamental dilemmas for business and the human community.

THE CENTRAL ECOLOGICAL VALUE PROBLEM

What, then, after all, is the central value problem that emerges from an understanding of ecological phenomena? Surely, the core issue is not, as so many popular accounts tell it, restoring nature's "balance" or "harmony," for there is none. Nor does the ecological value challenge call for humanity to stand aside while nature works its wonders in the splendid isolation of its wilderness areas, for humans are an integral part of nature itself and therefore incapable of a passive role. Neither does "preserving" wilderness and green spaces or any other manifestations of a pristine nature capture the essence of the ecological challenge (save for those few social-environmentalist elites whose esthetic sensibilities may be bruised by intrusive traces of "artificial" human artifacts such as discarded cans, plastics, and other civilizational detritus). "Preservation" of nature is impossible and has been since the beginning of life on earth, because all life forms constantly change and all ultimately fall prey to the second law of thermodynamics. In the long run, nothing is preserved; 99 percent of all species that have ever lived on earth are extinct. Not even "recycling," which now enjoys an unprecedentedly widespread allegiance, lies at the heart of the ecological conundrum.

Let us look instead through a broader and deeper field of vision that invokes the ancient lineages of evolutionary process, that acknowledges the place of humanity within nature, that accepts with equanimity the limits within which human purpose can be envisioned and sought, and that embraces the ever-changing life-scape that knows no fixed equilibrium and establishes no precise boundaries within or between the natural and cultural worlds. Emerging ever more clearly from that perspective is the core value issue presently facing business and society. The evolutionary forces and thermodynamic energy flows that spawned both economizing and ecologizing—along with their associated Value Clusters I and II—present humankind with a conundrum of immense proportions and nearly incomprehensible complexity.

The central challenge is to blend and harmonize these two value systems—economizing and ecologizing—in ways that sustain human purposes within the constraints and opportunities of the still evolving system of nature and culture. Reconciling economy and ecology is of central interest to both business and society. These two frequently opposed processes—each one rooted securely within both nature and culture—have indeed pitted business and society against one another in bitter and protracted struggles. Business has justifiably claimed to have been damaged and rendered less economically efficient as environmentalists have successfully pressed their case along a front including air and water pollution, chemical waste dumping, ozone depletion, global warming, acid rain damage, agricultural chemicals and farm-waste runoff, radiation perils, reduced biodiversity, and other environmental insults. The resultant public policy constraints, taking the form of laws, regulations, fines, and prison sentences, have purchased a measure of public protection and public confidence at the comparatively high price of lowered economic efficiency and diminished competitive standing.

Typically, both parties have continued to feel that their vital interests are threatened by the legislative compromises that tend to be produced. Rarely have business representatives and environmental groups risen above their own respective, narrowly perceived vested interests to confront the issues embedded in the clash of economizing values and ecologizing values.[47] Even when they do, each tends to remain committed almost maniacally to a preconceived notion of the common good and what it would take to realize that cherished condition. Common value ground has been notoriously difficult to find. Nor has the search been made easier by the persistence of power-aggrandizing values wielded by the leaders of both public and private institu-

---

47. For good examples, see Charles W. Powers, *The Role of NGOs [Nongovernmental Organizations] in Improving the Employment of Science and Technology in Environmental Management*, working paper, New York: Carnegie Commission on Science, Technology, and Government, May 1991; and Jay D. Hair, "A Second Look at Regulation," *Conservation Exchange*, vol. 11, no. 1, Summer 1993, pp. 2, 8.

tions, who with distressing frequency insist on exercising the privileges of the powerful, with little regard for the larger economic and ecological systems on which all life depends.

So, the central question arises: Is reconciliation possible? Can common value ground be discovered and taken? Can morals that embrace the global life needs of humans and their diverse, closely linked life companions of the plant and animal worlds be identified, cultivated, nourished, and brought forward to offset the ever-present entropic trends laid at the earth's doorstep by thermodynamic processes? Concerting our life-sustaining and life-expanding values—those of economizing (Value Cluster I) and ecologizing (Value Cluster III)—would seem to qualify as the highest of human priorities—but only, of course, if those values themselves are recognized and accepted as central to human purposes, a condition not yet widely realized. Finding the desired value base involves more than just developing an advanced understanding of nature, although such wisdom is a crucial part of the story. Showing a "respect for nature" is also compatible with the needed approach since it recognizes the presence and working out of natural processes that affect human purpose, but by itself it too is insufficient.

Nothing will do but to launch an active search that somehow rises above the rootedness of human cultural routine while remaining aware of our natural origins and of the anchors by which we are fixed within nature. The search can proceed in no other way than through the application of our collective intelligence, mediated by the tools and scientific understandings accumulated through cultural accretion over many centuries, and with an awareness that humans alone among all other creatures and organisms appear to conceive a conscious sense of purpose for themselves within a natural world. The key that opens this door of quest and discovery may well be the symbol skills that lie at the foundations of human culture. They too are one outcome of an evolutionary process that produced the human brain and thereby spawned symbol-based human culture. Language, play, tools and technology, ritual and ceremonial drama, and art forms of great variety, along with many other symbolic manifestations, are the likely raw materials from which humanly invented human purpose—and business purpose—can be reconciled and coupled with the life-giving forces of economizing and ecologizing. That story, or at least its prelude, is told in the following chapter.

7

The Values Within Technology

This chapter examines a commonly neglected source of normative guidance. It finds values and normative orientations embedded within the technological realm of human behavior. These technological values and principles are proposed as possible sources of reconciling the several value clashes that separate business and society, particularly the seemingly intractable issues that accompany rampant business economizing occurring within the constraints of finite ecological systems.

Seeking an answer within the technological component of human culture will seem odd to some. Religious figures, many scholars, common citizens, and a small cottage industry of social critics alike have long inveighed against technology's baleful influence on human affairs. Some of the choicest invective of social critics has been reserved for condemning technology's materialist orientation, its regimentation of behavior, the impersonal character it imparts to life's daily human exchanges, and the frustrating, impenetrable shell it seems to pull around itself after having subjected the citizenry to any number of technical abuses.[1]

While not denying that technology can exert negative influence on human affairs, this chapter argues for an alternative and more positive view of technology's normative significance for society. Doing so is not to say that there are technological solutions for all of today's major economic and ecological problems. Nor is it to aver, in the ways of many a witless optimist, that technology will save us from present and future dangers if only we persevere in engineering ingenuity and technical wizardry. Rather, the case is made that technology harbors a normative orientation that is fully compatible with humanity and humaneness, with nature and culture, with economizing and

1. A particularly strident example of this kind of criticism is Neil Postman's *Technopoly: The Surrender of Culture to Technology*, New York: Alfred A. Knopf, 1992.

ecologizing, and with the thermodynamic processes on which human affairs and all life rest. This normative platform comprises an evaluative standard for judging business-and-society issues and for coming to grips with questions of workplace ethics, which are discussed in the following chapters of this book.

The major thesis of the chapter is that *the values and logics within technology represent a way to address and help resolve the conflicts and contradictions between economizing, power aggrandizing, and ecologizing.* To grasp the normative possibilities inherent in the technological realm, one is required to reexamine and to imaginatively expand the very concept and meaning of technology itself, moving far beyond the machine-like and robot-like character normally attributed to all things technological. Technology has a human face that is frequently hidden from public view but that can be glimpsed, and even admired, if one can find ways to penetrate the dense obscurantist rhetoric of technology's social critics.

The central argument is supplemented by a subthesis: *the logics and values within technology are an outgrowth of genetics and culture, of evolutionary process and natural selection, and of thermodynamic energy flows.* Most remarkable of all, among all of the wondrous complexities of life on earth, is the emergence of this technological value set that enables human life in all of its variety to exist and persist in the face of entropic trends to the contrary. Technological value orientations are literally built into our very beings, found at our genetic core and lying deep within the structure of human culture. Once implanted in nature and culture, they have invited discovery and disclosure, have encouraged invention and elaboration, and have leaned toward improvement of the effects they exert on human affairs.

It is this deeply embedded normative orientation—supportive of both economizing and ecologizing—that can be a cause for hope that value reconciliation is achievable. If economy and ecology are to be concerted, if business and society are to live in harmony, then that concerted and harmonious outcome will be to a large extent a function of the technological values and logics that emerge from within the human genome and phenome and that find additional expression within human culture. There is nothing automatic or foreordained about it all. An outcome beneficial to humankind requires large doses of active human intelligence, sensitized to cultural and ethnic differences, and well informed about the constraints and opportunities presented by our natural origins. Entropy lurks without and within. Finding ways to fend it off for a while remains a useful, not to say essential, exercise. To explain just how technology may contribute to such a goal, and to the reconciliation of economizing and ecologizing, is the intention of this chapter.

The argument moves along four pathways. The first leads through some unexpected terrain in pursuit of technology's source, which is found to lie within both nature and culture. The discussion then reveals the cocoon-like nest that society constructs in which it cradles technology and shapes its uses. Business's stewardship of technology, and the subsequent societal dilemmas thus created, are then assessed. And a fourth pathway tells of a technological value system with a potential for helping to reconcile the value clashes that separate business and society.

THE WELLSPRING OF TECHNOLOGY

Until quite recently, tool use was cited as the distinguishing mark of humanity, a position that had to be abandoned when research and experimentation demonstrated that nonhuman animals (birds, apes, and others) displayed a suite of tool-using capabilities. A retreat was then made to tool *making* until still further research made clear that, among other tool-making creatures, chimpanzees are capable of manufacturing tools that they use to probe the tunnels of termites, to reach otherwise inaccessible food sources, and to perform other tool-assisted tasks.[2] The early anthropocentrically inspired efforts to distinguish humans from other creatures tended to coincide with a widespread view, largely urged by anthropologists, that the association of early tool use with the appearance of human culture hinted that technology was one of the early and most fundamental components of culture. From that time on, it has been the conventional view that technology—from crude stone and bone tools, clay pottery, and basketry to today's vastly more complex technologies—originated only as human culture emerged in the course of evolution. This functional linkage of culture and technology continues as a popular explanation of technology's point of origin.

That interpretation may well be partially accurate, because there is much archaeological and paleontological evidence to support the close functional and chronological connection between technology and human culture. But even if accurate, it is not the entire story. Technology is vastly older, much earlier, and more deeply implanted than even this early affiliation with human culture suggests. Technology's taproot extends far down into genetic systems of very ancient lineage, perhaps even to some of life's earliest and most rudimentary forms.

To grasp this view requires one to slough off preconceived conventional notions of technology as human-made objects, traits, procedures,

2. Carl Sagan and Ann Druyan, *Shadows of Forgotten Ancestors: A Search for Who We Are*, New York: Random House, 1992, pp. 391–399ff. J. W. K. Harris and Sileshi Semaw have found crude stone tools in Ethiopia that predate the earliest known humans by 500,000 years. *New York Times*, April 25, 1995, pp. B7, B9.

and systems. That which has been labeled "technology" has precursors within the genetic makeup of humans (and other life forms as well). One must be willing to extend the idea of technology backward through evolutionary time, beyond the threshhold of human culture, into the very processes that have made life possible and expandable. Calling these natural features "technology" may at first seem strange; it is certainly an unfamiliar usage. However, the rewards for doing so are considerable, for eventually it leads to a much richer and fuller understanding of human affairs and of the possibilities of achieving normative consensus on major issues facing business and society.

A Friendly Warning Label

Most discussions of technology begin by defining what is meant by the term, and so that will be the case here. Some accounts emphasize its physical aspects or components (tools and machines), others the technical traits (specialized knowledge and skills), still others the organizational implications (coordinated, disciplined, even regimented behavior), and a few acknowledge various cultural features that seem to accompany technological regimes (a receptivity to pragmatic rationality, an emergent scientific elite, and a tolerance for change and innovations). Finding a single label to convey the meaning of these (and other unmentioned) technical features is not easy and, in fact, is probably not feasible or plausible. Some of the great students of technology have tried using "technics" (Lewis Mumford), "technique" (Jacques Ellul), "instrument" (John Dewey), "machine process" (Thorstein Veblen), and "technology" or "life process" (Clarence Ayres), while others have preferred "tool," "machine," "mechanical process," "sociotechnical," "mechanical order," and so on. Each respective use tends to reflect the particular philosophic point of view taken by the user, which should surprise no one.

As will be argued in the following pages, the elusiveness or impreciseness of technology's meaning may well be due to its very character, so that it seems at different times and to different observers to project varying meanings that do not add up to a focused, universal image. The usage to be adopted here is a very broad, comprehensive one that spans both natural and cultural phenomena, and that version will be described in the following section. Such a view supports and is consistent with the general philosophic thrust, and the general evidentiary base, of the theory of business values being set forth in this book (also no surprise).

One way around the definitional difficulties is to realize that most meanings assigned to technology are metaphorical, not literal. They are intended to convey a character, a spirit, an inner trait that is larger, more encompassing, and closer to the truth being sought than the literal technical manifestations that can be seen, felt, handled, or encountered physically. That essential core character is sometimes detected as a sequential, ordered *process*, as when Ayres refers to "the life process" or Veblen to "the machine process" or Ellul to an all-embracing "technique." At other times, the spirit of technology may be realized more in the *effects or outcomes* it produces, such as a flow of goods or services, or a string of electronic signals conveying a decipherable message, or (for some) a commitment to materialistic ways of thinking and acting. Still others, though few in number, have envisioned artistic and aesthetic expressions as held together and given their meaning by the tools, symbols, and interwoven components of an artist's palette combined with an imaginative mind.

Regardless of outward form, all technology employed by humans rests on a symbolic base. This is true of physical tools and machines, the sociotechnical components of organization, and such abstract symbols as those employed in mathematical notation and analysis. Symbols are the root components of technology in all its forms. For that reason (which is to be explained more fully further along), *"technology" in the present account means the entire array of technical manifestations, physical tools and machines, behavioral features, organizational patterns, and abstract symbolic usages that can trace their functions and operations to a symbolic process rooted in genetic systems and expressed in sociocultural forms.*

To the possible objection that such a broad definition risks being too diffuse and general to be analytically useful, it is worth recalling the point made above that technology is not only many things at once but that its real significance at any one point is less in its tangible form than in the function it performs. Having a term that refers to the broad kinship that links diverse technological features to each other is an important reminder that technology's spirit—its essential significance—is more important than any physical, symbolic, or organizational features it may display. A physical tool is more important for what it can do than for the way it looks or feels. A mathematical symbol or a statistical concept is rarely sought for its aesthetic qualities (although it may have them) but rather for the contribution it can make to some analytic process. The tool and the symbol may both be referred to as forms of "technology," just as certain patterns of coordinated human behavior (as in a baseball or football team) owe their configuration to technical considerations. The element they share in common—the quality that identifies them as "technological" (rather than religious or political or mythological)—is a function and an operation that can be produced in no other way. That operational quality is set forth in the following pages.

Thus alerted, by means of this warning label, to the several definitional pitfalls that strew the path of any who seek to know the significance of technology, the reader is invited to explore yet one more account of how technology may play a central normative role in business affairs.

Technology and Economizing

Technology takes its core meaning from, and had its origins in, economizing. As told in earlier chapters, economizing is the core life activity of all biotic forms, from the simplest bacteria to the most complex, interlinked ecological networks of vegetation, animals, and humans. To economize is to absorb and process energy from the life unit's environment in sufficient amounts to sustain a basic life process. That is all that is required to establish viability, given an abiotic environment that does not exceed temperatures, chemical mixes, physical instabilities, and various meteorological conditions that render any part of the economizing process infeasible. Even the most violent episodes in the earth's past—giant asteroid and meteor impacts, vulcanism and mountain building, ice ages, mammoth wind and ocean storms, continental drift and submergence of vast land areas—have not stopped the surge of life on earth. In the course of evolution, millions of individual species have perished but millions of others have either survived or have emerged as new life forms in the very midst of cataclysmic and catastrophic events. Overall, life on earth has been a roaring economizing success story.[3]

For early and primitive life forms, economizing is carried forward through DNA genetic processing that encodes information and instructions in ways that make energy acquisition possible. This basic life process extends throughout all biota. Life units whose gene-based instructions prove to be compatible with the surrounding environment will succeed in obtaining the requisite food energy for economizing to occur and will perpetuate this particular set of encoded instructions in successive generations. For example, DNA instructions may direct an organism, say a plant, to behave in certain specified ways, such as sending down roots that process soil nutrients and producing flowers that yield nectar, which attracts bees or butterflies. Where DNA codes fail to provide sufficiently pliable or absorptive root systems or where the nectar supply is minimal or nonexistent, life falters. Natural selection simply means that some DNA-based traits (efficient roots and nectar production) are "selected for" and others (short, nonabsorptive roots and poor

---

3. Carl Sagan and Ann Druyan point out that although the earth is a vast graveyard, it also "brims over with life. . . . There is hardly a clod of soil, a drop of water, a breath of air that is not teeming with life. It fills every nook and cranny of our planet's surface." See Sagan and Druyan, op. cit., p. 411.

nectar production) are "selected against." In the one case, economizing goes forward; in the other, it does not. Hence, the economizing efficiency with which gene-encoded instructions function determines which life units live and which ones die out.

All life forms possess this kind of genetic technology. Without it, they would perish, either instantly or slowly. *It is life's most basic tool.* As natural selection reveals, some genetic tools are better, that is, more efficient, than others, as shown when some species and individuals become adept at economizing, while others become less adept to the point of being eliminated in the unceasing quest for life-sustaining energy. Genetic tools are not "manufactured," nor are they deliberately or with forethought designed, made, or constructed. They are simply part of natural biotic phenomena, a product of thermodynamic energy flows moving through chemical mediums and evolving evermore complex forms throughout the course of life's evolution on earth. If there were a genetic technology "factory," it would be found where genotypes send messages of economizing import to their host phenotypes, which then interact successfully (i.e., adaptively) with the environment. The factory's "output" would be diverse organic forms, functions, and behaviors—that is, the host phenotypes—that contribute to economizing.

The forms taken by genetic technology are legion within the organic realm. They are described in countless tomes of biology, botany, physiology, chemistry, physics, medicine, genetics, pharmacy, and so on. The genetic technology of most interest here is that which is characteristic of the primate order, which includes early and present human species. The reason for this focus is simple but profound: although inheritors of genetic technology, humans also possess cultural technology.

FROM GENETIC TECHNOLOGY
TO CULTURAL TECHNOLOGY

Because the concept of genetic technology is new and strange to students of technology, it will be helpful to describe the larger technological field that encompasses both genetic technology and cultural technology. These two technologies hold within their respective spheres all of humankind's potential for adaptation, survival, and flourishing. From each flow the vital impulses of economizing and ecologizing on which all life depends. The forms they take (or are given) and the functions they perform (or are permitted) can therefore determine the possibilities for reconciling these two life-supportive processes.

Genetic technology is endogenous, that is, it is self-contained within any given life unit. It is private and personal, though inherited genetically from many preceding generations. It consists of encoded "instructions" with economizing import acquired during conception as parents contribute their own respective halves to the newly formed genome; or perhaps more accurately, the new genome carries a potential for producing the genetic technology that will support economizing. The major forms of genetic technology that result will be described momentarily.

Cultural technology, on the other hand, is *for the most part* **exogenous**, that is, it works or operates only as life units interact with their environment *and with each other*. As will become evident in the ensuing discussion, some extremely important types of cultural technology are private and "internal," but most are decidedly social and interactive in operation and consequence. It is this exogenous, external, social trait of cultural technology that has contributed so heavily to the notion that human culture originated only when and as technology appeared, and vice versa. The surviving examples of early cultural technology, after all, are tangible in a real sense. Stone tools, stone lanterns, and stone and bone arrow and spear points can be seen, picked up, and measured. The stark reality of tools, as others have pointed out, may well have been responsible for a misreading of the early history of technology, particularly the belief that these artifacts were the beginnings of a phenomenon that, it is being suggested here, actually stretched much farther back into organic, evolutionary time. Perhaps the error lay in the attempt to define a beginning—an origin—that would mark out a distinctly *human* arena, anthropocentrically conceived, rather than with less drama to delineate the emergence of a new kind of life pattern rooted in the genetic past.

Figure 7–1, which depicts only bare outlines and relationships, may be useful in putting some order into the several different aspects of both genetic technology and cultural technology as the discussion goes forward. A subsequent figure fills in additional details.

Genetic Technology

Genetic technology among the evolutionarily later primates consists of two kinds of internal, gene-driven processes. One of these will be labeled "basal process." The other is called "symbolic process." From these two entirely organic processes is derived all of the genetic machinery needed for primate, and especially hominoid, economizing to occur prior to the emergence of human culture.

Basal process refers simply to the phenotypic features that are characteris-

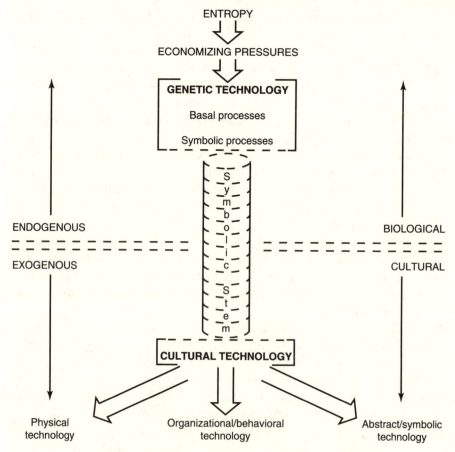

Figure 7–1. Genetic technology and cultural technology

tic of members of the primate order (some of which they share widely with other animal orders). These include *morphological traits* (body shapes and types, including bipedal and quasi-bipedal posture, binocular vision, body-covering hair, and other physical traits that permit their classification within the primate order); *physiological traits* (digestive systems, herbivorous and carnivorous appetites, heart-lung circulatory-respiratory systems, reproductive processes, and other bodily functions); and *behavioral traits* induced by genetic encoding (sociability, group and family bonding, territoriality, mating patterns, play and various random motility patterns, recognition and communication signals, and various other behaviors found among primates in general).

Such basal processes are, of course, the outcome of countless eons of evolutionary selection. While primates were evolving in these directions, other life orders were developing their own economizing "strategies" that permitted acquisition and processing of environmental energy.[4] What causes these particular basal processes to be classified as genetic technology is their participation in an economizing process that enabled this particular group of animals to survive and perpetuate these particular ways of ingesting and using energy. Plants—for example, temperate-zone trees—evolved different basal processes, with distinct ways of drawing nutrients from the soil, water, and air, and with a different suite of behavioral traits (very slow growth, periodic-cyclic nutrient uptake, acidic excretions to repel predators, a host of seed-dispersal techniques, etc.). Plant genetic technology has worked as well for plants' economizing needs as primate genetic technology has worked for the primate order's economizing needs. Natural selection produced each outcome. The variations in basal processes are simply another manifestation of the multiform patterns found within evolved life on earth.

Symbolic process is, most will acknowledge, a genetic-evolutionary phenomenon of overwhelming significance. The ability to form and manipulate mental symbols leads to a spectacular starburst of survival potential, an incredibly rich array of economizing feasibilities, an opening up of a vast menu of adaptive strategies upon which genetic process can play in "instructing" and "directing" phenotypic interactions with energy environments. It is truly an open door into a more secure economizing future for the simple reason that the door opens upon and reveals adaptive possibilities not available to those life forms that have not knocked at this particular genetic portal. The great ape and hominid groupings within the primate order manifest this symbolic process in greater degree than other orders and species. They therefore became the inheritors of a genetic technology whose eventual potential for economizing adaptivity has yet to be realized or even imagined. It was a genetic revolution worthy of being called the First Great Technological Revolu-

---

4. An unfortunate and erroneous connotation accompanies the use of "strategy" to describe economizing functions that stem from gene-based sources. A strategy is normally considered to be a consciously thought-out plan of action involving pursuit of a defined goal. Genes do not operate this way. They blindly and without forethought generate signals, impulses, and instructions that have an effect on the internal processes and external behavior of their host phenotypes. The result may be positive or negative insofar as harmonious interactions with the host's environment are concerned. Natural selection operating over long time periods favors gene-based traits that conduce to adaptation and selects against less adaptive ones. The entire process is unconscious, undirected, and nonteleological. The word "strategy" has acquired, whether justified or not, such an aura of preplanned, purposive, goal-seeking effort by individuals and organizations (especially large-scale business corporations) that one risks misunderstanding if it is used to describe gene-based economizing operations. Richard Dawkins in *The Selfish Gene* (Oxford: Oxford University Press, 1989) contributes to this terminological confusion, not only by the implications of the book's title but by many teleologically tinged passages throughout.

tion in evolutionary time (excepting, of course, those original life-generating and life-perpetuating processes that started it all).[5]

Symbolic process takes several different and successively linked forms. It permits—consists of—*mental abstractions*, that is, phenomena that exist in the imagination or are held in memory, images that somehow "exist" separated from the sentient, directly perceived context in which one lives and moves. Symbolic capability also allows the formation and expression of *concepts*, again an abstraction from immediate, "touchable" reality. *Foresight*—the ability to project onto a future time an imagined state of affairs—literally creates a new dimension of reality otherwise denied to those lacking such a mental function. *Hindsight*—memory, remembered experience—is immensely enriched and expanded when consisting of stored mental images (now fashionably called a "data bank") that can be called up on demand or when stimulated by particular environmental or behavioral cues. Symbolic process attains some kind of integrated plateau in nonhuman primates when mental images, abstractions, concepts, ideas, foreseen possibilities, and remembered experiences are brought together and focused on a problem facing the creature. At this point, *analysis* takes place. A chimpanzee, having been repeatedly frustrated by an inability to reach high enough to retrieve a food object, is seen to sit and apparently ponder this puzzle, followed by a quick move to shove a large box under the overhanging food that permits the chimpanzee to reach the prized object. Some rudimentary analytic process that involves abstraction, concept formation, foreseen possibility, and memory is surely manifest in these cases. One sees genetic technology at work as the chimp's symbolic processes swing into action to solve this problem.[6]

Symboling capability is a function of an elaborated neurological network found in varying degrees of development and complexity among the more recently evolved members of the primate order, mainly the great apes and hominids. Scholars still argue about the factors that brought on the emergence and further elaboration of this brain-neural system, but one does not need a definitive description or explanation of a particular evolutionary stimulus (even assuming there was one, or perhaps more) to realize that symbolic process in the primate order is one more outcome of genetic encoding interacting with diverse environments through primate phenotypes. Symbolic

---

5. One should not get too carried away about the glories of symbolic process. As noted in an earlier chapter, many nonsymbolically imbued creatures and plants have managed quite well as survival systems, outstripping the primates by several orders of chronological magnitude. Symbolic process may well serve adaptive functions for those creatures who inhabit changing and changeable environments, which would be true of primates, while other long-lived species (e.g., ancient redwood and juniper trees or cockroaches) occupy more stable environmental niches where species-specific basal processes serve well enough.

6. The episode is reported in Sagan and Druyan, op. cit., pp. 397–398.

process was "selected for" because it presumably provides its carriers with an array of economizing potentials that proved to have adaptive advantage. The frustrated chimpanzee seeking the out-of-reach bananas would have gone hungry but for a symbol-based analytic capability—and so would all such chimpanzees. Their economizing options were immeasurably extended, as was the adaptive potential of the entire species, as the components of the neural-brain symboling process emerged and were consolidated to permit rudimentary analytic thinking.

Cultural Technology

Cultural technology is an evolutionary outgrowth and extension of genetic technology. Though biologically rooted, cultural technology displays an extraorganic dimension that caused some earlier anthropologists to refer to all culture as the "superorganic."[7] Whereas genetic technology resides within each individual life unit (and is hence biologically and personally endogenous), cultural technology is largely an exogenous social possession that functions mostly through interactions among people (and among technological components themselves). Genetic technology is deeply rooted within the genome that imparts specific phenotypic traits to its host; cultural technology is much more public and external and can lead to myriad behavioral options. Cultural technology far outstrips genetic technology both in rate of change and in the range and power of its environmental influence. Mutational change in the genetic technology of individuals within a species most often displays a negative adaptive effect, while most changes that occur within the cultural technology of a society are, or are thought by many to be, advantageous and progressive (a matter to be examined further along). Cultural technology appears (perhaps falsely) to be so stupendously, so overwhelmingly more elaborated and outwardly more complex than genetic technology, plus making possible such an enormous array of behavioral and mental regimes, as to make comparison of the two technologies seem futile. Little wonder that the biological roots of cultural phenomena have found such meager (and often scornful) notice among most observers whose gaze has been transfixed by culture's splendors.[8]

7. A. L. Kroeber, *Anthropology*, Harcourt, Brace & World, 1923, 1948, p. 253: "'Superorganic' means simply that when we consider culture we are dealing with something that is organic but which must also be viewed as something more than organic if it is to be fully intelligible to us."

8. Attitudes may change as more is learned about the human genome, whose 3 billion base-pairs are being decoded by the Human Genome Project. Genetic complexity and variation may turn out to be vastly greater and more intricate than the cultural variations that can presently explain many different kinds of human behavior.

In spite of these obvious differences, it was across a bridge constructed of genetic materials that technology marched out of genome and across that elusive boundary between pre-culture, prehuman existence into the realm of culture and modern humanity. As it marched, human technology began to throw off some of its vestigial genetic constraints, acquiring a capacity for options, choices, and flexibility unknown in previous evolutionary time. The linking element was what might be called the **symbolic stem** or **taproot of technology**, which is depicted in Figure 7–2. The older evolutionary end of that stem lies within and gives effect to the basal processes and symbolic processes of genetic technology, as described above and shown in Figure 7–1. On the newer, more recent end, the symbol systems of primates take new and different forms and discharge unique functions.

Among those new operations, one observes a great expansion of the memory function as storage and retrieval become more efficient. Memory makes possible cumulative, generational learning, thus acquiring a social rather than a purely personal dimension. Symbolic language greatly en-

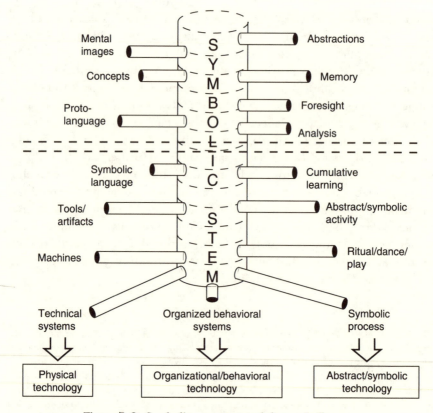

Figure 7–2. Symbolic processes and the symbolic stem

hances communication of complex ideas, concepts, and abstractions, and thus draws tighter links among the members of social groupings. Simultaneously, language injects a previously unknown flexibility into social relationships of affiliative groups. Rudimentary physical tools, those so-called "precursors" of culture, can be envisioned, crudely shaped, and their practice and usages passed on to others. Tools, traps, and cooperative hunting schemes, in turn, enable food to be obtained more effectively; again, the interactive nature of this newly emergent cultural technology becomes apparent.

At some phantom point in primate evolution, or perhaps at many different points repeated over extended periods of time, that astonishing genetically rooted symbolic stem had generated enough neurological potential to make possible these new forms of technology that somehow seemed to be manifesting something unique in evolutionary history. No one knows how large or of what chronological dimensions was the genetic-cultural vestibule through which the symbolic stem thrust itself in the course of evolutionary change. But when it emerged on the near side of evolutionary time, a new phenomenon had appeared. Cultural technology was on the march, shaping human affairs in both wondrously adaptive and evolutionarily problematic ways.[9]

The Elaborations of Cultural Technology

Figure 7–3 summarizes the three major forms taken by cultural technology: physical technology, organizational-behavioral technology, and abstract symbolic technology. Each will be discussed.

A glance at the technological landscape reveals a seeming litter and tangle of **physical devices**: Tools of every conceivable design for every conceivable use. Machines whose moving, meshed parts perform the myriad tasks and chores considered important to the human race. Physical artifacts ranging from household and office furniture to the buildings that contain them. Networks of tools, machines, and physical devices linked by electric wires and electronic signals. Vast collections of books, articles, records, and archives fill up libraries, while those somewhat mysterious, unseen collections of electronic symbols comprise computerized data banks. Also invisible but decidedly present are the swift communication microwaves that speed messages through the air, outer space, and around the globe. This physical realm of technology that bulks so large in everyday life is what many are accustomed to calling "technology."

9. The anthropologist Leslie A. White was an early social scientist who identified the symbol and symbolic behavior as defining the human condition. See especially Chapter II, The Symbol: The Origin and Basis of Human Behavior, in *The Science of Culture*, New York: Grove Press, 1949.

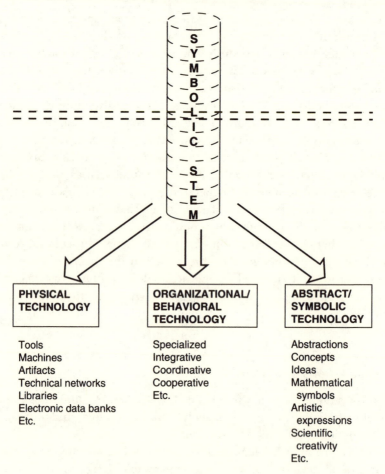

Figure 7–3. Forms of cultural technology

Others, however, have pointed to a second technological manifestation that is sometimes thought to be even more basic than the tool-machine-network component. If one is to have and enjoy the benefits of technology, a behavioral price must be paid. **Technology organizes human behavior**, requires a disciplined approach, calls forth specific human skills and talents, brings its users into patterned relationships, spreads out among the user-group a range of tasks to be performed in sequence and according to a logic that is found within the tools themselves rather than in the personal impulses of the users. At a rudimentary level, there is a proper way to drive a nail with a hammer; a mashed finger, a bent nail, and a failed task await the user who ignores the built-in demands of this simple technological device. At a more advanced level, a heart-lung organ transplant operation calls for intense coordination of a host of machines and skilled medical personnel, each performing a specialized part of the overall task, according to the most exacting technical and medical standards. In both cases, the technology itself has dictated the resultant behavior of the users.

This regimented, coordinated, cooperative, specialized behavioral trait of technology has exercised the fears of many observers who believe that it deprives humanity of freedom of action and initiative, strips away personal autonomy, imposes a collectivist regime on society, and creates an automaton-like personality ripe for the blandishments of political dictators and lunatic figures of all kinds. By contrast, others have felt that technology expands human options, while the behaviorally integrative trait of technology moves humankind closer to a sense of community and shared fate, as each person depends to a large degree on the skills and cooperation of many others if life's challenges are to be met successfully.[10] That controversy will be revisited further along in this chapter.

A third pathway taken by cultural technology is the **vast extension of genetic technology's most unique feature—the symbol**. It seems to be reasonably well established that the increasing size of the hominid brain, along with its continued specialization of mental functions, permitted the symboling capability of human primates to go beyond the relatively limited symbol-based behavior of the great apes. All of those primitive symboling functions known earlier—abstraction, concept formation, memory, foresight, analysis, proto-language—somehow broke out into more creative and complex manifestations. For all their tool-using and tool-making skills, chimpanzees do not have libraries or art galleries, nor have they invented computers, or journeyed to the moon, or devised the calculus, or gathered themselves into symphony orchestras, or composed the Koran. If one wishes to play anthropocentric games, it would be well to rest one's case on this aspect of cultural technology, for there is a clear human advantage present in advanced symbolic behavior.

Two additional features of cultural technology are worth noting. Each tends to be associated with the symbolic, abstract branch of technology. Cultural technology is very ancient; moreover, it both accumulates in volume and establishes firm habits of mind and behavior. Once possessed, it is not easily surrendered. Since it has served an adaptive purpose, one wishes to cling to it as a trusted friend. But, as will be told subsequently, technology is also progressive, so that old tools and practices become obsolete, bypassed by newer forms that serve human adaptive needs more effectively. New generations of tools may play havoc with the accustomed ways of older and passing

10. For the dire view, see Jacques Ellul, *The Technological Society*, New York: Alfred A. Knopf, 1964, 1967. For the more optimistic perspective, see Clarence E. Ayres, *Toward a Reasonable Society*, Austin: University of Texas Press, 1961.

human generations who neither welcome nor adapt to the new technical wonders. When habit and custom retain technology beyond its prime, one might be justified in referring to these obsolete forms as "technological shards"—broken pieces of once-useful devices and ideas. These shards are echoes, shadows, and phantoms of old technologies—old friends, so to speak—that one does not wish to abandon. They engender stories, legends, myths, oral traditions, dance, and ritual that incorporate cultural memories of past times, often preserved in such museums as the Smithsonian Institution. As such, they probably continue to give emotional comfort by easing the sometimes painful transition to newer practices and customs brought and imposed by technological progress. They also display a darker side in the role they are sometimes given by those who pursue power over others, by dint of the sentimental, romantic associations that may be captured and played upon (as in Hitler's appeal to Germany's past military, scientific, and technological mastery, along with the fantasy of racial superiority). As the technological shards sink into oblivion, their demise is accompanied by the dirge of myth, legend, and ritual—a mourning, so to speak, marking the passing of a beloved friend.

Beyond the bypassed technological shards is another remarkable phenomenon of cultural technology. This riotous realm of symbolic behavior is difficult to characterize in simple terms. Most have called it the creative component of human culture, although creativity also appears elsewhere within the technological context. Artistic and aesthetic expressions of all kinds gather here—poetry, music, painting, sculpture, staged drama, films, opera, photography, cinematography, mathematical discovery, theoretical speculation, scientific creativity, the play element and random experimentation (Thorstein Veblen's "idle curiosity"), the unceasing quest for novelty, and on and on throughout the imaginative wanderings of the human psyche and the human intellect. This intellectual fountain is most likely the "engine" that powers the symbolic process, the region of technological activity that is at the leading edge of continuing evolutionary emergence, the intellectual pathway into a yet unimagined symbolic future. This restless, ever-active, random-search function bursts the bonds of older economizing constraints and, within the brief but brilliant flash of human intellect at its finest, momentarily escapes the clutches of entropic doom. Here is to be found the seat of human intellectual exploration, whose full potential will be needed if the several economizing and ecologizing functions and services of technology are to be more clearly focused on both adaptive and creatively fulfilling human purpose.

While it is true that cultural-symbolic technology is purposive, pragmatic, and consciously created, it displays a kind of open-endedness that is not found in the more ancient genetic technology. With the exception of maladaptive mutations, genetic technology is devoted entirely to economizing, that is, to the survival needs of the host phenotype. Natural selection ensures this functional focus on economizing by "selecting against" the genetic technology that does not encode adaptive practices. But the human symbolic process opens up many diverse behavioral possibilities to which cultural technology may be devoted. They need not all be economizing in effect or result. They may carry well beyond adaptation and survival, greatly expanding the array of behavioral, emotional, and intellectual opportunities. Among these, as noted, are artistic, aesthetic, and many other kinds of creative symbolic expressions. Crossing that evolutionary threshhold was, in a sense, a bit like the Biblical dilemma faced by Adam and Eve when they ate the fruit of the Tree of Knowledge of Good and Evil. Having acquired god-like powers, they faced (as does humanity now) previously unknown choices. How, then, is that newly acquired creative intelligence to be used? For good or evil? For economizing alone? For power aggrandizement? For ecological harmony? For psychological enrichment? These are the choices to which a humanity that is fast losing its scientific innocence is being pushed.

All of (human) genetic technology and the vast bulk of cultural technology serve human economizing needs, for which we can be grateful. Both technologies also are caught up in power and domination impulses and practices, from which we suffer uncounted abuses. Whether the open-endedness and creativity displayed by abstract symbolic technology can be turned to the reconciliation of human economizing and human ecologizing purposes depends, in the final analysis, on the peculiar but very characteristic way that technology is encapsulated within a tissue of social institutions, habits, and practices. For all of its adaptive potential, technology in the end functions only as its human users and their particular cultures direct. Clarifying that link between human institutions and cultural technology is directly ahead. But first, the several logics of symbol-based cultural technology require attention. For they, too, have much to say about technology's fate in human hands.

THE LOGICS OF CULTURAL TECHNOLOGY

Were cultural technology to be left to its own impulses and internal processes, it would be seen to operate according to several diverse but interrelated logical regimes. Each of these logics seems to be built into the structure and functioning of technology. They have much to do with the general directions and the particular usages to which we humans put our technological adeptness. These logics shape and drive activities in all three realms of cultural technology discussed above—physical technology, organizational-be-

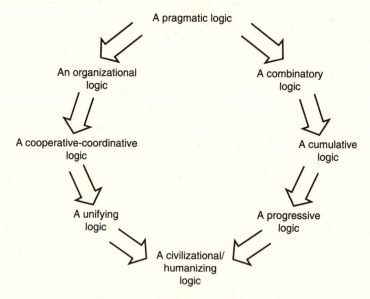

Figure 7–4. The circle of techno-logics

havioral technology, and abstract conceptual technology. This phenomenon we call technology displays sequence, regimen, pattern, and direction as it draws its human practitioners into behavioral combinations and attitudinal orientations congenial to its inherent operations and functions. These logics, which have been noted and described by many students of technology, have much—but not total and complete—influence on the ways that technology serves, or fails to serve, adaptive as well as creatively fulfilling human purposes.

Figure 7–4 displays nine major logics that govern technological operations. As the discussion proceeds, an interweaving kinship will be noted among the various logics. Some pairs and trios are more closely related to each other than to others, and certain interrelated patterns or spheres are discernible. Figure 7–5 may be a useful guide to the various patterned relationships. The sway that the logics hold over business affairs is treated later in this chapter.

A Pragmatic Logic

Technology is a way to get things done. Much of its appeal is in its usefulness and in the related satisfactions produced. Tools can be used to solve a problem, as hominoid apes discovered when they found that a stick could be inserted into termite nest tunnels to extract tasty treats. So too did early humans apparently find out that rocks could be shaped into tools for pounding,

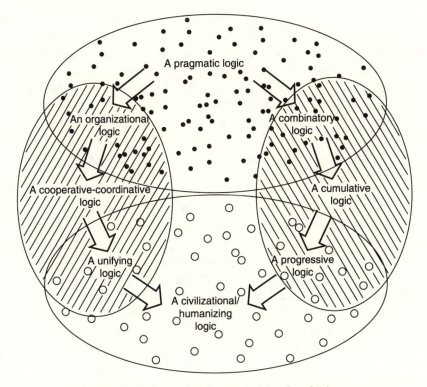

Figure 7–5. Interrelated patterns of techno-logics

breaking, grinding, piercing, and cutting. If symbolically produced sounds can be given specific meanings, as they were when symbolic communication emerged, they can be combined with hand and body signals in ways that enhance group communication, social interactions, and behavioral cues that contribute to more effective hunting, food gathering, and protection against predators. Ritual, dance, ceremonials, magical incantations, and other such symbolic imagery can convey a sense of shared fate and social solidarity, again supporting practical goals and satisfactions unachievable otherwise. Technology's pragmatic logic is without doubt an outgrowth and an extension of genetic technology's economizing function, which was the first great practical problem to be solved if life was to continue. "Getting things done"—tackling practical tasks in satisfying ways—is a hallmark of today's as well as yesterday's technology.

A Combinatory Logic

Interlinked parts and integrated functions are native to all of cultural technology. "Things fit together and function together" captures the spirit of this techno-logic. Many technological items themselves are combinations of previously existing components; this is true of an automobile, any common household appliance, and the countless machines scattered about the technological landscape. Newly assembled components function in an integrated fashion to produce effects not previously known; for example, the automobile carries more passengers further, faster, more surely, and in greater comfort than the covered wagon. The same "fitting-together" logic applies to the behavioral procedures and skills that are part of the technological phenomenon; for example, in performing an intricate surgical operation, doctors, nurses, and aides follow a tightly defined routine beginning long before the patient is brought to the operating theater and continuing throughout and well beyond the surgery itself. Serious deviation from this step-by-step regimen may defeat the operation's goal and threaten the patient's well-being or life. The things-fit-together logic applies as well within the realm of abstract symbolizing, as painters, sculptors, poets, and musicians realize when they create works of art by combining insights, expressions, sounds, materials, and thoughts into new patterns that convey unique meaning to themselves and others. Except for the technological shards that drop from functional use, technology's multiform component parts are drawn together for the simple reason that they function better that way.[11]

A Cumulative Logic

Technology accumulates over time, an observation so obvious as to require little elaboration concerning the overall volume and diversity of tools, machines, routines, and accompanying behaviors. However, the logic that impels this cumulative process deserves comment. Technology does not accumulate simply because more and more people acquire the *same kinds of tools* that others have previously possessed. For example, the greater number of cars on the world's roads is a greater tribute to marketing skills than to innovative production genius; it does not signify cumulative buildup to a new form of technology. The cumulative logic of technology can be seen in any sequence of technical development. Examples include the astonishing magnification of electronics that had its beginnings in the transistor; the successive waves or generations of computer technology built up from the microprocessor and the miniaturization of the patterned instructions that drive both software and hardware; and the increasingly complex tool kit of the auto repair

11. The phrase adopted here—"combinatory logic"—should not be confused with an identical phrase used in the field of symbolic logic. There it refers to a particular branch of symbolic logic. Here it refers to the combination of technological components, as well as the likelihood that, over time, tools and symbols will be fitted together into new patterns and relationships with each other.

garage, now largely dependent upon computer-assisted diagnostic technology and the ability to interpret computer output. "One thing (logically) follows another" is the core idea of technology's cumulative logic. Greater volume and variety of technological devices and symbols and greater complexity of operations, along with more complicated behavioral demands, are normally seen. This logic is closely linked to the combinatory logic previously discussed. It is, in a sense, the combinatory logic expressed over time. Because "things fit together" (the combinatory logic), "one thing follows another" (the cumulative logic).

A Progressive Logic

As Figure 7–4 is intended to suggest, *because* a pragmatic logic leads toward a combinatory logic and *because* the combining of technologies produces a cumulative effect, a fourth logic—a progressive one—emerges as technology develops over time.

The history of any distinct line of technological development exhibits a progression of form and functional outcome. This effect can be seen, for example, in dentistry equipment, computer technology, musical instrumentation, powered transportation, communication devices, lighting, mining equipment, art forms (painting, sculpture, music, dance, et al.), mathematical notation and symbols, and on and on. The pressure to solve problems, the fact that new combinations of tools prove pragmatically more effective, and the cumulative buildup of new technologies that occurs over time lead toward progressively more effective ways to confront the kinds of problems for which technology is required. The high-speed dental drill does its work faster, more thoroughly, and with less discomfort for the patient than the older and slower mechanical one. Today's computers calculate faster, store greater amounts of data, retrieve information more quickly, and offer users a vastly greater array of analytic and display possibilities than previous computer generations did. Coal miners extract more coal at less per unit cost, with fewer miners, penetrate further and deeper into coal seams, recover a greater proportion of coal not previously accessible, and do so with less risk of life than in earlier times. The piano, first introduced as a major instrument during the eighteenth century, not only proved to be superior to the harpsichord as a performing instrument (more flexible in dynamic range—hence, its name, "pianoforte"—and its tonal volume more audible to a large audience), but its successive versions also demonstrated constant improvement of its internal mechanisms, materials, framework, sounding board, strings, and overall durability. In all of these cases, the pragmatic work to be done is done better, more quickly, at less per unit cost, and with various other progressive effects associated with particular tools.

Technology's progressive logic simply means that improvement occurs over time in accomplishing the particular task or function that any given set of tools or symbols is intended to do. This is not to say—and this book does not argue—that these improvements are unmixed blessings. Building bigger and better bombs to pulverize one's enemies, or enhancing crop production by using improved chemical fertilizers, or storing sensitive personal medical information in computerized data banks, or finding technical ways to increase the speed and power of automobiles—these and other technologically progressive developments may introduce unacceptable risks, and they are discussed further along. Put another way, "progressive" is not being spelled with a capital "P" in a way that generalizes the improvement effects seen in technological development to all human affairs. Without doubt, some lines of technology (e.g., diagnostic medical technology) have inserted into human society an effect that unquestionably improves the lives and life prospects of those who can avail themselves of it. For them, life is indeed better; progress has in truth been recorded. Only the most willful and sentimental attachment or addiction to obsolete technological shards permits a contrary conclusion. But recognizing technology's inherent progressive logic need not commit one to a happy-go-lucky, mindless optimism that disregards the baleful effects that may accompany improved tools. More is said about this matter further along.

Once technology accumulates and demonstrates its pragmatic effects and potentials, there is strong pressure to change to new forms that will perform their functions in improved ways. The test of technological progressivity is a pragmatic one: Can the job be done more effectively, quicker, with greater overall impact, or lessen human burdens or pain, or provide more alternative ways to approach a given problem, or extend beneficial effects to larger numbers of people? As noted earlier, technology's midwife was pragmatism and its first word was "economize." From that pragmatic cradle, technology has extended its combinatory, cumulative, progressive vocabulary into countless human realms. And even today, its leading innovative edge moves constantly outward to seek more effective ways for humans to solve their practical problems and achieve their genetic and cultural potentials.

A Cooperative-Coordinative Logic

Because tools, procedures, and symbol-based ideas fit together functionally, technology induces cooperative behavior from its users. The cooperative, coordinative impulse stems from the technology itself and requires no other motive.

There does appear to be an exhilaration, a pleasurable sense of working together, a "teamwork" motif that is frequently sensed when all the pieces of a technologically based procedure are brought together to accomplish a group's goal. That may explain the exuberant though physically bizarre actions of sports teams when they make a goal, win a pennant, or secure a championship. Scientists and engineers also have been seen to celebrate, though somewhat more soberly, a successful space launch or the winning of a Nobel prize or the accurate anticipation of a volcanic eruption (as occurred in the 1991 eruption of Mount Pinatubo in the Philippines). What is being celebrated is a realization by team members that they have managed to bring the pieces of a technological complex together in functionally correct ways, whether in the rough-and-tumble of sports, in the complicated realm of the research laboratory, or amid the irregularities of volcanic forces. In each case, cooperation and coordination are brought forth by the necessity of adhering to technological routines. Sports games define the permitted range of goal-scoring offensives and strategies; laboratory scientists work within well-defined research values and methodological guidelines; and vulcanologists depend upon the reports and impulses coming from several different kinds of instruments. Technology, by its very nature, induces and favors cooperative, integrative, coordinative interactions among its users.

As noted in an earlier chapter, business firms attempt to build teamwork within their labor force, knowing the importance of coordinating all of the intricate parts and functions of, say, an automobile assembly line. Well-known manufacturing experiments have demonstrated the utility of creating small-scale production teams of workers who then provide for themselves the needed division of tasks, the assignment of individual responsibility, and the coordination required by the task at hand. The technology of automobile production defines a behavioral necessity—tools must be brought together in functionally meaningful ways, and that calls for close cooperation among the tool users. "Doing one's own thing" or, as one source has advocated, pursuing on-the-job "personal projects" contradicts the coordinative logic found in technological operations.[12] Such a self-willed autarchy leads to technological anarchy by eroding the cooperative basis on which complex technologies depend. A price paid for advanced technology includes a willingness to coordinate one's behavior with others, along with the routines and operations of the tools themselves.

---

12. See R. Edward Freeman and Daniel R. Gilbert, Jr., *Corporate Strategy and the Search for Ethics*, Englewood Cliffs, NJ: Prentice-Hall, 1988, especially Chapter 8.

An Organizational Logic

Technology's organizational logic is embedded in, and draws strength from, two other logics already discussed: the combinatory logic and the cooperative-coordinative logic. As tools and symbols are combined into ever more complex and newer patterns, the human behavior surrounding the new combinations must necessarily adjust to the changed circumstances. An example is seen in the sprawl of suburban communities brought about by the automobile, with all of the attendant changes in household routines, shopping patterns, traffic congestion, and urban finance. People follow where tools and symbols lead them.

The coordinative tendencies brought forth by advanced technological systems do indeed induce cooperation among those who work with tools, for the simple reason that the work cannot go forward on any other basis. People must therefore be related to one another, that is, they must be organized along technical lines if they wish to enjoy the fruits of technology's productive potential. The organizational design springs from the technology itself and from what the tools are capable of doing. A symphony orchestra, for example, lends itself to a certain proportion of different kinds of musical instruments that are arranged (i.e., organized) in patterns that contribute to a balance of musical sounds. The same kind of organizational impulse is present in enterprises ranging from a dry cleaning plant, to a hospital, to a school, to a stock exchange; in each case, the core technology draws its operatives and directors into organizational systems suited to the technical functions to be exploited. People follow tools.

Technological organization is not hierarchical in the sense of the status hierarchies discussed in an earlier chapter. There, graded levels of status rank separate one group from another, and ceremonial precedence typically defines how these different ranks should address one another and how they are properly to interact. The core organizing principle of rank-order hierarchy is the consolidation and preservation of power. This is accomplished by a careful delineation of behavior permitted to the occupants of organizational status roles. Whereas technological organization establishes relations among participants on the basis of the functions they can contribute to the successful operation of the tools being manipulated, hierarchical organization links people together (and also keeps them apart) based on the desire of those who wield organizational power to maintain their favored position in, and to preserve the entire structure of, the rank-order hierarchy. Coordination of technical operations (as in the symphony orchestra) is the impulse underlying technology's organizational logic. Consolidation of power (as in an autocratically run corporation or a military brigade) is the inspiration for organizing rank-order hierarchies.

The idea of people following tools is offensive to some. For these observers, it suggests a craven, mindless subservience to mere technical or mechanical devices and their routines. It seems to strip humans of their freedom to judge and to participate freely in deciding what they will do and how they will do it. It binds imagination into an unyielding mold of regimented routine that slowly transforms the free spirit into an unthinking automaton, or so the argument goes.[13] The view is compelling but overdrawn.

When people follow tools, they do only what they have been doing since the early forms of cultural technology appeared. Whether it is the symbolic imagery of dance and ritual or the well-known stone and bone tools found by anthropologists and paleontologists, technology has always shaped human behavior, has organized it into patterns and designs, has caused its human users to gather around it in coordinated ways so as to better utilize its potentialities for human purposes. In the process, it has released and yielded great stores of human imagination and expression; it has enhanced and expanded human intelligence and mental alertness; it has allowed countless living experiments in how best to organize human interactions; and it has provided the multiform pathways through which the human intellect has freed itself from earlier commitments, and found innovative and liberating ways to express and pursue human aspirations.

When people follow tools, they acknowledge the organizational logic implicit in technology. There is no other way to reap technology's many benefits. As new technological forms appear, human behavior shifts. True, the habit of acting as one did in the past may change as new tools call forth new routines, new functions, and new arrangements of the human users. True, technologically dictated routines can be monotonous, dulling of one's senses, and habituating to the point of encouraging automaton-like motions. True, once some technologies are put in place, they can operate without further mental intervention by their tenders. Perhaps what is most put at risk by technological routine are human resiliency and a flexible, plastic intellect, both of which can yield great organizational dividends. A securities analyst who stares at a stock quotation computer daily for several years may lose in imaginative creativity what is gained in analytic judgment. However, these changed behaviors need not impose a societal cap on freedom or on an individual's options, nor make unthinking automatons of either the machine operators or others not directly involved, nor commit a society to a way of life that squeezes out all spontaneity, expansion of intellectual inquiry, aesthetic awareness, and artistic expression and exploration.

13. Ellul, op. cit., and Postman, op. cit.

A Unifying Logic

One of Marshall McLuhan's most felicitious phrases was "the global village," which he envisioned as one outcome of the worldwide adoption of television.[14] Instantaneous communication, delivered in attractive, dramatic imagery that conveys and reminds all viewers of common problems and experiences, could bind humanity into a whole not unlike that found in the small-scale village. While McLuhan's typically imaginative language captured one of television's potentialities, he might well have generalized this insight to the entire network of technology that is the common possession of humanity. Ships, trains, airplanes, automobiles, and trucks also bind people together, as do telephones, facsimile messages, electronic mail, radio, and news services. Medical technology is remarkably similar (though not uniform) throughout much of the world, as are pedagogical techniques and routines, systems of public finance, construction methods and routines, along with the technologies employed in sports, drama, recreation, art, and food preparation, as well as many mundane though important tools such as sewer systems, public water systems and water treatment plants, heating and cooling systems, basic farming techniques, and on and on.

Technology displays a unifying impulse because many human problems are commonly faced and because of the existence of a common human heritage of many basic tools and symbols that have been pragmatically effective in confronting and resolving some of those common problems. Personal computers, television sets, and transistor radios comprise a common language well understood across many societal and cultural boundaries, giving tangible meaning to yet another famous McLuhan phrase, "the medium is the message." These and other common technologies, or media, create a type of universal culture, one not without strife and conflict (which may even be aggravated by technology) but one that causes human behavior around the world to begin to look remarkably similar everywhere. The "message" of technology—that tools help solve problems—is well understood by people everywhere.

Not too much should be claimed for the present realization of this potential for human unification, but neither should the achievements to date or the future possibilities be overlooked. Common experiences, common tools, and shared successes in resolving basic human problems comprise one of the sources of human value formation.[15] Such common values carry a potential

---

14. The phrase appears in Marshall McLuhan and Quentin Fiore, *The Medium Is the Massage,* New York: Bantam, 1967, p. 63.

15. See Robin Williams, "Change and Stability in Values and Value Systems," in Milton Rokeach, *Understanding Values,* New York: Free Press, 1979, pp. 22, 45; and William C. Frederick, "The Moral Authority of Transnational Corporate Codes," *Journal of Business Ethics,* vol. 10, 1991, pp. 165–177.

for greater cross-cultural understanding among people from diverse sociocultural traditions. Technology, by providing a common culture of human accomplishment, may prove to be one of the major pathways leading to McLuhan's global village.

A Civilizational-Humanizing Logic

Technology has long driven humans in the direction of civilizational arts. It is technology that makes possible a technical-humanist infrastructure that has led away from the crude, barbarous harshness of a life centered exclusively on competitive economizing. When organic-based genetic technology was supplemented with symbol-based cultural technology, a door was opened onto behavioral and intellectual potentialities previously unknown. If one seeks a point in life's evolution where unique human pathways emerged, it surely must be found here when human potentials experienced outlet in a resplendent burgeoning of symbol-based activity. No longer anchored to genetic technology's single-purpose economizing impulse, human intelligence now flowed into multiform diversities bounded only by whatever limits were encoded into the symbol-making operations of the human brain. Over time, with many hesitations, false starts, and dead ends, humans seized on these opportunities and potentialities, moving their new-found cultural technology forward in the general directions laid down by the techno-logics that have been described.

The organizing, coordinative, unifying logics have concerted human activities and driven them toward accomplishments never imagined by—and totally beyond the reach of—our hominoid ancestors. The cumulative combinations that display progression from one era to another, from one instrument to another, as successively more complex human problems have been confronted, hint—indeed, shout—that cultural technology has brought the human enterprise to a level of expression, accomplishment, and yet-to-be-realized potential not seen elsewhere among the earth's many life forms.

We take this rich technological heritage so much for granted that we leave it largely exogenous to our economic theory and moral philosophy. It has, after all, produced the technical infrastructure that makes civilization possible: systems of agriculture, production, distribution, transportation, communication, education, water supply, power supply, and waste disposal; urban centers with their architectural creations, monuments, temples, cathedrals, universities, public buildings, plazas, parks, gardens, and fountains; systems of governance, public finance, laws and judicial systems; the great literatures of painting, poetry, drama, music, dance, religious belief, and cultural legends; the books, newspapers, magazines, periodicals, and libraries, along with their modern electronic counterparts, that record and store accumulated knowledge. This common civilizational heritage, which is rooted firmly in technological soil, defines and contains a humanizing impulse that has carried human endeavors far beyond the economizing horizons of genetic technology. We may flatter ourselves that this accomplishment outdistances the lives and experiences of our predecessors, just as we may attach such lofty labels as "civilization" and "humanism" to the results, risking hubris of the worst kind. Still, it seems entirely within reasoned judgment to acknowledge that cultural technology has built a house that molds and holds the accomplishments of past ages and whose halls continue to echo with the full range of apparently limitless human abilities and aspirations. If this be not civilization and the core of humanity's achievements, what then shall it be called?

Techno-Logics—A Summation

The logics of technology show what can be expected from the inner impulses of cultural technology. They suggest the potentials of technological systems, the implicit tendencies and directions that arise from the nature, the structure, and the operations of technology. The pragmatic logic or impulse is a direct outgrowth of the economizing functions of genetic technology; pragmatism is in that sense the leading edge of the burgeoning technological capabilities manifested by early humans. Their first crude tools, along with whatever group-bonding behavior they engaged in—genetic-kinship affiliations, ritualistic dances, magical incantations and spells, cooperative hunting practices, and so on—improved their economizing chances in a rough-and-tumble world. The basic pragmatic impulse—use this tool to get that job done—underlies all subsequent forms of cultural technology. It is technology's most basic logic. On this original impulse, all other techno-logics were built and elaborated into the overwhelmingly complicated skein of technology that we know today and that sustains life on an unprecedented global scale and at a level of well-being not attainable otherwise.

The results have not always been happy ones, as many of technology's critics never tire of pointing out. Focused pragmatic attitudes do indeed tend to squeeze out alternative ways of dealing with issues and problems, thus often discouraging experimentation and flights of creative fancy. The combinatory-cooperative-coordinative impulse may and probably often has overwhelmed the solitary, awesome creativity of potential geniuses; it has also pushed people into relationships with others whom, left to their own tendencies, they would have preferred to avoid. Likewise, when technology accumulates and provides progressively better ways to get things done, older technologies are left behind, creating a sentimental vacuum that is difficult to fill; for example, steam locomotives still elicit regretful sighs of "the good old days" from some railroad buffs. Others recoil from the unifying and organizational pressures brought on by acceptance of large-scale technological systems such as mass production, television, electronic mail, global air travel, and so on, feeling that old options are irretrievably lost as new unifications and community patterns emerge. A sizable cottage industry of social criticism keeps these negative effects of technology's logics ever in the public eye. Their jeremiads still carry wide appeal.

But the world's peoples long ago embraced technology enthusiastically, accepting its logics as the necessary conditions for using technology to their advantage. Perhaps they have realized something that technology's jeremiahs have failed to note or have insufficiently stressed: *The logics of technology are everywhere caught up within the folds of culture. Technology never stands alone.* There is constant struggle—a kind of warfare—between the inner impulses of techno-logics and a broad range of sociocultural practices, habits, and conventions. Therein lie the cultural safeguards against the supposed technological terrors envisioned by the doomsayers. Culture buffers humanity against the full expression of technology's logics. But cultural practices also impel technological forces along pathways that can and do threaten vital life impulses. If one wishes to find reasons to fear technology, it is best to look deeply into the sociocultural surround that encloses, shapes, and directs technology toward its users' purposes and goals. It is to that part of technology's story that we now turn. As the story unfolds, it will become apparent that the continuing onslaught by technology's critics has produced a peculiar but unfortunate effect: it has overridden and overlooked a technological value system that holds the promise of reconciling economy and ecology, and bringing business and society into a more harmonious relationship.

TECHNOLOGY IN SOCIETY: THE MUMFORD PRINCIPLE

Technology, though having roots in genetic processes, is always and everywhere also linked to and expressive of sociocultural practices. Its uses are a culture's uses. Its operations, even when shaped partially by nature, reflect also a culture's purposes and goals. The pathways it takes are largely, though not completely, those laid down by a culture's institutions, its values, its habits and conventions. Technology exists only within a cocoon of human purpose and practice as defined by a prevailing culture. Its forms are those given it by its practitioners, who are impelled by a multiplicity of complex sociocultural goals. It runs in channels carved out by habitual experience. It never stands alone as an autonomous agent, free of either natural or sociocultural influence, nor is it free to go where it may of its own volition.

This simple but profoundly important trait of technology will be referred to here as The Mumford Principle. Lewis Mumford (1895–1990), this nation's foremost scholar of technology, set forth this technology–society linkage first and most eloquently in his path-breaking study *Technics and Civilization*, published in 1934. And in his last major books on technology, *The Pentagon of Power* and *The Myth of the Machine*, where his early optimism about technology's human promise wavered, Mumford illustrated once more the central idea that technology, though rampant and often destructive of cherished human linkages and traditions, is (and should be, he thought) cradled by social systems and constrained by human purposes. For him, the terror invoked by technology was that its human operators might be, and frequently had been, willing to use it for evil and humanly devastating ends, *driven by their cultures* to harness technology's power to their vaulting ambitions and paranoid fantasies. "The world of technics is not isolated and self-contained; it reacts to forces and impulses that come from apparently remote parts of the [cultural] environment."[16]

Applying this principle to the business arena yields great dividends, for it reveals that the technology commanded by business decision makers is used for purposes defined by the value clusters that dominate the business institution. The technology itself does not dictate the outcome or make the decision. What *does* shape the use of technology within business is the blend of characteristic values found there, as The Mumford Principle holds.

Business and The Mumford Principle

Technology is inherently and unavoidably bound up in business operations. The core function of business is to economize. Economizing is the root operation—the basic techno-logic—of both genetic technology and cultural technology. *Economizing can be accomplished in no other way than by technological means.* That is the first and most fundamental charter that business has been issued by society (and ratified by nature). But as also discussed in an earlier chapter, business decision makers seek more than economizing. The attrac-

---

16. Lewis Mumford, *Technics and Civilization*, New York: Harcourt, Brace & World, Harbinger Edition, 1962, originally published in 1934, p. 6. Those who wish to absorb Mumford's comprehensive views of technology and its influence on human affairs should be forewarned that there is an "early Mumford" and a "late Mumford." He began his studies as a technological optimist, believing that the mechanistic grip on the human psyche was loosening as technological diversity allowed human organic potentials to be released. His optimism never completely faded, although his later books invoked a "megamachine" that threatened to pulverize all of those qualities and traits that he considered to be quintessentially human. One need not accept this later austere view of technology's influence to appreciate the cultural perspective he brought to bear on the meaning and functioning of technology. See Lewis Mumford, *The Myth of the Machine: Technics and Human Development*, New York: Harcourt, Brace & World, 1966, 1967; and Mumford, *The Pentagon of Power*, New York: Harcourt Brace Jovanovich, 1964, 1970.

tions of power aggrandizement pull them away from strict economizing efforts. Profits derived from economizing become less important than power itself. The technologies of organization and behavior, of symbolic persuasion, along with the underlying physical tools and machines, become the means of achieving, consolidating, and perpetuating power within and for the business system. The technology commanded by business thus runs along twin tracks, one toward economizing, the other toward power aggrandizement.

Here is a prime example of The Mumford Principle at work. The technology that falls under the sway of business decision makers is not free to function according to its inherent techno-logics. At every single point within the circle of techno-logics diagrammed in Figure 7–4, technical operations are constrained by the two master value sets to be found within business. On the one hand, the pragmatic thrust is strong, for that is business's primary societal function and the premier logic of technology. Economizing technology is highly favored and sought. Business mentality welcomes and supports efforts that seem to produce an economizing outcome for the firm.

On the other hand, the hold of power is great on business minds, especially those minds that direct and manage the firm. In the pursuit of power, economizing technology and its potentials may be compromised: "satisficing" replaces "maximizing"; "optimum profits" seem more acceptable than "maximum profits"; and regulated prices seem preferable to freely competitive prices, for they stabilize an unruly market that may otherwise rupture established industrial systems and the power network through which this qualified economizing is accomplished. Worse, power seekers may consciously, cynically, or carelessly promote those technologies—physical, organizational-behavioral, and symbolic—that not only diminish or even threaten to destroy their firm's economizing capabilities but that may carry grave and widespread threats to societal stability or to life itself. The potential harm that resides in business technology can therefore be activated either by single-minded economizing or by power-aggrandizing impulses.

In either case, the problem lies not in the technology but in the forms and expressions given it by the dominant values of the business institution. The techno-logics themselves can lead to vitally needed economizing gains of great and lasting value to society. Placing the stewardship of this technological potential in the hands of business decision makers means that business values will chart the course of much technological development. The promotion by business of economizing values and power-aggrandizing values tends to channel and compromise the potentials inhering in techno-logics. That is the lesson taught by The Mumford Principle. Over and over again, The Mumford Principle demonstrates that it is *the values of dominant institutions*, and not the technology itself, that direct the course of technological usage and innovation. If something is to be done either to encourage or to curb technology's societal effects, one must look beyond the technology to a society's principal values and its value-inculcating institutions, such as business.

THE VALUES WITHIN TECHNOLOGY

If one looks deeply into the circle of techno-logics diagrammed in Figure 7–4, a technological value system is discoverable. Like other value clusters, it consists of beliefs, relationships, and standards of judgment derived from human experience in coping with life forces. This normative structure is present in all human societies, although it varies as sociocultural systems vary in their respective contents, their stage and complexity of development, and their accumulated historical traditions and experience. Because technology is not distributed uniformly among human societies, one finds still other variations in the depth of commitment to technological values that those societies may exhibit. Technological value systems never stand alone or free from the influence of other kinds of values.

Normative technological systems are not usually accorded standing as genuine value systems. Frequently, they are dismissed as mechanistic technical routines that lie well outside the arena of values and norms. Nevertheless, if one looks closely enough, values can be found to be rooted as firmly within technological systems as in any other aspect of sociocultural life. Moreover, those technological values are a vital part of every human endeavor, and in that sense are perhaps more commonly encountered than most other values. Their very commonness may contribute to the notion that they lack the quality and uniqueness conventionally assigned to value phenomena.

The Technological Value Cluster (Value Cluster IV)

Technological values cluster together in much the same way as do the clusters of economizing values, power-aggrandizing values, and ecologizing values described in earlier chapters. In each case, the clustering signals the presence of interlinked values that support and reinforce one another. Such value clusters are extrusions of human experience that have over time been conceptualized and eventually recognized as values, that is, as beliefs, relationships, and judgmental standards emerging from human life experiences. Technological values owe their existence to nature and culture as surely as do the economizing, power-aggrandizing, and ecologizing value clusters. The core technological values are listed in Figure 7–6.

Technological values are an outgrowth of the techno-logics discussed earlier, and they closely parallel many of those logical qualities. Techno-logics generate techno-values by creating the conditions that encourage certain be-

```
+-----------------------------------------------+
|                                               |
|              VALUE CLUSTER IV:                |
|             TECHNOLOGICAL VALUES              |
|                                               |
|                                               |
|      Instrumental pragmatics                  |
|                                               |
|      Cooperative-coordinative relations       |
|                                               |
|      Technical expertise                      |
|                                               |
|      Public openness                          |
|                                               |
|      Participatory leveling                   |
|                                               |
+-----------------------------------------------+
```

Figure 7–6. Value Cluster IV: Technological values

liefs, relationships, behaviors, and standards of performance to emerge and to be widely accepted. In other words, as people use tools, they find certain patterns of behavior and belief to be a necessary and desirable part of effective tool use. As the entire complement of technology grows in size and complexity, still other relationships and behavioral traits are seen to be essential. From such tool-using experiences, a cluster of beliefs emerges and forms the core of a society's technological value system.

The most readily apparent technological value is **pragmatics**. Using instrumental means to achieve practical, tangible results is at the core of all technological activity. This is true of the simplest technical task, such as brushing one's teeth, as well as the more complex operations entailed, for example, in writing a computer software program. Finding the appropriate means to achieve identifiable goals is a familiar activity within business firms, whose central goals are set by a devotion to economizing and power aggrandizement. In the business lexicon, this basic means-ends process now bears the label of "strategic planning," a rhetorical upgrading presumably thought to confer greater dignity on the sometime grubby utilitarian actions of business planners. If well executed, pragmatically inspired operations carry the firm toward a resolution of the various problems it encounters from day to day and year to year. A whole host of technological devices and procedures is arrayed, running the entire gamut of physical tools and machines, organizational and behavioral systems, and intellectual software—all of them chosen and used for the practical, pragmatic results they promise to deliver. Pragmatics is a deeply cherished technological value.

Technological practitioners intent on achieving pragmatic results also learn to value **coordinative, integrative,** and **cooperative relationships** among tool users. These valued relationships are an obvious reflection of several of the techno-logics, including coordinative-cooperative logic, organizational logic, and combinatory logic. Acceptance of a technological way of life by humans (they had little choice in the matter!) brought about a concertedness of human activities and laid the foundations of organizational systems amenable to technical operations and cooperative human endeavors of all kinds. One aspect of the teamwork so highly valued and sought by business practitioners is its contribution to the smooth coordination and integration of workplace activities. The oddball maverick who persists in out-of-step behavior gums up the works, and strenuous efforts are bent to eliminate such occurrences. A failure to "get in step" can be particularly risky when the effective operation of a complex or even dangerous technology (e.g., a nuclear power plant or a jet airliner) is involved. Technologists are strongly devoted to the value of coordinated, cooperative routines.

If practical ends and coordinated behavior are to be achieved, it will be because **technical talent, skill, expertise,** and **know-how** are present. Technology both calls forth and reinforces these human traits. They are the necessary accompaniments of any technological operation, whether applied directly (as by a talented pianist playing a sonata) or indirectly through a programmed procedure (as by a mechanical robot welding joints on an automobile assembly line). Technical expertise is a value widely embraced and admired, for it is only by having and applying that value that technology can yield its fruits. Cultivating talent through education and training, and providing an experimental setting in which practice can hone one's skills (as in a music academy, an experimental theater, or an industrial training center), have a long history in industrial societies. Tools, whether of the physical, organizational-behavioral, or purely symbolic variety, do not move themselves but are totally dependent on the human know-how and expertise that surround and activate the tool function. Expertise is valued and becomes a cultivated value.

Technical expertise invokes the complementary technological values of **trust, openness, honesty,** and **truth telling**. Technologists have little or no reason to be secretive or to mislead their work mates. An aboveboard approach to problems and an open attitude will move tool users more securely toward the goals they seek in any given technological task. An aura of trust and honesty must suffuse any technological endeavor if the concerted efforts of all are to be successful. This is not to say that contrary motives are absent. Technological needs and values can be subordinated to the psychological and emotional impulses of tool users: vital information can be withheld, technical data can be falsified, one's technical colleagues can be misled or lied to, and a person's dreams of technical prowess can override and sabotage the need to extend trust and honesty to others. But this kind of psychopathic workplace sabotage only serves to confirm that technological systems cultivate the opposite effects and values. Honesty, openness, and trust are core normative principles of technological systems.

Technology, in a historical sense, has long exerted a leveling influence within society, as tools once the possession of only a few become more widely owned by the citizenry. Over time, a technological commons emerges and becomes a taken-for-granted part of life within that society: automobiles replace horse-drawn carriages, superhighways connect urban centers, air terminals become more common than rail or bus stations, stylish ready-to-wear clothing is seen on the backs of all classes and not just an upper-class elite, television sets and transistor radios are found in the humblest hut in the world's poorest country. The spread of technology to wider and wider realms of society creates the conditions for another technological value, which might be labeled **participatory leveling**. When, for example, there is much talk about an "information highway" capable of linking into one vast, interconnected computer network any and all persons who can "plug into" global electronic systems, then there is a thrust to ensure that the largest number of people are included. Being left out means virtual banishment from worldwide society, where possession of information is vital for citizenship involvement. Technology can level social-class orders and expand the boundaries of social participation to the precise extent that deliberate steps are taken to place tools in the hands of citizens and simultaneously to educate them in the tools' complexities and various usages. In this way, technology is compatible with, and helps to reinforce, a democratic conception of how human affairs ought to be arranged. The value of participatory leveling works directly against an elitist, class-oriented control of a society's technology.[17] So too can participatory teamwork schemes adopted by business firms exert a leveling influence within the workplace and create a more democratic environment there. These programs often struggle for acceptance within a corporate culture that is resistant to the leveling implications for a controlling managerial elite.[18]

Other technological values hover hesitantly within human culture, displaying a not-yet-realized normative potential for exerting positive influence

17. For an example, see "News That Falls from the Sky," *The Wall Street Journal*, October 25, 1993, p. A18, which tells of efforts by the Chinese government to forbid the use of satellite-dish television receivers by private citizens as a way of "propagating the people's patriotism, preserving the superior tradition of the Chinese race, expediting the construction of socialist spiritual civilization *and maintaining social stability*" (emphasis added). The author of this article goes on to say, "Beijing's hand is not high enough or wide enough to stop the information and entertainment that falls from the clouds."

18. Denis Collins, "Self-Interests and Group Interests in Employee Involvement Programs: A Case Study," *Journal of Labor Research*, vol. 26, no. 1, 1995, pp. 57–79; Larry Hatcher, Timothy L. Ross, and Denis Collins, "Why Employees Support (and Oppose) Gainsharing Plans," *National Productivity Review*, vol. 8, no. 2, 1992, pp. 17–27; and "Computer Links Erode Hierarchical Nature of Workplace Culture," *The Wall Street Journal*, December 9, 1993, pp. A1, A7.

in human affairs. The **progressive material betterment** that can be observed within a given line of technology—for example, heart and organ transplant techniques—does not automatically generate a broader societal progressiveness. In other words, technical progress is not equivalent to Social Progress. But progressive material betterment that can be produced by technological advancement is without question highly valued and cherished for giving a powerful boost to human life prospects.

So too does the **community-unifying potential** of technology fall short of what is clearly implied by the unifying techno-logic. The unifying potentials of technology are frequently restricted to strengthening a particular organization or corporation (by making it more efficient), rather than toughening the sinews of the broader community (by protecting the rights of its weakest members and securing just relationships). The globe's need for a broad, easily accessible, instantaneous information and communication network that has the power to bring people into closer understanding of one another may take a back seat to the more immediate goals and focused strategies of media corporations. Nevertheless, one can glimpse the powerful potential of earth-straddling technological systems to knit diverse societies together, if not into common ways of life, then at least into broader communities of understanding and sympathy for the common problems faced by all.

This cluster of technological values—**instrumental pragmatics, cooperative-coordinative relations, technical expertise, honesty-trust-openness,** and **participatory leveling**, along with the value potentials of **material betterment** and **community building**, is latent in technological operations wherever they occur and whatever form they may take. Acceptance of a technological way of life means acceptance of technology's implicit values. Each of these normative orientations has become part of any human society's value system—that is, its normative beliefs, its ways of relating people to one another, and the standards it uses to judge the outcome of technologically assisted human activity. All technological values, whether fully active or only a normative potential, are subject to the discipline of The Mumford Principle. This means that their strength and the direction in which they drive human affairs are always conditioned by sociocultural practices and institutions. Thus, the civilizing-humanizing-unifying-progressive potentials inhering in technological values are realized only insofar as a society's institutions and other kinds of values permit those conditions to emerge and flourish.

TOWARD VALUE RECONCILIATION

Technological values may, in time, contribute importantly to the reconciliation of economizing and ecologizing forces, as well as to other normative issues that divide business and society from one another. The intention of setting them forth here is to offer an additional, alternative normative standard for thinking through some of these complex problems and issues. Technological values are too central to human existence to be disregarded. They are, after all, an outgrowth of natural evolutionary processes. They also have been shaped and channeled by sociocultural practices to become an important part of the way we humans make value judgments. The case for accepting technological values as an evaluative standard rests on four propositions.

Proposition One: *Economizing and ecologizing are a single intertwined process of energy transformation, each process exerting antientropic, life-supporting effects.* This relationship was discussed in the preceding chapter and will not be described again here. Its importance for value reconciliation is as follows. Since neither economizing nor ecologizing can occur without the other, they cannot be conceived in isolation from each other. They differ only in the magnitude and comprehensiveness of their respective impacts on life. Therefore, reconciliation cannot imply that ecologizing values are *superior* to economizing values (for both are equally supportive of life, though on different scales) or that ecologizing values must *replace* economizing values (for that is clearly impossible in view of their interlinked association). Clearly, any evaluative scheme must find room for both kinds of processes and both kinds of values. One needs to find a value set capable of releasing from each of these two life forces whatever potential they have for sustaining life and, at the same time, curbing their built-in tendency to work against one another. Applying the evaluative standards contained in the technological value cluster may help to clarify the choices that need to be made. A later chapter attempts to demonstrate this possibility.

Proposition Two: *Technological values are compatible with the values of both economizing and ecologizing, and they can therefore serve to link the two antientropic processes together whenever either threatens the integrity of the other.* Every one of the technological values shown in Figure 7–6 contributes directly to the economizing goals sought by business firms. Productivity, growth, and organizational integrity (the economizing goal-values) are enhanced by the application of pragmatic methods, by technical expertise, by cooperative-coordinative workplace relations, by attitudes of honesty-trust-openness, and by full participation of all technically qualified personnel (all of these being techno-values). Ecological processes, particularly those involved in community building, may also be advanced by the application of technological principles and values. Technical expertise not only reveals ecological risks and dangers created by runaway economizing but is increasingly employed to find ecologically safe solutions to these problems. The techno-logics of unification, coordination-integration-cooperation, combination, and civilizational humanizing give powerful reinforcement to modern tendencies to discover common threads that tie diverse societies closer together into ecological wholes. This consistency and compatibility of technological values (Value Cluster IV) with economizing values (Value Cluster I) and ecologizing values (Value Cluster III) lays the groundwork for a normative analysis that draws on all three value clusters.

Proposition Three: *In actual fact, ways are presently being explored and found to reconcile several economizing–ecological conflicts, and new institutions are being created to resolve specific types of ecological controversies. All such emerging institution-building activities incorporate technological values into their basic approach and methods.* The Montreal Protocol that outlined a retreat from the use of high-level ozone-depleting chemical compounds drew heavily on techno-logics and techno-value principles. There was broad acceptance of a pragmatic approach; technical expertise helped to define the problem and recommend alternative solutions; an attitude of trust-honesty-openness prevailed; the need to cooperate-coordinate-integrate the actions of both producers and users of the chemicals was recognized; and all parties were involved participatively in reaching agreement on the compact's provisions and timetables. The same can be said for other new organizations and environmental initiatives, such as Clean Sites, the Health Effects Institute, the Institute for Evaluating Health Risks, Resources for Responsible Site Management, the National Wildlife Federation's Corporate Conservation Council, and other similar undertakings.[19] These bridging institutions bring environmentalists and industrialists together to work out problems of waste cleanup, automotive emissions, and the hazards of pesticides, asbestos, and toxic releases. Hence, in actual fact, technological values are already relied upon to help resolve economizing–ecologizing conflicts.

Proposition Four: *Technological values resonate with other, better-known ethical principles and value orientations that are widely respected and consistent with established societal institutions and practices.* Business ethicists speak often of the importance of honesty, truthfulness, and openness. They favor full and open participation of all who hold a stake in corporate actions. They advocate a cooperative approach that brings corporate managers and stakeholders together to consider the social impact of corporate practices. Clearly, they believe in community-building efforts and outcomes where a sense of social justice prevails and where those least well off do not suffer greater injustice as policies are formed and programs are launched—a condition that is more easily attained when the material betterment that is brought about by techno-

---

19. Several of these organizations are described in Charles W. Powers, *The Role of NGOs [Non-governmental Organizations] in Improving the Employment of Science and Technology in Environmental Management*, working paper, New York: Carnegie Commission on Science, Technology, and Government, May 1991.

logical advances is encouraged. Where there is a compatibility of well-known ethical principles and technological values, the prospects seem improved for erecting a powerful normative system for evaluating the many conflicts that separate business and society. This would be particularly true if the evaluative standards within techno-logics and techno-values could be deliberately conjoined with the more conventional ethical principles of business ethicists. The following chapters explore such possibilities.

If economy and ecology are to be reconciled, both business and society will need to accept a commonly shared set of normative guidelines that reflects their shared interests and their shared experiences in coping with an environment shaped by thermodynamic forces. This chapter has argued that technology, techno-logics, and techno-values are a central part of such a normative system.

But surely, one will be tempted to say in protest, these technological values are not what most people mean by values; they are not expressive of the normative meanings that commonly arise in daily interchanges; and they do not provide obvious guidance as one confronts a sometimes bewildering array of ethical workplace dilemmas. Where within the technological complex, for instance, may one find a concern or a standard for judging fairness or achieving social justice? And what of human rights and related entitlements? Are they not frequently trampled and sacrificed in the technologically driven utilitarian-instrumentalist quest for business profits? Are not individual spontaneity, freedom, and autonomy at risk within institutions and organizations that adopt techno-logics as a way of relating people to one another? And particularly within the business corporation that displays such an abiding love affair with technological pragmatics, what is to become of those sometime-fugitive personal (X-factor) values that are at variance with workplace demands?

These central normative puzzles have been tackled in recent years by applied philosophers, whose answers comprise the principal body of business ethics literature. Approaching the same kinds of value issues from a somewhat different disciplinary angle have been students of corporate social responsibility and of organizational behavior.[20] It is only the peculiarities of academic organization and disciplinary classification that have produced parallel, though not entirely identical, streams of normative literature. Organization and management theorists, lodged in business schools and raised in the positivist traditions of social science, have tended to shy away from a di-

---

20. For a description and classification of this second body of literature, see Donna J. Wood, "Corporate Social Performance Revisited," *Academy of Management Review*, vol. 16, 1991, pp. 691–718. The other literature field, which has been produced by business ethicists, is examined in the next two chapters.

rect approach to controversial value issues involving business. They have viewed business from an inside-looking-out perspective. The philosophers of business ethics, hampered neither by institutional loyalty to business nor (for most) by any significant contact with the subject of their concern, have been bolder and more caustic in their analysis of business behavior. Their perspective has been from the outside looking in.[21]

It is time now to assess the success and to reveal the shortcomings of these related bodies of literature that have generated the bulk of scholarly dialogue that seeks reconciliation of business values and social values. Though flawed, that dialogue can be helpful in finding a way out of the conflicts that separate business and society.

21. One is reminded of President Lyndon Johnson's vulgar but colorful aphorism for dealing with and coopting internal critics of his policies: "I'd rather have them inside pissing out than outside pissing in."

8

The Business Ethics Question

For close to half a century, scholars who study business operations have sought a normative base from which to judge the moral adequacy of business motives and business goals, as well as the consequences of business decisions, policies, and practices. This is not to say that concern about business ethics arose only toward the middle of the twentieth century, for there is an ancient history that reflects widespread doubt about the moral probity of business people, their motives, and their goals throughout many centuries and across a wide spectrum of societies and cultures. In the West, no lesser figures than Aristotle, Thomas Aquinas, Adam Smith, and Karl Marx, not to speak more broadly of the founders of the world's major religions, have considered such questions. Rather, the intention in this chapter is to focus upon the efforts of contemporary business scholars to find acceptable ways of describing, analyzing, and evaluating the normatively tinged activities of business as it is practiced in corporate America.

The view to be developed is at times critical of ethics theory, although there is no intention to denigrate the impressive theoretical contributions of business ethicists. The purpose is rather to lay the groundwork for linking the **theory of business values** being developed in this book with the established and still evolving body of **business ethics principles**. Without doubt, fundamental differences separate the two formulations, and they will be noted, but a guiding belief expressed here is that a new normative synthesis is achievable, thus clearing the way for an improved understanding of the moral tensions found at the interface of business and society. That synthesis is proposed in the following chapter.

What is needed at the outset is a grasp of the major themes and analytical strategies, along with their sometimes unspoken preconceptions and assumptions, that have been characteristic of business ethics theorizing. It will be helpful, as a way of identifying the methodological issues involved, to adopt

209

convenient labels, albeit overly simple ones, for the most prominent approaches. For these purposes, the discussion concentrates on what will be called **Responsibility Ethics, Philosophic Ethics,** and **Behavioral/Organizational Ethics**. Though treated separately for purposes of expositional clarity, the three are frequently interwoven within the published literature of the field, and these interweavings are noted where appropriate.

RESPONSIBILITY ETHICS

The earliest and most enduring normative formulation has emphasized the responsibilities of business corporations to those affected by a company's decisions and policies. From the beginning, it has been felt that business has fiduciary duties and obligations of performance that extend beyond the company's legal boundaries and economic goals. This view is tantamount to declaring that those who own the company should run it, or hire professional managers to run it, with an eye to the interests of others as well as their own. Hence, business owners and managers are said to have a range of *social* responsibilities in addition to being responsible for the normal economic functions that one expects to find in a well-organized and well-run firm.[1]

To sustain and rationalize this perspective, its advocates have drawn on various economic, political, ideological, and sociocultural sources, although rarely acknowledging them as such.[2] Two quasi-philosophic, quasi-religious axes orient Responsibility Ethics within the field of normative analysis: the Charity Principle and the Stewardship Principle. Both of these principles are rooted in ancient practices associated with concentrated political and financial power, and Responsibility Ethicists simply updated them to fit within the institutions of advanced capitalist business systems.

1. The classic statement of this doctrine is *Social Responsibilities of Business Corporations,* issued in 1971 by the Committee for Economic Development, a group of leading corporate executives and public figures. Social responsibility theorists of the day welcomed the report with two rather weak cheers, because they believed that it compromised important moral principles in order to protect corporate interests. Opponents and skeptics of the social responsibility concept believed that the CED, by insisting on a broader social role for business, had not only shot itself in the foot but had grievously wounded the business community in another vital organ somewhat higher on the corporate body. These critics of the doctrine subsequently had their day and their say within CED circles. For the story of the CED's change of mind, see William C. Frederick, "Free Market versus Social Responsibility: Decision Time at the CED," *California Management Review,* vol. XXIII, no. 3, Spring 1981, pp. 20–28.

2. An exception is Richard Eells's and Clarence C. Walton's *Conceptual Foundations of Business,* Homewood, IL: Irwin, 1961, 1969, which traces the debt of American social responsibility theories to political, constitutional, and ideological orientations. The same can be said of Gerald F. Cavanagh's *American Business Values,* 2nd edition, Englewood Cliffs, NJ: Prentice-Hall, 1984.

According to the Charity Principle, corporate owners and their hired managers who command large accumulations of capital are to be "their brother's keeper" by extending a charitable, philanthropic corporate hand to needy groups and worthy causes unable to generate enough support to be self-sustaining. This *noblesse oblige* attitude tended to be the sole meaning given by most business leaders to the social responsibility notion until it was roughly swept aside by corporate critics as a self-serving, feudal-like, and totally inadequate managerial response to the social turmoil of the 1960s and early 1970s. Until then, though, to be charitable and caring toward others was advocated as a moral requirement of top management, though one never knew just how widely adopted in practice was this putative moral imperative. It spawned the institutions of corporate philanthropy, including such pools of corporate largesse as the Ford Foundation, the Carnegie Corporation, the Russell Sage Foundation, and many other similar foundation adjuncts. In most communities, one finds some version of the United Way, whose annual fund drives are typically headed by local corporate titans.[3]

The Stewardship Principle was to prove a more enduring business belief, partly because it reflected a persistent and comforting theme in Judeo-Christian Biblical lore that those entrusted with "talents" were to exhibit prudence and foresight in their use, leading to their multiplication. The business mind easily transmogrified this hoary maxim into the corporate context by adopting for executives the mantle of "steward" of the public interest, "trustee" of business resources, and "corporate statesman" expected to manifest a broad social vision, while not denying their company's economic purpose and objectives (nor, it might be added, did it disturb their power). For the most part, these attributions of moral peerage were what might be called self-coronations or simple assertions, since no visible public selection process had elevated these corporate worthies to such vaunted peaks of public influence and function.[4]

Thus endowed with self-annointed, regal-like responsibilities, corporate executives everywhere were urged to adopt an "enlightened self-interest" perspective in approaching business decisions and formulating corporate policies. To act otherwise was to risk serious inroads on business-as-usual. As the Committee for Economic Development put it, "The doctrine of enlightened self-interest is also based on the proposition that if business does not accept a

---

3. The story of corporate philanthropy's beginnings is told in Morrell Heald, *The Social Responsibilities of Business: Company and Community*, Cleveland: Case-Western Reserve Press, 1970.

4. Milton Friedman made this telling point about self-annointment in a scathing denunciation of the social responsibility doctrine that has become a minor classic of its own. See "The Social Responsibility of Business Is to Increase Its Profits," *New York Times Magazine*, September 13, 1970, pp. 33, 122–126. An earlier version of his position is found in Milton Friedman, *Capitalism and Freedom*, Chicago: University of Chicago Press, 1962.

fair measure of responsibility for social improvement, the interests of the corporation may actually be jeopardized. . . . By acting on its own initiative, management preserves the flexibility needed to conduct the company's affairs in a constructive, efficient, and adaptive manner." The report averred that looking beyond today's bottom line would pay off in the long run by reducing social costs, dampening radical antibusiness protest, and lessening the likelihood of government intervention into business affairs. Indeed, the stability and public acceptance of business itself were said to be at risk: "Indiscriminate opposition to social change [by business] not only jeopardizes the interest of the single corporation, but also affects adversely the interest *all* corporations have in maintaining a climate conducive to the effective functioning of *the entire business system.*"[5]

Hence, Responsibility Ethics has rested upon the twin normative pillars of Charity and Stewardship. Each moral principle had its origins deep within long-accepted sociocultural practices and customary outlooks regarding the uses of power and wealth. The Biblical shadows they cast upon the business scene served to justify and reinforce their presence within the business conscience. Once acknowledged, or better, once accepted, these moral orientations were a way to create an expanded moral category for business activities, filled with the warmth and goodwill of charity and burnished with the glories and rewards of an enlightened stewardship.[6]

However, for those with strong appetites for the fruits of ethical analysis, this doctrinal creed was pretty thin moral gruel. It seemed to buffer corporate decision makers from the charge of being uncaring so long as they professed an attitude of stewardship and charity, even as their companies fixed prices, sold defective and unhealthy products, gouged competitors, polluted the environment, and discriminated against women and various minorities. It also seemed to place the entire moral burden of corporate social performance on an elite corps of top managers who, common sense suggested, might well vary widely in their commitment to social purposes and goals.

Thus, but for one additional feature of Responsibility Ethics, this somewhat quaint normative methodology might well have passed quietly from the purview of those who seek to judge business on moral terms. The theoretical component that proved, in the long run, to be the most attractive to moralists, and that was to sustain Responsibility Ethics well into the final decade of the twentieth century, was the notion of "corporate claimants" and "con-

---

5. *Social Responsibilities of Business Corporations*, pp. 28, 29. Emphasis added.

6. Standard Oil (New Jersey) CEO Frank Abrams told his executive counterparts throughout the corporate community that "We must re-establish the common touch with our fellow men. We must reappear in the role of warmhearted human beings—which is what we are." Frank Abrams, "Management's Responsibilities in a Complex World," *Harvard Business Review*, May 1951, p. 33.

stituencies" or, more recently, "corporate stakeholders." This key concept deserves further attention.

Corporate Stakeholders

The moral nub of the stakeholder idea is that a wide range of groups have a stake—said to be a moral interest—in what corporations do, therefore requiring corporate decision makers to consider the moral, as well as the economic, aspects of their actions. The germ of this idea appeared sporadically in the American business mind early in the twentieth century but became entangled with and was overridden by the Charity Principle during and well beyond the Great Depression years of the 1930s. For reasons not entirely clear and never explored thoroughly by social and intellectual historians, the Stewardship Principle mutated into a proto-stakeholder notion around midcentury. Or at least, one can by that time hear business dialogue suggesting its bare outlines.[7]

The idea began as a relatively simple and straightforward proposition. Since corporations not only depend on but also affect the lives of numerous identifiable groups, someone in the executive suite ought to pay some attention to their rights and to the impact of corporate operations. Those who could claim such a relationship included owner-investors, lenders, employees, suppliers, customers, and the communities and neighborhoods where facilities are located. Frank Abrams' 1950 list named stockholders, employees, customers, and the general public. A decade later, Richard Eells added security holders, competitors, local communities, and governments.[8] After another ten years, the Committee for Economic Development lengthened the list measurably by including labor unions, a wide variety of interest groups, the educational system, and the news media. Over the years, the perceived corporate stakeholder population has continued to expand, now including ethnic minorities and their advocacy organizations, women and their support groups, handicapped persons, war veterans, environmental advocates of all

7. Three sources capture this early dialogue: Abrams, op. cit., pp. 29–34; Howard R. Bowen, *Social Responsibilities of the Businessman*, New York: Harper, 1953; and Francis X. Sutton, Seymour E. Harris, Carl Kaysen, and James Tobin, *The American Business Creed*, Cambridge, MA: Harvard University Press, 1956. The stakeholder notion was hinted at in 1950, though apparently not developed, by Robert Wood, CEO of Sears-Roebuck. For the latter claim, see Thomas Donaldson and Lee E. Preston, "The Stakeholder Theory of the Corporation: Concepts, Evidence, Implications," *Academy of Management Review*, January 1995, p.71, who also suggest an even earlier source in E. M. Dodd, Jr., "For Whom Are Corporate Managers Trustees?" *Harvard Law Review*, vol. 45, 1932, pp. 1145–1163. The main sources suggest that stakeholder thoughts were finding fertile soil in representative business leaders' minds around midcentury.

8. Richard Eells, *The Meaning of Modern Business*, New York: Columbia University Press, 1960. Eells called these groups "direct contributor-claimants" and "indirect claimants."

stripes, governments at all levels across the entire global landscape, the ever-present media, health care organizations, trees and other ecological manifes-tations, political terrorists, baby seals and veal calves, and on and on through an almost inexhaustible list of claimants to the corporation's largesse or ap-peal for relief from its alleged depredations.[9]

Although the lists varied from one commentator to another, there was a tendency to divide stakeholders into two fairly distinct groups, one that was directly and vitally involved in company operations (e.g., employees, suppli-ers, and investors) and others standing somewhat aside while nevertheless feeling the burdens or benefits of the firm's activities (e.g., governments and local communities). This division was a commentary on the market-oriented mind of stakeholder theorists, because the "direct" or "primary" stakeholders, it turned out, were those who enjoyed contractual market relationships with the corporation, while the "indirect" or "secondary" stakeholders' ties to the company were extralegal, noncontractual, and nonmarket in nature.

Lee E. Preston and James E. Post made (and probably originated) this dis-tinction in their landmark book *Private Management and Public Policy: The Prin-ciple of Public Responsibility.* The idea caught on, and in time became an article of faith in business and society textbooks and in stakeholder theory gener-ally.[10] Preston and Post did not use the term "stakeholder." Their equivalent is "publics," and they occasionally refer to "constituencies" (which was used earlier by Frank Abrams and Richard Eells) and "interest groups" (the latter in a negative, pejorative sense, as far as corporate response is concerned). Nor did they propose an explicit stakeholder theory of the firm or a stake-holder concept, although one is foreshadowed and implied in their distinc-

---

9. What may well prove to be the apogee of definitional imperialism regarding the meaning of "stakeholder" occurred in 1993 when one enthusiast argued that the entire environment con-ceivably could be treated as a corporate stakeholder. The possible candidates, in addition to the usual ones, were, in the author's own words, nonhuman physical entities; Earth's atmosphere, hydrosphere, lithosphere, and biosphere; the natural environment itself; [perhaps] hominoids, mammals, pets, vertebrates, animals, plants, endangered species, sentient species, bacteria, viruses, rocks, air, water; the entire sun–Earth system; dead ancestors; future generations; one's house, car, computers, equipment, and personal products; whatever we care about, whatever we value; and mental-emotional states, conditions, or elements, such as love, honesty, goodness, community, success or failure. Although intended to alert theorists to the definitional problems surrounding the term "stakeholder," such an all-points definition causes the concept to lose all useful analytic meaning for scholars and any operational meaning for business practitioners. See "Essay by Mark Starik," *Business and Society,* vol. 33, no. 1, April 1994, pp. 89–95.

10. A citation analysis by John F. Mahon and Patti N. Andrews, "Social Issues in Management Lit-erature: A Preliminary Citation Analysis," *Proceedings,* Academy of Management, 1987, revealed that the Preston and Post book was the most frequently cited work in this field from 1980 to 1986. See Exhibit 3 of their paper. The primary–secondary distinction is found in *Private Manage-ment and Public Policy: The Principle of Public Responsibility,* Englewood Cliffs, NJ: Prentice-Hall, 1975, pp. 9, 95–96.

tion between the "primary" and "secondary" social involvements of corporations. Their concern was less with specific groups and more with the transactions that make up what they called an "interpenetrating system" that linked business firms with their host society. An additional parallel to the work of later stakeholder theorists was their belief about the importance of a company's primary involvements: "Without them, the organization cannot be what it is."[11]

As for the moral responsibilities of business, these two authors were quite wary. They distrusted the usefulness and meaning of what others had called "social responsibility" and rejected the notion that executives' personal values should guide a company's social decisions and policies. They preferred to speak of business's social "involvement" rather than social "responsibility" because "the former is ethically neutral" (p. 9). In the end, they finessed questions of morality and ethics by folding them into the "public policy process," where normative matters might receive whatever attention and remedy the society's political system could or would produce. With moral matters shunted off to the political realm, the stakeholder framework was morally denuded, remaining only as a way of describing a company's interactions with other groups. At the same time, corporate executives were presumably relieved of burdensome and possibly diversionary normative deliberations.[12]

Another public policy theorist demurred, arguing that values may be found at the very core of a society's public policies, therefore exerting a powerful influence on the way public questions are addressed and resolved: "Public policy reflects the values of society or at least of significant segments of society that are active in the public policy process . . . [and] in some sense values are the basic building blocks in . . . public policy."[13] The clear implication of this view is that business executives do not have the luxury of passively relying on an impersonal "public policy process" to resolve normative issues of public responsibility from which they can presumably stand apart. Their values and the values of their companies are injected actively into public policy by lobbying, organizing political action committees, serving on govern-

---

11. Ibid., p. 10. Over a decade later, Post added "stakeholder model" to other models originally described in *Private Management and Public Policy*, seeming to distinguish it from the "interpenetrating systems model." See James E. Post, "Perfecting Capitalism: Perspective on Institutional Responsibility," in Robert B. Dickie and Leroy S. Rouner (eds.), *Corporations and the Common Good*, Notre Dame, IN: Notre Dame University Press, 1986, pp. 54–56.

12. In a later paper, Preston noted the descriptive power of the stakeholder concept but went on to acknowledge that "the ultimate justification for the stakeholder theory is to be found in its normative base." For this shift of emphasis, see Donaldson and Preston, op. cit., pp. 87–88.

13. Rogene A. Buchholz, *Business Environment and Public Policy*, 5th edition, Englewood Cliffs, NJ: Prentice-Hall, forthcoming 1995 (ms. pp. 142, 144, and 168).

ment boards and commissions, and so on. Hence, ethical neutrality toward a company's stakeholders seems both implausible and impossible.

For others, the moral reasons given for attentiveness to stakeholders' fortunes were not made very clear. However, a general sense of the responsibilities that accrue with power sufficed for a while. As such it did not represent much of an advance beyond the earlier ideas of the social responsibility pioneers. But events were to give the stakeholder approach a powerful boost into theoretical glory, not for its moral claims but rather for its serviceability as a pragmatic management tool. Several leading corporations discovered that stakeholder management made sense at a time when fierce demands were being made upon business by a host of disaffected social groups and protest movements. Business leaders were now ready to endorse an idea that had originated as a moral yardstick—but they had other, more pragmatic reasons in mind. Knowing all about a company's stakeholders and how to deal with them might help to dampen the fires of social protest raging just outside the corporate bastions.[14]

It was not until the mid-1980s, some thirty-five years after the rudimentary idea surfaced, that the stakeholder concept was given serious theoretical attention within management circles. R. Edward Freeman's *Strategic Management: A Stakeholder Approach* became, and remains, the bible of stakeholder thinking. According to the theory, being actively aware of a company's stakeholders is the key to successful management of the firm. Stakeholder maps can be drawn up, thus revealing the breadth and complexity of any given company's stakeholders. Their values and motives might be found so that transactional strategies, both "offensive" and "defensive," could be plotted. All of the core business functions—marketing, finance, personnel, manufacturing, and so on—became potential candidates for reform in light of stakeholder perspectives. The board of directors and top-level executives were exhorted to adopt this wider view of a company's operations, thus giving the firm a better chance of surviving in the rough-and-tumble competitive business world. Freeman's central message was clear: "My focus is on how executives can use the concept, framework, philosophy and processes of the stakeholder approach to manage their organizations more effectively." With this strong pragmatic appeal, there was little or no explicit help offered to business executives who might seek ethical ways of dealing with their company's stakeholders. It was only on the book's final page that Freeman noted the importance of a normative standard that was to become a central tenet of busi-

---

14. A good account of the main attacks made on corporations by various interest groups during the 1960s and 1970s is found in David Vogel, *Lobbying the Corporation: Citizen Challenges to Business Authority*, New York: Basic Books, 1978. A flavor of the era's rhetoric is preserved in Charles Perrow, *The Radical Attack on Business*, New York: Harcourt Brace Jovanovich, 1972.

ness ethicists: "Ultimately, the 'stakeholder issue' must be resolved in the arena of 'distributive justice.'"[15] This afterthought was pursued vigorously by Freeman and others in subsequent years.

Freeman's more advanced treatment of the stakeholder idea was an analytic improvement over earlier models, but the managerial outcome was identical: stakeholder management was reputed to make a company more effective in reaching its goals. Its appeal, in the end, was more instrumental than moral, more economic than social, more managerial than normative. At most it seemed to marry a rather nonspecific sense of moral responsibility with a more readily understandable market success, an outcome even Milton Friedman might celebrate.

In truth, after a journey of some four decades, Responsibility Ethics came to rest in a moral fog not far from where it began. It seemed as if managers could have their moral-and-economic layer cake—and eat it, too. As Frank Abrams had told his managerial audience in 1951, "in the long run the public interest corresponds with the basic interests of [your] individual businesses."[16] Freeman delivered essentially the same message in 1984: acting responsibly toward a company's stakeholders was the way for managers to be strategically effective, economically successful, and publicly admired. In reaching this conclusion, Freeman was in effect agreeing with the similar view of Preston and Post, who advised some ten years earlier, act as public policy directs (i.e., to satisfy stakeholder groups) and your business fortunes are likely to improve.[17] This melding of public and private interests did little to point the moral way forward for business, and it left many questions unanswered.

Toward the end of its useful life, Responsibility Ethics was beset by friend

15. The passages in this paragraph are from Freeman, op. cit., pp. 27 and 249, respectively. Freeman later acknowledged the strategically instrumentalist thrust of this work. A footnote in *Corporate Strategy and the Search for Ethics*, coauthored in 1988 with Daniel Gilbert, says that "The approach there [in *Strategic Management: A Stakeholder Approach*] was completely a process approach, vulnerable to the criticisms we level at that genre in Chapter 7 [of the 1988 book]."

16. Abrams, op. cit., p. 34.

17. Freeman does not cite Preston and Post, suggesting that these two versions of stakeholder theory were an example of what anthropologists have called independent inventions representing parallel discoveries rather than an evolutionary kinship. A sociologist of knowledge might find interesting the fact that although all three authors were housed in (two different) business schools, Preston's degree is in economics and Post, his former student, is academically credentialed in management, while Freeman holds a doctorate in philosophy. The slight normative spin put on Freeman's first formulation of stakeholder theory can probably be attributed to his membership within the brotherhood of the Philosopher Knights (to be described further along), while Preston's and Post's reluctance to declare a direct normative function for the business executive reflects their own positivist training, which is more typically found in business faculties than in philosophy departments.

and foe alike. No one seemed to like it. Milton Friedman believed it to be subversive of the free enterprise system, while Theodore Levitt saw it as a reversion to feudal paternalism. John Kenneth Galbraith belittled it as an optional goal pursued only after a firm's economic purposes were achieved. Ralph Nader trashed the notion as just another smokescreen concealing nefarious profit goals. Neil Chamberlain argued that society itself, not business indifference or greed, imposed the most powerful restraints on companies seeking social goals, because social programs imposed costs, offered only long-run benefits, and posed a threat to the consumer's market-centered quest for material well-being. Preston and Post, as noted, wanted to substitute the political realities of "public responsibility" for the abstractions of "social responsibility." Harvard's Raymond Bauer and Robert Ackerman eschewed talk of "moral judgments" and social responsibility, favoring analysis of a company's social responsiveness *sans* pesky normative questions. The popularity of the Bauer-Ackerman view was confirmed in a citation analysis of the literature of social issues in management. After Preston and Post, their books were among the most frequently cited items in this field from 1980 to 1986.[18]

In the end, Responsibility Ethics remained attractive to two groups: the general public and business managers. It is worth pondering the reasons for their loyalty to a doctrine so thoroughly doubted by management theorists. Had the public and business practitioners sensed something of a moral nature in business operations that was not detected by business theorists? Or if detected by some theorists, did that discovery create for them a sense of deep philosophic unease that could be relieved by relegating the entire doctrine to the trash can of failed theory? An answer to that question can best be appreciated after exploring a second major effort to address the issues of business morality. The Age of the Applied Philosopher dawned even as Responsibility Ethics sank into a presumed oblivion.

PHILOSOPHIC ETHICS

Among the shortcomings of Responsibility Ethics was its seeming inability to come to grips with the specific meaning of social or moral responsibility and

---

18. Mahon and Andrews, op. cit., Exhibit 3. For representative critiques or dismissals of Responsibility Ethics, see Milton Friedman, op. cit.; Theodore Levitt, "The Dangers of Social Responsibility," *Harvard Business Review*, September-October 1958, pp. 41–50; John Kenneth Galbraith, *The New Industrial State*, New York: New American Library, 1967, p. 186; Ralph Nader and Mark J. Green (eds.), *Corporate Power in America*, New York: Grossman, 1973; Neil Chamberlain, *The Limits of Corporate Responsibility*, New York: Basic Books, 1973; Robert Ackerman, *The Social Challenge to Business*, Cambridge, MA: Harvard University Press, 1973, p. 4; and Robert W. Ackerman and Raymond A. Bauer, *Corporate Social Responsiveness: The Modern Dilemma*, Reston, VA: Reston, 1976.

how to make the desired responsibility operational. That moral fog persisted throughout the long vigil of Responsibility Ethicists but began to dissipate in the morning light as a new band of Philosophic Ethicists appeared on the scene. As applied philosophers, they provided the moral fiber and wielded a moral methodology that had been lacking or was unexpressed by their predecessors. A new vigor, both analytical and emotional, was injected into questions of business ethics.

These Knights of the Moral Roundtable proclaimed a Quest not previously heard in business realms: It was to seek and lay before the corporate barons a Normative Code, no less than a set of declared moral principles that would chart for these worthies and their firms ethical pathways through the field of temptations they might tread in the workaday world. The Knights displayed little patience with the bland moral generalities of Responsibility Ethics. They dismissed as self-serving rationalizations the moral refuges some earlier theorists and business practitioners had taken in the blandishments of enlightened self-interest and Adam Smith's market-driven "invisible hand." From their moral aerie, they scanned "the moral low ground on which business resides" and asserted that the only escape route lay in "addressing important business issues in moral terms."[19]

The Normative Code

In commenting on business operations, the applied philosophers' great advantage, which turned out to be their unique contribution, was to draw on normative principles long and deeply embedded in the history of Western thought. Such ancients as Aristotle, Plato, and lesser classical Greek thinkers were conjoined with others of later centuries, particularly Thomas Hobbes, Jean-Jacques Rousseau, Immanuel Kant, Adam Smith (as moral philosopher), John Locke and David Hume, Jeremy Bentham, and, later still, John Stuart Mill and the twentieth century's John Rawls. From this philosophic stew they extracted the essence of a normative code thought to be applicable to modern business practice.

The code rests primarily on twin and somewhat interlinked philosophic concepts: **rights** and **justice**. Rights are derived from Kant's critique of pure reason and his argument for what he labeled the "categorical imperative." This analysis concludes that one should "Act so as never to treat another human being merely as a means to an end." It follows that respect for all persons and—what amounts to the same thing—an obligation to acknowledge their dignity as human beings is a cardinal moral principle, particularly when

19. R. Edward Freeman and Daniel R. Gilbert, Jr., *Corporate Strategy and the Search for Ethics*, Englewood Cliffs, NJ: Prentice-Hall, 1988, p. 175.

the full development of the principle argues for its universal applicability. The Kantian rights principle became the central component of the philosophers' Normative Code, a preferred anchor in turbulent ethical seas.[20]

Justice is the Code's second ethical component. The contemporary philosopher John Rawls refurbished the ancient notion of social justice in his widely influential book *A Theory of Justice*, which has become the main underpinning of most current philosophic theories of business ethics. In a bow to the ancients' hoary ideas of justice, Rawls averred that "There is no reason to think that Aristotle would disagree with this [i.e., that principles of justice are derived from social institutions]. . . . There is no conflict with the [Aristotelian] traditional notion." He also rendered obeisance to John Locke, Jean-Jacques Rousseau, and Immanuel Kant, who are credited with the notion of the social contract that Rawls set out to carry "to a higher level of abstraction." The ghost of Kant was summoned to fortify the importance of justice as a moral principle: "Each person possesses an inviolability founded on justice that even the welfare of society as a whole cannot override." Indeed, "Justice is the first virtue of social institutions" and those institutions that are unjust "must be reformed or abolished."[21]

This was truly a sharp and menacing sword with which to arm the Philosopher Knights as they entered the lists to joust against any and all unjust institutions, not the least of which were contemporary profit-seeking business firms. Business practices that violated the rights and entitlements of individuals, that failed to respect people as human beings, that did not accord them the proper dignity, and that did not adhere to the principles of social justice were to become the focus of the philosophers' ethical analysis and critique.

Moral ethicians, along with any business *naifs* who might venture into moral reasoning precincts, were cautioned to be wary of a third moral methodology that had long occupied a central place in the calculus of business success or failure. **Utilitarian reasoning**, *when employed by business to decide a course of action* (such as whether to close a U.S. plant and/or move it to a new Third World location), attempts to describe and measure the economic benefits and economic costs to the firm. A net positive sum accruing to the company gives a green light to proceed, on grounds that the firm is better off economically. Utilitarian philosophers have been quick to point out that this kind of restricted utilitarian analysis falls short of considering all of the relevant costs, particularly social, familial, emotional, and psychological costs

20. This view is routinely found in business ethics textbooks. A good example is Manuel G. Velasquez, *Business Ethics: Concepts and Cases*, 2nd edition, Englewood Cliffs, NJ: Prentice-Hall, 1988, especially Chapters 1 and 2.

21. John Rawls, *A Theory of Justice*, Cambridge, MA: Harvard University Press, 1971. The quotations are from pp. 10–11 and 3, respectively.

(e.g., of a plant closure or relocation) that might not be revealed or considered when only monetary yardsticks are used and only company interests are calculated. This foreshortened version of utilitarian reasoning—some thought it could aptly be called "corporate utilitarianism"—was laden with problems that dulled its usefulness for confronting the most critically important kinds of ethical issues in business.

However, not everyone doubted utilitarianism's usefulness. Philosopher Richard DeGeorge may have been registering a minority opinion when he maintained that "Utilitarianism, far from being a self-serving approach to moral issues, demands careful, objective, impartial evaluation of consequences. It is a widely used—but often misused—approach to moral evaluation. A powerful tool of moral reasoning, it is a technique well worth mastering."[22] In truth, business ethics philosophers have split on the admissibility and uses of utilitarian concepts. When used narrowly to justify self-centered, egoistic behavior, or when it fails to account for all relevant costs and benefits, the approach is typically rejected. Perhaps one might be justified in speculating that the reluctance of many applied philosophers to embrace utilitarian reasoning has been tied to its accustomed usage by business decision makers, who after all are believed by some philosophers to stand on "moral low ground" and who, in truth, frequently seem willing to limit their fleeting moral considerations to a hasty and shallow cost–benefit calculation that ignores both rights and justice.

In some accounts, the philosophers' Normative Code encompasses all three principles—rights, justice, and utility—but finds moral finality in none. An ethics authority puts it this way:

> Our morality therefore contains three main kinds of moral considerations, each of which emphasizes certain morally important aspects of our behavior, but no one of which captures all the factors that must be taken into account. . . . These three kinds of moral considerations do not seem to be reducible to each other yet all three seem to be necessary parts of our morality. . . . This suggests that moral reasoning should incorporate all three kinds of moral considerations, even though only one or the other may turn out to be relevant or decisive in a particular situation.[23]

Even more troublesome has been an inability to locate what might be called the Code's normative core:

22. Richard DeGeorge, *Business Ethics*, 3rd edition, New York: Macmillan, 1990, p. 61.

23. Velasquez, op. cit., pp. 116–117. This textbook, which is especially clear in setting forth the Normative Code, is taken as broadly representative of several others where similar views are found.

We have at this time no comprehensive moral theory capable of determining precisely when utilitarian considerations become "sufficiently large" to outweigh narrow infringements on a conflicting right or standard of justice, or when considerations of justice become "important enough" to outweigh infringements on conflicting rights. Moral philosophers have been unable to agree on any absolute rules for making such judgments.[24]

Richard DeGeorge also has struggled with the question of moral priority:

There is no procedure or algorithm that we can automatically apply and rest assured that it will produce a satisfactory [ethical] solution. . . . When different approaches lead to different moral evaluations or to conflicting second-order principles . . . we must ultimately decide on the basis of which argument is stronger or clearer, and which result coheres better with our other moral judgments.[25]

But if one is forced to choose among the three principles—rights, justice, and utility—a respected authority advises that "standards concerned with moral rights have greater weight than either utilitarian standards or standards of justice. And standards of justice are generally accorded greater weight than utilitarian considerations."[26] While not all business ethicists would necessarily agree with this conclusion, it echoes a widely shared outlook about the moral priorities that are to be applied to business's ethical problems.

And so, Kant's rights and Rawls's justice trumped Bentham's and Mills's utilitarian approach as the Normative Code took shape. As the Code emerged and the Quest neared its goal, the Normative Code could be rendered as The Philosophers' Formula, in the following way:

$$EBB = f(R_k + J_r + U)$$

24. Ibid., pp. 117–118.

25. DeGeorge, op. cit., p. 82. DeGeorge pointed out that the failure to find a common moral methodology may not be so critical after all. "Despite the fact that the approaches differ, in the great majority of cases either method, if carefully, subtly, and conscientiously applied, will produce the same moral conclusions with respect to the morality of the practice or act." He also said, somewhat refreshingly, that "Solving moral issues requires a certain amount of common sense" (pp. 83, 84).

26. Velasquez, op. cit., pp. 117–118. Velasquez and two colleagues stated a similar position in a widely cited and admired article dealing with organizational politics. There decision makers were urged to consult their "conscience" and told that they might use yet other moral norms "as long as they are arrived at conscientiously." Unable to establish a valid theoretical claim for the superiority of one method over another, the authors simply asserted (in the article's final sentence) their personal belief that "respect for justice and human rights should prevail for its own sake." See Gerald F. Cavanagh, Dennis J. Moberg, and Manuel Velasquez, "The Ethics of Organizational Politics," *Academy of Management Review*, vol. 6, no. 3, 1981, pp. 363–374.

where

EBB is Ethical Business Behavior,

R_k is (Kantian) Rights reasoning,

J_r is (Rawlsian) Justice reasoning, and

U is Utilitarian reasoning.

This formulaic rendering of complicated issues is, of course, inadequate and incomplete but is intended to summarize the priorities assigned by applied philosophers to the various modes of ethical reasoning. By all odds, the Kantian rights principle is supreme, followed closely and in overlapping fashion by the Rawlsian justice principle. Utilitarian reasoning is thought to be useful but only if undertaken comprehensively in a way that includes consideration of all kinds of costs and benefits experienced by a wide range of parties throughout society. Corporate utilitarian reasoning that is focused solely on the economic and financial interests of a company is rejected as morally inadequate.

In offering this oversimplified formula there is no intention to denigrate the detailed and sophisticated presentations to be found in the works of many business ethicists. Without their contributions, the search for a normative methodology to judge business activities would be feeble indeed. Rather, the purpose here is to reduce the philosopher's approach to its essentials, so that it may be identified as one of the major ways proposed for teasing out and analyzing the many ethical complexities of the business institution. Supplementing and extending the Philosophers' Formula are additional insights of great analytic usefulness. One of the most powerful is the idea of a social contract between business and society.

Social Contracts and Moral Communities

The main path taken by contemporary ethical analysis of business operations leads through social contract theory. Thoroughly indebted to John Rawls's theory of justice, the version of social contract theory employed by business ethicists has also spawned a new and expanded concept of corporate stakeholders, one with a new set of ethical clothes not worn by the earlier version. Additionally, some social contractarians, as they are known in the trade, have managed to stretch their concepts to cover the entire business order, thus generating what has been called "Kantian capitalism." To the Philosophers' Formula, then, one must add these three components: social contract, an ethically refurbished corporate stakeholder concept, and the business system conceived as a Kantian moral community. Each bears further attention.

Social Contract. Thomas Donaldson was first into the field with a fully developed social contract interpretation of modern business. It is best to let him state the case in his own words:

> The point of applying social contract reasoning to business is to clarify the moral foundations of productive organizations, of which corporations happen to be one kind. As we look at the moral foundations of business, we are to presume that rational individuals living in a state of "nature"—in which everyone produces without benefit of the direct cooperative efforts of others—attempt to sketch the terms of an agreement between themselves and the productive organizations upon which they are considering bestowing status as legal, fictional persons, and to which they are considering allowing access to both natural resources and the existing employment pool.

> All productive organizations, then, are viewed as engaging in an implied contract with society, not unlike that employed by Locke, Rousseau, and Hobbes in understanding the moral and political foundations of the state. The raison d'etre for the productive organization turns out to be its contribution to society, tempered by a set of reciprocal obligations existing on both sides of the organization/society divide.[27]

The moral obligations laid on business firms by the social contract are "to enhance social welfare through satisfying consumer and worker interests, while at the same time remaining within the bounds of justice."[28] If that phrase sounds familiar, it should, because it is nothing less than the Normative Code written into the social contract between business and society. Rights—at least those of consumers and workers—and justice are to be the central moral directives for establishing right and wrong in business operations.

The analytic maneuvers used by social contract theorists to present their case normally raise the hackles of social scientists, who charge that several of the necessary assumptions are wildly at odds with contemporary knowledge of human behavior and institutional development. Following Rawls's lead, a "veil of ignorance" separates the contractors from knowledge of their own particular standing in the society for which a social contract is to be designed. This hypothetical device consciously removes the deliberations from any existing sociocultural interests and actual social contexts, as well as from any historical traditions or any social change that may be occurring at any given

---

27. Thomas Donaldson, *The Ethics of International Business*, New York: Oxford University Press, 1989, pp. 47–48. Donaldson's first formulation of the social contract for business is found in *Corporations and Morality*, Englewood Cliffs, NJ: Prentice-Hall, 1982.

28. Donaldson, *Corporations and Morality*, p. 57.

time. The contractors are then presumed to be rational actors frozen in a moment of time and capable of reasoning with exquisite precision. Unsullied by any suggestion of racial bias, ethnic identification, social standing, or gender perspective, and detached from all historical associations and events, they are to devise a logical, rational system for protecting the presumed rights of the contractors, thereby ensuring that social justice prevails for all. An often unstated, unrecognized, or unacknowledged assumption is that the participants are driven by rational self-interest to want to ensure for themselves as favorable a position as possible in the subsequent social arrangements so that they will, since shielded by a veil of ignorance, attempt to establish what they individually consider a minimum level of acceptable standing for themselves. The outcome of this "thought experiment" is said to be a system that reflects the most just and moral conditions that can be devised for all people living in such an organized society.

The flavor of social scientists' objections to this way of thinking about society is captured in the following passage:

> The idea of autonomous individuals choosing everything—their beliefs and values, their history and traditions, their social forms and family structures—is a vainglorious idea, one that could be invented only by thinkers who felt compelled to construct society out of theories. . . . [M]en are not born into a state of nature, they are born into a social compact that has long preceded them and without which their survival would have been impossible.[29]

These and other arguments between social contract philosophers and their detractors have a long history, too long to recount here. Donaldson has mounted a vigorous defense of his position.[30] Later in this book, an attempt is made to reconcile these differing perspectives so as to preserve something of methodological worth from each inquiring tradition.

The analytic outcome, and the probable intention, of social contractarian thinking is twofold. It established a mode of moral reasoning that could claim to be superior to and more comprehensive than that commonly employed by business professionals, who typically rely on narrower market-oriented utilitarian reasoning. The social contract approach simultaneously denies to business the moral defense that its market function alone justifies its existence, as well as the customarily favored treatment extended to the shareholder-owners. Emphasizing that older moral conventions were to lose their prior standing, Donaldson proposed that business and society "should act *as if* they had struck a deal, the kind of deal that would be acceptable to free, in-

29. James Q. Wilson, *The Moral Sense*, New York: Free Press, 1993, p. 234.

30. Donaldson, *The Ethics of International Business*, pp. 56–61.

formed parties acting from positions of *equal moral authority* [emphasis added]." Hence, if social contract thinking were to win out, the way would be opened for a wholesale moral attack on any business practices that could not be made to fit logically within the rationalist provisions of the presumed social contract. Of productive organizations that violate the terms of the social contract, Donaldson sternly warned (echoing Rawls's similar stricture), "They must reform themselves, or lose their moral right to exist."[31]

Stakeholder Theory Ethically Resuscitated. When last encountered earlier in this chapter, stakeholder theory had emerged as a strategic planning tool for managers striving for market success in a competitive world. As such, its advocates either did not attribute much moral significance to it beyond managers' fiduciary duties to stockholder-owners, or broader questions of ethics were simply not addressed or included. The concept was as appealing to strategy specialists who sought market efficiency for the corporation as to those who were trying to fathom the complexities of business and society linkages. The most that might be said for the theory in the mid-1980s was that it dealt with a company's *pragmatic responsiveness* to social and economic pressures but not with matters of *moral responsibility*.

The shift that brought stakeholder theory to the moral forefront is captured symbolically in the titles of two books published ten years apart. Freeman's pioneering theoretical study, published in 1984, was called *Strategic Management: A Stakeholder Approach*. As noted earlier, whatever wisps of ethical wisdom it contained were overridden by its focus on market-oriented strategic considerations. In a subtle shift of terminology, Joseph W. Weiss's 1994 classroom textbook, which acknowledged its debt to Freeman, bears the title *Business Ethics: A Managerial, Stakeholder Approach*. For Weiss, *business ethics*, not *strategic management*, is the major focus of stakeholder theory. He states that "a stakeholder approach includes moral, political, ecological, and human welfare interests as well as economic factors . . . [, is] a means of studying managers' social and moral responsibility strategies, actions, and outcomes toward other stakeholders . . . [and] a pragmatic way of understanding . . . moral claims of a host of constituencies."[32] For Weiss, the stakeholder concept that grew out of the older tradition of Responsibility Ethics becomes a

---

31. The first quotation in this paragraph is from Donaldson, *The Ethics of International Business*, p. 61. The second quotation is from Donaldson, *Corporations and Morality*, p. 54. For an alternative and less harsh presentation of the social contract's potentialities as a community-building device, see Denis Collins, "Adam Smith's Social Contract: The Proper Role of Individual Liberty and Government Intervention in 18th Century Society," *Business and Professional Ethics Journal*, vol. 7, nos. 3 and 4, 1988, pp. 119–146.

32. Joseph W. Weiss, *Business Ethics: A Managerial, Stakeholder Approach*, Belmont, CA: Wadsworth, 1994, p. 29.

central tenet of Philosophic Ethics, for it gives corporate managers a tool they can use to deal with workplace-generated *moral* issues. Indeed, Freeman's stakeholder emperor now sported new ethical garb.

But it turned out to be familiar clothing, nothing more or less than a modish style of the Philosophers' Formula. With an over-the-shoulder glance toward social contractarians, Weiss avers that companies are morally responsible if they "respond to [stakeholders'] legitimate *rights and claims* according to ethical standards of *fairness and justice,* as well as *utilitarian costs and benefits analyses.*"[33] Weiss's formulation, of course, reflects, as do all textbooks, what is considered to be a field's conventional wisdom. Others had previously laid the groundwork on which he built. Philosophers Norman Bowie and Ronald Duska focused on a company's *moral* responsibilities to stockholders, employees, consumers, and local communities. William Evan and Freeman restated in a morally expanded way Frank Abrams's assertion (almost word for word) that the job of management is to "keep the relationships among stakeholders in balance" and that a corporation's purpose is "to serve as a vehicle for coordinating stakeholder interests." With his coauthor, Daniel Gilbert, Freeman noted a variety of possible stakeholder approaches that had varying normative effects, but in the end these two authors seemed to turn away from all of them in urging companies to adopt a "personal projects enterprise strategy."[34]

One additional symbol of the conversion of stakeholder theory from strategy tool to ethical precept can be seen in the rather remarkable evolution of Thomas Donaldson's thinking about the matter. In his 1982 *Corporations and Morality,* which, as noted above, advocated a social contract approach, neither the term "stakeholder" nor the concept itself appears at all. When he tackled the ethical issues confronting international corporations in 1989, Donaldson declared that "The so-called stakeholder model of corporate social responsibility . . . is a genuinely normative . . . model" but that it "lacks any explicit theoretical moral grounding." Finding this shortcoming compelling, he preferred "either replacing or augmenting the stakeholder model" with his original social contract construct. By 1993, though, in a paper written with economist Lee E. Preston, Donaldson concluded that "the ultimate justification for

---

33. Ibid., p. 92, emphasis added. Weiss's readmittance of utilitarian reasoning into the charmed circle of acceptable ethics methodology is noteworthy, although it is not entirely clear whether he refers only to corporate utilitarianism. The question of utilitarianism's place in ethical analysis will be readdressed in a later chapter, where an attempt is made to develop a normative synthesis among the various approaches discussed here.

34. Norman E. Bowie and Ronald Duska, *Business Ethics,* 2nd edition, Englewood Cliffs, NJ: Prentice-Hall, 1990; William M. Evan and R. Edward Freeman, "A Stakeholder Theory of the Modern Corporation: Kantian Capitalism," in Tom L. Beauchamp and Norman E. Bowie (eds.), *Ethical Theory and Business,* 3rd edition, Englewood Cliffs, NJ: Prentice-Hall, 1988, p. 103; and Freeman and Gilbert, op. cit., p. 72 and Chapter 8.

the stakeholder theory is to be found in its normative base" because "the interests of all stakeholders are of *intrinsic value.*" In spite of this gradual and somewhat grudging acknowledgment of the normative component of the stakeholder concept, his central interest remained with the social contract, whose ethical reach he extended and enriched in yet another paper.[35] One result of Donaldson's endorsement of the normative import of stakeholder theory was that other ethicists were then able to find moral meaning in a corporation's stakeholder relationships by adopting the Rawlsian social contract principles advocated by Donaldson.

Kantian Capitalism and the Moral Community. Standing somewhat to one side but still part of the larger normative net being cast over business affairs is a variant of the social contract model that perceives the modern corporation to be a moral community. The most articulate exponent of this view has been philosopher Norman Bowie, who probes for a normative structure that may lie concealed within business practices. Bowie reasons that Kantian rights require that all stakeholders of a company be respected and that their claims be given full consideration. That means that their views should be sought whenever their rights are affected by any contemplated corporate actions. Rawlsian justice can be approximated only if a company has procedures and policies that acknowledge and can actually implement and protect all stakeholders' rights. When a company and its managers accept such conditions and constraints, the corporation can be viewed as "a moral community" where "the management of the firm will be done from the moral perspective. The other stakeholder groups would in a similar fashion honor their moral obligations. . . . In such a firm all the stakeholders would be treated with the respect required by morality."[36]

This Kantian corporation, it turns out, would bear a normative burden even heavier than those imposed by the social contractarians. Also incurred would be a responsibility and an obligation to solve social problems *for altruistic reasons.* A company would fall short morally if it were to achieve only the "moral minimum" of avoiding harm in its actions, even if in doing so it also respected individual rights and justice. Not only would a business's financial interests be enhanced by altruistically driven operations that improve and re-

35. The 1989 quotation is from Donaldson, *The Ethics of International Business*, pp. 45–47. The 1993 passages are from Donaldson and Preston, op. cit., pp. 87–88 and 67, respectively. Donaldson's extension of social contract thinking is found in Thomas Donaldson and Thomas W. Dunfee, "Towards a Unified Conception of Business Ethics: Integrative Social Contracts Theory," *Academy of Management Review*, vol. 19, no. 2, April 1994, pp. 252–284. The latter perspective receives further attention in Chapter 9 of this book.

36. Norman E. Bowie, "The Firm as a Moral Community," in Richard M. Coughlin (ed.), *Morality, Rationality, and Efficiency: New Perspectives on Socio-Economics*, Armonk, NY: M. E. Sharpe, 1991, pp. 176–179.

spect the rights of its labor force, but it would in the process create a "public good" for the entire business system.[37] An alert ear attuned to this argument could detect faint echoes of an "invisible hand" of altruism replacing Adam Smith's equally unseen hand of profit-driven market competition, for in both cases a greater (public) good not intended by their initiators was to be the outcome of actions motivated by lesser purposes. Bowie's full position, which is not developed here, builds on Kant's three formulations of the categorical imperative. These draw on such items as truth telling, trust building, respect for persons, procedural justice, and equity. For him, the motives of managers, including altruistic ones, are important components of the Kantian corporation, helping to move it in morally correct directions.[38]

The optimistic outlook that pervades Bowie's rendition of the Kantian business firm includes positive answers to the question of whether such an altruistic company can operate at a competitive advantage and make a profit. His position is supported by Toronto University's Max Clarkson, whose study of forty-two large corporations demonstrated that a deliberate attempt by managers to balance profit goals and the social concerns of stakeholders paid off in average or above-average profit levels. Companies that sought to maximize profits without a balanced response to social demands recorded below-average profit performance compared with their competitors. Clarkson insists that "The corporation's economic orientation will not come at the expense of its social, or moral, orientation. Profits and ethics coexist. [They] are integrated into the strategic planning and decision making of the corporation." Based as they are on empirical research findings (unlike the abstract theorizing of many philosopher-ethicists), Clarkson's views bear serious consideration. From the larger population studied, he has described specific companies that exemplify the essential meaning of Bowie's Kantian corporation.[39]

37. Norman E. Bowie, "New Directions in Corporate Social Responsibility," *Business Horizons*, July-August 1991, pp. 56–65. In other writings, Bowie has maintained that the corporation's main purpose is to provide "meaningful work" for its employees, a position close to that of Freeman and Gilbert's "personal projects enterprise strategy" mentioned earlier. See Bowie's "The Paradox of Profit" in N. Dale Wright (ed.), *Papers on the Ethics of Administration*, Provo, Utah: Brigham Young University, 1988, pp. 97–120. For a somewhat related but practitioner-oriented argument that corporations should act altruistically, see Rabindra N. Kanungo and Jay A. Conger, "Promoting Altruism as a Corporate Goal," *Academy of Management Executive*, vol. VII, no. 3, August 1993, pp. 37–48.

38. Bowie has written a brief precis of his approach to business ethics, entitled "Enough Already," for *The Society for Business Ethics Newsletter*, vol. 4, no. 4, February 1994, pp. 3–4.

39. Max B. E. Clarkson, "The Moral Dimension of Corporate Social Responsibility," in Coughlin, op. cit., p. 194. See also Clarkson, "Corporate Social Performance in Canada, 1976–1986," in Lee E. Preston (ed.), *Research in Corporate Social Performance and Policy*, vol. 10, Greenwich, CT: JAI Press, 1988, pp. 241–265; and Clarkson and Michael C. Deck, "The Stakeholder Management Model in Practice," The Centre for Corporate Social Performance and Ethics, Faculty of Management, University of Toronto, January 1992. Clarkson's inclusion of economic performance within the sphere of a company's social responsibilities will be revisited later in this chapter.

Philosophic Ethics, in the end, can be fairly said to have injected an analytic edge into what had previously been the morally flabby discussions of Responsibility Ethics. The Normative Code that stresses rights and justice does, even its detractors have to admit, provide substance and content to the empty prattlings that had earlier passed for moral dialogue. The Philosophers' Formula that attempts to level the moral playing ground by reducing business's reliance on utilitarian reasoning might be thought unfair, unbalanced, pragmatically unrealistic, and abstractly ideal in the most impracticable manner, but it at least puts business practitioners and their defenders on notice that tangible moral principles for evaluating business's performance are available if and when needed.

But questions remained. To their credit, even the boldest of the Philosopher Knights hesitated to assert that the Grail itself had been found. Their deeds of valor had driven them onto ground contested by other seekers of moral yardsticks who, while partaking of some of the Kantian-Rawlsian moral potions, believed that yet other ways might be found to rein in the rogues and rascals found within the business kingdom. Still small in overall numbers and with unknown strength, another group now began to gather on the ethics battlefield. Their banners proclaimed a Behavioral/Organizational Ethic.

BEHAVIORAL/ORGANIZATIONAL ETHICS

A third kind of normative explanation of business practices has been produced by observing how the workplace itself can exert an influence on the people who work there. In these accounts, the interplay between work context and working behavior generates normative questions, issues, and dilemmas. For example, the personnel director of a company who must implement a reduction-in-force may face painful choices in deciding how to administer the required layoffs in a fair manner. Or a purchasing manager under orders to reduce costs may be required to sever relationships with a reliable but high-priced suppplier whose business may then founder. In such cases, the manager's ethical discomfort—and the way it is resolved—are an outgrowth of workplace pressures and a person's ethical conscience. How people act in such circumstances can reveal much about the normative content of business decisions. Even greater ethical insights are possible when actual behavior is related to the attitudes, the preconceptions, the reciprocal assumptions made by the actors, and the motivations embedded within individual psyches and encouraged by organizational arrangements. It is true that simple descriptions alone, absent a contextual ethical orientation to life-affecting human experience, tell little or nothing per se that is of evaluative interest. But somewhere within the actual practices and behaviors (i.e., the everyday experiences) of human actors—who rarely, if ever, act in isolation from a sociocultural tradition rich in ethical dimensions—one can seek and perhaps locate the ethical components that cause business activities to be either praised or blamed. Certainly, say some, to search *outside* this behavioral/organizational arena is to look in the wrong place.[40] It is from such a contextualist perspective that management theorists have proposed ways of judging business behavior. Taken collectively, their views can be labeled **Behavioral/Organizational Ethics**.

If Philosophic Ethics evokes an image of questing Philosopher Knights, the management theorists who seek normative clues within the business firm call to mind the White-Coated Laboratory Scientist. The White Coats fine-tune their observational instruments in an attempt to resolve into crisp images the otherwise fuzzy blurs that pass for normative behavior. And if they cannot catch a glimpse of the actual behavior itself, they at least hope to capture the tangible factors that produce the behavior and that cause it to be identified as normative in nature. They frequently affect a morally detached manner, as if—in contradistinction to all that is now known about observational science—they can separate themselves and their own normative inclinations and attitudes from the subjects and objects they study. One should not take such objective posturing seriously. Where not motivated by a simple effort to ensure honesty and integrity in research, it merely bespeaks the presence of the hovering (and now discredited) phantom of positivist science. In spite of such methodological lapses, the actual research findings of the White Coats far outweigh in importance their occasional philosophic timidity.

A Value-Laden Workplace

Shakespeare's plays sometimes begin with a prologue played out on the proscenium, as a way of providing the theater audience with a suitably descriptive account of events that have preceded the action that is to follow, when the actors will take their places and begin the play. So it is now with those contextualist scholars who, as Chorus, precede the main action by telling of the arena in which the ethics drama is to occur. Once they have set the scene, the main actors—business managers and others who populate and give life to the corporate body—enter to play their parts. As the plot unfolds, one begins to sense the important role played by the intersections—the moral crossroads, so to speak—where organizational context and real people

---

40. One is reminded of the simpleton who one evening, in searching for a lost glove, was asked if he dropped the glove at that location. He replied, "No, but the light is better here."

come together to confront normative issues of much significance. First, then, to the ethical realm of business operations.

Ethical Work Climates. Business behavior is strongly affected by a company's culture and by the groups of people who live their professional lives within that culture. As one management scholar has said, "Work organizations provide the social context within which behavior takes place. . . . Theory and research . . . offer strong support for situational variables [i.e., an organizational context] having a profound effect on ethical/unethical behavior in most people." Another claims that "The necessity and advantages of an ethical organizational culture to promote ethical behavior at work have never been seriously challenged," while a third points out that some business cultures are capable of "creating a climate which not only discourages ethical behavior among employees but may actually *encourage* blatantly unethical practices."[41] Some of these effects were discussed earlier in Chapter 5, where ethical climates were seen to embody and give tangible expression to economizing and power-aggrandizing values. The emphasis in this chapter is to reveal how powerfully an ethical workplace climate can dictate the meaning of morality to business practitioners.

Workplace climates display an identifiable normative content. Believing that "individual characteristics alone are insufficient to explain moral and ethical behavior," the primary researchers have attempted to demonstrate that "ethical climates identify the normative systems that guide organizational decision making."[42] These ethical work climates exist as *perceptions* in the minds of employees and managers, who learn that certain normative behaviors are permitted and encouraged while others are forbidden and perhaps punished. The climate, as such, is never seen. One knows of its presence only by getting into the minds of those who create it through their own perceptions of what is considered right and wrong. A subtle notion, ethical climates are hidden yet present, controlling but unvoiced, detected largely through indirect and sometimes furtive but knowing signals (a lifted eyebrow, a shrug of the shoulders, a cynical wink), yet clearly recognized by all of those who both create these climates and fall under their normative sway.

41. The quotations in this paragraph are, respectively, from Linda Klebe Trevino, "Ethical Decision Making in Organizations: A Person–Situation Interactionist Model," *Academy of Management Review*, vol. 11, no. 3, 1986, p. 614; James Weber, "Institutionalizing Ethics into Business Organizations," *Business Ethics Quarterly*, vol. 3, no. 4, October 1993, p. 422; and Deborah Vidaver Cohen, "Creating and Maintaining Ethical Work Climates," *Business Ethics Quarterly*, vol. 3, no. 4, October 1993, p. 355.

42. Bart Victor and John B. Cullen, "The Organizational Bases of Ethical Work Climates," *Administrative Science Quarterly*, vol. 33, 1988, pp. 101–125. The quotations are from pp. 103 and 123, respectively.

Ethical climates seem to pervade entire companies, departments, and divisions within a single company, varying from company to company and within subdivisions. Researchers say that "organizations have combinations of ethical climates." What is acceptable ethically in one company or department may not be perceived as welcome in another, or varying ethical precepts may dominate different climates. For example, caring for one's fellow employees or for a firm's customers may count for much in one firm, while in another business more attention might be paid to simple instrumental ways of promoting the company's economizing goals without special regard for the needs of others. As these signals are sent through perceptual pathways, they simultaneously help establish and reinforce ethically acceptable ways of behaving and making workplace decisions.

The methodological contrast here between the Philosopher Knights and the White Coats is striking. Rather than imposing pre-defined, abstract normative categories on a company's inhabitants, the contextualists elicit ethical meanings by *taking testimony* from organizational actors (through interviews or questionnaire responses) based on their *workplace experiences*. Not devoted to the rigors and glories of a Normative Quest, the White Coats *do not seem* to prescribe a preferred normative direction. Organization scientists Bart Victor and John Cullen, who pioneered the study of ethical climates, have said that "[W]e are unwilling to judge whether one type of normative system is inherently more moral than another."[43] Moreover, they claim to be more interested in identifying the *process* of ethical reasoning found within these climates than in whatever moral outcomes those climates may encourage (or discourage) company employees to produce. Pushed to a logical conclusion, this posture would be equivalent to saying that the procedures used by dictatorial governments to suppress dissent, or by a theocracy to stifle alternative religious views, are more worthy of scholarly attention than to know what moral outcomes might be produced by political dissent and religious pluralism.

However, close examination reveals that moral categories are deliberately invoked and built into the very concept of ethical work climates. The same researchers acknowledge that "[E]thical philosophy and theories of ethical behavior guided our selection of ethical issues that possibly form the bases of work climates." Climate theorists rely on either the moral learning and development theories of educational psychologist Lawrence Kohlberg or the simi-

---

43. Ibid., footnote 1, p. 106. One wonders whether this comment was urged on the authors by the editors and referees of the journal that published their research, which is noted for adhering to a positivist form of reporting research. In some cases, though, the positivist habit of mind is so ingrained that it becomes a self-policing device, requiring no prompting by editorial guardians of the faith.

lar theories of psychologist James Rest. The research instruments used to detect ethical climates are designed to reflect such moral orientations. In these methodological ways, morality is insinuated subtly into the workplace and shown to be perceived as an ethical work climate.[44] These "normative control systems for organizations"—which, to repeat, are purely perceptual phenomena—stem from the larger society's norms of behavior (e.g., showing respect for others), from various types of bureaucratic structures typical of organizations (e.g., hierarchical authority versus horizontal participation), and from a company's history and its success in inculcating a more or less uniform view in its work force of what is meant by ethical behavior there (e.g., Johnson & Johnson, which became well known for its successful handling of tainted capsules).

Researcher Barbara Toffler found similar forces at work during her in-depth interviews with corporate executives, citing "the [positive] presence of policies, rules, or procedures that either tell them what to do or back up their decisions [which] makes dealing with ethical situations less painful." She also discovered that an organization's culture, the "design and implementation of personnel and information management systems," and routine institutionalized habits can contribute to unreflective and unethical business decisions.[45] So powerful is this "self-reinforcing organizational mind-set" in acting as an organizational arbiter of right and wrong that it has been called a "stacked deck" to suggest that it disproportionately weights ethical rules to favor the company's interests over all others. This effect is particularly likely when linked to what is called "the performance ethic [which] is the heart of America. Growth, wealth-creation, achievement, and performance are some of the principal reasons we created organizations. . . . In a word, organizations must be able . . . to resolve internal conflicts between 'business as usual' and a higher level of morality in such a way that *the organization's affairs, as these are understood by its leaders, do not seriously suffer.*"[46]

Ethical work climates appear capable of supporting unethical or even criminal behavior, although that outcome may be only one unintended and unrecognized function of an organization's structure, its customary rules or standard operating procedures, and unexamined assumptions of how people will behave under certain circumstances. For example, the research of James Waters records instances of corporate bribery and price fixing as a direct

---

44. For a general acknowledgment of their debt to social scientists for providing behaviorally relevant moral categories, see Victor and Cullen, op. cit., pp. 102–108. The quotations in this paragraph are from pp. 103 and 119, respectively.

45. Barbara Ley Toffler, *Tough Choices: Managers Talk Ethics*, New York: Wiley, 1986, pp. 24–28.

46. H. R. Smith and Archie B. Carroll, "Organizational Ethics: A Stacked Deck," *Journal of Business Ethics*, no. 3, 1984, pp. 95–100. Emphasis added.

function of company structure, and M. Cash Mathews has outlined the various ways in which managers learn to commit on-the-job criminal acts.[47]

Thus, the normative stage on which business decisions are made seems amply supplied with normative cues about the kinds of decisions perceived to be ethically appropriate. But what about the actors who are to play their parts in the drama of everyday business life?

The Managerial Actors. There is every reason to believe that the real people who live within business firms bring preconceived attitudes and orientations to any normative question that they may encounter at work. These turn out to be remarkably similar to the kinds of approaches taken by most adults. That means that corporate managers reason their way through moral dilemmas by considering the impact of their decisions on their close workplace associates, as well as whether those decisions are legal. Few venture beyond group loyalty or society's legal standards in thinking about ethical constraints or opportunities. Not even threats to personal integrity or violations of professional standards seem to override the executive's tendency to reason at a moral level centered in company loyalty and law.[48]

Managers' values play a related role in creating behavioral possibilities. One study of over 400 managers found that nearly three-quarters of them preferred to emphasize competence values rather than moral values. By linking personal, ego-centered values with competence values and moral values with a social orientation, an even bleaker result was discovered:

> . . . most managers [53.5%] place greater importance upon personal and competence values as guiding principles in their lives than on social and moral values [6.3%]. . . . This finding is understandable when one considers that managers are immersed in a work environment where economic and psychological incentives to perform and achieve are overwhelmingly present. Most managers adopt those values that will enable them to compete more successfully against their peers or competitors.[49]

Important as a person's *value commitments* and *moral reasoning skills* are, they are not the entire story. Two other business researchers point out that actual on-the-job ethical decision making depends also on the desire a man-

47. James A. Waters, "Catch 20.5: Corporate Morality as an Organizational Phenomenon," *Organizational Dynamics*, Spring 1978, pp. 3–19; and M. Cash Mathews, *Strategic Intervention in Organizations: Resolving Ethical Dilemmas*, Newbury Park, CA: Sage, 1988, especially Chapter 3, and the Foreword written by Marshall B. Clinard.

48. James Weber, "Managers' Moral Reasoning: Assessing Their Responses to Three Moral Dilemmas," *Human Relations*, vol. 43, no. 7, 1990, pp. 693–695.

49. James Weber, "Managerial Value Orientations: A Typology and Assessment," *International Journal of Value Based Management*, vol. 3, no. 2, 1990, pp. 49–50.

ager may have for *moral approbation* from others. Since individuals vary in the amount and degree of moral approval they seek, some managers are likely to approach moral issues and make decisions differently from their peers. Extant research suggests that the moral quality of managers' decisions will be higher "when the stakes are high, when they know the act in question is immoral, when they are intimately involved, and when pressure to behave immorally is low." When these conditions are present, "individuals will assign themselves the greatest moral responsibility for their actions, and . . . will anticipate the greatest amount of moral disapproval from themselves or others if they fail to behave ethically." In a laudable effort to link observed behavior with philosophical moral principles, these particular research scholars say that "we are trying to show that actual human beings draw (approximately) the same normative conclusions that moral philosophers do with respect to the elements of moral responsibility."[50] Managerial actors can likewise be influenced by the *kinds of moral issues* they encounter. The "moral intensity" of an issue—for example, the amount of harm that may be done, how close one is to the action both physically and temporally, how many people agree about its ethicality, and so on—exerts a moral pull that is hard to resist. The higher the intensity, the greater is the likelihood that moral standards will be brought to bear.[51]

Left untouched by the White Coats—perhaps an oddity spawned from their empirically grounded research methods—is the question of how an individual's *character* might influence ethical perceptions and actions. Long ago displaced by the psychologist's concept of personality, "character" conveys a quaint, antique connotation, one not attuned to the precision sought through the use of rigorous social science methods. There is no small degree of irony here, for as one commentator has noted, character encapsulates many of the qualities thought by the White Coats to be a part of ethical action. "When directed toward developing a constellation of qualities like sensitivity, loyalty, courage, fairness, honesty, and openness, the manager reveals a particular and visible moral identity. Direction, determination, movement— all reflect the operation of a developed character guided by a developed con-

---

50. Thomas M. Jones and Lori Verstegen Ryan, "Moral Approbation and Ethical Decision Making in Organizations," unpublished manuscript, pp. 33 and 16–17, respectively.

51. Thomas M. Jones, "Ethical Decision Making by Individuals in Organizations: An Issue-Contingent Model," *Academy of Management Review*, vol. 16, no. 2, 1991, pp. 366–395. James Weber also reported the possibility that managers are influenced by the type of ethical issue they confront, applying a more advanced level of moral reasoning in some cases than in others, thus suggesting the presence of a "hierarchy of moral issues." See Weber, "Managers' Moral Reasoning," op. cit., pp. 698–699; and James Weber, "Assessing the Influence of the Moral Issue and Its Intensity upon Managerial Decision Making," in Jean Pasquero and Denis Collins (eds.), *1993 Proceedings, International Association for Business and Society*, San Diego, CA, March 1993, pp. 390–394.

science. What we do morally is determined not solely by rules or responses to one particular situation but by what we have become through our past history."[52] Perhaps this is to suggest that the delineation of character is best entrusted to poets, portraitists, novelists, and playwrights than to White-Coated Laboratory Scientists.

"Character" has recently been resurrected as an explanatory variable accounting for some aspects of business behavior. Much of this work, usually bearing the title of "virtue ethics," is pridefully derived from Aristotle's thoughts of over two millennia ago, now given a modern gloss by today's philosophers of both applied and nonapplied inclination. If these insights were to be joined with those of contemporary students of organizational behavior, a new way of understanding on-the-job ethical needs might be revealed.[53]

In these various ways—some related to values held, others to moral reasoning applied, yet others reflecting a search for moral approval, and some linked to types of issues faced—the organizational actors play their parts. They interpret their roles in varying fashion, as one expects from any compelling drama. It remains now only to see the moral intersection created when the staged scenery of the workplace and the players' individual interpretations come together in the final act's denouement.

The Moral Crossroads. Perhaps the simplest and most profound insight developed by the White Coats is what might be called the Interactionist Principle: The amount and degree of ethical activity to be found within business is a function of organizational context *and* individual actor. Neither one alone determines the outcome of any ethical situation. A work climate that seems to foster principles of justice, fairness, and caring may fall short of realizing such ethical ideals if it is populated or managed by people who are only instrumentally inclined to seek contrary goals for themselves or the company. They may interpret the ethical climate correctly but be unwilling or unable to conform to its moral directives. For example, managers who sincerely wish to deal fairly with loyal employees with many years' service to the company at a time when personnel layoffs are required may find themselves boxed in morally by market forces threatening the company's existence. Or a young professional employee asked to falsify a report to save face for an organiza-

52. Clarence C. Walton, *The Moral Manager*, Cambridge, MA: Ballinger, 1988, p. 177.

53. A step in this general direction has been taken by Robert Solomon in *Ethics and Excellence: Cooperation and Integrity in Business*, New York: Oxford University Press, 1992. For a compact review and bibliography of "virtue ethics," see David Kirkwood Hart, "Administration and the Ethics of Virtue," in Terry L. Cooper (ed.), *Handbook of Administrative Ethics*, New York: Marcel Dekker, 1994, pp. 107–123.

tional superior or to help the company escape government scrutiny faces a cruel moral dilemma (and possible job loss) if no support is forthcoming from an established and enforced ethical code of conduct. The ethical outcome in such cases depends upon a blend of organizational culture and personal commitment to ethical precepts.

The major research finding of organizational ethicist Karen Newman was precisely in support of the Interactionist Principle. The more ethical a work climate is, the more likely are the people who work there to make ethical decisions. Even better news is that the amount of "principled moral reasoning" increases with a more clearly delineated ethical work climate. "An ethical climate encourages those with more principled moral reasoning capacity to use that capacity in making principled moral judgments. . . . The context within which behavior takes place has a powerful effect on behavior, limiting and shaping options. When context is not taken into account . . . the true relationship between moral reasoning and behavior is masked." For Newman, principled moral reasoning displayed by an individual includes consideration of "justice, concern for the rights and well-being of others, and maintenance of cooperative social systems." She views "the moral climate of the organization as a signalling device, indicating the legitimacy of using different classes of criteria in decision making." As workplace climate and employees interact, they create the moral crucible that gives form and meaning to the course of a company's normative actions.[54] The Interactionist Principle is given further support by research showing that individual practitioners interact differently with the particular ethical issues they encounter, so that even a work climate strongly supportive of ethical behavior may fail if a given ethical issue is not perceived to be compelling by an otherwise moral employee.[55]

And so, it is the skill (or carelessness) of those who design the stage set, together with the actors' imaginative moral creativity (or lack thereof), that drives the plot and that finally brings down the curtain on the ethical drama played out daily in the workplace.

Plus ça change . . .

A major distinction separates Behavioral/Organizational Ethics from Philosophic Ethics. For Behavioral/Organizational Ethicists, the ethics, the norma-

---

54. Karen L. Newman, "Principled Moral Judgment in Decision Making: Individual and Organizational Determinants," unpublished manuscript, April 1993. The quoted passages are from pp. 29–30, 2, and 4, respectively. Newman's primary method was an in-basket simulation using MBA students as respondents, and her conclusions are therefore only suggestive of what might be true for an actual company. She reports, though, that the simulation's developers claim that "managers' behavior in the simulation is remarkably similar to their behavior on their actual jobs" (p. 21).

55. Jones, "Ethical Decision Making," op. cit, and Weber, "Managers' Moral Reasoning," op. cit.

tive orientations, and the moral inclinations of the workplace are *in* the organization and its climate, *in* the people who work there, and *in* the interactions between organizational context and workplace inhabitants. Whether a business firm and its people will act ethically depends, not on externally derived, abstract philosophic principles but on the values that employees and managers bring with them as they come to work, as well as the values they find in the company's past traditions and present practices. The White Coats look for those values, seek to identify just where on a scale of moral reasoning one might find business people to be located, and they search especially for the normative pressures exerted on business people by their company's organizational systems.

Perhaps most distinctive of all, theirs is an *experiential* theory of ethics that derives normative meaning from the collective experiences of people working together. For them, justice, fairness, caring, and moral entitlements become a function of organizational dynamics, reflecting the necessities of work and cooperation, as well as the aspirations and desires of employees to be considered a worthy part of the collective undertaking that is business. They conclude that normative phenomena are generated *within* the workplace. In this respect, they differ from both Responsibility Ethics and Philosophic Ethics, whose advocates believe that the sources of morality are *external* to the firm and require acceptance by business of abstract ideal principles, rather than deriving morality from experiences acquired in the workplace. As one behavioral theorist put it, "Where the philosophical discussion of ethics is often highly abstract, business ethics includes an explicit reference to the *experience* of the individual organizational actor; it attempts to reflect, to some degree, the difficulties faced by real individuals making ethical decisions in real situations in the hope of helping them to make a more ethical choice in the future."[56]

Some of the more enthusiastic White Coats maintain that organizational restructuring and internal controls alone may bring business to heel:

> For those upper-echelon executives who wish to foster a corporate culture in which illegal or unethical behavior is "unthinkable," a workable method of implementation is a two pronged, long-term intervention approach. First, structural changes within the corporation can be undertaken. Secondly, reinforcement contingencies can be analyzed and revised to promote prosocial behavior. Such a two-

56. Nelson Phillips, "Understanding Ethics in Practice: An Ethnomethodological Approach to the Study of Business Ethics," *Business Ethics Quarterly*, vol. 2, no. 2, April 1992, pp. 223–224. Emphasis added. The importance of context is emphasized also by anthropologist Fredrik Barth: "[T]o study what we may choose to call values, we must embed our data in the particular context of concepts and practices within which the actors themselves are positioned." Barth, "Are Values Real? The Enigma of Naturalism in the Anthropological Imputation of Values," in Michael Hechter, Lynn Nadel, and Richard E. Michod (eds.), *The Origin of Values*, New York: Aldine de Gruyter, 1993, p. 44.

pronged approach is essential to the establishment and *maintenance* of an ethical and law-abiding corporate culture.[57]

Others who seek to introduce "ethics formally and explicitly into daily business life" say that it "requires behavioral influence, and behavioral change if necessary" but that the desired behavior must be linked to some specific (philosophical) meaning of ethics. For example, "[E]thical action is justified when it maximizes the greatest good for the greatest number (utilitarianism), when it adheres to the ethical principles of justice, fairness, and a respect for individual rights, or when it complies with the moral duty entrusted to the individual (deontology)."[58] That prescription is only another version of the now-familiar Philosophers' Formula. Other White Coats have invoked its moral message as well. Management theorists Robert Gatewood and Archie Carroll say: "[N]orms emanating from a consideration of *rights*, *justice*, and *utilitarianism* should be brought to bear on the [ethical] standard-setting process." Climate theorists Victor and Cullen propose "three classes of ethical theories . . . [which] are labeled egoism, benevolence, and [deontological] principle" and are their equivalent terms for *utilitarian, justice-fairness*, and *rights* principles. Newman speaks of "principled criteria" as "norms of *justice, fairness*, the *rights* and well-being of others, . . . and cooperative social systems." And socioeconomist Amitai Etzioni favors "moderate deontology" (i.e., a reliance on moral duty as well as moral consequences) in formulating a moral dimension for economic behavior.[59]

Hence, these two inquiring traditions, one based in philosophy and the other in social science, converge at the all-important point of defining the meaning of ethical actions. In the end, the White Coats seem to join forces with the Philosopher Knights, the latter certain of the goal they seek, the former convinced that their lamps will illuminate the paths that must be trod if the Quest is to succeed. This normative convergence tells much about the course taken in recent years by ethical analysis of business. However, the

---

57. Mathews, op. cit., p. 136.

58. James Weber, "Institutionalizing Ethics into Business Organizations: A Model and Research Agenda," *Business Ethics Quarterly*, vol. 3, no. 4, October 1993, pp. 420, 421.

59. The quotations here are respectively from Robert D. Gatewood and Archie B. Carroll, "Assessment of Ethical Performance of Organization Members: A Conceptual Framework," *Academy of Management Review*, vol. 16, no. 4, 1991, p. 677, emphasis added; Victor and Cullen, op. cit., p. 105; Newman, op. cit., pp. 2, 3, emphasis added; and Amitai Etzioni, *The Moral Dimension: Toward a New Economics*, New York: Free Press, 1988, pp. 11–13, 253. Not all White Coats rely on these conventional normative categories. Thomas Jones, op. cit., admitting that substantive definitions of ethics are hard to come by, settles for a relativistic meaning. Linda Trevino, op. cit., who relies on Lawrence Kohlberg's stages of moral development for her concept of ethics, eschews the Philosophers' Formula altogether, saying, somewhat dismissively, that "The profile of each stage has meaning without any background in ethics or philosophy"—a point others might dispute.

reappearance of the Philosophers' Formula, while welcome in one sense, also signals the presence of one of the principal, though unrecognized, obstacles to further progress in the search for the normative base of business operations. It is an obstacle that impedes the way of all three groups—the Responsibility Ethicists, the Philosophic Ethicists, and the Behavioral/Organizational Ethicists. A full airing of this theoretical shortcoming is reserved for the following chapter, after first outlining the core moral message sent by today's business ethicists to business practitioners.

THE MORAL MANDATE—AND ITS MISSING LINKS

The collective moral lesson taught by business ethicists goes something like this. Business is more than an economic enterprise. It is also a social institution, succoring large numbers of people who work there, and supporting others who supply it with resources and trade with it in the marketplace. Its operations extend far beyond its immediate neighborhood, having an impact on the environment and on host governments and citizens of diverse nations. The Responsibility Ethicists emphasize the social and human responsibilities that accrue to business corporations. For them, the power and influence of business call forth (or at least they say it should) a commensurate amount of social and moral responsibility. For those companies not inclined to accept this social mandate, an Iron Law of Responsibility operates to remove or reduce their influence over others: Act responsibly or lose your power.

To this general social charge, the Philosophic Ethicists add more pointed moral requirements. It is not good enough simply to compute the costs and benefits of contemplated business decisions and policies when assessing their morality. A high-benefit, low-cost action that satisfies a majority bloc—the greatest good for the greatest number—might override minority interests, ignore just entitlements, and deprive some people of their legitimate rights. The clearest path toward moral probity is marked out by showing a deep respect for persons, a dignity due them by their status as human beings. They—whether employees, customers, suppliers, competitors, or neighbors—should never be seen or used exclusively as simple means to business ends alone. If the ends of justice are to be served in the workplace, a sense of caring must emanate from the executive suite and pervade shop, factory, and office alike. Opportunities for significant participation in decisions must be present and realistic, and recourse and appeal of unjust actions must be granted. These are the tangible directions implied in the Philosophers' Formula and toward which a business firm is to be led by Philosophic Ethics.

The Behavioral/Organizational Ethicists add yet another moral requirement if business is to measure up to an acceptable ethical standard. They believe that morality is a direct function of workplace context and the moral potentialities of those who work there. For that reason, all efforts should be made to structure the firm (and restructure it, if necessary) so that an open, caring, fair ethical climate will be present and perceived. Ethical role modeling by upper-level executives, ethics training programs, ethics committees, ethics audits, and an ethics director are part of the organizational machinery to be put in place. Ways should be found to encourage managers and employees who display advanced moral reasoning capacity to break the bonds of narrow company loyalty and to go beyond minimum legal requirements when faced with ethical workplace dilemmas. Ethics is essentially an experiential phenomenon, so that finding ways to affect one's working experience is more likely to have moral impact than exhortations to adopt abstract philosophic principles, laudable as they may be.

Thus sayeth the Moral Mandate of contemporary business ethics theory.

Economics, Nature, and Technology—Quo Vadis?

Three oddities stand out as one reflects on what is now the conventional wisdom of business ethics. The role assigned to *economic behavior* is peculiar inasmuch as it is generally ignored, denigrated, or dismissed as harboring unworthy and unsavory motivations. And there is no role at all spelled out for *nature*—no room at the inn, so to speak. Nor is *technology* given any better treatment, being ignored by most ethicists or, when noticed, it is said to be antinormative, morally neutered, or amoral in ethical significance. This peculiar state of affairs deserves brief attention, particularly given the prominent and positive role all three of these components play in the theory of values being outlined in this book. How could such a gaping chasm separate the latter theory from the conventional wisdom of business ethics, particularly when both attempt to find common moral ground on which to judge business activities?

Part of the explanation is found in disciplinary habits of thought. For the Business Ethicists as a group, all substantive normative principles are derived from one or more of the following sources: (1) sociocultural features, including organizational characteristics (e.g., workplace ethical climates), (2) personal attributes (e.g., attained stage of moral development), and/or (3) imposed abstract, analytic, moral categories (e.g., asserted rights or social justice). Philosophers do not normally consider economic behavior to be a source of moral guidance, seeing it instead as capable of generating quite the opposite moral effects. Nor do social scientists readily welcome explanations that are not sociocultural in origin, hence manifesting an ingrained disciplinary bias against nature as an explanatory variable. Both groups have looked askance at and have placed the greatest emphasis on technology's baleful impacts on society.

Although these omissions of economics, nature, and technology from the main body of business ethics theory may therefore seem to be a product of disciplinary traditions only, with each one therefore unrelated to the other, the truth lies elsewhere. Economics and nature are but two sides of the same coin—a coin forged in the crucible of thermodynamic forces. As this book has argued throughout, economizing behavior originated within natural evolutionary processes and it continues to serve an antientropic, life-supporting function for humankind. The technology of economizing makes that outcome possible. To admit one of these critically important processes to the inner sanctum of ethics theory would require opening the door to the others as well. Their virtual exclusion *as a linked trio* is no mere coincidence attributable to disciplinary bias alone.

The record speaks plainly about this general reluctance. Among all those who think and write about business ethics, only a handful admit economic factors into their conceptual frameworks, and even then, it is often a grudging acknowledgment. Economic responsibilities are one component of management theorist Archie Carroll's concept of corporate social responsibility, although he remarks that "It may seem odd to call an economic responsibility a social responsibility, but this is, in effect, what it is." However, for stakeholder theorist Max Clarkson, "The first and most important social responsibility is *economic performance*," and he identifies the central "normative element" of his stakeholder theory in these words: "The economic purpose of the corporation is to create wealth by using its resources effectively." Even more intriguing is Karen Newman's research-based observation that "Principled moral climates and principled moral judgments are not . . . necessarily inconsistent with or incompatible with moral climates and judgments based on economic rationality. . . . Use of one set of criteria does not appear to *replace* the other in [management] decisions. . . . [E]thical quality and economic quality need not be negatively correlated." It remains true, though, that many business ethicists, rather than welcoming economics into their models, frequently equate economizing with unprincipled greed, and speak of economically motivated activities and business profit making as the opposite of moral behavior.[60]

As for nature, it too is denied entrance into the hallowed halls of ethical discourse. It appears never to occur to most ethicists, who are schooled in so-

---

60. The quotations in this paragraph are respectively from Archie B. Carroll, *Business and Society: Ethics and Stakeholder Management*, Cincinnati: South-Western, 1989, p. 30; Max B. E. Clarkson, "Corporate Social Performance in Canada, 1976–86," in Lee E. Preston (ed.), *Research in Corporate Social Performance and Policy*, vol. 10, Greenwich, CT: JAI Press, 1988, p. 250, and Clarkson and Michael Deck, "The Stakeholder Theory of the Corporation," *Proceedings of a Workshop on the Stakeholder Theory of the Corporation and the Management of Ethics in the Workplace*, vol. 2, University of Toronto, May 20–21, 1993, p. 5; and Newman, op. cit., pp. 2, 33.

cial science or philosophy, even to acknowledge nature's presence. Two leading ethics scholars, however, go further to warn explicitly against relying on naturalistic explanations: "We begin by noting that economic systems are not products of nature. . . . [E]conomic systems are products of artifice, not nature, and their structures can and do vary immensely. . . . Such systems . . . are, in a word, *artifacts.* People create them. People make them what they are, and people might have chosen to make them differently. . . . The definitions of economic practices are *stipulated* rather than given by nature."[61] Such confident, vainglorious assertions, delivered *ex cathedra,* deserve the further attention they receive in the following chapter, where attempts are made to establish a normative synthesis from the many diverse theoretical themes that characterize the thinking of business ethicists. As will become evident there, the somewhat muffled part played by economics in theories of business ethics is attributable directly to the omission of nature from those same theories.

For the moment, it may suffice to observe that the dominant collective approach to questions of business ethics fails to acknowledge—and at times rejects—the naturalistic base on which all business values and all economic enterprise rest. Surely, this outcome is awry and unintended. What might be done to set things aright, and therefore to move toward a clearer conception of what it means to be ethical while at work, is worth exploring in the chapter immediately ahead.

---

61. Donaldson and Dunfee, op. cit., pp. 257–258.

9

A New Normative Synthesis

The earlier chapters of this book have set forth a theory of business values derived from two dynamic developmental processes—nature and culture. It has been argued that those values, when pursued by and in business, are responsible for the typical behavior and practices found there. Many of these values are life-supporting, life-expanding, and societally vital, while others constrain or diminish life. The normative significance of business values arises from these positive and negative outcomes. Collectively, the values that comprise the four central value clusters—economizing, power aggrandizing, ecologizing, and technologizing—provide a basis on which the operations and performance of business can be judged as right and proper or as wrong and misguided. The standards of normative judgment encompass both natural and sociocultural factors, and neither type of standard can be usefully ignored or discounted. Both are needed if a clear picture is to be had of business's ethical standing in today's society.

This chapter moves toward a synthesis of the normative views of business ethicists, which were examined in the preceding chapter, and the theory of business values being developed in this book. This New Normative Synthesis draws what is valid from existing theories of business ethics, which owe much to tradition and accumulated wisdom, and blends those ideas with naturalistic and sociocultural perspectives that have emerged within the last half century. The goal is to find a satisfying and analytically effective approach to understanding business's ethical and social responsibilities.

The New Normative Synthesis is developed in several steps. A critique is first made of some central theoretical weaknesses of conventional approaches to business ethics. This discussion is followed by a reinterpretation of the basic analytic categories used by business ethicists—rights, justice, and utility—in order to harmonize them with this book's theory of business values. After defining some critical theoretical choices that need to be confronted, a set of convergence theorems—which together constitute a normative commons—is offered as one way to move toward a New Normative Synthesis. Achieving that goal should also provide an answer to the question of what it means to be ethical while at work.

REPAIRING AND RENOVATING
BUSINESS ETHICS INQUIRY

Before a theoretically adequate normative structure can be erected, it is necessary to acknowledge weaknesses in the prevailing infrastructure of ethics inquiry. While modifications are needed, they fall considerably short of complete rebuilding from the ground up. If certain repairs are made to portions of the older structure, it may then support the course of ethical inquiry more securely and direct it toward its intended goal with greater assurance that ethical investigations will arrive where and when needed by both practitioners and theoreticians. Attaining that desirable end is the guiding spirit of this chapter. Three major weaknesses appear in the main body of business ethics theory: a disregard of nature as an acceptable explanatory device; a tendency to think of ethical processes as focused almost exclusively within individual persons; and an inability to deal with the relativity of values. Each of these shortcomings is worth further comment.

Far and away the most serious omission of extant ethics theory is the disregard, the inattention, or in some cases the outright rejection of natural forces as an explanatory factor. Rejecting naturalistic explanations and refusing to give them theoretical standing is equivalent to omitting the basic experiential and behavioral rationale that establishes a legitimate claim for business functions. Economizing constitutes that function. Treating economizing—which is typically mislabeled as the pursuit of profits—as a greed-soaked, egoistic, and therefore personally and socially undesirable business practice overlooks economizing's naturalistic origin and continued function as a socially vital offset to entropy. Likewise, an antinaturalist attitude deprives ethics theory of a possible explanation for the stubborn persistence of power-laden and socially problematic business practices that might be traced to phylogenetic power-aggrandizing urges and motives of business executives and their companies. Refusing to acknowledge that technology is a culturally elaborated outgrowth of genetic process tempts theorists to believe that technology is antihuman, antisocial, and antivital, whereas it may well exert just the opposite effects on human (and business) affairs. A naive and at times exaggerated conception of ecological forces, which often finds its way into deliberations about business's ethical responsibilities, carries the possibility of misdirecting, misinterpreting, and underemphasizing the normative significance of ecologizing factors as a community-building force. Hence, one kind of needed repair to existing ethics theory involves finding ways to give legitimate standing to natural processes as an explanatory component of human behavior, including that found in business.

An illustration of the theoretical difficulties that can arise from inattention to nature is the ethical rootlessness of that part of Responsibility Ethics that has found the greatest favor among corporate theorists, namely, the stakeholder concept. Lacking a naturalistic component, stakeholder theorists are reduced to simply asserting that stakeholders *do possess* certain rights that should not be overridden or disregarded by corporate management. As such, the stakeholder concept emerges as a political notion, an assertion of claimed privilege that is open to dispute by others who do not like or accept the claim itself. Further, in the hands of self-interested businesses that have been urged to be "socially responsive" to stakeholder pressures, an expedient and opportunistic attitude may encourage reliance on utilitarian rationales narrowly conceived, and a company-centered cost–benefit analysis may allow a rejection of stakeholder claims entirely, which then may be bolstered by resort to coercive government regulations. In the absence of nature-grounded standards on which to judge business behavior, self-interested businesses may pick and choose among those groups to which they will be responsive rather than being held to principles that protect their own as well as others' interests. Possibly even worse from a normative point of view, the legitimate basis for stakeholder claims cannot be made clear without a framework that roots their behavior within natural and sociocultural processes acceptable to all. Failure to provide such a rationale grants a hearing for the putative claims of lunatic groups alongside others.

If, on the other hand, stakeholders are conceptually presented as economizing groups intent on offsetting entropic forces that weigh not only on themselves but also on society, then they enjoy the same normative theoretical standing as do the economizing business firms of which they are the stakeholders. Or if stakeholders are visualized as part of a cooperative production process that rests on a naturalistic technological base, their role can be grasped as both essential and equally important to the technological roles being played by corporate managers and other business professionals.[1] It is even possible theoretically to argue for the normative superiority of stakeholder claims over the economizing needs of a business firm if the stakehold-

---

1. John Kenneth Galbraith once referred to this cooperative grouping as a company's "technostructure." The fact that he cast his technical net too widely across the corporate organization, thereby capturing some business professionals whose function supports only a firm's power-aggrandizing goals rather than its technologically productive functions, does not invalidate the general technological insight that he had, which remains useful. See John Kenneth Galbraith, *The New Industrial State*, New York: New American Library, 1967, Chapter VI and passim.

ers in question base their claims on vital (naturalistic) ecological factors that encompass societal and human interests that outrun those of the firm. Current concerns about global warming and rain forest depletion illustrate this possibility.

In these and similar instances, what stakeholder theorists are attempting to say could be better and more accurately established by resting their case on a substantive normative base rooted in nature. For example, consumers, employees, suppliers, and entire communities (all of them types of corporate stakeholders) are economizing entities whose ability to economize is as vital to each of them as is a corporation's need to act in antientropic ways. A corporation that ignores or inhibits stakeholders' economizing needs by marketing shoddy or unsafe products, exploiting its employees, dealing dishonestly with its suppliers, or polluting its host communities has interfered with natural processes that sustain stakeholders' livelihoods and enhance the quality of their lives. When these natural processes are paired with the array of sociocultural demands for fair and just treatment of employees, honesty in market transactions, consumer protections, and environmental care, then stakeholder claims can rest on a more secure normative base comprising both nature and culture. Expanding stakeholder analysis in this way not only advances the legitimacy of many stakeholder claims but avoids the sometimes irrational, political nature of some stakeholder assertions that leaves them vulnerable to refutation as little more than self-interested rationales of questionable ethical worth.

As earlier chapters of this book have made plain, a vast, constantly expanding, and normatively promising body of naturalistic knowledge awaits exploration by business ethicists. Those who dare to explore it may find intellectual and philosophic riches of untold proportions not unlike the precious metals, exotic food crops, and natural resource bonanzas that were the delight of early adventurers in the New World, Africa, Asia, and other lands. Surely, the larger normative significance of all such forays, whether undertaken by booty hunters or by the intellectually curious, can be enhanced by looking outward to the edge of evolving knowledge rather than only to that which is already well known or to roads well traveled and perhaps intellectually rutted. Incorporating nature into theories of business ethics carries much promise that new lands will be discovered.

A second conventional orientation of extant business ethics thinking bears critical reexamination. Philosophic Ethicists have focused on the dyadic, face-to-face relations that might at one time have been typical of business transactions undertaken within localized markets—long before massive multinational corporations operating across multiple societal boundaries and overseeing complex, highly advanced technological networks appeared on the scene. A methodology apt for resolving village disputes is put forward as a way to work through the ethical complexities faced by global corporations. An appeal is made for today's multilingual, multicultural, multitalented, multitechnological, multimarket, multiracial, multigendered corporate management to heed the simple nostrums that may have served well as sources of ethical guidance for a small group of village elders, all of whom were typically patriarchs rooted within a limited geographical area and a stagnant technological tradition, and bereft of significant experience with "outsiders" from radically different cultures.

One is entitled to ask, if Truth is captured so easily and so obviously within a few everlasting principles, why has it taken so long to bring these views forward and why have the legions and generations of business practitioners, especially today's, been so resistant to the lessons they teach? Does the persistent adherence to these oversimplified, individualized precepts say more about the judges than the judged, and about their latent attitudes toward business activities? Does it bespeak a secret conviction too terrible for them to sound out—namely, that business in general (regardless of its present level of complexity) and individual business practitioners are believed by some Philosophic Ethicists to be thoroughly corrupt and that those who practice its arts are to bear forever the curse of Cain, never to find ethical surcease or forgiveness from their academic judges? Could the philosophers' focus on individual, face-to-face behavior be the problem rather than the solution?

A third well-accepted and frequently discussed theoretical precept in the field of business ethics concerns the relativism of values. Haunting the dreams of business ethicists is the specter of cultural and moral relativism, which is resisted with vigor and indignation. This feared nightmare not only turns ethical theorists toward a search for supracultural, universalist moral principles—as admirable a task as are the complexities it invokes—but also turns them away from the realities of evolved sociocultural life and institutions, particularly contemporary business life and practices. Human cultural patterns, with their embedded ethics and value systems, are *in fact* relative to time and place and evolved tradition, that being one of the marvels of culture as both an adaptive process and a humanly expansive experience writ large and with much variation across the ages. One might well ask, to what else are values related (besides nature)? Were values not culturally relative, human life itself would be placed in peril by trading away cultural adaptability for the seeming security of a more uniform, unvarying way of life. That is one of the lessons taught by natural evolutionary process. Extreme specialization tends to drive its carriers into adaptive dead ends, while their generalized counterparts remain open and flexible in the face of environmental and cultural change. The much discussed question of bribery and related kinds of nonmarket payments as tools of international commerce is an example. By restricting or forbidding U.S. companies from making the most blatant of such payments, U.S. law has injected an element of rigid moralism into an international trading process where cultural flexibility and adaptability to local custom carry great competitive advantage. One need not endorse bribery as a mode of commercial trading to grasp the point being made.

The variability and relativism displayed by culture are a source of strength, not weakness, and the multiple ethical systems spawned through cultural variation are testimony to moral ingenuity, imagination, and creativity, rather than signaling a craven retreat into an amoral muddle of lesser normative dimensions. Such a perspective is lost on those whose minds are set upon discovering and broadcasting everlasting normative principles that may be brought to bear in judging business practices. The irony here is double-edged, for in rejecting naturalistic explanations, ethics theorists have been left with little more than humanly invented sociocultural explanations. But that has led them to confront the perceived perils of moral relativism, a doctrine they also reject. Fleeing from nature, they have run straight into the waiting arms of a relativist cultural realm, only to find relativism to be a morally repugnant position. This seems to leave only two possibilities: a supernaturalist conception of ethics and morality, and a search for secular ethical principles that transcend cultural boundaries. (The latter need not be seen as an extension of the former, nor vice versa.) The proportions in which business ethics theorists divide among these two paths is not securely known, but it is obvious that some theorists have struggled to articulate a secular transcultural ethic to guide business practitioners. Thomas Donaldson's set of ten "fundamental international rights" and Richard DeGeorge's discussion of moral integrity in international business are examples.[2]

It is time to ask whether other theoretical outlets beyond the prevailing theories of business ethics exist or can be developed. The answer given here, which will come as no surprise to those who have read this far, is "yes." We turn now to a search for contact points that encourage a harmonization of established ethics theory and a theory of business values founded on naturalist-experientialist-behavioralist perspectives. What follows is offered in the spirit of a commentary by John Rawls when he referred to the complexity of moral conceptions:

> [T]he corollary to recognizing their complexity is accepting the fact that our present theories are primitive and have grave defects. We need to be tolerant of simplifications if they reveal and approximate the general outlines of our judgments. Objections by way of counterexamples are to be made with care, since these may tell us only what we know already, namely that our theory is wrong somewhere.

2. Thomas Donaldson, *The Ethics of International Business*, New York: Oxford University Press, 1989, pp. 81–86; and Richard T. DeGeorge, *Competing with Integrity in International Business*, New York: Oxford University Press, 1993.

The important thing is to find out how often and how far it is wrong. All theories are presumably mistaken in places. The real question at any given time is which of the views already proposed is the best approximation overall. To ascertain this some grasp of the structure of rival theories is surely necessary.[3]

REFURBISHING THE PHILOSOPHERS' FORMULA

The preceding chapter argued that normative analysis of business operations rests primarily on the concepts of **rights** and **justice**. In this formulation "rights" embraces the notion of entitlements, as well as reciprocal duties by all to protect and nourish those entitlements. "Justice" is equated with a sense of fairness and equity, as well as an attitude of caring for the well-being of others. As developed in the literature of the field, both rights and justice are conceived as more than analytic abstractions, having behavioral and moral implications and applications in the workaday world. In some accounts, a third concept—**utility**—is employed to determine the ethicality of workplace actions, although utility has tended to occupy a decidedly inferior analytic position relative to both rights and justice. Summing up the relationship of these three concepts to each other produced what was earlier labeled the Philosophers' Formula: $EBB = f(R_k + J_r + U)$, in which ethical business behavior is understood to be a function of a respect for (Kantian) rights, an observance of (Rawlsian) justice, and a utilitarian net sum where benefits exceed harms. The cost–benefit utilitarian claims that reflect only a company's self-interested, market-based advantage are seen as morally narrow and inadequate.

As a way of reconstructing normative methodology, it will be useful to reassess and modify this conventional approach to judging business behavior and operations. Examination reveals that each component of the formula may serve normative purposes consistent with the theory of business values proposed in this book. In what follows, each of the three concepts—rights, justice, and utility—is reinterpreted to make it compatible with current knowledge of natural and sociocultural processes.

Rights: From Privileged Assertion to Experiential Values

No philosophic concept is more important in contemporary theories of business ethics than the idea of "rights." Any reformulation of ethics theory to make it more effective in coping with workplace ethical dilemmas needs to

---

3. John Rawls, *A Theory of Justice*, Cambridge, MA: Belknap Press of Harvard University Press, 1971, p. 52.

find a place and a meaning for rights. In what follows, two questions are addressed: What is wrong with current formulations of rights? and What might be done to strengthen this strategically important analytic concept? First, we turn to the question of what seems to be amiss.

In the literature of business ethics (and elsewhere), "rights" are typically presented—usually without question or doubt—as absolute, inherent, intrinsic entitlements. This is particularly true of *human* rights, although similar claims have been made on behalf of other life forms and for various inanimate features of the biosphere. Business ethics philosophers are quick to credit Immanuel Kant, the eighteenth-century philosopher (1724–1804), for this way of understanding people's rights to life, well-being, personal security, property, and other entitlements. Kant is said to have viewed human beings as inherently worthy because possessed of an intrinsic rational will, which should be directed so that no person should treat another human being as a mere means to one's own ends. This kind of rational human nature, possessed by all normal people, requires that each person be approached with dignity and accorded a basic respect that acknowledges his or her intrinsic moral standing in all human interactions.[4]

Not only, therefore, does one find a particular assumption or declaration about human nature to lie behind the concept of Kantian rights, but the claim made for rights itself is a simple assertion, a proposition to be tested, and a claimed entitlement or privilege that is usually attached to and rationalized by the concept of human nature from which it is derived. Leaving aside for a moment the question of continuing to rely on a sense of human nature developed in the eighteenth century, rights in the conventional formulation appear to be mere declarations of privilege, that is, the privilege of being treated in a special, particular way. Rights also are coercive regarding other persons, for they *must* be acknowledged and respected because they are said to be intrinsic, that is, a part of human nature.

The coercive nature of rights has been noted by one philosopher in these words:

---

4. The special status granted to Kant as the principal author of rights doctrine is disputed among philosophers. John Locke and John Stuart Mill may be more responsible for elaborating and popularizing the notion of rights. One philosopher has declared that the concept of a right does not appear in Kant's major works: "And nowhere in his account of the three forms of the principle of the categorical imperative or in the proof or 'deduction' he gives us does Kant make any reference to rights, and wisely so. Indeed, the current widespread idea that Kant thought he was expounding, in his account of the treatment one ought to give either oneself or anyone else, anything that has to do with rights, is only evidence of the fashionable tendency to engage in morally inflated rhetoric by supposing that there is a right whenever there is an ought—by supposing, to consider an extreme example, that since one ought to protect the environment, the latter, along with human and other animals, has its rights." A. I. Melden, *Rights in Moral Lives: A Historical-Philosophical Essay*, Berkeley: University of California Press, 1988, p. 56.

> *To assert one's right is . . . to exercise a power*—to use Locke's term—that is, a moral authority that a right holder has, over the person or persons against whom the former has a right. . . . The figure of a chain by which one person is bound, the other end of which is held by another, is sometimes employed to represent the moral relation between two persons, the latter being the right holder and the former the person under the correlative obligation [to respect the rights of the chain holder]. Asserting a right would be represented by having the person holding the end of the chain pull it and thus force the other to move in the right holder's direction.[5]

Rights in this sense are indeed coercive assertions that define obligatory behavior or duties by others to protect the claims of those who assert them.

One does not have to look far in the final decade of the twentieth century to discover how the assertion of what are said to be intrinsic rights—for example, to possess disputed territory, to have a share of scarce economic benefits, to enjoy adequate health care, to acquire or reinforce ethnic recognition—invites a resort to power as a way to resolve conflicting and sometimes contradictory rights. Where equal legitimacy can be claimed for contending parties because each side is believed to be expressing intrinsic rights, power is a frequently chosen way to seek to secure such rights, as ethnic strife around the globe demonstrates all too well. Nor does the business sphere escape its share of similar claims and power plays, as hosts of corporate stakeholders, each proclaiming some rights-based privilege (i.e., a particular treatment), besiege corporate suites, flooding the willing media with the kind of drama the public has come to expect (and enjoy), and pressuring legislative bodies to help coerce firms into a *de jure* acknowledgment of such rights. Business also plays this power game, and plays it well, enjoying many well-known advantages in media and legislative battles for the hearts and minds of those willing to listen, view, and read. The point being made should be obvious: intrinsic rights as an expression of human nature can become coercive assertions of privilege that invite resort to power to resolve conflicting and contradictory rights. Neither business nor society can afford to proceed on such a basis, although both have seemingly done so for long years.

The idea that people have these kinds of rights is both chronologically and culturally relative, a point not always acknowledged by business ethicists. The term "rights" itself is said to have first appeared in the work of the fourteenth-century scholastic philosopher William of Occam, who spoke of a "natural right." As noted above, the eighteenth-century's Kant did not use the term, but it found fuller flower in the thinking of the seventeenth-century's John Locke and the nineteenth-century's John Stuart Mill. All of these fig-

5. Ibid., op. cit., pp. 81, 82. Emphasis added.

ures, of course, stand in the philosophic traditions of Western culture, which should at least arouse suspicion that the notion is far from being able to claim universal (nonrelativist) standing.[6]

By holding constant an eighteenth-century concept of human nature—that is, that all normal persons possess a rational will that should lead them to acknowledge others' rights—while trying to cope with the complex ethical dilemmas of twentieth-century business firms, business ethicists have worked themselves into an awkward position, both philosophically and analytically. Social science, primarily cultural anthropology, sociology, and psychology, over a century ago began a revolution that has by now drastically reformulated earlier notions of human nature. Kant's version now appears not only antique but quaint. Human nature is said by social science to be a function of learned and acquired sociocultural patterns, and hence is relative to time and place. Moreover, as earlier chapters of this book have made plain, biological, physical, ecological, and ethological sciences have identified nature-based human behavioral proclivities that were unknown to earlier generations of philosophers. Nor have scientists yet discovered the *intrinsic* rights posited by Kant and his many followers over the years, nor have they observed the *intrinsic rational will* said by Kant's supporters to underlie the entire notion of rights. Additionally, if rights are, as argued above, little more than asserted claims rooted in the self-defined interests of contending groups, the validity of the normative analytic structure erected by philosopher-ethicists is endangered. If it is not strengthened, a strong aftershock may bring it tumbling down.

It is likely that the reluctance to accept or acknowledge the changed, relativistic conception of human nature is a simple artifact of habitual thinking, combined with the undoubted attractiveness of a rights theory that exhibits much analytic (and political) power. That this may be the case helps to explain the appearance in recent years of efforts by some business ethics philosophers to identify overarching, transcultural, universal ethics principles.[7] Such common normative principles, particularly if they were to embody the notion of Kantian-like human rights, could conceivably exist side by side with ethics and values that are clearly relative to different societies. This initiative might well contribute importantly to rewriting the terms of the Philosophers' Formula, a possibility that is explored more fully in the following chapter.

---

6. A debate continues among philosophers about whether, or the extent to which it may be claimed that, ancient and revered Greek philosophers thought in terms of rights. See Melden, op. cit., whose essay is devoted to the topic.

7. The best example is Donaldson, op. cit. Another is William C. Frederick, "The Moral Authority of Transnational Corporate Codes," *Journal of Business Ethics*, vol. 10, 1991, pp. 165–177.

More important at the moment for rebuilding a more secure analytic approach to business ethics is the question of how the putative rights discussed by business ethics philosophers are related to the concept of values articulated by social scientists (and by this book). They are not the same for several reasons. Rights are typically made to appear as noncontextual, abstract assertions of privilege. Values, by contrast, are treated as behavioral traits, beliefs, and intellectual orientations that are thoroughly contextual in their origin and subsequent development. Rights tend to be imposed upon a context of human action, with the term itself suggesting a coercive or insistent claim not to be disputed, as in the declaration "But I have a *right* to so and so!" Values grow out of a given sociocultural context and its history, and the moral reasoning based on a person's or a society's values has a life history that can be observed and documented. Values may and usually do become firmly embedded in individuals and organizations, thus superficially resembling the imperative character ascribed to rights. However, unlike rights, values are not usually assigned, nor do they deserve, a superior standing within the total array of human traits observed by social scientists, as sometimes occurs with regard to rights. If values are conceived, as they are in this book, as beliefs and standards having both naturalistic and sociocultural origins, then it would be possible to argue that various rights are *derived from* values. For example, some might want to argue that each human being has a "right" to pursue economizing values and practices in order to survive as a life form, or that religious worship constitutes a "right" emergent from a society's value structure and religious belief systems.

The business values set forth in this book are not presented as the "rights" of business practitioners. Rather, those values are described as beliefs and standards that tend to guide business behavior. Whatever *rights* business people have acquired by virtue of being business practitioners are matters of sociocultural convention. This would be true, for example, of acquired property rights to the technology of production, various (legal) contractual rights, and the right to direct business affairs toward profit goals. On the other hand, the *values* that shape their actions in the workplace—for example, an impulse to economize by minimizing production costs—are manifestations of natural processes that are then subsequently influenced by sociocultural (including market) forces. The normative justification and legitimacy of business activities rest far more on the life-sustaining value clusters of economizing and technologizing than on the putative rights that the vagaries of sociohistorical development may have ceded to business practitioners.

To the first question, then, of what is wrong with the usual way of presenting the rights concept, several answers have been given. Rights appear to be simple declarations of privilege rather than intrinsic human traits. Rights, as traditionally conceived, are rooted in a questionable and now outmoded concept of human nature. Rights are historically and culturally relative; they are not an unchanging constant found identically in all times and places. Rights are not the same as values, the latter being responsible for shaping and channeling human behavior (including business behavior), so that sociocultural rights appear to be less compelling determinants of human actions than nature-based and socioculturally elaborated values.

If the discussion and analytic use of rights are flawed in these ways but the concept itself remains viable as an analytic tool, what can be said to align it with the theory of business values? This is the second question posed at the beginning of this discussion of rights. A view that melds the two approaches would propose that rights are created objects of sociocultural origin that mark out (i.e., call attention to) spheres or traits of human behavior that exhibit life-adaptive significance. Rights are, in a sense, a kind of cumulative human wisdom, compiled from many experiential sources, and a product of applied human intelligence regarding how life can be lived and made to flourish. The test of their validity and legitimacy is their service to these adaptive and life-flourishing purposes. The insistent, imperative character that has been imputed to rights could be seen as a (sometimes unconscious or not well understood) recognition of the role that rights play in sustaining, securing, and expanding life, rather than as a manifestation of a universalist and intrinsic rational human will.

Quite clearly as human, sociocultural experience evolves, accumulates, and encounters new and changing environmental conditions, our ability to apply our mental capacities to these new challenges is likely to reveal and to create new rights (e.g., freedom from slavery) and to apply existing ones more widely (e.g., various rights for women, submerged ethnic groups, disabled persons). Rights, being relative, are almost bound to expand in number and variety to match an emerging consciousness of what is needed to cope with life's many complexities. In the business arena, such an evolution of rights can clearly be seen in the increasing numbers of corporate stakeholders who demand job rights, rights to workplace safety and health, equal and/or comparable pay, safe and effective products, clean air and water, and so on. If stakeholders' rights are understood, not as absolutist assertions of privilege but rather as marking out legitimate ways of carrying on life's basic activities that need to be considered when corporate decisions are made, *then* business ethicists' arguments for them sound reasonable and should be heeded by corporate management. Doing so is equivalent to acknowledging the economizing needs and values of *all* the parties involved in or affected by business operations. Such an approach also permits consideration of the entire range of values that have an impact on the firm and its stakeholders, including power-aggrandizing, ecologizing, and technologizing effects. In this (re)formulation, no rights are seen as inherently superior by virtue of proclamation alone. Rather, they need to be judged with others and for their effects in interaction with others.

This interdependent nature of rights and their links to a life-flourishing process is captured in the following passage by the philosopher A. I. Melden, who could just as easily have had the corporation and its stakeholders in mind (but probably did not).

> [T]he members of the moral community are not individuals who go about their affairs independently of and with indifference toward one another. Each is disposed to stand in moral relations to the other, prepared to engage in ties that bind them together as they go about their affairs. Each, of course, is an individual in the commonplace sense that he or she has a distinctive personality, a set of personality traits, interests, abilities, hopes, and aspirations; but each is also a social being as a member of the moral community with a life that is in important respects joined with those of others. It is not only that we need one another in order to obtain goods no one can procure unaided; it is also that we are concerned about others, even the total stranger, and are prepared, if we live up to the normative requirements imposed upon us by our membership in the moral community, to care for each other if need be. For as moral agents, the members of the moral community have rights, if for no other reason than that they *are* moral agents. . . . We owe others the help we can give them without which they cannot live lives worth living; their title to this help is simply the fact that they are moral agents.[8]

A modified rights concept can become a powerful analytic tool for judging business operations. This would be especially true if rights were visualized as emergent from a naturalistic-sociocultural value process that gives them their meaning and normative significance.

Justice: From Social Status to Social Involvement

Justice, too, might be made into a normative marker of greater analytic usefulness if modified to be more consistent with contemporary knowledge of value formation and value function than the present version that dominates business ethics theorizing. "Justice," the second term in the Philosophers' Formula, is closely linked to rights, and, in a sense, the two concepts cannot be separated from one another, at least in the most popular Rawlsian version. Rawls himself seemed to believe that justice is the key component, for he refers to justice as "the first virtue" of institutions, with rights being subsumed within the processes he advocates as being most likely to lead toward justice and fairness. It might be noted also that this dominant theory of justice is thoroughly relativistic and is presented as such by its author, who re-

8. Melden, op. cit., pp. 102–103.

marks that "the primary subject of justice is the basic structure of society . . . [by which] I understand the political constitution and the principal economic and social arrangements." Justice, in other words, is relative to the way a society is organized, particularly in its political and economic life. Noting the difficulties of constructing a general theory of justice applicable to all societies, he says, "It [i.e., the theory] should not be dismissed because its principles are not everywhere satisfactory," a point not always remembered by those of his followers who are inclined to interpret justice principles in absolutist and universalist terms.[9]

Rawls also acknowledges that all of the thorny, controversial issues associated with a society's status-and-class order are brought to the fore by his discussion of distributive justice. "[T]he institutions of society favor certain starting places over others. These are especially deep inequalities. Not only are they pervasive, but they affect [one's] initial chances in life. . . . It is these inequalities, *presumably inevitable in the basic structure of any society*, to which the principles of social justice must in the first instance apply."[10] Given the "inevitability" of such injustices, the prevailing Rawlsian-Kantian theory of justice is little more than an analytic device by which to question a society's existing distributions and distributive processes. It emerged, as did Kant's ideas, in a period of societal ferment and (in the United States) in the midst of a furious national debate about, not only the distributive shares allocated among various social, economic, political, and ethnic groups but also about the fairness of the distributive mechanisms governing those shares.[11]

The Rawlsian theory rests on two dubious premises, already questioned earlier: (1) that human nature expresses an intrinsic prudential rational will and (2) that historical and contemporary sociocultural contexts can be safely set aside while rational, self-interested humans deliberate the questions of distributive equity. Using Kantian absolutist rights to justify claims to distributive shares has surely increased the decibel level of social protest from those seeking redress along with the counterprotests of those wanting to retain present distributive arrangements, as in programs of social welfare, health care, and affirmative action, plus the tax structures and bureaucratic vested interests that support such activities. In other words, Rawlsian justice is *defined* through a set of procedural principles based on a Kantian claim of privilege—that is, a "right" to participate and to receive a "fair" status-and-class share of benefits. The resultant distributive share, along with the procedure

---

9. Rawls, op. cit., pp. 3, 7, 9.

10. Ibid., p. 7. Emphasis added.

11. Two useful accounts of Kant's life, times, and ideas are Arsenij Gulyga, *Immanuel Kant: His Life and Thought*, Boston: Birkhauser, 1987; and Ernst Cassirer, *Kant's Life and Thought*, New Haven, CT: Yale University Press, 1981.

for establishing it, are both made to appear as the mere working out of an intrinsic rational will to which everyone (being rational) should agree. Little wonder that business professionals have registered less than enthusiasm for what may appear to them as philosophic legerdemain, especially when their own "rights" (to property, to freedom of decision making, to economic growth and expansion) seem so often to be portrayed as needing reexamination and subjected to what might be called "ethical downsizing."

What if, on the other hand, an alternative view of justice more compatible with business's central economizing function were to supplement—but not supplant—the business ethicists' perspective? Might that not dampen the fires of controversy that are all too frequently stoked to white-hot heat by absolutist stakeholder demands? Would that not pose the possibility of transforming business from a reluctant, foot-dragging participant to a more willing supporter of workplace justice? A heady thought, it nevertheless seems worth pursuing.

Paradoxically, Rawls himself may be the source of this alternative view. In the opening pages of his book, he notes that agreeing on what justice is and how it is to be achieved is not the entire story of what produces "a viable human community." It is best to let his own words make the case, even though the passage is lengthy. He continues:

> There are other fundamental social problems, in particular those of coordination, efficiency, and stability. Thus the plans of individuals need to be fitted together so that their activities are compatible with one another and they can be carried through without anyone's legitimate expectations being severely disappointed. Moreover, the execution of these plans should lead to the achievement of social ends in ways that are efficient and consistent with justice. And finally, the scheme of social cooperation must be stable: it must be more or less regularly complied with and its basic rules willingly acted upon; and when infractions occur, stabilizing forces should exist that prevent further violations and tend to restore the arrangement. Now it is evident that these three problems are connected with that of justice. In the absence of a certain measure of agreement on what is just and unjust, it is clearly more difficult for individuals to coordinate their plans efficiently in order to insure that mutually beneficial arrangments are maintained. Distrust and resentment corrode the ties of civility, and suspicion and hostility tempt [people] to act in ways they would otherwise avoid. So while the distinctive role of conceptions of justice is to specify basic rights and duties and to determine the appropriate distributive shares, the way in which a conception does this is bound to affect the problems of efficiency, coordination, and stability. *We cannot, in general, assess a conception of justice by its distributive role alone,* however useful this role may be in identifying the concept of justice. *We must take into account its wider connections;* for even though justice has a certain priority, being the most important virtue of institutions, it is still true that, other things equal, one conception of justice is preferable to another when its broader consequences are more desir-

able. . . . *Fully to understand a conception of justice we must make explicit the conception of social cooperation from which it derives.*[12]

"Coordination, efficiency, and stability": These are ideas that business professionals know well, for each is a condition essential to and expressive of economizing business operations. If justice *derives from* the necessities of social cooperation and social coordination, as Rawls maintains, would it not therefore be possible to define it in ways thoroughly compatible with business's societally essential core function of economizing? Do not complex systems of production demand the cooperative participation of a wide range of workers (and their technology) whose workplace coordination is sought by skilled managers? And do not these workplace systems have to be harmonized with others and with a society's expressed economic needs and social aspirations? And to achieve these ends, is it not important that all contributing parties should feel that a sense of justice and fairness governs the cooperative-coordinated efforts of all? A business mentality that is resistant to "justice demanded and imposed" (through government regulation, media coercion, and public confrontations) may well be more receptive to "justice as participation and social involvement."

Where the participation and involvement of corporate stakeholders refer to the ability of those stakeholders to economize their interests and needs within the orbit of a company's economic influence; where those economizing efforts are made possible by technologizing processes and values, which therefore contribute by their nature to the "coordination, efficiency, and stability" of business (and societal) operations; and where the blended activities of stakeholders and corporate management produce offsets to entropy—*there* is where an operational justice and the naturalistic principles that support it may be observed and applauded by business. The proof of justice within the workplace then could be understood instrumentally and pragmatically as those social shares found to be necessary to sustain economizing and technologizing by the firm and its stakeholders. Were that end to be attained, so too would be the coordination, efficiency, and stability recognized by Rawls as a "prerequisite for a viable human community."

In a broader sense that carries beyond the business firm, social justice emerges as the recognition of instrumentally legitimate claims of individuals and social groups to share in the bounty created by society's economizing-technologizing-ecologizing processes, as well as a need to shoulder some of the unavoidable burdens and risks that arise. Social justice need not be yoked to a social status-and-class system based upon power, privilege, and prestige or to a dubious notion of intrinsic rights. Questions of justice can and should

---

12. Rawls, op. cit. pp. 6, 9–10. Emphasis added.

be couched as questions of intelligent participation and involvement in life's benefits and burdens, without invoking social, religious, political, or ethnic labels to bolster one's claims or to reject another group's claims. *Justice, in the end, has more to do with social involvement than with social status.*

Utility: A Standard for All Seasons

Perhaps the greatest point of disagreement between the generally accepted way of approaching ethical issues in business and this book's theory of business values is the dismissive treatment of utility and utilitarian analysis by many ethics theorists. There is no intention here to endorse the specific use and definition of these notions as found in the earlier work of Jeremy Bentham or John Stuart Mill and their many followers. Rather, it is to suggest that utility may help to bridge the gap that separates conventional philosophic analysis and an experiential-behavioral analysis. "Utility" connotes usefulness, practicality, functionality, efficacy, purpose, worth, value, serviceability, pragmatism, practice—and, yes, its conventional philosophic meaning of pleasure or human satisfactions. This broader meaning of utility puts a different light on its normative significance than if one thinks only of a narrow range of economic utilities sought in the marketplace. It also vastly extends the complexity of attempting to calculate and measure the total costs and benefits that might be the outcome of any given action. Only one of the several meanings of utility—or the various reciprocals of utility devised by successive generations of economists—is particularly congruent with the operation of markets, and with attempts to find and apply a measure of economic worth and progress. Utility as happiness, having captured the imagination of earlier generations of economists, is not the entire story. Nor need (nor should) the happiness and satisfaction component of utility be discarded. Indeed, pleasure has found a secure place in one recent account of socio-economic behavior, where a bi-utility concept of human behavior is advocated: people seek pleasure without abandoning a sense of moral duty.[13]

Within the theory of business values developed in this book, utility lies at the core of economizing, is a direct function of technologizing, and is one effect of ecologizing. Hence, utility is an expression of the three major value clusters that sustain and expand life. Given the negative attitudes toward economics and technology manifested by many ethics theorists, their disdain for utilitarian methodology is therefore more understandable. But is it justified? If utilitarian traits such as usefulness, adaptive function, instrumental practicality, and technological accomplishment lead toward economizing activities, who is to say, and on what grounds, that the pursuit and cultivation of utility

13. Amitai Etzioni, *The Moral Dimension*, New York: Free Press, 1988.

by business practitioners is ethically questionable? Moreover, if one goes beyond "mere" adaptability of humans within their evolving environment—a utilitarian consequence with obvious normative import—one encounters more than instrumental success writ only in the script of genetic process. The many enjoyments, satisfactions, imaginative flights of fancy, creative outbursts and insights, sublime felt experiences, and aesthetic encounters—that is, all such "utilities"—carry humankind well beyond the grubby business of survival, important as it is. Utilities in the broader sense being used here extend human purpose, expand human potentials, bring imagination and creativity into play, build yet unimagined futures—*and, most important for this account of business values, utilities make plain the vital link between business economizing and technologizing and the humanly vital needs and satisfactions pursued by the members of society*. Without the former, there can be none of the latter.

Rather than being opposed to society, as maintained by some theorists, business's principal economizing operations, which encompass utilitarian modes of thought and action, undergird human society's quest for present survival and its exploration of future potentials. Utility, when viewed from a broad societal perspective, functions as a normative yardstick to help pass judgment on which human goals, pleasures, and satisfactions are worthwhile and which ones are best discarded. The ability to distinguish between utilities and disutilities is what evaluative judgments are all about. When a plant closes or moves, utilitarians want to know who benefits and who loses, Kantians want to know if rights are protected or trampled, Rawlsians want to know if the move or closure is fair or unfair. In their own respective ways, each is safeguarding a "utility"—a value, a right, a just outcome—that is considered to be morally indispensable. Such utilitarian judgments are inherent within the economizing-technologizing-ecologizing evolutionary process that sustains and expands human life as we know it. Humans decided long ago that mere survival of the species was not sufficient for human purposes, that is, it was not good *enough*. Additionally, they have wanted to know, have wanted to judge, how that survival might be exploited and expanded in ways that fulfill broader aspirations, including the values we call "rights" and the sense of fairness and social participation we call "justice." Life's utilitarian joy ride will indeed be cut short if the life-sustaining processes that make it all possible are not preserved and protected. Utilitarian judgments about how to achieve those results are an indispensable part of the needed normative framework used to judge business actions and motives. Were that view to be adopted by business ethicists, an important block to further progress would have been removed.

In sum, the modified and expanded perspectives suggested here for rights, justice, and utility may contribute to a theoretical synthesis that draws from both older and newer inquiring traditions. The intention has been to show that these key concepts can be reinterpreted and made consistent with today's knowledge of value formation processes. They contain hints of the value orientations and moral principles that have proved, in the course of genetic and sociocultural evolution, to be more selectively adaptive and life-liberating than if they had been ignored or scorned. Steps taken to identify and highlight the somewhat shadowy value orientations that lurk behind their conventionally expressed philosophic facades multiply the analytic power of ethics inquiry. Perhaps recognizing these contact points that link the older and the contemporary ways of thinking about ethics has been The First Giant Step toward building a different and more effective paradigm for working through the dilemmas of workplace ethics. The succeeding steps naturally follow, and they are discussed next.

A NEW NORMATIVE SYNTHESIS

Finding common ground on which ethicists can judge business operations is important work. By drawing deeply from the philosophic storehouses well stocked by respected thinkers of the past, today's philosophers have shed much needed light on many contemporary ethical puzzles that arise within business. The same can be said for the social scientists and organizational theorists who build models and theories about the various ways corporations and their managers might be expected (or can be observed) to behave in the social arena. All such efforts register gains, not only for scholars but for business practitioners who daily wrestle with thorny questions of ethical and social priority. The ethical and practical import of these valuable insights might well be greatly multiplied if the most analytically powerful components of each scholarly tradition were to be conjoined and focused anew on business behavior. Doing so requires one to search for contact points, common elements, and what might be called "convergence theorems" that draw into a single inquiring orientation the best efforts of those who would understand and guide business operations toward normatively acceptable goals and purposes.

Choosing Grounded Premises

Before theoretical integration of the kind being proposed can go forward, and before there is agreement on convergence theorems, one must confront and attempt to deal with the irreconcilable elements that have accumulated within these disparate methodological approaches. Choices are inevitable if integrated inquiry is to go forward. We ask therefore: What choices (beyond those already noted in the earlier discussion) would have to be made if this book's theory of business values is to be harmonized with the salient analytic features found in established theories of business ethics and corporate social performance? Four such choices are apparent and important.

A central choice entails either acceptance or rejection of an evolutionary, biological, genetic explanation of human origins and of that part of human behavior derived from the evolutionary base. The prevailing tradition within social science holds that human behavior is the outcome of *acquired learning* of sociocultural practices, customs, and artifacts. Human origins are believed to coincide with the appearance of rudimentary cultural practices and artifacts. Little or no room is permitted for naturalistic, biological-genetic explanations of behavior or origins. By contrast, the theory of business values offered here posits that business activities, in their most fundamental sense, are a direct function and outgrowth of natural thermodynamic processes that, in turn, have spawned biological-genetic behavioral features displayed by humans and other life forms. This is not to deny the equally valid processes of sociocultural accretion and their subsequent influence on human (and business) behavior. However, at some point within scholarly deliberations about how and why humans, including people in business, behave the way they do, the role of natural processes must be considered. There appears to be no valid reason why business behavior cannot be accepted as arising from and expressing both natural and cultural forces. A business firm, a market, or an economic system—composed of people, technology, and financial instruments—can be viewed as a blend and outcome of many interacting cultural and natural processes. It would be remarkable if the same people who claim familial links, bring forth newborns, sleep, eat, fall ill, age, become angry, feel sympathy, cry, laugh, and otherwise manifest their biological-genetic heritage were to act, while performing business work, as only the directives of their sociocultural heritage encourage. Firms, markets, and economic systems are far more comprehensively structured than is normally recognized; they feel the tugs and impulses of nature as well as culture. What theorists have called "corporate *social* performance" is not sealed off from a corporate *economizing* process that owes its origin and societal legitimacy to nature.

Closely related to this first choice is another that poses the question of human variability and malleability. Modern scholarship has established beyond any reasonable (current) doubt that human beings are socially multicultural, psychologically multileveled, and biologically multigenetic. In spite of the existence of common sociocultural patterns, common psychological profiles, and a more or less characteristic (i.e., identifiable) human genome, humans are a remarkably plastic and variable life form. Beginning from a *generalized* biological-genetic platform, humans have evolved a fantastic array of multiple life possibilities and behavioral outcomes. That generalized human trait has been one of the central strengths of the human species, especially of the more recently evolved *Homo sapiens* whose members have confronted and exploited nearly all dimensions of the earth's biosphere. This view of human plasticity and variability contrasts sharply with the unidimensional, unicultural, unichronological version of human nature often invoked (perhaps only subconsciously) by business ethicists. Kantian analysis, for example, often proceeds as if human nature and human rights are "intrinsic" or are framed by inherent and unyielding qualities that outlast and override all temporal, historical, geological, ecological, ethological, institutional, and cultural conditions. Clearly, scholars must choose between these two ways of viewing the prospects and the nature of humanity—one evolutionary and variable, the other static and one-dimensional. So too must students of business decide whether business practitioners are to be placed theoretically within a behavioral straitjacket that channels their operations within limited human purposes (however laudable or dreadful—take your pick) or whether business theory might better be served by adopting the view that business's economizing-technologizing-ecologizing normative potentialities are best understood (and pursued) in widely imaginative and innovative ways.

A third choice entails establishing the legitimacy of stakeholder claims against the business corporation. It will not do simply to declare that such claims arise from the mere interaction of a corporation and any given group alleging harm or benefit from such contact, for proximity alone establishes no moral claim. Further, if the demand for redress is premised upon the possession of, and injury sustained by, an "intrinsic (Kantian) right," one might well question this basis of legitimation, as noted several times in the foregoing discussion. Stakeholder assertions of privilege (i.e., "rights") are frequently little more than just that—simple assertions lacking self-evident, substantive, normative grounds.[14] By contrast, a strong case can be made for any stakeholder claim premised upon a need to economize, or to have access to the technological components that make economizing possible, or to preserve the ecologizing potentialities of ecosystems and life networks. If business operations seriously impinge upon or defeat these core processes that sustain life for all, one might then have revealed the substantive and legitimate basis of stakeholder claims against the corporation. The choice is stark: Shall it be Kantian political assertions of privilege that underwrite stakeholder claims, or should it be the stakeholder's need to participate in life-sustaining activities?

More difficult still for some will be to choose between positive and nega-

---

14. The importance of power in establishing and consolidating stakeholder claims has been emphasized by management theorist Steve Wartick. He recognizes that power is "a critical dimension of stakeholder management" and asserts that "the engine which drives it is power relationships." A somewhat more diffuse acknowledgment of power's importance is noted by Donna Wood, who asks, "Why in the world would any manager voluntarily give up any power, control, or autonomy just because some stakeholder group says s/he ought to?" For these two discussions of power, see "Essay by Steve Wartick" and "Essay by Donna J. Wood," *Business and Society*, vol. 33, no. 1, April 1994, pp. 114 and 104, respectively.

tive images of business's function. Shall business economizing and profit making, along with reliance on a rational, pragmatic calculus of gains and losses, be accepted as socially essential and both biologically and socioculturally driven? Or will scholars prefer the view that business is a flawed human institution, a historical and cultural anomaly with mainly negative human impact, scarred by the self-interested motives and (ultimately) the greed of those who populate its ranks? One need not admire business—indeed, one might even wish that things were otherwise and that some of the seedier aspects of business were not a part of our lives at all—to pose this choice. But sooner or later, those who study business must come to terms with one fundamental fact: Business is, and shall long remain, among the premier institutions of society. Is it to be understood as fatally flawed and normatively irredeemable—or as worthy, though imperfect? A prevailing tendency of many commentators both inside and outside the academy is to take the former view, thereby spawning all manner of ethical nostrums administered more in despair than with hope for the patient's recovery. A more optimistic outlook would acknowledge the essential (thermodynamic) nature of the business function within society, while attempting to guide its operations into channels that serve the broad needs and normative inclinations of complex sociocultural communities and their host ecosystems.

The four choices posed here raise questions related to the premises on which ethics inquiry should proceed. A theoretical harmonization is more likely to be achieved, and ethics issues are more likely to be understandable, if those premises are grounded securely in extant knowledge of natural and sociocultural processes.

Convergence Theorems

Business ethicists of all stripes, in spite of sometimes bitterly contested theoretical differences, share certain normative orientations about business, and these are worth emphasizing. These common elements tend to draw into a single inquiring tradition the best efforts of scholars who have trod different disciplinary pathways. At some point (or perhaps at several such points) their thoughts converge in shared understandings, which might usefully be labeled "convergence theorems." These theorems—they could also be called a "normative commons"—register the central gains and accomplishments of a half-century's inquiry into the moral links between business and society.[15] Collec-

---

15. These convergence theorems, while echoing similar themes, are not identical to the Moral Mandate of business ethics described in Chapter 8. The latter bears the marks of constricted and compartmentalized disciplinary habits and perspectives, while the convergence theorems blend and harmonize multidisciplinary discoveries and insights that are potentially acceptable to all scholars who pursue the meaning of business ethics.

tively, they stand at the center of present-day understanding of business's ethical and social responsibilities to humankind and to the ecosystems on which life depends. As they unfold here, it will become apparent that, at some point not easily defined, a boundary is crossed where the older traditions of ethical inquiry encounter the newer ways of thinking about the ethics of business. Different observers will want to place that boundary line earlier than later, while still others may want to insist that the dividing line is more like a barrier to integration than a pathway leading toward theoretical convergence of the two modes of inquiry. The spirit in which they are offered here is one of convergence. Figure 9–1 diagrams the logic that binds them together. If there is to be a New Normative Synthesis, it will find its beginnings expressed in these theorems.

Theorem One: *Business is an inherently normative activity, calling for moral evaluation and judgment of its operations, motives, decisions, policies, and goals.* All

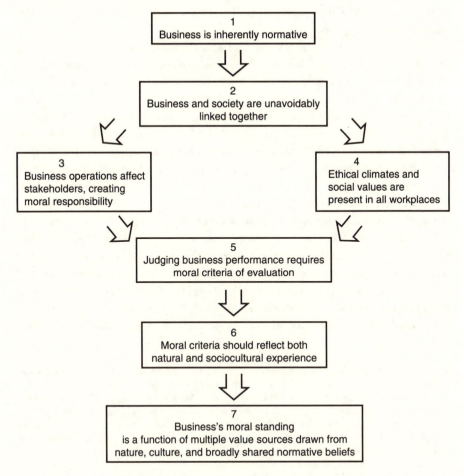

Figure 9–1. Normative convergence theorems

parties who seek answers to ethical issues in business accept this theorem, either explicitly or by the implicit assumptions that guide their inquiry. The view is rejected that business can be fully understood as a self-contained, socially isolated, value-neutral, solely instrumental activity.

Theorem Two: *Business and society are unavoidably linked together in functional ways, so that what one of them does directly affects the other, posing the possibility that each will suffer harms and/or experience benefits stemming from the other's activities.* Whereas students of corporate social performance tend to emphasize the social harms (actual and potential) produced by business operations, others who are more inclined to defend business interests have countered by stressing the restrictive inefficiencies laid upon business by government regulators and other public pressures. Both sets of commentators can claim to have found at least part of the truth. The reciprocal moral responsibilities owed by business and society to each other stem from their interlinked nature. Business is both *in* and *of* society, while society penetrates deeply into every aspect of business operations. Their respective fates are tied to what each does and how it is done.[16]

Theorem Three: *Business's societal impacts are divisible and variable among identifiable groups (called "stakeholders"), whose interests cannot and should not be disregarded or discounted by those who direct and carry out business operations.* This theorem translates the generalized principle expressed in Theorem Two into the specific interactions and transactions that occur as business firms go about their daily activities. Many people, both adjacent to and far from the center of business operations, may be drawn into the orbit of business influence, and when that occurs, business incurs a moral responsibility of greater or lesser magnitude for those effects that may be either beneficial or harmful.

Theorem Four: *The workplace is an arena saturated with values and ethics that are a function of several factors: a company's history of dealing with ethical issues, the organizational structure relating managers and employees to one another, prevailing ethical attitudes expressed by the company's organizational leaders, the particular personal values brought into the workplace by employees and managers, and the actual (observable) response of organizational authority figures (i.e., managers and professionals) to ethical issues that arise during the workday.* This theorem is equivalent to acknowledging the presence of ethical work climates as a part of any given

16. See Robert H. Hogner, "Social Fabric or Economic Threads: Thoughts on the Corporation as Non-Object," a paper presented during the fifth annual conference of the Society for the Advancement of Socio-Economics, New York, March 1993. Hogner, following Karl Polanyi, has long maintained the inseparability of business and society as conceptual constructs. In this paper, he questions the usefulness of objectifying the "corporation" and then analyzing its ties to an equally objectified "society." Such an approach, Hogner maintains, fails to realize that both concepts are only inventions stemming from certain intellectual and philosophic preconceptions embedded deeply in Western traditions of inquiry.

business firm's culture. It is intended to counter the myth (widely held among cynics, skeptics, and amoralists) that business work goes forward in a moral vacuum.

Theorem Five: *Moral measures, standards, principles, and criteria are required to judge and evaluate business performance that impinges upon the moral interests and needs of stakeholders and society generally.* Economic, financial, technical-engineering, and accounting measures *by themselves* are incapable of generating the insights and information needed to understand business's normative impacts on others. Just as other disciplinarians develop and apply criteria of market performance, financial success or failure, technical effectiveness, or legal compliance, so too have business ethicists developed and applied standards and principles that enable an assessment of business's normative behavior. These have been described in this and preceding chapters. The measurement and evaluation of business performance that omits these moral methodologies falls short of telling the entire story of business's function and its import for society.

Theorem Six: *The moral interests of business, corporate stakeholders, and society at large are a function of* acquired experience *within an array of evolving human communities, where normative meanings may vary in time and place but where they converge toward the sustenance and expansion of life's potentialities.* Human values, including the particular value sets found in specific business firms, thus simultaneously register the uniqueness of diverse cultures while being open to and expressive of common existential human needs. Values, as noted at the outset of this book, are conceptualizations (beliefs, standards, relationships) born of life-affecting experiences. The reason business values are worth studying is that they reflect human experience in coping with the problems posed by an entropic universe.

Theorem Seven: *Business acquires moral standing in society by carrying out a socially vital economizing function, but reliance upon that function* alone *provides an incomplete justification of business values, behavior, and operations.* An earlier chapter argued that business operations are driven partially by power-aggrandizing values that typically produce proentropic effects, thus diminishing life prospects for others. Moreover, the X-factor values present in any given business firm may comprise a volatile, potentially destructive mixture of personal values reinforced by an authoritarian corporate culture. Of even greater normative significance are the ecological transactions between firm and ecosystem, where the pursuit of economizing goals may override and endanger ecological processes of great importance to society. Hence, the overall normative significance of business can be assessed only by going beyond business's core legitimating function of economizing to consider the effects stemming from other values both inside and external to the business firm.

These theorems, taken collectively, comprise a normative commons that has emerged from the separate (and, at times, disparate) inquiries of business ethicists and students of corporate social performance. They can serve as a beginning point for a unity of discourse on business's moral and social responsibilities. They make possible a conjoining of traditional philosophic inquiry and a theory of business values derived from naturalistic and sociocultural sources.

The Social Contract Revisited

An initiative of compelling theoretical significance has been proposed by the business ethicists Thomas Donaldson and Thomas Dunfee. They advocate a revised concept of the social contract, whose earlier versions were discussed and criticized in the preceding chapter. The new approach has been labled "integrated social contracts theory (ISCT)" by its authors. It is quite possible that their theory will comprise a major linchpin connecting and consolidating the older philosophical and the newer naturalist-sociocultural ways of conducting normative analyses of business activities.[17]

ISCT distinguishes between a "macrosocial contract" and "microsocial contracts." The former is modeled along the traditional lines of a Rawlsian-rationalist derivation of overarching normative principles said to be proper for arranging the just rights and claims of people who populate a society's social, economic, and political institutions. Since this concept was discussed in the preceding chapter, it will not be described further here. Microsocial contracts are "agreements or shared understandings about the moral norms relevant to specific economic interactions." These smaller-scale contracts may be endorsed by a wide variety of groups within society, including business firms, departments within firms, larger industrial associations, and so on.

The two kinds of social contract are linked together by an imaginative, ingenious argument that preserves the "pure," abstractly and rationally derived ethical principles of a *macrosocial* contract, while allowing room for the *microsocial* contract's rather messier, less precise, socioculturally embedded social values and ethical rules of thumb by which most people guide their daily lives. "Moral free space" is granted to microsocial contractors in one society

---

17. See Thomas Donaldson and Thomas W. Dunfee, "Toward a Unified Conception of Business Ethics: Integrative Social Contracts Theory," *Academy of Management Review*, vol. 19, no. 2, April 1994, pp. 252–284. The theory's provenance sheds interesting light on the virtues of cross-disciplinary inquiry. Donaldson, a philosopher, and Dunfee, a legal scholar, seem to have blended their respective intellectual traditions to produce a quite new way of thinking about old puzzles. The interplay between the two is fascinating, with Donaldson willing to find room within traditional philosophic categories for experiential components, and with Dunfee accepting a broad philosophic framework in which to place the specifics of everyday behavior so familiar to the lawyer.

to agree on culturally prescribed ethical rules that may be at variance with
the ethical customs of another society. For example, where negotiating intent
differs from one society to another, bluffing (or less than full disclosure) may
be an expected and acceptable practice in one place but not in another. As
the authors say, "it does not follow that there is only one set of efficient ethical rules for all systems of negotiation."[18] A "bounded moral rationality" that
limits everyone's moral vision leads people to settle for less than may be abstractly and logically desirable in an ethical sense, thereby putting an emphasis on "commonsense moral convictions and preferences." A kind of moral
insurance is offered that protects against the abuses arising from an ethically
"authentic" norm of one society's microsocial contracts that might endorse
practices depriving people there of fundamental rights otherwise implied in
the overarching and ethically superior principles of humanity's macrosocial
contract. These more comprehensive principles are called "hypernorms,"
which the authors believe may reflect a convergence of ethical beliefs found
in religions, cultures, and philosophies throughout the world.

Although Donaldson and Dunfee offer their theory as a way to integrate
"normative" and "empirical" approaches to business ethics, the theory's integrative possibilities go far beyond that somewhat dubious usage.[19] Much
more important, ISCT opens a door onto a theoretical platform that blends
the powerful normative tools of philosophic analysis with the equally sharp
tools of the evolving social, physical, and biological sciences. To a philosopher, that prospect may seem to be precisely what Donaldson and Dunfee
mean by ISCT's ability to integrate normative values and empirical facts. But
to a theorist who derives values and moral norms from an evolving set of
physical and biological phenomena—as this book proposes—ISCT's analytic
potential seems far greater.

In a departure from traditional social contract thinking, ISCT seems to
proclaim that philosophy's normative principles find their moral meaning
within, *and only within*, a double-sided field of *human experience*. On one side
are the culturally specific experiences responsible for the "commonsense
moral convictions and preferences" found in microsocial contracts; examples
might be the acceptance by one society of noncommercial side payments, or
bluffing, during commercial negotiations. On the other side are the *shared*
(religious, cultural, and philosophic) experiences of people from many sociocultural traditions from which the morally binding "hypernorms" of the

18. Ibid., p. 261.

19. Although self-quotation and self-referencing are best avoided, see William C. Frederick, "The
Virtual Reality of Fact versus Value," *Business Ethics Quarterly*, vol. 4, no. 2, April 1994, pp.
171–173, for a critique of this venerable philosophic phantom. This entire issue of the journal is
devoted to the pros and cons of the fact-versus-value proposition when applied to business ethics.

macrosocial contract have been derived; an example might be the general acceptance of truth telling and honesty as ethical precepts. The Rawlsian "veil of (sociocultural) ignorance" behind which "rational" moral solutions are to be found dissolves, replaced by reliance on human judgments embedded within sociocultural settings. Further, by accepting micro moral norms that measure up to the superior moral requirements of hypernorms (and rejecting those that do not), ISCT retains that part of moral relativism that is consistent with observable sociocultural behavior while giving full rein to the transculturally-legitimate conventional principles of applied philosophy, such as respect for persons, promise keeping, and so on. Voila! Nature-based and socioculturally elaborated human experience is married to philosophy's most cherished principles. This is substantive, not merely methodological, normative integration of the greatest significance. It is a bold move that begins to tie together two inquiring traditions long held apart.

One can note various analytic imperfections of ISCT. There is a hesitancy and uncertainty still about the question of moral relativism. The relativism issue is not entirely settled by the device of restricting a society's "moral free space" by deferring to the moral superiority of "hypernorms," for the latter are themselves, as acknowledged by the authors, reflective of human sociocultural experience on a global scale. The fact that such experience, plus the values thereby inculcated, are acquired in common ways by diverse peoples does not make them less relative. Quite to the contrary, it suggests a wider (perhaps global) realm of relative human experience that has been and can be the seedbed of normative orientations. That broader normative dimension is explored more fully in the following chapter.

A curious relic of philosophic tradition—the rejection of a naturalistic foundation of economic behavior—continues to mar dialogue and analysis based on integrated social contracts theory. It is a remnant of positivism's now-declining heritage, ironically embraced by those who most wish to escape the clutches of this enduring, "value-free" intellectual tradition. Economic processes are not value-neutral, contrary to the hoary arguments of economic positivists. Nor are economic practices only "stipulated rather than given by nature," as claimed by Donaldson and Dunfee. The "naturalness" of economic behavior is what underlies many of the "commonsense moral convictions and preferences" of people in business. For example, agreeing on fair and open exchange rules that govern market transactions is a prerequisite for effective economizing. Moreover, accepting economics as emerging from nature-based processes might contribute to a "general theory of the ethics of economics" that ISCT's creators note as a desirable and necessary condition for valid ethical inquiry. Even the notion of "rationality," which plays such an indispensable part in social contract theory, might be matched in a theory of business values to the equally vital role played there by "human intelligence" that rests securely on a genetic-sociocultural base. More striking still is nature's ability to underwrite "hypernorms," which (according to the authors), "by definition, entail *principles so fundamental to human existence* that they serve as a guide in evaluating lower level moral norms." Given the entropic nature of the universe, it is difficult to imagine principles more "fundamental to human existence" than the nature-based values of economizing, technologizing, and ecologizing. The authors themselves leave open such a possibility when they ask whether hypernorms may eventually be found to exist "in some natural law sense."[20]

These theoretical hesitations and uncertainties, while disappointing, need not block further progress in moving toward a harmonization of different inquiring traditions. The importance of integrated social contracts theory in making such a contribution cannot be denied, nor can the theory be ignored by anyone interested in establishing firm grounds for judging business's ethical performance.

Normative Cores and the Ghost of John Dewey

Yet another step, though a hesitant one, may have been taken on the road to revamping the popular, well-nigh indispensable stakeholder concept that has so charmed business-and-society theorists. The theory's patron saint, business philosopher Edward Freeman, recently has proposed that "there is no stakeholder theory but that stakeholder theory becomes a genre" and that the idea of a single stakeholder theory "can be unpacked into a number of stakeholder theories," each with a somewhat distinctive "normative core."[21] An example given is of "a normative core that reflects the liberal notions of autonomy, solidarity, and fairness," which is proposed as a basis for contractual agreements among business parties and affected stakeholders. Other arrangements, each with varying normative cores embodying other ethical notions, can be visualized. Freeman's suggestion is a bold one (at least for business ethics philosophers), because it implies that normative principles are variable from place to place and from time to time, thus reflecting people's differing encounters with experienced problems. It is a theoretical modification that edges away from previous assertions and arguments made by some ethicists that convey a more absolutist or foundationist ring.

Perhaps of greatest theoretical import is Freeman's suggestion that business ethicists need, above all, to understand the value-creating activity in

20. The longer quotations in this paragraph are from Donaldson and Dunfee, op. cit., pp. 258, 265, and 278, respectively.

21. The quotations are from an unpublished paper by Freeman, "The Politics of Stakeholder Theory: Some Future Directions," Charlottesville: The Darden School, University of Virginia, February 1994.

which business is engaged, for only in that way, he avers, can a link be established between moral principle and economic operations. As Freeman says, "We cannot divorce the idea of a moral community or of a moral discourse from the ideas of the value-creation activity of business." Such a position is, or at least can be interpreted to be, consistent with this book's theory of business values, because economizing *is* business's central (i.e., original) "value-creation activity." Freeman's idea of a morality-economizing relationship is also closely related to the links between macrosocial contracts and microsocial contracts proposed by Donaldson and Dunfee. In both cases, moral principles bubble up from human experience (i.e., from Freeman's normative cores and from Donaldson's and Dunfee's microsocial contracts) and percolate down from an overarching moral system (i.e., Freeman's moral community and Donaldson's and Dunfee's hypernorms). In this sense, all three theorists seem to invoke the ghost of John Dewey, the instrumental pragmatist who long advocated that values and valuational processes stem from the realm of human experience as lived within sociocultural communities.[22] While the three well-respected business ethicists continue to cling to Rawlsian-rationalist notions of social contract, their theories sound increasingly consistent with the pragmatic world of work in which business practitioners dwell and make daily decisions of ethical import. If such a trend were to continue, one might hope and expect that business ethics theory would draw ever closer to touching the needs of business practitioners for an ethical understanding that fits the context in which they and their corporate companions work.

WHAT DOES IT MEAN TO BE ETHICAL WHILE AT WORK?

The New Normative Synthesis proposed in this chapter exhibits much greater explanatory power than alternative ways of defining ethicality in the workplace. By anchoring business behavior within a nature-based, antientropic economizing process, business practitioners can be seen as carrying out societally vital, life-sustaining activities, which thereby acquire great positive normative significance. By recognizing that much business activity involves the pursuit, consolidation, and magnification of coercive power that hobbles

---

22. Freeman acknowledges explicitly that his reinterpretation of stakeholder theory is closely related to Dewey's brand of pragmatism. For an insightful discussion of pragmatism's potential contribution to business ethics theorizing, see Rogene A. Buchholz and Sandra B. Rosenthal, "Toward a New Understanding of Moral Pluralism," a paper delivered during the annual conference of the International Association for Business and Society, Hilton Head, SC, March 18–19, 1994.

business's own and others' economizing efforts, as well as rupturing vital ecological processes, it is possible to conclude that these proentropic business
tendencies are unethical in the sense of diminishing the life prospects of
many people. By acknowledging that business cannot go forward without the
involvement and cooperation of a wide range of stakeholders, a pragmatic,
utilitarian basis is established for recognizing and accepting the validity of
stakeholder claims that make their full participation desirable and possible.
Workplace justice emerges as a blend of respect for the personal and intellectual integrity and security of those who participate in a company's economizing activities, along with a tangible recognition that individuals vary greatly in
what they are able to contribute to the firm and in what they need in order to
sustain a humanly meaningful life both within and outside the workplace. Because any given workplace is a complex crossroads where many individuals
bearing personal values encounter not only each other but also the core values of a company's culture, ethicality will vary immensely from one company
to another, as well as among industries and in companies doing business in
diverse societies.

Since business ethics is thus relative to nature's economizing and ecologizing processes, to varying sociocultural conventions, to a company's culture
and ethical climate, to a firm's commitment to power aggrandizement, to
practitioners' personal values, and to stakeholders' involvement and participation, *ethical business behavior has no single meaning.* It is a thoroughly relativistic phenomenon, although that need not mean that it lacks substantive,
morally bound meaning, which can arise from any one of the value sources
just listed. Being ethical while at work takes many different forms because
ethicality is given multiple meanings by nature, by culture, by society, by organizations, by individuals, by stakeholders, and by all who practice business.
From this ethics stewpot of human experience, we have learned to extract
moral orientations that preserve life, enhance its quality, reveal present
threats and future dangers, and teach us what it takes to maintain a humane
life process within the limits and possibilities set by nature and culture. In the
final analysis, ethicality in business is relative to *and is sustained by* these experiential moral orientations. It is therefore both relative to diverse moral traditions *and* incorporated within enduring experience-based principles.

By using an analytical device such as, for example, integrated social contracts theory, it is possible to sift a variety of business behaviors through a normative screen to test their ability to meet widely agreed and commonly
shared ethical standards. This emphasis upon a *process* of arriving at ethical
judgments is akin to John Rawls's effort to establish a set of principles, rather
than only a substantive meaning, for deriving justice. Nevertheless, the New
Normative Synthesis proposed here comprises more than just an evaluative
process for judging business's normative behavior.

The normative *substance* of business operations—the larger ethical significance of this premier social institution—cannot be found by looking simply within the precincts of the workplace or the economy or a single society. A much broader field of view is needed if we are to find the proper place and role of business in society. A final chapter explores those broader realms.

10

Business and the Moral Process

The normative bill of particulars brought against American corporate business is lengthy, shocking, and saddening. From many quarters and over long stretches of time, a clamorous chorus has sounded out a damning indictment of specific business practices and, in some cases, a condemnation of the institution itself. Greed, selfishness, ego-centeredness, disregard of the needs and well-being of others, a narrow or nonexistent social vision, an ethnocentric managerial creed imposed on nonindustrial cultures, a reckless use of dangerous technologies, an undermining of countervailing institutions such as trade unions, a virtual political takeover of some pluralist government agencies, and a system of self-reward that few either inside or outside business have cared to defend as fair or moral—all of these attributes have been credited to the business account.

Case study after case study has documented these and other abuses, while countless conferences and workshops have agonized over the social irresponsibility and ethical transgressions of corporate America. Activist protests have been raised by consumers, employees, environmentalists, ethnic minorities, women, gays, the mentally and physically disabled, pensioners, military veterans, trade unionists, Third World citizens living in the shadow of some corporate installation, and on and on through a long and dreary list of corporate stakeholders (and stockholders) who have found themselves to be the victims of corporate depredations of one kind or another. Occasionally (though rarely), questions about business's social and ethical irresponsibilities are even brought forward by a few business practitioners themselves, who timidly admit that business performance is sometimes less than socially and morally acceptable.

There seems to be little disagreement, among both friends and foes, that business at times lacks—even profoundly lacks—a conscious, well-developed, and active moral sense to guide its decisions and operations. How otherwise to explain the financial excesses and fraudulent schemes of various Wall Street investment bankers, some of whom were jailed and fined for criminal acts? How to account for the company that exposed its workers to fatal chemical fumes, and whose convicted managers were imprisoned for workplace homicide? How to explain the pharmaceutical company or the tire manufacturer or the car maker that secretly knew (sometimes for years) of life-threatening design features of their products yet continued marketing them to trusting customers, many of whom died or were maimed and injured as a result? How otherwise to understand the widespread, almost casually delivered misleading commercial claims, the sly half-truths of much advertising, the price-fixing conspiracies, the misrepresentation of insurance policies as retirement plans, the advantage taken of elderly retirees by home repair firms and unscrupulous health care insurance outfits? If morality is not taking a holiday from the executive suite, how might one answer the charge that closing a plant and moving to another location also closes the professional and cherished work lives of loyal employees? If the answer is that the newly opened plant creates work for others, how then is one to morally justify the truly enormous gap that yawns between the hourly pay of these new workers (or the non-pay of the laid-off workers) and the lofty salaries of the managerial-executive cadre at headquarters? As corporate downsizing proceeds apace, what meaning of morality can be offered by corporate decision makers to reassure those whose professional careers and work lives are disrupted or ruined irretrievably? If competitive pressures present a business firm with a move-shrink-or-die market edict, can its managers then escape a moral obligation to advocate nonmarket ways to protect the firm's discarded employees?[1]

These many documented moral abuses, and the answers implicit in the questions they raise, testify to an uncertain moral awareness within American corporate enterprise. Moral considerations tend not to be assigned a high priority, nor are they significantly or deliberately rewarded within many American business firms. Indeed, moral discussions rarely occur within the workplace, where the language of morality is generally considered to be off limits.[2] Even in those instances where a company or an industrial association draws up a code of ethical conduct or a set of principles as recommended practice to all within a given sector, the moral impact is compromised. Re-

---

1. To hear the voices of some of the hapless victims of industrial transition, read Carrie R. Leana and Daniel C. Feldman, *Coping with Job Loss: How Individuals, Organizations, and Communities Respond to Layoffs*, New York: Lexington Books, 1992. As one among many said (p. 30), "I feel tossed aside, like an old shoe."

2. Frederick Bird and James A. Waters, "The Moral Muteness of Managers," *California Management Review*, vol. 32, no. 1, 1989, pp. 73–88.

search has demonstrated that corporate ethical codes are designed primarily to protect *companies* against ethical abuses by their employees and the potential legal claims of other stakeholder groups, not to extend moral precepts in comprehensive ways that would provide protection for what the company may do to others.[3] On the few occasions in which corporate titans have seemed to endorse moral principles, their statements, though sincerely crafted and perhaps well motivated, exhibit a marshmallow consistency.[4] They invariably endorse the central motivational, organizational, and institutional components that provide shelter for the business corporation against the principal moral charges being brought.

That this regrettable state of affairs exists, and has persisted throughout a century of corporate enterprise, is a cruelly ironic commentary on the working out of moral processes within human society. Here is an institution that carries in its bosom clusters of values that help to define and sustain, not just its own meaning but that of humanity writ large. As this book has argued, without those economizing and technologizing values, the human condition would be radically different and woefully less admirable even than its present uneven and uncertain state. The generic business function has occupied a central place in winning and consolidating the layer of civilization that humans have managed to win from their natural environment. Within the more recent chapters of this saga, the American business corporation has been an indispensable instrument in this struggle, making possible through its economizing and technologizing operations a veritable cornucopia of resources, products, and services that literally define large components of our way of life. Few if any dimensions of our individual, familial, organizational, societal, and cultural lives are untouched by the business corporation's positive and beneficial functions. How, then, can there have been created such a wide chasm, a bottomless pit, a seemingly unbridgeable gap between the many benefits brought forward by the corporation and the morally dubious record it has compiled?

This chapter explores this difficult, painful conundrum, with only the faintest hope or expectation that firm and convincing answers or solutions are to be found. What may be reasonable to expect, though, is the emergence of some useful insights and perspectives shaped by the theory of busi-

---

3. Donald R. Cressey and Charles A. Moore, "Managerial Values and Corporate Codes of Ethics," *California Management Review*, vol. 25, 1983, pp. 53–77; and M. Cash Mathews, *Strategic Intervention in Organizations: Resolving Ethical Dilemmas*, Newbury Park, CA: Sage, 1988, Chapters 4 and 5.

4. Examples are the Committee for Economic Development, *Social Responsibilities of Business Corporations*, New York: Committee for Economic Development, 1971; and The Business Roundtable, *Corporate Ethics: A Prime Business Asset*, New York: The Business Roundtable, 1988.

ness values proposed here, particularly when set within the context of what will be called a "culture of ethics."

THE CULTURE OF ETHICS

A principal premise of this book is that business is necessarily imbued with normative qualities. It cannot help but be bound up within a cocoon of moral meanings. Its core values of economizing and power aggrandizement, along with the diversity of X-factor values stemming from its work force—plus the intersection with and impact of all these on ecological processes—guarantee that all business decisions, policies, and operations carry significant normative weight. Even though these interacting value systems are very comprehensive and extensive, it may be possible to visualize yet another, even broader and more inclusive realm of valuing phenomena that lends additional normative meaning to business activities. That more extensive value complex is the "culture of ethics."

This concept embraces the notion that normative judgments, including those about business operations, originate within a broad realm of shared understandings and shared life experiences that tend to be found wherever humans congregate and live together. It is not a culture in the sense of being tied to any particular society or to any delimited or unchanging point of historical time. Nor is the culture of ethics a seamless, uniform set of normative directives, rules, or principles to which all might give moral allegiance. No one society can claim to be its originator, or its exclusive proprietor or guardian, for the culture of ethics is found throughout the human realm, taking diverse forms and found within multiple institutional organs in each society. It is something like a normative seedbed from which ethical and moral understandings are cultivated and allowed to grow to maturity in light of experiences acquired through living within human society and within natural ecosystems. Neither is it morally overarching or more ethically authentic than contrasting normative systems found within specific human societies. The culture of ethics simply reflects a commonness of human experience in coping with the multiform problems of living together in fair, just, and moral ways. Diverse and varied in content at any one time, as well as changing its focus and emphasis throughout historical time, it incorporates the widest range of normative orientations without asserting the moral superiority of any particular one and without blending all varieties into a single set of preferable ethical alternatives.

This culture of ethics—this normative seedbed—evolves and functions alongside the societally vital economizing, technologizing, and ecologizing values, and because it is supportive of those values, it carries humankind along against the tides of entropy. In this sense, business as an economizing institution is and has always been deeply and irretrievably bound up within a normative process of the utmost importance. *This all-embracing moral process gives central meaning to business, defines its societal legitimacy, and means that business cannot be severed from moral considerations.* If this proposition is true, the linkage of business to a broad moral order would mean that no explanation, description, or analysis of the business institution could be considered complete or wholly true without an explicit acknowledgment of this relationship.

Moreover, the existence of this link begins to define an obligation of business practitioners, not only to affirm the moral embeddedness of business but also to accept and act upon it. But affirmation must precede such action, thus raising the question of moral awareness. The gap between business performance and the moral expectations of society may be partially explained by a failure of moral awareness, a kind of moral astigmatism that does not blind but that seriously distorts the perception of the moral reality in which business operations are normally and necessarily carried on. While most business professionals are acutely attuned to (what they consider to be) *economic* reality, their grasp of a broader *moral* reality may be constricted or blocked by organizational factors or competitive market factors over which they have little or only limited discretionary control. This is not to excuse inaction or to imply that if only more business practitioners had a developed sense of moral awareness, the gap between business performance and the moral expectations of society would be narrowed, although the latter argument might well be sustained. Rather, it is to wonder how fully it is understood, *both within and outside the business firm*, that all business operations are unavoidably value-laden; that those operations and values have both pro- and antientropic consequences; that business's central economizing, power-aggrandizing, and technologizing values intersect with ecologizing values that underpin a humane community life; and that all business practitioners—for all of these reasons—are continuously and profoundly engaged in a moral process. It is not simply that a moral shell surrounds a rationalist, pragmatic business operation, with a firm boundary separating the two, but rather that moral qualities penetrate throughout and saturate the entire business-in-society complex. In this sense, business *is*—that is, it exists only as—part of a moral process to which it is a positive contributor but that also is more comprehensive and extensive than normative business activity itself.

If true, this concept of business-in-and-of-a-moral-process means that the grounds for judging any business activity, motive, or goal must come from within that moral process. No aspect of business operations either stands alone or can be judged as if it were separate from the moral dimension within which business itself is embedded. This is tantamount to saying that a culture of ethics, drawn from many diverse sources within nature and culture, is the most comprehensive source for judging the normative significance of business. If there is indeed this broader realm of human experience to which business activity could be referred in seeking a better course than that already recorded, one might be able to believe that normative inquiry would make a difference in the lives of business practitioners. For business ethicists, that is, after all, inquiry's primary justification. Thus, one is led to consider the viability of the notion that a culture of ethics actually exists and can exert normative force within business.

THE SEARCH FOR ETHICAL CONSTANTS

Business ethicists in recent years have joined and extended the search, undertaken by others before them, for universal ethical principles. These ethical constants frequently have been proposed as guides to business decision making—an ethical tool kit, so to speak. Each such effort, arising from the widest variety of motives and purposes, has managed unwittingly to reveal some portion of the fabric that comprises the culture of ethics. All suffer an inherent limitation that is a product of the designer's conscious purpose in bringing such a scheme forward, that is, the constants named are intended to support a larger philosophic framework that is being proposed or that is unconsciously implicit. (The same observation may be made about this book's proposals concerning values and ethics.) Nevertheless, when viewed collectively, such attempts to find universal ethical principles are impressive, and perhaps they contain a normative significance not yet fully recognized or articulated. Some of the most salient and compelling proposals are worth mention and brief discussion.

Common Morality

Business philosophers Edward Freeman and Daniel Gilbert assure corporate managers that a "common morality" can be the starting point of ethical analysis.[5] They refer to "that set of rules that most of us live by most of the time." Included are promise keeping, nonmalevolence (do no physical harm), mutual aid, respect for persons (the Kantian concept), and respect for property. Without promise keeping, they aver, "social interaction would grind to a halt." The "bedrock of social intercourse" rests on the rules of promise keeping, doing no harm, and mutual aid. So the authors are telling business decision makers that moral rules have important instrumental usefulness. Just

---

5. R. Edward Freeman and Daniel R. Gilbert, Jr., *Corporate Strategy and the Search for Ethics*, Englewood Cliffs, NJ: Prentice-Hall, 1988, pp. 55–57.

how widely these rules are thought to apply is not made clear, although two of the rules—respect for persons and property—are identified as "the corner-stone of our Western society," therefore seeming to delimit any broader claims for universality. In other words, the "common morality" they invoke is to some extent culture bound, while some principles seem applicable to "so-cial interaction" and "social intercourse" wherever they may occur.

Virtue Ethics

Virtue ethicists, on the other hand, do not hesitate to find universalist traits in human nature.[6] They trace common ethical constants to personal charac-ter and to virtues such as prudence, justice, fortitude, temperance, benevo-lence, and harmonious self-acceptance. These and other virtues "represent the essential aspects of our common, transcultural, transtemporal, human na-ture," according to David Hart's authoritative account. An "innate human na-ture" therefore becomes the source of omnipresent virtues that underlie ethi-cal behavior, and these virtues are presumably to be found wherever there are humans—that is, in all societies,. Virtue ethicists emphasize the develop-ment of internal strength of character rather than the acceptance of external ethical rules. Being a virtuous person, that is, having developed the virtues as a part of one's character, is more important and a greater accomplishment than simply learning to obey moral edicts issued by others. Moreover, the virtues are not a free gift but must be gained through effort, study, and reflec-tion. They, too, like Freeman and Gilbert's common morality, have instru-mental force: "the cardinal virtues are to guide action in practical affairs," and "they are the only solid ethical foundation upon which to construct a so-cial, economic, or political system," including administrative or managerial systems such as business.

An attempt to translate these generalities into specific business contexts has been offered by the philosopher Robert Solomon, who in a sense turns aside from a strict belief in universal ethical guides.[7] He understands the rele-vant virtues to be "context bound, 'relative' to various practices and activities, and that means that not only will new practices produce new virtues . . . but that a virtue that is of little importance in one situation may be a cardinal virtue in another or vice versa." The business virtues—honesty, fairness, trust,

6. The quotations and interpretations here are from David Kirkwood Hart, "Administration and the Ethics of Virtue," in Terry L. Cooper (ed.), *Handbook of Administrative Ethics*, New York: Mar-cel Dekker, 1994, pp. 107–123.

7. Robert C. Solomon, *Ethics and Excellence: Cooperation and Integrity in Business*, New York: Oxford University Press, 1992. The longer quotations in this paragraph are from pp. 190–192 and 198, respectively. See especially Chapters 16–22.

toughness, friendliness, honor, loyalty, shame, caring, compassion, and justice ("the ultimate virtue of corporate life")—are set forth as desirable traits to be cultivated by business professionals. His view is obviously less sweeping and less universalist than that claimed by many virtue ethicists, though Solomon's is no less instrumentalist: "Virtues are essentially social traits. . . . A virtue fits in with people in a particular kind of community . . . [and is] essential to the life of the community and [is] socially sanctioned." Like all good virtue ethicists, Solomon invokes "generic virtues" that for him have a focused place in business, and the reader emerges with an impression that it is within virtuous character, and not in overarching ethical rules, that one is to find enduring ethical constants.

International Human Rights

By far the most thorough, best argued, most theoretically consistent, and most logically compelling argument for universal principles of ethics applicable to business is found in the philosopher Thomas Donaldson's book *The Ethics of International Business*.[8] He offers a list of ten fundamental international rights as "a moral minimum" which all corporations doing business across national borders are obligated to observe in practice. They range from the right to freedom of physical movement, to nondiscriminatory treatment, to subsistence, to freedom of speech, and on to others. A close reading reveals that this set of ten rights is believed to be universalist in nature: they are "*transnational* moral obligations"; are "justified claims from the standpoint of *all members of the human community*"; are "applicable to peoples *even when those peoples would fail to compose an identical list*," thus seeming to exist in a sense above and beyond any given society's ethical traditions; and are "a *universal, objective minimum*." Donaldson deals forthrightly with issues of relativism, and he proposes "an ethical algorithm" for working through and finding ways for corporate managers to observe and apply the fundamental rights to their companies' operations that occur in diverse cultural settings. Though quite comprehensive, Donaldson's ten fundamental rights, by taking specific form, are less sweeping and general than either the "common morality" of Freeman and Gilbert or the "innate" character traits proposed by virtue ethicists. They nevertheless define a core of moral behavior that should apply in all locations where multinational corporations do business, and in that sense they comprise a type of universalized moral principle.

Contemporaneous with Donaldson's formulation, and somewhat akin to his, was an argument I put forth that claimed that basic human rights, de-

---

8. Thomas Donaldson, *The Ethics of International Business*, New York: Oxford University Press, 1989. The quotations are from pages 5, 7, 91, and 100, with emphasis added in all cases.

rived from Kantian philosophy and taking tangible form in various transnational compacts, agreements, and declarations, were the basis for a universalist ethic that should be used to guide international corporations.[9] This account displays all the signs of serious intellectual schizophrenia, for it also posits a second, overlapping argument for a universal standard of business ethics. It argues that human values grow out of commonly shared experiences encountered in confronting life's many problems and challenges, and that the ethical principles embedded in transnational declarations and compacts such as the United Nations Universal Declaration of Human Rights reflect the widespread existence of these common experienced-based value systems. An apparently forked tongue seems to speak the language of human rights to Kantian philosophers, while another message is sent to pragmatic philosophers who favor an emphasis on experiential value formation. In either case, though, the argument is that it is possible to identify and apply universalist moral principles relevant to business operations.

Competing with Integrity

One seasoned business ethicist, Richard DeGeorge, is less sanguine that agreement will be reached on enduring ethical meanings that can be applied to all business contexts. Although there is, for him, a core of commonly accepted ethical norms for conducting business transactions—promise keeping, honoring contracts, telling the truth, and so on—societies differ in the meaning they assign to some of the most basic ethics concepts, such as justice. DeGeorge recognizes what anthropologists have long maintained, namely, that ethical norms are embedded within "accepted customs, laws, and institutions" and that at present there is no globally uniform cultural pattern of this kind that would support a common ethic. He believes that "a workable set of such background institutions is more valuable and more likely to be achieved than is agreement on an overarching set of ethical norms or principles upon which all people from all nations must agree." Whereas an "international ethical theory" may not be achievable, there might be agreement on "a set of international practices that all can agree to as ethical, no matter what ethical perspective they hold."[10]

---

9. William C. Frederick, "The Moral Authority of Transnational Corporate Codes," *Journal of Business Ethics*, vol. 10, no. 2, 1991, pp. 165–177.

10. Richard T. DeGeorge, "International Business Ethics," *Business Ethics Quarterly*, vol. 4, no. 1, January 1994, pp. 1–9. DeGeorge's views, always refreshingly sensible and well argued, are set forth in much greater detail in his book, *Competing with Integrity in International Business*, New York: Oxford University Press, 1993, where he places considerable emphasis on the importance of virtuous character.

International Policy Regimes

Just such background institutions and international agreements favored by De-George have been identified by Lee Preston and Duane Windsor, who prefer to call these arrangements "international policy regimes."[11] Such regimes include "principles, norms, rules, and decision-making procedures" that regulate the activities of governments and enterprises regarding such international matters as air transport, ocean shipping, environmental protection, use of the oceans, consumer protection, technology transfer, and so on. Increasingly, these and similar "rules of the game"—thirty-two major regimes are named—regulate international trade and commerce and form a framework through which much global business is being conducted. Of the principles and norms found in these agreements, two are said to be of "critical importance"—"*efficiency*" (largely, economic efficiency is meant)" and "*equity, or fairness*," the latter becoming "increasingly important in more recent years."[12] In other words, the authors seem to say that policy regimes rest on a solid foundation of ethical principles and that they are not mere technical agreements to ease world trade.

Moreover, policy regimes consist not only of the kinds of "background institutions" that DeGeorge seeks as supports for ethical business actions in international trade and commerce, but they also include normative elements governing the behavior of those who adopt and are governed by the agreements. Preston and Windsor report that "although most important regimes contain significant *institutional elements (formal agreements, organizations)*, the *understandings and norms* governing the behavior of participants are of primary importance."[13] In other passages in the book (p. xvi), they speak of the importance of "*mutually acceptable norms and patterns of behavior*," as well as "*common understandings and norms*" needed for "an increasingly interdependent world economy," thus evoking language that adumbrates but does not specifically invoke ethical concerns. The omission is deliberate, as the authors explicitly put aside any intention of dealing directly with the normative aspects of policy regimes.[14] However, their choice to keep their own distance

---

11. Lee E. Preston and Duane Windsor, *The Rules of the Game in the Global Economy: Policy Regimes for International Business*, Drodrecht: Kluwer, 1992.

12. Lee E. Preston and Duane Windsor, "Policy Regimes for International Business: Concepts and Prospects," Occasional Paper No. 7 (revised), College Park: Center for International Business Education and Research, University of Maryland, n.d., pp. 4–5.

13. Ibid., p. 20, emphasis added.

14. Even the most determined positivist stance can fall afoul of the illogic involved in trying to keep "values" and "facts" separate from one another. For example, Preston and Windsor say, "This study is positive rather than normative in character," only to conclude that same paragraph by declaring that "it is important to understand that different regime features yield different outcomes and *to seek ways in which the diverse interests of regime participants can be harmonized*." But "harmonizing diverse interests" is frequently and characteristically a large portion of what normative ethical analysis seeks to accomplish. See *The Rules of the Game*, p. xix, emphasis added.

most of the time from the ethical content of these regimes does not preclude others from pointing out the obvious normative substance of many such agreements. Examples include the World Health Organization's code on marketing of infant formula, the Vienna and Montreal Protocols on air pollution and ozone depletion, the proposed United Nations code on acceptable practices of multinational enterprises, various consumer protection agreements, provisions governing the treatment of employees and child labor, and regimes regarding ocean usage, exploitation of the Antarctic, and other cross-border or "global commons" environmental issues, along with a concern for "long-run sustainability" (which the authors acknowledge expands the notion of "efficiency" as one of the two critically important guiding principles of most policy regimes).

The significant point is that such compacts *in fact* operationalize what are understood to be normative relationships among peoples and their institutions, whether or not they are couched in the language of morals and ethics. They are indeed a portion of what DeGeorge calls background institutions that sustain and make possible cross-cultural agreements on actions believed to be right or wrong. "The rules of the game" governing international business transactions clearly include transnational normative orientations. In that sense, those rules appear to be part of a broad culture of ethics from which business operations may be judged.

Religious Universals

The influence of religious belief and doctrine on economic life is a much discussed matter that is entirely too complex for more than brief attention here. Without question, religious faith is a major component of the culture of ethics, bringing its influence to bear in many ways, not the least of which is to teach moral values and normative principles to the faithful, who then carry those ethical orientations with them wherever they may find themselves. In the language of earlier chapters of this book, the X-factor values that play such a large role in developing the overall value profile of any given business firm owe much to the religious conditioning and personal moral commitments of employees and managers. However hemmed in by corporate culture or channeled by prevailing ethical workplace climates are those who work in business, it seems unlikely that deeply held religious beliefs could be so squelched as to be totally inoperative. For the most part, the forms taken by this kind of influence are highly varied and diverse, reflecting the pluralistic architecture of religious belief as found around the world. The sheer diversity of religious beliefs, official doctrines, sacred writings, and localized expressions of overarching religious faith tells of a deep well or an inexhaustible spring of normative inclination among peoples everywhere. Beyond the personal realm are all of the organized institutional energies of religious organizations that are frequently focused on questions and issues of public import and normative significance, including many that occur within the business arena.

A recent attempt to draw together into one document the strands of religious belief that collectively would define a "global ethic" is worth noting.[15] The sponsor of this effort is the Parliament of World Religions, a coalition of over 200 representatives of all the world's major religions (and many lesser-known ones, as well). "Toward a Global Ethic" declares the need for an overarching set of moral guides for societies everywhere and, like other seekers of universal ethical rules discussed above, maintains that its basis already exists within "a common set of values . . . found in the teachings of the [world's] religions." The declaration speaks of "a minimal *fundamental consensus* concerning binding *values*, irrevocable *standards*, and *fundamental moral attitudes*." These are said to be "norms which are valid for all humans regardless of their social origin, sex, skin color, language, or religion." The global ethic's core consists of "four broad, ancient guidelines for human behavior which are found in most of the religions of the world." They are a commitment to (1) nonviolence and respect for life, (2) solidarity and a just economic order, (3) tolerance and a life of truthfulness, and (4) equal rights and partnership between men and women. (Close examination reveals that the four pairs logically divide into eight distinct principles.) These "irrevocable [moral] propositions" are proposed as guides to people, organizations, institutions, and societies everywhere. Somewhat like Donaldson's ten fundamental human rights, they constitute "a moral minimum" that in this case draws moral authority from religious teachings and precepts.

Interestingly enough, though it has been endorsed by religious authorities from many diverse societies and religious traditions, the global ethic clearly expresses the Kantian principle of respect for persons, which is a central precept of Western philosophy (though similar principles are found in non-Western societies): "Humans must always be the subjects of rights, must be ends, never mere means, never objects of commercialization and industrialization." Toward that end, the declaration is sprinkled with references to ecological harms and the need for ecological protections, the exploitation of peoples and nations by excessive economic initiatives, the need to find humane ways for production to go forward, and the importance of easing the burdens imposed by economic progress.

The World Parliament's declaration is broadly suggestive of a consensus among religious thinkers and leaders that something like a common morality or a moral minimum does in fact exist, and that it finds powerful reinforcement in religious doctrine and religious teaching. As such, the moral aware-

15. Parliament of World Religions, *Toward a Global Ethic*, Chicago, 1993.

ness that it encourages among the faithful would have to be counted among the component parts of a culture of ethics that stretches around the globe and comprises a moral presence that business firms are bound to encounter in the course of their operations wherever conducted.

The Moral Sense

Is it possible that such broad-scale moral orientations as seem to be revealed by disparate groups of business ethicists, economists, and religious representatives are traceable to natural forces operating through evolutionary processes? So believes James Q. Wilson, one of America's leading social scientists, who has set forth his persuasive arguments in *The Moral Sense*.[16] He argues that "people have a natural moral sense, a sense that is formed out of the interaction of their innate dispositions with their earliest familial experiences. To different degrees among different people, but to some important degree in almost all people, that moral sense shapes human behavior and the judgments people make of the behavior of others." He rejects explanations based solely on sociocultural grounds:

> Two errors arise in attempting to understand the human condition. One is to assume that culture is everything, the other to assume that it is nothing. In the first case there would be no natural moral sense—if culture is everything, then nature is nothing. In the second, the moral sense would speak to us far more clearly than it does. A more reasonable assumption is that culture will make some difference some of the time in the lives of most of us and a large difference much of the time in the lives of a few of us.[17]

Nor does he find universal moral rules to be a necessary precondition of a commonly shared sense of morality.

> Most important human universals do not take the form of rules at all. . . . But what is most likely to be universal are those impulses that, because they are so common, scarcely need to be stated in the form of a rule. . . . To find what is universal about human nature, we must look behind the rules and the circumstances that shape them to discover what fundamental dispositions, if any, animate them and to decide whether those dispositions are universal.[18]

The moral impulses and dispositions Wilson identifies are "the consequence of biological predispositions selected for over eons of evolutionary

---

16. James Q. Wilson, *The Moral Sense*, New York: Free Press, 1993.

17. The two quotations here are from ibid., pp. 2, 6.

18. Ibid., pp. 18, 226.

history." An innate moral sense—a predisposition to consider the interests of others as well as one's own—develops from an infant's interactions with and bonding to a mother, and this moral sense is reinforced by familial ties and practices, and later extended, though problematically and uncertainly, to others outside the family circle. Moral sentiments such as sympathy, fairness, self-control, and duty have been behavioral imperatives for family units that subsequently have served as shelters and guarantors of family lineages. Although these moral sentiments are the outcome of a natural evolutionary process, "gender and culture will profoundly influence which of them—sympathy or duty, fairness or self-control—are most valued. And since these senses are to a degree indeterminate, culture will affect how they are converted into maxims, customs, and rules."[19]

If Wilson's view is correct, it would help explain the widespread prevalence of moral orientations that so many observers seem to have sensed. His four moral sentiments clearly overlap Freeman and Gilbert's "common morality," as well as many of the cardinal virtues proclaimed by virtue ethicists, the respect for human rights advocated by Donaldson, the integrity favored by DeGeorge as a guiding principle of international business, the soft-spoken moral norms invoked by Preston and Windsor's international policy regimes, and the Parliament of World Religions' four "irrevocable" moral propositions that undergird the declaration of a global ethic.

Morality, in this view, is integral to the human condition, a product of natural evolution, elaborated and extended in many diverse directions and toward many varied purposes by sociocultural practices. Wilson's "moral sense" is the natural evolutionary underlayer on which sociocultural ethical systems, principles, and rules are subsequently built up. As such, it helps explain why it becomes possible to find convergence and mutual support about the prevalence of moral sensibilities and moral consciousness throughout the world.

Feminist Morality

Closely akin to Wilson's concept of a moral sense, and lending strength to the global prevalence of a culture of ethics, is what Virginia Held presents as "feminist morality."[20]

---

19. Ibid., pp. 123, 229.

20. Virginia Held, *Feminist Morality: Transforming Culture, Society, and Politics*, Chicago: University of Chicago Press, 1993. Held's book draws on a large, diverse array of feminist writings and is used here as generally representative of feminist views, although Held clearly develops her own distinctive perspective and she does not claim to include the views of all who have developed and who continue to formulate feminist thought.

Her interpretation of the roots of morality is based within the mother-child relationship, including an extended process of deciding whether to give birth, whether the child is desired and valued or not wanted and devalued, whether the child will be nourished or neglected (and perhaps even allowed to die), and especially the long period of caring for the developing child as it grows to physical and social maturity. Within the extended process of conception, pregnancy, lactation, nursing, and postnatal-postpartum closeness, mothers evolve and give expression to a wide range of feelings (both positive and negative) about the child, about themselves, and about the decisions they make and the experiences they encounter during all stages of the birth-and-early-caring process. This mothering experience is offered as the moral seedbed from which the mother's and the child's notions of morality are formed and reinforced. It is here within mothering that is created, not just a new human being but experiences that are inherently moral and that begin to define for the child and for society the kinds of relationships essential for the continued existence of both. In Held's own words:

> When we bring the experience of women fully into the domain of moral consciousness, we can see that the most central and fundamental social relation is that between mother or mothering person and child. It is mothering persons and children who turn biological entities into human social entities through their interactions. It is mothers and mothering persons who create children and construct with and for the child the human social reality of the child. The child's understanding of language and of symbols and of all that they create and make real occurs through cooperation between child and caretakers. Mothering persons and children thus produce and create the most basic elements of human culture. The development of language and the creation within and for each person of a human social reality thus seems utterly central to human society.[21]

The view is especially compelling, given the universality of mothering, birth, and the essential period of direct care that follows birth. This is indeed the time when what is identified as distinctively "human" begins to be created and formed. This is the period when the fundamental symbolic roots of human culture are first made known to the child—through the mothering

21. Ibid, p. 70. See Chapters 4, 5, and 6 for an elaboration of the mothering experience as a basis of moral conception and development. Held points out that mothering and caretaking can be done by persons other than the biological mother. Held is also aware that an emphasis on mothering risks perpetuating traditional sex-role stereotyping of women, but she believes that the need to reveal the moral significance of the mothering-birthing process overrides this risk. Held's keen interest in securing a firm and equal foothold for consideration of women's experiences leads her to reject mothering-birthing as "nothing but" (my quotation marks) an aspect of biological function. The argument of this book, by contrast, is that biologically rooted processes (of which birthing-mothering is but one of many instances) are the beginning of human experiences that eventuate in the formation of values and moral conceptions.

person's (or persons') actions and expressed feelings. This is when the biological entity is made into a cultural entity—through contacts and links dominated by the mother's (or in some cases a mother-substitute's) culturally conditioned behavior. It is the beginning of behaviors, feelings, attitudes, and reactions that bear the stamp of approval or disapproval and from which the child slowly (and painfully, as parents and children know) acquires a sense of values and morality. It is an experience literally known to everyone, regardless of sociocultural setting. While not all women become mothers, all persons are born, nourished, and cared for long enough to assume some semblance of cultural identity, thus being exposed to a process that brings them into the realm of humanity and the beginnings of morality. The (mothering) sources of morality quite obviously are embedded within varying sociocultural traditions that diversely condition the specific, substantive content of this initial morality wherever it is found. But Held's argument is not vitiated by the existential fact of culturally relative moral beliefs, for the mothering-birthing-child-development process that is the source of morality presents mothers and children everywhere with situations that call forth similar types of needs, attitudes, emotional feelings, and bonds as the child passes through this early vestibule into human society. In fact, it is the particularistic character of diverse sociocultural traditions that lends special weight to the feminist argument that generalized universalist principles and rules of morality are not to be trusted to reveal the true nature of values and value formation.

Feminist moral theory in general is constructed on a firm base of human experience, not just experience in general but specific, particularistic experiences encountered in everyday living (as in mothering and birthing). Such an experiential, contextualist focus draws feminist conceptions of morality into close kinship with this book's theory of (business) values and value formation. The view here has been that values come into existence and acquire their meaning and function within sociocultural contexts as extrusions of experiences that affect human life.

Held, once again, on the importance of contextual experience:

> In my view, not only must moral theories be applicable to actual problems, they must in some way be "tested" in actual experience. They must be made to confront lived reality; they must be found satisfactory in the actual situations people find themselves in. Otherwise, they are intellectual exercises that may be intriguing and impressively coherent, but they are not adequate as *moral theories*. . . .

> The central category of feminist thought, at least in its contemporary phase, is experience. It is not the constricted experience of mere empirical observation. It is the lived experience of feeling as well as thought, of acting as well as receiving impressions, and of connectedness to other persons as well as to self.[22]

22. Ibid., pp. 23–24.

Hence, if Held has found a type of morality-inducing and value-creating experience that is widely known and shared wherever humans congregate, she and her feminist colleagues have surely described yet another dimension—perhaps the central one—of the culture of ethics. Combined with James Q. Wilson's notion of a moral sense that grows out of familial experiences, the feminist theory of human morality constitutes a powerful reinforcement of this chapter's contention that a culturally overarching panoply of values and ethics exists and has been built up from an underlying biological base in ways that give life to the most comprehensive meaning of human morality.[23]

The Culture of Ethics—A Summation

No argument is improved by overstatement, and that should be borne firmly in mind in assessing the significance of the culture of ethics. That some such generalized consensual acceptance of broad moral understandings can be invoked seems evident. That there is much overlap and consistency among many of these universalist-like schemes is also patent. Some will say that this very generality is a source of weakness, that is, that the moral principles involved are so general and so subject to varying cultural interpretations as to be worthless for any practical tasks of deciding right and wrong courses of action, perhaps especially so for business decision makers. That may be true, although Donaldson's "ethical algorithm" and Preston's and Windsor's international policy regimes provide specific behavioral guides to government officials and business practitioners who genuinely seek to follow ethically acceptable pathways. So, too, do the many other international economic agreements and compacts negotiated over the years, many under United Nations sponsorship.

The problem would not appear to be an absence of agreed-upon moral principles or that such principles lack operational significance for business. A culture of ethics does indeed seem to exist as a widespread, generalized acceptance of a few core moral orientations. They are the essential moral framework within which societies everywhere insist that business be conducted. Though varying in shape and force and mode of expression from society to society, the core principles keep reappearing. And for very good reason: they speak the voice of nature, they tell of an irreducible core of moral meaning that natural evolutionary processes have laid at the human

---

23. Held's commentary on feminist thought is rich in passages that touch on many of the points raised in several chapters of this book. I believe there is a close logical link between the theory of (business) values set forth here and the evolving view of morality described by Held and other feminist scholars, particularly the derivation of values from an experiential base of actual, context-conditioned behavior, along with this book's acknowledgment of power aggrandizement's likely origins in a blend of phylogenetic male assertiveness and patriarchal culture.

doorstep, have inserted into human mentality, and have insinuated into the human heart. It will not do for business practitioners to disregard such powerful and compelling moral directives. The question of greatest interest then becomes how a moral sense rooted in nature and culture can be made an active component of business operations.

ON JUDGING AND ADVISING BUSINESS

This book's opening chapter confidently claimed that the theory of business values developed here would reveal "what is needed to lessen [business and society] tensions and to find managerial systems that are apt for dealing with complex business problems" and that it would provide "guidelines for knowing what might be involved in achieving a more economically effective, humanely caring, and ecologically sensitive business organization." Alas, we may be witnessing another case of hubris triumphant over intellectual frailty, for those claims have not been made good in any explicit or particularistic sense. But their presence as ideal but unrealized goals should not go unremarked, for they may reveal something worthwhile about all similar attempts to judge business behavior on moral grounds.

At the end of any analysis or discussion of the ethical dilemmas confronting business practitioners, it appears legitimate, even imperative, to provide answers to the "so what" questions. What should managers do? What practical course of action is recommended? What behavioral guides can be offered? How are the many tensions between business and society to be resolved? Not to respond to such questions, particularly when they are frequently asked by business practitioners whose sincerity and good intentions are not to be doubted, seems more than morally churlish and may be seen in itself as a form of irresponsibility.

Faced with such challenges, an optimist would prefer to proffer guidelines that can be translated into a program of organizational reform seeking to rechannel the practitioner's activities and provide checkpoints and safeguards against ethical backsliding. Many business ethicists are not merely disinterested observers of the business scene but fervently desire to lift practitioners from the "moral low ground" on which, as noted in an earlier chapter, they perceive business to operate. Without wishing to discourage such laudable and well-intentioned initiatives, it is worth examining the philosophic premises on which they are undertaken.

In one sense, there is no "program," nor is there any "practical action" to recommend. The so-what queries, which take interrogative form, only appear to be questions, or may be considered to be questions only if one grants the assumptions that lie behind them. The questions typically assume the pres-

ence somewhere of a foundationist ethic carrying an enduring moral authority that, once discovered or revealed, can be converted into behavioral guides
or drawn up into a program of practical action for the business firm to follow.
Whether the ethical foundations might be found in virtuous character traits,
or enumerated as inalienable human rights, or glimpsed within the folds of
religious doctrines matters less than the presumption that such underlying
and justifying principles exist, can be revealed, and can then serve as action
guides. If virtuous character can be identified, the presumption is that it can
be cultivated and emulated by business practitioners. If key human rights are
defined, then correlative duties to protect those rights can be set forth as action guides for any business firm. If justice can be envisioned through rational, disinterested analysis, then both governmental and corporate policies
and programs to promote it can be outlined.

The foundationist view, from which these many action approaches take
inspiration, stands in opposition to the position taken in this book's theory of
business values and which was given special attention in the preceding chapter: *Business ethics bears no single meaning, is defined by no single ethical standard,
but rather is imbued with multiple meanings stemming from diverse sources produced
in pluralistic sociocultural settings and derived in large part from natural evolutionary
processes.* The dimensions of business ethics cannot be encompassed by any
single foundationist concept. In short, there is no "formula" for the ethicist
to present for the edification of the business practitioner, no "secret" to reveal that offers a practical way out of workplace ethical dilemmas, no "key" to
unlock the cabinet of ethical medicines that can be administered to those in
need of moral repair. The best advice for practitioners is to beware the
bearer of ethical solutions, for buried somewhere within such advice is a
foundationist precept that may be, but is probably not, relatable to the ethical needs of the workplace.

However, this need not mean that ethicists should pack their bags and
head back to the campus. Ethics consultants are at their valuable best when
acting as did the troubadors and minstrels of the Middle Ages, telling stories,
bringing tidings of others' misfortunes, giving their hearers ways of seeing
themselves against a broader backdrop of experience than they can produce
for themselves. It is quite likely that the kinds of corporate morality tales that
appear frequently in the columns of *The Wall Street Journal* carry greater moral
weight and spread ethical lessons to a wider range of business practitioners
than all of the business ethics consultants taken together. The consultant's
greatest responsibility and most valuable function is to convey up-to-date theoretical insights and to raise the troubling ethical questions that business
practitioners are reluctant or resistant to ask for themselves. It is not the
ethics adviser's task either to create a belief that all will be fine if only X-foun-
dationist principle is accepted, or to raise fears if it is rejected, or to leave be-

hind guilty consciences or, worse, to leave an impression that little or nothing is to be done. Business is not mired hopelessly in a bog of self-seeking, egoistic greed (which is another frequently peddled foundationist idea) for which its practitioners are to be pilloried, drawn, and quartered by their ethicist guardians. Most business people who have thought about the matter at all are most likely ready to consider what might be done to improve their company's ethical posture. Actions indeed can be taken—and recommended—but those actions will rest on processes *already* underway, *already* familiar to the practitioner, *already* within grasp rather than out in some imagined ideal place beyond the world of practical action. Values are, and always have been, experiential, that is, reflective of behavior taking place within known settings. Such values, however firmly clasped and cherished, may change as the experiential horizon of those who hold them is modified. It is to that sphere that we now turn to note what might be conveyed to practitioners that will be of some operational value.

A dash or two of realism first sets the stage and blocks excessive expectations. The business-and-society tensions that inspired the development of this book's theory of business values, along with the many ethical and social abuses noted at the beginning of this chapter, are built-in and ongoing features of American business for the simple reason that those tensions and abuses reflect the working out of natural evolutionary processes spawned from thermodynamic forces. The value clusters that drive business practitioners and their firms to take the actions they take register in one way or another the interplay of such natural forces. The gap we observe between actual business performance that is based within these enduring natural processes, on the one hand, and the preferred ethical directions that are defined in largely sociocultural terms, on the other hand, will likely persist. In one sense, the gap is reducible (if at all) only in small increments over long periods of time. Only as these natural and sociocultural processes are better understood— and not necessarily even then—is it possible to envision a closer adhesion of practice and desired ethical function or purpose.

Of these various value clusters, power aggandizement is the most problematic and troublesome, for it works against ecologizing values and purposes; when in the ascendant, it drives economizing to excessive and destructive ends; it is capable of capturing, distorting, and overwhelming the beneficial components of techno-logics and techno-values; and, as many a business ethicist has pointed out, power-aggrandizing impulses can, have, and often do pulverize the many positive X-factor (personal, role-conditioned) values borne by those who work in business. To say that these abuses occur as a function of naturalistic forces is not to accept, rationalize, or justify them or to throw up one's hands in despair. To the contrary, there is every reason to believe that this darker side of nature is, at least to some extent, counterbalanced by more positive impulses. Thermodynamics, as noted in earlier chapters, has built dikes that keep entropy at bay. Without conscious purpose, ecologizing processes blend and harmonize multiform, highly diverse life entities into interwoven networks and integrated communities. So too have techno-values and techno-logics brought humanity forward and beyond the behavioral and intellectual thresholds of our biotic companions with whom we share life on this planet. Quite possibly, a nature-based moral sense is one outcome, though an unplanned one, of the affiliative kinship bond that succors each of us from early infancy. There is also that vast normative quilt woven from many patches of contrasting natural and sociocultural materials—the culture of ethics—that brings moral warmth and comfort to all who shelter under it.

From this moral melange, it is possible to discern the general points at which sociocultural levers can be applied at an organizational level if humanity—and in particular, business practitioners—are to be moved toward more acceptable moral ground. Here, the best counsel comes from behavioral and organizational scientists, from educational psychologists who command a knowledge of how people develop and grow toward moral maturity, from organizational sociologists whose research reveals the pressures that lead toward both desirable and undesirable workplace actions, and from those who design organizational levees that can nudge the flow of workplace activities into ethical channels—for example, ethics committees, in-house ethics advisors, ethics audits, ethics training programs, and similar devices and routines.[24] All such organizational innovations must lean against the powerful inertial forces of nature and of sociocultural habit long ingrained in the business institution. Even when sincerely adopted and skillfully launched, they cannot be expected to yield revolutionary results. But because such reforms begin within the organizational context where business people live their working lives—that is, where the values they hold and the values of the business firm constitute the stuff of everyday intercourse—there is at least the prospect that behavioral and attitudinal changes can be encouraged.

As for the larger tensions and value conflicts that occur outside the corporate walls along the business-and-society interface, an impressive but far from perfect array of pluralist institutions, practices, laws, regulations, and informal social controls operates to mediate conflict, to deflect the worst of the antisocial impulses, and to help repair the sociocultural fabric when torn

---

24. Linda K. Trevino, "A Cultural Perspective on Changing and Developing Organizational Ethics," in R. Woodman and W. Pasmore (eds.), *Research in Organizational Change and Development*, vol. 4, Greenwich, CT: JAI Press, 1990, pp. 195–230; and James Weber, "Institutionalizing Ethics into Business Organizations: A Model and Research Agenda," *Business Ethics Quarterly*, vol. 3, no. 2, October 1993, pp. 419–436.

asunder by irresponsible business actions. A stakeholder apparatus works, though at times hesitantly and uncertainly, to reconcile conflicting claims brought by persons, groups, and communities against the corporation, and vice versa. The market, though itself a source of ethical mischief and conflict, acts to mediate a wide range of value differences, such as those between management and labor, between a company and its suppliers, and between competing business firms. That the methods and outcomes are not always just diminishes but does not cancel the worthwhileness of all such institutional processes. As the economic historian Karl Polanyi pointed out many years ago, business and economic activities in all societies throughout recorded history and earlier have always been subject to the influence of social values and institutional controls, except for one brief, humanly and socially catastrophic period of laissez-faire market capitalism.[25] This is not to say that all is now well, for that social skein needs constant attention and strengthening to contain what would otherwise be an unrestrained and possibly destructive expression of the natural forces undergirding the core values of business.

To counter that possibility, as two of our wisest cosmologists have written, we humans are challenged to do that which humans do best—to draw on the intelligence that is part of our natural heritage to forge supportive links with each other and with the ecosystems that sustain us against the relentless entropic forces without and within. They remind us in these words:[26]

Even in the fossil remains of the earliest lifeforms, there is unmistakable evidence of communal living arrangements and mutual cooperation. We humans have been able to design effective cultures that for hundreds of thousands of years have fostered one set of inborn characteristics and discouraged another. From brain anatomy, human behavior, personal introspection, the annals of recorded history, the fossil record, DNA sequencing, and the behavior of our closest relatives, a clear lesson emerges: There is more than one side to human nature. If our greater intelligence is the hallmark of our species, then we should use it as all the other beings use their distinctive advantages—to help ensure that their offspring prosper and their heredity is passed on. It is our business to understand that some predilections we bear as remnants of our evolutionary history, when coupled with our intelligence—especially with intelligence in the subordinate role—might threaten our future. Our intelligence is imperfect, surely, and newly arisen; the ease with which it can be sweet-talked, overwhelmed, or subverted by other hardwired [natural] propensities—sometimes themselves disguised as the cool light of reason—is worrisome. But if intelligence is our only edge, we must learn to use it better, to sharpen it, to understand its limitations and deficiencies—to use it as

25. Karl Polanyi, *The Great Transformation*, Boston: Beacon Press, 1944.

26. Carl Sagan and Ann Druyan, *Shadows of Forgotten Ancestors*, New York: Random House, 1992, p. 407.

cats use stealth, as walking sticks use camouflage, to make it the tool of our survival.

So, to the question—What is to be done?—it is well to be reminded of the larger dimensions that are bound to give shape to any practical actions recommended or undertaken. As noted earlier, we are not dealing with easily malleable forces, for this book has offered a view of the taproots of human nature and human culture that extend deep into the soil of inexorable thermodynamic processes. The products of those forces—people, our nonhuman life companions in the plant and animal worlds, the earth itself and its planetary and galactic counterparts—have persisted through unimaginably immense eons of time, and there is little apparent reason to believe that they will not endure for many more. The chronological and planetary vastness of this theater is seemingly matched by the continuum of natural forces that have brought it all about.

As important as any other perspective is the discovered knowledge that there is no arrival point, nor is there an apparent final destination, where all matters are to be resolved. The stunningly complex forces at work throughout what we perceive as a vast universe are a continuum, not a platform. All is provisional, and impermanence is written into nature. Transformation is the only constant. Thus, a search for permanent, everlasting rules to guide human conduct is bound to bump up against the provisionality of nature and to be frustrated by the inexorableness of thermodynamic transformations.

Accepting this truth need not produce despair or cynicism, or cause one to give oneself up to a deterministic philosophy where little is to be done. Within the ever-changing hues of nature's kaleidoscopic processes, one can glimpse treasured, delightful, inspiring, valued, and valuable patterns worth preserving—and worth the hard struggles needed to keep them in view. These moments in time are what might be called "pause points" in the long journey taken by Time's Arrow. They are the platforms of achievement built by collective human strivings to which we attach the label "wisdom." It is on those transitory platforms where one can both find and invent "rules" and "principles" of conduct that reflect the accumulated wisdom of human experience. They are, like all else in the long run, temporary and transitory but no less salient and essential for the moment in time when they serve human purposes. The search, then, should be directed toward finding and creating new pause points, new collective experiences that express and stand for what has been found—and what is yet to be discovered—as ethically acceptable.

Also to be remembered is that all discovered and invented ethical precepts will be diversely interpreted and differentially applied by the varying sociocultural traditions in which they appear. Whatever ethical rules or principles are devised as guides for business conduct are unavoidably related to both nature and culture. Business morality in the end is less than absolute because qualified by diverse cultures but is more than culturally relative because it also is a function of nature.

I leave readers with two final thoughts, each one a plea. One is to scholars whose professional lives are dedicated to plumbing the mysteries of business-and-society relationships. The second is to business practitioners whose individual and collective decisions transit that phantom boundary linking business with society.

To my scholarly friends and colleagues, I reaffirm what many will already find congenial. Our inquiring enterprise must seek and find new ground, must break out of well-worn ways of thinking about business's ethical and social dilemmas, must build on what is presently known about human nature and human values, must infuse ethics and values inquiry with a larger range of scientific insight than is customarily used, must be willing to relinquish the tight grip on cherished concepts, must help forge a new normative synthesis out of the best that philosophy, social science, and the natural sciences can offer. If we, as scholars, do not encourage the building of new perspectives from constantly evolving, multiple sources of knowledge, how can we expect business practitioners to grasp the realities and complexities on which ethical discourse must go forward?

And I say this to all business practitioners who may read these pages or who may hear of them through others: You are societal custodians and caretakers of one of nature's most important and vital forces from which many draw sustenance and find their way toward life goals. The influence you are able to exert on that economizing process—whether supportive of life goals or denigrative of human purpose—will be judged on moral grounds. Those companies are well and fairly judged that liberate and release rather than restrain and hamper human intelligence and human aspirations; that house and reward managers who display mature moral character as they make day-to-day workplace decisions; that have created and activated organs of moral awareness and moral astuteness; and—most important of all—that transform nature's impulses into forms and actions and outcomes that preserve business's own essential functions while also nourishing and protecting humanity's ethical and social core. The business professions are, and long have been, cocooned within a moral dimension that defines the ethical course and meaning of business activities. Accepting that meaning—and acting upon it—is more than just an ethical and social responsibility of business. It is no less than an imperative moral summons that lately swells in ever mounting crescendos out of the shadowy deeps of nature and echoes insistently and urgently across the sunny uplands of human culture.

Epilogue

If we shadows have offended,
Think but this, and all is mended,
That you have but slumb'red here
While these visions did appear.
And this weak and idle theme,
No more yielding but a dream,
Gentles, do not reprehend:
If you pardon, we will mend: . . .
So, good night unto you all.
Give me your hands, if we be friends,
And Robin [and Norm, three Eds, three Toms, three Richards,
      Manny, Pat, Diane, Nancy, Rogene, Denis, Jim, Bob, Lyman,
      Bill, Carroll, Curt, et al.] shall
restore amends.

WILLIAM SHAKESPEARE [with help]
A Midsummer Night's Dream[1]

---

1. Stanley Wells, Gary Taylor, John Jowett, and William Montgomery (eds.), *William Shakespeare: The Complete Works*, Oxford: Clarendon Press, p. 375, by permission of Oxford University Press.

Bibliographic Note

The book's footnotes provide sufficient bibliographic references for most purposes. This bibliographic note lists a small number of key works that are particularly worthwhile for anyone interested in exploring the theoretical underpinnings of this book's theory of business values.

Conrad, Michael. *Adaptability: The Significance of Variability from Molecule to Ecosystem.* New York: Plenum Press, 1983.

Coveney, Peter, and Roger Highfield. *The Arrow of Time.* London: W. H. Allen, 1990.

Eibl-Eibesfeldt, Irenaus. *Human Ethology.* New York: Aldine de Gruyter, 1989.

Eldredge, Niles, and Marjorie Grene. *Interactions: The Biological Context of Social Systems.* New York: Columbia University Press, 1992.

Goldsmith, Timothy H. *The Biological Roots of Human Nature: Forging Links between Evolution and Behavior.* New York: Oxford University Press, 1991.

Jackall, Robert. *Moral Mazes: The World of Corporate Managers.* New York: Oxford University Press, 1988.

Keddy, Paul A. *Competition.* London: Chapman and Hall, 1989.

Sagan, Carl, and Ann Druyan. *Shadows of Forgotten Ancestors.* New York: Random House, 1992.

Schein, Edgar. *Organizational Culture and Leadership.* San Francisco: Jossey-Bass, 1985, 1988.

Wilson, Edward O. *The Diversity of Life.* London: Allen Pane The Penguin Press, 1993 (and Cambridge, MA: Harvard University Press, 1992).

Wilson, James Q. *The Moral Sense.* New York: Free Press, 1993.

Name Index

Subject Index

Page numbers in italics refer to a figure.